SPORT

in

AUSTRALIA

Jacket illustrations:
District School Football Team, 1929, West Wyalong; Harry Hall 1838–1886, West Australian, winner of the Triple Crown, 1853, with Frank Butler up [ca. 1853] oil on canvas 35.8 x 45.8 cm; Jantzen — finely tailored for perfect fit, in *Australian Women's Weekly* 5/5/1954; J. M. Crossland 1800–1858, Portrait of Nannultera, a young Pooindie cricketer [1854] oil on canvas 99 x 78.8 cm; Australia's undefeated soccer girls 1973; Surf board riders shoot the breakers at Tamarama beach, Sydney, Photo: John Tanner ANIB; Melbourne cup 1965, ANIB; all reproduced by permission of the National Library of Australia.

South Bondi Baths, school children on holidays line up for a cool plunge, reproduced by permission of Australian Consolidated Press; Mal Meninga, reproduced by permission of Rugby League Week, Australian Consolidated Press.

SPORT

in

AUSTRALIA

A SOCIAL HISTORY

Edited by:

WRAY VAMPLEW

and

BRIAN STODDART

CAMBRIDGE
UNIVERSITY PRESS

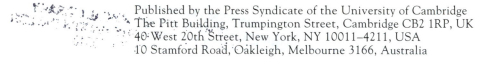

Published by the Press Syndicate of the University of Cambridge
The Pitt Building, Trumpington Street, Cambridge CB2 1RP, UK
40 West 20th Street, New York, NY 10011–4211, USA
10 Stamford Road, Oakleigh, Melbourne 3166, Australia

© Cambridge University Press 1994
First published 1994

Volume Editors: Brian Stoddart, Wray Vamplew
Associate Editor: Ian Jobling
Picture Research: Sean Brawley, Phillipa McGuinness
Copy Editor: Janet Bunny
Indexer: Michael J. Ramsden
Design and Typesetting: Mark Davis/text-art
Printed in Australia by McPherson's Printing Group

National Library of Australia cataloguing-in-publication data

Sport in Australia
Bibliography.
Includes index.
1. Sports – Australia – History. 2. Sports – Social aspects –
Australia. I. Vamplew, Wray. II. Stoddart, Brian
796.0994

Library of Congress cataloguing-in-publication data

Sport in Australia: a social history / edited by Wray Vamplew
and Brian Stoddart.
Includes bibliographical references and index.
1. Sports – Social aspects – Australia. 2. Popular culture –
Australia. 3. Australia – Social conditions. I. Vamplew, Wray.
II. Stoddart, Brian.
GV706.5.S7326   1994
306.4'83–dc20   94—19932
                                                              CIP

A catalogue record for this book is available from the British Library.

ISBN 0 521 43513 7 Hardback

Contents

The Contributors

Daryl Adair is a PhD. candidate in history at the Flinders University of South Australia where he is researching ceremonial crowd events in early twentieth-century Australia. He has published articles on spectator disorder and professional sculling in *Sporting Traditions*.

Douglas Booth gained a master's degree in social sciences at the University of Natal and completed his doctorate at Macquarie University in New South Wales. His doctoral thesis examines the trilogy of race, politics and sport in South Africa. He has written numerous articles covering the history, sociology and politics of sport. He currently teaches in the School of Physical Education at the University of Otago.

Richard Cashman, who teaches sports history at the University of New South Wales, is the author of *Patrons, players and the crowd, 'Ave a go, yer mug!, Australian cricket: the attendance cycle, The 'Demon' Spofforth* and *Wicket women*. He also edited *Early cricket in Sydney* by Jas Scott. He has twice won the Literary Award of the Australian Cricket Society. Currently he is editor of *Sporting Traditions*.

John Daly is an associate professor at the University of South Australia where he lectures in the history and sociology of sport. He is the author of four books and numerous articles on Australian sport. He has been associated with the national athletic team for twenty years as head coach (1974–84) or team manager (1985–92). In 1991 he was awarded the Medal of the Order of Australia for services to Australian sport.

Ian Jobling is Associate Professor and Director of the Centre for Physical Activity and Sport Education, Department of Human Movement Studies at the University of Queensland. His main research and teaching interests pertain to sport in Australian society, especially the Olympic movement and gender issues. Dr Jobling and Pamela Barham received a grant from the Applied Sports Research Programme of the Australian Sports Commission and the All Australia Netball Association to undertake the research for the report entitled *Netball Australia: a socio-historical analysis*, which was published in 1988.

Graeme Kinross-Smith is a poet, prose fiction writer and academic, and until recently Senior Lecturer in Australian Studies and Creative Writing at Deakin University, where he is now an honorary associate of the Faculty of Humanities. His publications on sports history include *The sweet spot*, articles in *Sporting Traditions* and contributions to the *Oxford companion to Australian sport* and the *Oxford book of Australian sporting anecdotes*.

Louella McCarthy is a PhD candidate in History at the University of New South Wales. She has been project officer for the University of New South Wales Community History Programme since 1987, and is also currently working as historian for the University of New South Wales oral history project. Her publications include 'How to write the history of a sports club' in *Locating Australia's past* and she is editor of the Community History Programme's magazine *Locality*.

Philip Mosely has been a lecturer in the centres for sports studies and communication at the University of Canberra. His doctorate was on *A social history of soccer in New South Wales 1880–1957* and he is currently the director of an Australian Sports Commission project on *The history of ethnic involvement in Australian soccer since 1950*.

Bill Murray teaches history at La Trobe University in Victoria. His publications on sport include two books on 'the Old Firm' (the Rangers and Celtic football clubs in Glasgow), and articles on the Olympic Games and workers' sport in France. Currently he is writing a world history of soccer.

John O'Hara is an associate professor of history and head of the Division of Arts in the Faculty of Arts and Social Sciences at the University of Western Sydney, Macarthur. He is the author of *A mugs game: a history of gaming and betting in Australia* and a general editor of the *Oxford companion to Australian sport*. He was a founding member of both the Australian Society for Sports History and the National Association for Gambling Studies and has served both societies in executive capacities, including being immediate past editor of *Sporting Traditions*.

Murray Phillips is a lecturer in sports studies at the University of Canberra. He has recently been awarded his Doctorate for a thesis on Australian sport and the First World War and has also published articles on golf and rugby football in Australia.

Brian Stoddart is Professor of Cultural Studies and Dean of the Faculty of Communication at the University of Canberra. He has written *Cricket and Empire: the 1932–33 bodyline tour of Australia* (with Ric Sissons), *Saturday afternoon fever: sport in the Australian culture* and *The Royal Sydney Golf Club: the first hundred years* (with Colin Tatz) and is a regular commentator on sports issues for the electronic media.

Wray Vamplew was Pro-Vice-Chancellor at Flinders University before taking up a chair in sports history at De Montfort University in the United Kingdom in 1993. He has published extensively on sports history including *Pay up and play the game* which won the inaugural North American Society for Sports History Book Award. He was foundation editor of *Sporting Traditions*.

Bernard Whimpress comes to history from sports journalism. He is the author of *The South Australian football story* and was editor of the *South Australian Football Budget* and *Football Times*. In addition he has written two books on cricket: *Adelaide Oval Test Cricket 1884–1984* (with Nigel Hart) and *Understanding Cricket*. At present he is engaged in postgraduate research at Flinders University of South Australia on the subject of Aborigines in first-class cricket.

Illustrations

Preface

The origins of this book were twofold. One lay on the pine-surrounded beach at Manly, site of William Gocher's 1902 defiance of the local council's ban on daylight bathing. Eighty-five years after Gocher, the editors of this volume trudged that same sand in a welcome respite from an intensive brainstorming weekend mapping out a television series on the history of Australian sport. While pushing that set of programmes towards themes in Australian sports history, we also spent our seaside sojourn bemoaning the absence of a history of the major sports which had been played in Australia. Individual histories, varying in quality, existed for many sports but there was no book which brought them together. One day, we promised ourselves, we would produce such a volume. Busy with other projects, however, we consigned the scheme to the back burner. Then in 1992 Robin Derricourt of Cambridge University Press approached one of us with a proposal to produce an Antipodean version of Tony Mason's *Sport in Britain: a social history*. Memories of Manly were revived, beachfront ideas were resurrected, and authors were recruited.

The contributors cover a spectrum from the new wave of younger academics to those with established reputations in sports history. Regrettably we were able to attract only one female historian. An inability to recruit expert authors also forced us to omit some sports despite their importance in Australia's sporting history. Among these were cycling, a major attraction for spectators at the turn of the century and, more recently, the locus of Australia's medal grab at the Olympic and Commonwealth Games; motor sports in which Australia has produced world champions on both two and four wheels and the late developers, at least on the international scene, of Australian basketball and hockey, and the mass participation sport of squash.

We owe a great deal to our authors, including worries about meeting deadlines and incompatible computer discs! Seriously however, we are indebted to them for their expertise and their willingness to write within a framework for, in order to provide some cohesion, we requested authors to consider certain sub-themes where relevant in each chapter. These were the role taken by women in the particular sport; indigenous, ethnic and international influences; participants and spectators; and regional differences within Australia, including those between city and country areas. The concluding chapter pulls these common threads together.

Finally we would like to thank Marilyn Chandler for her word-processing and patience in dealing with edited manuscripts, Sue Wright for her work in Canberra, Janice Cameron for her research skills, and Ian Jobling for taking responsibility for illustrative material.

Wray Vamplew, De Montfort University
Brian Stoddart, University of Canberra

1 Australians and Sport

Wray Vamplew

Loving Old England with a child's affection
I'm to her fame and honour ever true,
But then my heart has form'd a new connection,
Hardly less strong — I love Victoria too.
But should 'Old England' win, we shall admire
The height to which they've brought their noble game,
And our Victorians, vanquished, may acquire,
A knowledge which may lead them on to fame

Melbourne Punch, 2 January 1862

SPORT WAS part of the cultural baggage brought out to Australia by the convicts, the free settlers and the accompanying administrative and military personnel, though initially the limited size of the community and the priority given to the establishment of a viable settlement delayed the commencement of organised sporting activities. Although the still imperfect knowledge about British sport at the time of the founding of Australia makes it difficult to determine the exact extent to which Britain's sporting heritage was transferred to the new Antipodean colonies, there is general acceptance that such a transfer occurred.[1] The migrant Englishman, hankering for home, could find cricket matches between teams named after county sides; early horse-racing followed the pattern of English provincial meetings with heats, hacks and owner-riders; British sporting equipment, horse-flesh, game birds, greyhounds and even foxes were imported; and old rustic sports — greasy poles and pigs, Aunt Sallies and sack races — featured at organised picnics. One diarist in the newly-established colony of South Australia was in no doubt that in the first decade of settlement 'all the purely English sports [were] kept up'. Additionally the Scots held their Caledonian games and pioneered golf while the Irish played their versions of football and celebrated St Patrick's Day with sports and race meetings.[2] In importing their traditional sports, the British were no different from other immigrant groups such as the Germans who brought with them skittles, crossbows, target rifle-shooting and, later, gymnastics, but the numerical superiority of the Britons inevitably led to their activities dominating the colonial sporting calendar.

In an environment where the seasons did not match the accustomed months and the landscape was far from familiar, sport provided a link with what had been left behind: indeed news from 'home' in the press included much sporting intelligence. Nostalgia no doubt led to the adoption of many British sporting activities, but others were the result of deliberate attempts by the colonial wealthy and educated classes to replicate English social life, including its social structure. Whatever the reason, such was the desire in some quarters to emulate British, particularly English, sporting practices that attempts were made even when inappropriate. There were far too few quality horses in the Australian colonies for the Derbies and St Legers to resemble their English classical counterparts and heavy morning suits were clearly unsuited to the dusty paddocks of many Australian racecourses.

Ultimately, beating the mother country at her own sports became regarded as a sign of colonial maturity. Initially, however, deference was shown to visiting English sportsmen, particularly cricketers who played the great imperial game. Measuring performance against the English, not only at the select levels but also in the frequent British-born versus colonial-born matches, was a yardstick of how the Australian environment — physical, climatic and social — might have undermined traditional British qualities. How transplantation had affected bodily and mental prowess was the question raised by *Bell's Life in Victoria* in 1858.[3] In fact the pupils were becoming the masters. Victories by XVIII of Victoria and by XVIII of New South Wales over W. G. Grace's team led the *Sydney Morning Herald* to comment that British blood 'had not yet been thinned by the heat of *Australian* summers' and the *Australasian* to point out that 'in bone and muscle, activity, vigour and success in field sports, the Englishmen born in Australia do not fall short of the Englishmen born in Surrey or Yorkshire'.[4] Soon the visiting English cricketers began to play the Victorian, New South Welsh and South Australian teams on equal terms rather than with eighteen or fifteen on the home side. On the 1876–77 tour of Australia the hosts beat the English professional team led by James Lillywhite though, since many star English cricketers had not joined the tour, followers of the game in England treated the loss less seriously than the colonists took their victory. Then in August 1882 came one of the great boilovers — at least to the English mind — when an Australian XI, inspired by Fred Spofforth's fourteen wickets for ninety runs, beat the Marylebone Cricket Club at the Oval by seven runs, leading the *Australasian* to comment that 'the translation of stock to this country has improved rather than impaired the physique'.[5] Deference had disappeared to be replaced by self-confidence and, in some quarters, arrogance. During the 1890s English touring cricketers reportedly were 'insulted, hooted at and hissed' on every ground in Australia.[6]

By this time Australia had had its first sporting world champions. Although the American boxing authorities refused to acknowledge 'Young Griffo's' claim for the world featherweight title after he outpointed New Zealander Billy Murphy in Sydney in 1890, there was no such dispute in sculling circles about Ned Trickett's defeat of the Englishman, Saddler, on the Thames in 1876 to become world champion, Australia's first in any sport.[7] His achievement was emulated by other Australians Bill Beach, Peter Kemp, Henry Searle, Jim Stanbury, John McLean and George Towns. Indeed between them these seven New South Welshmen held the world title for twenty-two of the years from 1876 to 1908.[8]

Political independence and national unity has not diminished the Australian desire to beat 'the Poms' at anything. The use of the word 'test', which originated as sporting terminology in the cricketing trials of skill and pluck between Australia and England, on this side of the globe is applied now for publicity purposes to all sporting contests between the two countries. Yet other enemies have surfaced. The United States and, to a lesser extent though not in all sports, New Zealand have joined Britain as the nations Australia must defeat. Australia cannot challenge the world's super power politically, but occasionally

The Victorian team practising on the Melbourne Cricket Ground for the match against W. G. Grace's All-England XI, December 1873.
(*Australasian Sketcher*, December 1873, Mitchell Library, State Library of New South Wales.)

on the Davis Cup tennis courts or in the Olympic pool Australians have upstaged the Americans. The most notable upset occurred in 1983 off Newport when *Australia II* wrenched American hands from their 139-year-old grip on their self-titled trophy. America, however, has exacted revenge by influencing the nature of Australian sport, particularly basketball, using American razz-a-matazz, sporting gear virtually unchanged for the Antipodean market and a media use of statistics which takes the quantification of games way beyond the traditional batting and bowling averages. Kiwis, along with 'Septic Tanks', have become nations to be beaten in the sporting area. Although united with Australia in an Australasian team for early Davis Cup and Olympic ventures, New Zealanders have often proved difficult sporting opponents: not so much in cricket in which Australia refused to grant them test-match status until 1946[9] and even ranked them alongside state sides in the 1970s limited-over competitions, but certainly in rugby (the union version), and horse-racing, in which equine performers have often crossed the Tasman to collect Australian prize money. It is worth noting that both Carbine and Phar Lap, perhaps the two most famous Australian racehorses, were in fact bred in New Zealand.

Occasionally too Australia has challenged the world. Indeed Australians have participated in every summer Olympics — one of only three nations to do so — since the establishment of the modern Games in Athens in 1896. Although Edwin Flack won both the 800 metres and 1500 metres track events in that initial gathering, success on this particular world stage has been limited with the notable exception of the Melbourne Games in 1956, the first and only time so far the Olympics have been held in the southern hemisphere. Revelling in the support of a home crowd, and with many events being held 'in-season', Australian sportsmen and women won thirty-five medals, thirteen of them gold. Disappointing later results, particularly the failure to win any gold medals at the Montreal Olympics in 1976, forced Australians to realise that basic talent alone was no longer sufficient and led to the formation of the Australian Institute of Sport with a charter to apply sports science to the coaching and training of top-ranking sportspeople.[10]

Whether the investment in the institute is warranted is still debated, but at the recent Barcelona Olympics Australia finished tenth in the (unofficial) medal count, prompting the then Federal Sports Minister, Ros Kelly, to proclaim that 'we have re-established Australia as a world sporting power'.[11] The truth is that currently Australia ranks as world champion in both rugby codes and has several world-class performers in golf and motor-cycling, none of which is an Olympic sport. In terms of world sporting interest Australia's best performance at Barcelona was fourth — and out of the medals — in soccer, a sport which struggles for recognition in Australia.

Sports nationalism has played an important role in unifying Australia, in sublimating albeit temporarily the inequities of race and gender and the rivalries of internal geography. Indeed, historian Bill Mandle has argued persuasively that the performances of the Australian cricket team in the 1890s helped pave the way for political federation.[12] The down side of such unity has been the occasional xenophobic or chauvinistic outburst. Worse still, the nationalism of other lands has been brought to Australia, though fortunately Australian tolerance has generally channelled this into open, non-violent activities. One major exception in the sporting arena has been soccer, where the game has suffered not from the hooliganism of Britain but from the homeland hatreds of ethnic groups.[13] The ethnic mix of Australian cities has meant that the historical

The official poster of the 1956 Melbourne Olympic Games. The 2000 Sydney Olympic Games will mark only the second occasion the Summer Olympics have been held in the southern hemisphere. (International Olympic Committee.)

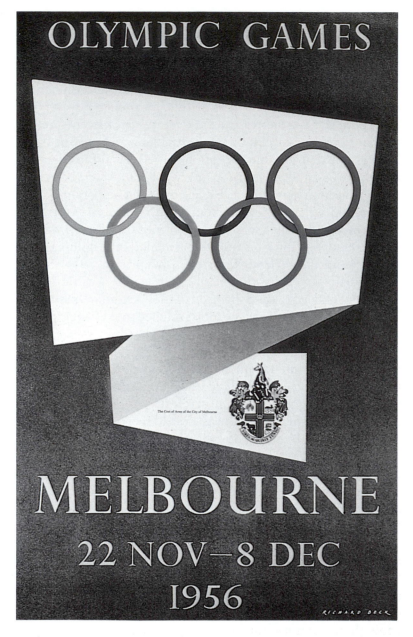

and contemporary political problems of Europe are condensed into a relatively small area and the large distances between Australian cities have forced rival groups to play soccer against each other, whereas in Europe they might have been in leagues with teams of similar ethnicity. Often issues other than football have been at stake: for example, in the 1960s when Croatia played Yugal, whose support came mainly from Serbs and

Slavs, past Yugoslavian political struggles and Second World War experiences were symbolised and re-enacted.[14] More recently a crowd riot occurred when Preston Makedonia played Heidelberg Alexander in Melbourne; the issue which provoked the trouble was a dispute thousands of kilometres away in Europe over whether or not Greece had patent rights to the Macedonian name.[15] Nevertheless there is a strong case that the benefits of soccer as a socialisation mechanism for migrants have outweighed the costs of intermittent violence and indeed for arguing that such nationalistic violence might have been much worse had not soccer provided an outlet for some of the politically-based aggression.[16]

The continued flow of migrants to Australia from Britain throughout the nineteenth century reinforced the early cultural continuity in terms of sporting activities. Among the newcomers were muscular Christians, imported educators who transmitted the games ethos and its emphasis on the character-building aspects of many sports to young Australians, particularly those attending private schools.[17] Other immigrants brought with them the new sports of athletics, tennis, cycling and golf. Nevertheless, as argued earlier in the context of cricket, towards the end of the century there was a growing self-confidence within Australia about sport and other issues and Australian participants no longer simply followed a lead set by Britain.

It could be said that the development of Australian rules football was a first sign of a desire to go it alone; in reality 'footy', soccer and rugby probably all shared a common ancestry in traditional folk football. When the first rules of Australian (or Victorian as it was then) football were formulated in 1859, there was not a standardised game in Britain on which to model an Australian version. Thus there was no conscious decision to reject *the* British game for none existed, and in fact the football rules of the English public schools, all of which varied, were scoured by the rule-makers of Melbourne.[18]

A clearer break from Britain came in horse-racing with the Melbourne Cup which, within a few years of its inauguration in 1861, became acknowledged as the premier race in Australia.

A crowd listens to the Melbourne Cup broadcast outside the Modern Radio Store in Martin Place, Sydney, 6 November 1934. Darby Munro rode Peter Pan home; it was the horse's second win in the race. (Hood Collection, State Library of New South Wales.)

Previously major races had taken their titles from the English classics, even though the scarcity of high-quality thoroughbreds in the colonies forced them to be handicaps rather than events at equal weights. The Melbourne Cup openly acknowledged the Australian situation. Run as a handicap over a testing two miles (now 3200 metres), it attracted owners because it offered good prize money for a small entry fee and was popular with gamblers because the best horse need not win. Once established it has remained a major feature of the Australian racing and social calendar.[19] Later in the nineteenth century the enclosed gate-money course, the starting gate and the totalisator all made their appearance in Australian racing ahead of their adoption in Britain.[20]

Other sports too witnessed Australian innovations. By the 1880s cricket at the metropolitan level was organised in local competitions rather than the 'friendlies' so common in England, or at least in the south of that country, and matches were often played over two successive Saturdays. At the inter-colonial level the timeless first-class fixture was introduced. Football too was played in competitive leagues with the Victorian (1877), South Australian (1877) and West Australian (1885) football associations all preceding their counterparts of the round ball code in England (1888) and Scotland (1892). By the 1890s, both in cricket and in all codes of football, competitions in the Australian capital cities were based on suburbs, often organised around electorates, a feature unique to Australia.[21] The development of such electorate sport was a concession to the vast distances between major inhabited areas in Australia. Weekly matches were feasible only at the metropolitan level. This is not to say that inter-colonial sports competition did not occur. A natural desire to challenge further afield was strengthened by political rivalries between the colonies. Victoria had been created out of New South Wales in 1851, obtaining responsible government four years later, and Queensland was separated from New South Wales and simultaneously granted responsible government in 1859. For the new colonies, proving that they were better than the original settlement from which they sprang stimulated competition in many fields, including sport. Additionally, boundary disputes between them were common throughout the nineteenth century and these too heightened the feelings of rivalry, as did South Australia's often vaunted claim of being the only colony settled without the aid of convict labour.

Horse-racing was one of the first sports to feature a promoted inter-colonial contest. Following a newspaper challenge in 1857 Veno, from New South Wales, defeated Victoria's Alice Hawthorne by three lengths in a match race for one thousand sovereigns. Two years later, however, Victorians celebrated as Flying Buck beat all comers in the first Australian Champion Sweepstakes which had been inaugurated by Melbourne turf interests so as 'to give the colonies of Australia an opportunity of testing the rival merits of their best horses'. Subsequently inter-colonial championships were staged during the 1860s in all the Australian colonies except Western Australia, where distance still proved an intractable problem; its metropolis, Perth, was nearly three thousand kilometres from Adelaide, the nearest neighbouring capital. Highlighting the contemporary transport difficulties was the fate of The Barber, which travelled from South Australia to Melbourne for that first inter-colonial sweepstakes. The horse survived a shipwreck in which eighty-one lives were lost; then was walked several hundred kilometres to Geelong where it was put aboard a train for the last fifty or so kilometres to Melbourne.[22]

These equine contests had been preceded in the mid-1850s by competitions in archery and rifle-shooting in which metropolitan clubs would shoot on their own butts or ranges and then transmit the score, initially by post and later by telegraph. Such competition at a distance of course was not feasible in team games and, although following an advertised challenge the first inter-colonial cricket match took place in 1856 (NSW defeated Victoria by three wickets and only 193 runs were scored), regular events had to await improvements in transportation. It is worthy of note that for several decades English cricket teams played in more of the Australian colonies than any neighbouring colonial team. Ventures by clubs generally paved the way for visits by representative teams and in the last quarter of the nineteenth century, among other sports, intercolonial contests began in rowing (1878), Victorian (later Australian) rules (1879), bowls (1880), rugby (1882) and soccer (1883); mostly these were organised on an annual basis. Designated Australian championships were held in cycling (1888) and athletics (1893).[23]

Population and geography determined that New South Wales versus Victoria would be the inaugural fixture in most inter-colonial sporting events, but, by the time of Federation all states were participating in some sports. Although inter-colonial cricket matches had been played fairly regularly since the 1870s, it was not until 1892 that a formal competition was organised following the donation of a trophy by the visiting Lord Sheffield. The Sheffield Shield is still a coveted prize and the competition has been expanded to include Queensland (1926), Western Australia (1947) and Tasmania (1977). The survival of this traditional competition is indicative of the fact that Federation has not diminished interstate rivalry, though in some sports, notably basketball, soccer and Australian rules football, sponsorship has assisted the development of inter-city competition in recent years with the formation of national leagues.

Australian rules football aside, what has Australia contributed to modern sport? It has given the world the winged keel in ocean yachting, the Australian-crawl swimming stroke, the eight-ball over in cricket, the starting block in athletics, and the nomenclature 'rugby league' though not the game itself. Australian claims to the invention of speedway (dirt- or cinders-track motor-cycle racing) have not been upheld, but it did originate cricko, cricket under lights, polocrosse, sphairee, trugo and vigoro, none of which have found much international favour.[24] However, it was an Australian entrepreneur, Kerry Packer, who revolutionalised cricket and its telecasting in the 1970s, a move which has had ramifications not just in the cricketing world but in many areas of televised sport.

In a seminal essay on the Australian language the late Barry Andrews estimated that 'something like one in thirty of the words we use is a sporting word — and that of these sporting words, perhaps one in five is a sporting Australianism'.[25] This lends linguistic support to those who have argued that Australians are besotted by sport: that they are possessed of an obsession which lasts from the cradle to the grave, from the wearing of nappies in their team's colours to the scattering of their ashes at a favourite sporting venue. Such allegations have a long history and usually follow a time-honoured trail of quotations from visitors, mention of world champions in the 1950s and 1960s, and reference to a 1960s survey in *Sports Illustrated* which concluded that, on a per-capita basis Australia was one of the leading sporting countries in the world.[26]

Paradoxically Keith Dunstan, scarcely a sports fan as his foundation of the Anti-Football League testifies, has done much to create the image of a sports-obsessed nation. His book *Sports*, a highly readable account detailing the Australian passion for a wide variety of sporting pursuits, has had a major influence on public perception, perhaps because of the absence, at the time of publication in the early 1970s, of a strong academic interest in sport, which consequently left the field open to folklore and a journalistic approach.[27]

This view of the importance of sport to Australians has been reinforced by the Australian media, who have seized on the self-image as a promotional device; by politicians, who have seen votes in supporting bids to host the Olympics and in becoming number-one ticket-holders of sporting clubs; and by advertisers such as the biscuit manufacturers, Arnotts, who in the 1960s hoped to secure sales by pushing the line that

> If you couldn't kick a ball
> Or you couldn't hold a bat
> . . .
> Then you wouldn't be an Aussie
> You wouldn't be true blue.

11

Historian Richard Cashman has attempted to put the alleged sporting obsession into perspective by comparing Australia with other countries. He rejects any reliance on the qualitative, impressionistic views of visitors and looks to harder, quantified data and argues that, in terms of television coverage of sport, spectator access to top sport and crowd size at lesser events, Australia lags behind the United States; that on a per-capita basis New Zealand has a better Olympic record; that specialised sports journals have not developed on any scale here; and that sports participation is significantly less here than in some other countries. Nevertheless he is still led to conclude that Australians are passionate about sport, although he argues that such a passion is not unique.[28]

One aspect of the passion which requires further investigation is whether there is (and was) a dichotomy between the avowed interest in sport and actually playing a game. Two pieces of statistical data, on crowds at sporting events and at sporting funerals, support the idea of sport being an important ingredient in Australian popular culture. There is clearly spectator allegiance to Australia's own game: aggregate seasonal attendances at Australian (formerly Victorian) Football League minor-round matches have topped the two million mark since 1946 and the three million since 1978, with grand-final crowds of well over 100 000 since 1963.[29] In fact one ardent Scottish soccer fan has noted that twice the percentage of Victorians attend Australian football matches than the proportion of Scots who view the real 'fitba'.[30]

Then there has been the adulation of sportsmen who have died whilst at their sporting peaks. Most recently this was seen in the Collingwood supporters' response to the death of footballer Darren Millane, killed in a drink-driving incident. Such veneration has a long history in Australia beginning with the sculler Henry Searle, who died from typhoid that he contracted while returning home from a successful defence of his world title in London in 1889. A huge crowd paid their last respects to the 'Clarence Comet' as his Sydney funeral procession passed by.[31] Nineteenth-century Melburnians too turned out to pay homage to their deceased sporting heroes. When jockey Tom Corrigan died from injuries received in the fall of his mount Waiter in the 1894 Caulfield Grand National Steeplechase, thousands of mourning spectators lined the funeral route from his Caulfield home to the Melbourne cemetery.[32] The most famous Australian sporting funeral, however, was that at Maitland in 1917, when local boy Les Darcy was laid to rest following his death in the United States from blood poisoning. He had left Australia under a cloud, many believing that he had fled his native land to avoid conscription and earn money overseas: his reputation as a world-class boxer, his modesty, clean living and family loyalty all rendered meaningless by taunts of cowardice and avarice. In death all was forgiven and Australian sports fans awarded Darcy martyr status.[33] Yet too much should not be read into these instances of mass public mourning. The funerals of the explorers Burke and Wills, politician W. C. Wentworth, and militarist General Monash also drew large crowds and surely no-one would claim that Australians were obsessed by their activities![34]

Sports participation is less obviously an Australian trait. Player registrations are available on a national basis for very recent years only and undoubtedly the 9.4 million (from an Australian population of 17.3 million) cited in the 1991 *Australian Sports Directory* includes substantial double, treble or even quadruple counting, plus figures most likely inflated for the purposes of securing a better public image or perhaps greater financial assistance from the Australian Sports Commission. What is clear from the statistics is that a substantial proportion of the registrations (46.5 per cent) are of children and youths, groups which may have missed out on sport historically. That Australian adults are not playing sport to any great extent may also be inferred from physical-activity surveys which show that only fifteen per cent of the population aged eighteen and above were 'highly physically active' and that the average Australian exercises neither long enough nor sufficiently vigorously to maintain a reasonable level of fitness.[35]

Despite some reservations on one side and hyperbole on the other, there is truth in the perception that significant numbers of Australians are interested in sport. Any nation which utilised sportsmen's regiments — 'show the enemy what Australian sporting men can do' — as a recruiting device in the First World War, has declared public holidays for race meetings and regattas and televises the *counting* of votes for the Brownlow Medal must see sport as a major ingredient in its lifestyle and culture.

Supporters of the obsession hypothesis have tended to regard Australians as an homogeneous group and have ignored the fact that for too long Australian sport has been mainly the preserve of the white, Anglo-Saxon male. Although sports advocate William Bundey, Attorney-General of South Australia, maintained in an 1880 lecture that 'one of the greatest charms connected with manly exercises is that ... they level all social distinctions', historically sport has not proved to be an agent for social equality and indeed has more often than not emphasised rather than lessened differences of class, race and gender.[36]

Certainly the leading citizens in Bundey's own colony used sport as a means of demonstrating their social status by participating in sporting activities rendered exclusive to their group. This was partly achieved by cost in that imported game birds, cruising yachts and thoroughbred horses for hunting, racing and playing polo were expensive status symbols.[37] Sporting dress too could be expensive but essentially hunting 'pink', riding habits, archery costume and yachting uniforms were intended as an ostentatious public display to mark out the participants from the mob.[38] The timing and location of events further restricted participation to a select band. Clearly midweek race meetings and hunting were organised for the leisured élite and the use of private property for polo matches and the grounds of Government House for archery practice enabled social vetting of both players and spectators to be enforced.[39] As increased affluence and leisure time opened up the range of sporting activities available to the bulk of the population, there were some unwelcome intrusions into select preserves. Football was a prime example of a game which lost caste through popularisation. In South Australia it had initially been a sport of the younger gentry but as mass participation converted 'manliness' into 'violence' it acquired a less reputable image. Those who did not wish to participate alongside the newcomers either withdrew from the sport, resorted to old-scholars teams, or became patrons of clubs, thus reminding the community who its social leaders were.[40]

Sport in Australia, as in many other nations, has been a prime means of gender-fixing; a way of socialising the populace into sex-based social roles; a method of informing, even dictating to both men and women how they should behave on and off the sports field.[41] Thus for most of the nineteenth century, and perhaps even into the twentieth, almost half the Australian population was excluded from sports participation by virtue of its gender. The focus was on Bundey's 'manly exercises' which by definition relegated women to a spectator role. To emphasise the manliness of sports, women had to be excluded. Thus medical 'evidence' was marshalled to demonstrate that physical exercise was inimical to motherhood and social pressures were applied to restrict women to gentle sports where the emphasis was on fashion and social chitchat. In the South Australian press, for example, ladies' golf was reported under the heading, 'Adelaide gossip'.[42] This, of course, served to reinforce the stereotype of the fragile female.

Only slowly did Australian women begin to participate in sport though, even in the third quarter of the nineteenth century, this seems mainly to have been in class-based, genteel activities such as archery and croquet, more recreational activities than competitive sport. Tennis also began this way, but its social base was later broadened by church groups taking it beyond the private courts. By the turn of the century there was a small but growing participation of women in sporting activity; most were involved in non-competitive events such as gymnastics, calisthenics, skating and, of course, cycling which spearheaded the female liberation movement in recreation, though rowing and hockey were also in evidence, especially in some of the girls' private schools which thought that these sports helped promote team spirit and create an institutional identity. Gradually in the years between the First and Second World Wars, Australian women began to participate more in competitive sport but some avenues were firmly blocked. Football, combat sports, long-distance running and even some track and field events remained strictly men only.

From the 1960s women increasingly have challenged the male view of their role in Australian society. In sport they have undermined the idea of female weakness by taking up horse-racing, long-distance running, weight-lifting and body-building, previously the domain of men. Yet equality of opportunity to participate in sport has not been achieved. Although females are the majority of the Australian population, they still receive a disproportionate share of sporting resources; they have only slowly, and often very reluctantly, been accepted into traditional male sports; and even in mixed clubs and associations they have been generally excluded from positions of influence and authority.[43]

The prime reason for this has been the attitudes not just of males but also of many females who share the predominant male view that high-exertion, highly competitive, physical contact sport is unfeminine. Some believe that women should not participate at all; others feel that they should concentrate on those sports such as gymnastics, diving, synchronised swimming and ice-skating which emphasise grace, flexibility and

Doug Nicholls ready to run in the Warracknabeal Gift in 1929, which he won. *From left:* V.R. Foster, F. Speakman, R.P. Wilhelm, M.J. Dunne, D.R. Nicholls and G. Sykeso. His prize money of £220 would have been one-fifth of the annual income of Cummeragunja Mission New South Wales, Nicholls' home. Nicholls was an outstanding Aboriginal athlete and Australian rules footballer in the period before the Second World War. (Source unknown.)

co-ordination, widely accepted feminine characteristics; the more radical minority seek equal access, equal rights, equal rewards and possibly genderless sport. The dominant masculine viewpoint of female sport has been nurtured and reinforced by the Australian media which, until recently, featured little serious discussion of women's sport and instead, when they deigned to offer any space gave a largely discriminatory presentation of female athletes and their performances.[44] Despite legislation designed to promote equality of sporting opportunity, community attitudes mean that for many Australian women anatomy determines their sporting activity or, more likely, their non-activity. Successful sportswomen still have to overcome opposition and discrimination: to use an Australian colloquialism, women in Australian sport have not yet had a 'fair go'.

The activity in which Aborigines have received most acknowledgement from the Australian white population is sport. World boxing titles, Australian rugby captaincies, and Sandover and Tassie medals have caught white imagination more than any prowess in bush skills or artistic pursuits.[45] Yet Aborigines have often been denied access to white sports and sporting facilities. In that doors to ski lodges and polo stables have been shut firmly in their faces the Aborigines are little different to the bulk of the Australian working class. However, within their own domain most Aborigines have lived on government settlements and Church missions where pools and gyms, courts and tracks and, for many, even grass, have not been part of their life experience. Their poverty, their geographical remoteness and the attitudes of whites with whom and against whom they might have played have kept Aborigines out of most white sports.

In the twentieth century, although vastly under-represented in most sports and virtually non-participatory in many others, Aborigines have been disproportionately successful at the high levels of three major sports, Australian rules football, rugby league football and boxing. Perhaps two dozen Aborigines have played with distinction in the Australian Football League and its predecessor, the Victorian Football League, but in the west they have been much more successful. On eight occasions since 1955 Aborigines have won the Sandover Medal for being the best player in the Western Australian Football League (WAFL) and three of the recipients also gained the Tassie Medal as the best player in the interstate championships. In the late 1980s some ten per cent of WAFL footballers were Aboriginal, almost ten times their proportion of that state's population. Prior to the Second World War Aborigines may have faced selection bias in rugby league but certainly from the 1950s their merit appears to have overcome prejudice. In 1987 some thirty-two Aboriginal footballers played in the New South Wales premiership competition and a further fifteen in the Queensland championship. At least fourteen Aboriginal players have represented Australia. However, it is in boxing that Aborigines have really made their sporting mark. At professional level they have won at least one hundred state titles, fifty-one Australian titles, six British Empire or Commonwealth titles and, with Lionel Rose, the world bantamweight championship. Three others have fought unsuccessfully for world titles.

These particular sports have attracted Aborigines partly because they are mainstream Australian activities which offer blacks a chance of success in a white world: indeed opportunities might have been given to Aborigines for their entertainment value as a special breed of gladiators. That some Aborigines have been successful has provided over time a number of role models for young blacks. Access to these sports has also been easier than in the more class-conscious rowing or rugby union or in tennis and golf which have frequently been organised around private clubs. Yet no Aborigine has represented Australia at cricket, a somewhat ironic statistic considering that the first team of Australian cricketers to tour England was virtually all-Aboriginal, though significantly the captain-manager was a white man.[46] Since that tour in 1868 perhaps only eight Aborigines have played first-class cricket in Australia.[47]

Weight of numbers has meant that British migrants have influenced Australian sporting development more than any other group. Nevertheless other nationalities have contributed to 'new Australian' sporting traditions, particularly with the mass European migration of the two decades following the Second World War.[48] They brought with them handball, bocce and volleyball and stimulated water-polo, ice-hockey, table-tennis, basketball, skiing, fencing and, above all, soccer. Unlike the workplace, the soccer field offered them the opportunity to demonstrate their skills without fluency in English. The soccer clubs which developed also provided a link with home and a base for the socialisation of their Australian-born children. So much did the game become identified with ethnic communities that soccer became disparagingly referred to as 'wogball'.[49] The extent to which non-British migrants and their offspring have participated in mainstream Australian sport has not yet been quantified, but it can be asserted that few have played cricket, more have ventured into Australian rules football and boxing, and even more into rugby league, which seems to have become the most democratic of Australian sports.

Claims that in sport 'all social distinctions are broken down' and 'all meet on equal terms' have proved unfounded.[50] Indeed class prejudice, sexual segregation and racial discrimination have permeated Australia's sporting history. Clearly sport in Australia has not taken place on a level playing field.

2

Australian Football

Bernard Whimpress

The great objection to the rules in New South Wales was that they
were styled The Victorian Rules of Football.

> Football Reporter of 1881,
> quoted in Geoffrey Blainey,
> *A game of our own* (Melbourne, 1990)

You do meet good blokes from Collingwood. But they have to be away
from the club or finished with football.

> Jack Dyer, *Captain Blood* (Melbourne, 1965)

AUSTRALIAN football is not just the Australian Football
League although strong emphasis will be given here to
the major competitions. Across the country there are
nearly half a million registered footballers comprising 138 720
adult male players and 338 868 juniors.[1] On ovals dotted
throughout the country men, women and children enjoy the
game without the need for electronic scoreboards, huge corporate sponsors and television coverage.[2] This football at the
grassroots level enables patrons to park their cars around the
ground and toot their horns when their team scores a goal; it
allows supporters to enter the arena to listen to the coaches'
pearls of wisdom at the quarter and three-quarter time breaks;
and it allows youngsters to kick their footballs on the field
before the match, during the intervals in play and when the

game is over. In the cities many of the teams play under the auspices of amateur associations although a lot of players receive payment. In the country, players are often paid although the pleasures are principally derived from personal satisfaction. The exception might be the fringe league player looking to pick up easy dollars in the bush, but if his attitude is too mercenary it is not likely that he will last long. In such competitions, rivalries are as fierce as anywhere else but attention to physical condition is not always paramount.

Australian football contains a number of contradictions. From humble beginnings in the 1850s it has developed into Australia's major sport and been described as a 'significant contributor to the national economy and Australian lifestyle'[3] but the world's oldest codified football game only in the 1980s decided on a change of name. For most of the last hundred years it has been known as Australian rules football but if the alteration to 'Australian football' is intended to be symbolic it also provokes several main questions. To what extent is the game Australian and is it football? To what extent is it, or has it been national? To what extent is it Australian made? And to what extent is it Australian in spirit?

Victorians, South Australians, Western Australians and Tasmanians have had little difficulty recognising the game as football and it is likely that it was never queried seriously as football until Australia's post-war migrant community, coming from soccer traditions, began to give it labels like aerial ping-pong. The Australianness of the game is more complex. It preceded the Commonwealth of Australia by forty years but it has never been able to establish Australia-wide supremacy as the rugby codes dominated in New South Wales and Queensland.

Founded in Victoria, the Melbourne Football Club rules predominated before giving way to Victorian rules and there are those both inside and outside that state who would argue that it has remained thus ever since. The history of the game's growth has been largely one of separate development with the colonial and state associations and leagues responsible for the conduct of the sport within their borders but deferring to the National Australian Football Council[4] on matters regarding

the laws and permit regulations. At the same time the real controlling power of the game has remained in Melbourne.

In 1877 the Victorian Football Association had been formed partly with the aim of arranging football matches with the surrounding colonies. This met with initial resistance in Sydney from the Southern Rugby Football Union although, three years later, the New South Wales Football Association was formed and Victorian laws adopted. The following year the New South Wales team did play the Victorians but they were humiliated by margins of nine goals to nil in Melbourne and nine to one in Sydney. These heavy defeats were a blow to the national progress of the sport, although as *Melbourne Punch* explained, it was not being adopted in Sydney because of colonial rivalry and the insistence of Melburnians in maintaining the name 'Victorian Rules'.[5] It was then that the call was made for it to be changed to Australian rules.

This occurred in 1883 and in the same year the first intercolonial football conference was held with delegates attending from Victoria, Queensland, South Australia and Tasmania (but not New South Wales). This conference was noteworthy in that it followed close upon the first trade union congresses (1879) but preceded conferences on federation (1891) and cricket (1892) as part of moves towards national expression.

An early game. (*Illustrated Australian News*, 1877, Mitchell Library, State Library of New South Wales.)

The pioneering years were full of hope. In 1877 inter-colonial club matches began when the Melbourne and St Kilda clubs visited Adelaide. These club tours, first undertaken by coastal steamship and then rail, were a regular feature of the game for the next fifteen years and games between respective colonial association premiers were billed as championships of Australia. Although football in Melbourne was more powerful, as evidenced by their dominance of the first fully-fledged inter-colonial matches which began in 1879, the club champion-ships were sometimes won by South Australian teams such as Norwood, which defeated Victorian premiers South Melbourne three matches to nil in 1888.[6]

By this time, observers could note several characteristics:

Football, as now carried on here, is not only often rough and brutal between the combatants, but seems to me to have a decided moral lowering and brutalizing effect upon the spectators.

The records of the past season show that several promising young men have been crippled for life in this 'manly sport;' others have received serious temporary injuries, and laid the foundations of future ill-health, the luckiest getting off with scars which they will bear with them to their graves.

Society is demoralised by such public exhibitions as the 'last match of the season' between the Melbourne and Carlton Football Clubs, which I witnessed ... The six or seven thousand spectators comprised representatives of nearly all classes. It was a truly democratic crowd. Ex-Cabinet Ministers and their families, members of parliament, professional and tradesmen, free selectors and squatters, clerks, shopmen. bagmen, mechanics, larrikins, betting men, publicans, barmaids (very strongly represented), working girls, and the half world, all were there.

From the want of reserved seats, or any special accommodation for ladies, the mixture all round the ground was as heterogeneous as well might be ... The Carlton Club were playing on their own ground, and the feeling of the majority was in their favour, and from the com-mencement was so expressed rather offensively towards the Mel-bourne Club, which is considered, I believe, to be a little more high-toned, and consequently antagonistic to democratic Carlton.

It is true that, as a spectacle of bodily activity and endurance, the show was a fine one, but the cruelty and brutality intermixed with it, and which the crowd loudly applauded, and appeared to consider the principal attraction, was anything but a promising evidence of a high civilization.

I was told by several that it would be a pretty rough game, and they gloated to the fact. As the play went on, and men got heavy falls, and rose limping or bleeding, the applause was immense. 'Well played, sir,' always greeted a successful throw. 'That's the way to smash 'em,' said one of my neighbours. 'Pitch him over!' and such cries were frequent, and the whole interest and applause seem centred in such work.

It was no fair conflict either; a man running after another who has the ball, seizing him by the neck, and throwing him down, does not, to my mind, do a particularly manly thing. It inculcates bad blood, as the victim is sure to spot his oppressor, and be down on him when occasion offers.

Early in the game it was apparent that a bad feeling existed between the players . . . the umpire took up his stick, and walked off the ground, and the game was suddenly stopped. I asked this gentleman what was the matter, and he said the Carlton players used such blackguard language to him that he would not stand it; and in this, I think, he was right.

One friend said, however, that he was wrong. 'The umpire always has a hard time of it,' said he; 'the only thing he can do is to wear several brass rings, if he hasn't got gold ones, and let the first man who disputes his decision have it straight.' This idea was received with great favour by the crowd, and is an instance of the good feeling generally engendered by this 'manly sport'. The 'scrimmages' were frequent, and altogether the violence used was often totally unnecessary and gratuitous. I watched several individual players. One man would throw or push another down after he had kicked the ball, and without, as far as the play was concerned, any excuse or provocation. The aggrieved one would 'spot' his antagonist and repay in like manner.

This system of aggression was altogether, to my mind, cowardly and uncalled for, and yet was loudly applauded by the spectators.

The victory of the Melbourne Club proved unpopular with the larrikins, who commenced stoning the players outside the gates. One offender, however, received a good thrashing for his pains.

I consider that football, as played at this match, is a disgrace to our civilization.[7]

Australia's centenary year provided an opportunity to take the sport into the international arena at a crucial time in the growth of the world's football codes.[8] An English football team led by the test cricketing entrepreneurs James Lillywhite and Arthur Shrewsbury played rugby in New South Wales and New Zealand and then were coached in Australian rules football in order to play the leading Victorian and South Australian clubs. The Englishmen used their greater body power to move the ball with a sustained charge and won fourteen of twenty-five matches playing the Australian game but more importantly the offer was made for a series of return matches in England. Unfortunately, however, this was never finalised as the Victorian Football Association, then the major administrative body in the country, thought the move beyond their capacities and postponed final arrangements.[9]

A number of conferences were held which led to the formation of the Australasian Football Council (AFC) in 1905 but calls for the proper promotion of the nationalisation of the Australian game of football by the 'co-operation of the organisations in the various states'[10] did not gain the impetus it might have expected as the Victorian Football League began to take the dominant role in the AFC that it has never relinquished.[11] The AFC became 'Australian' in 1924 and like the South Australian Football League inserted the word 'National' into its title in 1927 as evidence of the redirected ambitions of some of its administrators, although the body would never be democratic while the Victorian Football League had the largest block of votes. Essentially the achievements of the various so-called national bodies have thus been small, and limited principally to organising triennial carnivals between 1908 and 1980 as showcases for national expansion. For most of this century the Victorian Football League's prime interest has been its member clubs, interstate matches have been restricted to one or two per season and the premiers matches for the Championship of Australia were revived briefly only in the early 1970s. Almost all of these games were well attended but were dominated by Victorian teams except for a North Adelaide side let by the talented Barrie Robran which triumphed over Carlton in 1972. It has only been in the 1980s that the game has been interested in expanding nationally but this has been chiefly for commercial gain. The attempt to take Australian football to international audiences has seen matches played in London, Japan, America and Greece but these have been novelty events, and the Gaelic football test matches against the Irish republic have not been continued.

There is strong evidence for Australian football being made in Australia. While it is true to say that it was built on existing traditions and not codified in a vacuum,[12] it had also become distinctive within a year, combining the merits of the kicking and handling games played in English public schools.[13] The crucial factor for the Australian game was that it was first played before either rugby or soccer had been codified. If it had begun fifteen years later it may not have invented its own rules although it did draw inspiration from a number of sources.

In the beginning, rugby influenced Australian football: captains were the sole judges of infringements of the rules before the appointment of umpires; the game began with a kick-off from the centre of the ground; the Australian game adopted rugby positions of goal-keepers and goal-sneaks; the mark derived from the rugby 'fair catch'; goals from the field had to be kicked by drop kick or place kicks; goals could be forced through by scrummaging; and a rugby-shaped ball was introduced from 1860.[14] As time went by, however, the scrum was removed and goals had to be kicked between the posts without touching another player. From the outset Australian football differed from rugby in that there was no off-side rule; players could not run with the ball further than necessary to kick it except by touching it to their boot or bouncing it; and the ball had to be punched rather than thrown.[15]

In framing the code then creating the rules during the late 1850s and early 1860s the founders wanted a 'manly' game but one which was not too rough. On the one hand the emphasis on kicking allowed that it was suitable for 'true gentlemen' for whom scarred legs and blood in their boots as a result of repeated kicks in the shins was perceived as 'noble'. On the other hand serious injury was to be avoided if a man was to make a living.[16] Henry Harrison pioneered fast and open running play although he also favoured a vigorous approach. 'Football is essentially a rough game the world over, and it is not suitable for menpoodles or milksops'[17] he once wrote in the *Australasian*, the sort of statement which has since been used to legitimise thuggery.

Australian football was also shaped by a number of other influences including cricket and spatial considerations. Like cricket, football matches began with the toss of a coin and the winning team had the choice of goal; the first players wore long white trousers and shirts and the early Melbourne Football Club teams were known as the Invincible Whites.[18] Football matches, like cricket, were interrupted for refreshment breaks and extended over more than a day with play often continued until bad light intervened and were even suspended for rain. For the first twenty-five years umpires only adjudicated in response to players' appeals for decisions on the rules.[19]

The large amounts of open space also had an impact on the game's development. Although Tom Wills' letter to *Bells' Life in Victoria* on 10 July 1858 had suggested that cricketers could keep fit by playing football during the winter and that cricket grounds would benefit by being 'trampled upon', this did not automatically follow. Indeed, for the first fifteen years in Victoria the Melbourne Football Club played its games on the paddock outside the cricket ground and on the one exceptional occasion in June 1869 when the club played against the 14th Regiment its captain was bluntly told: 'Harrison, you have ruined our ground!'[20] Most football matches were played on more or less rectangular grounds often a quarter of a mile (402 metres) long and up to two hundred yards (183 metres) wide. The vast size of the grounds led to an emphasis on a kicking game but Australian football did not transfer to the largely fenced cricket grounds until the 1870s when it became necessary to keep the large and enthusiastic crowds off the playing arena.

Before closing on the subject of Australian football's origins it seems appropriate to dispose of a couple of myths which have long prevailed. One, which has been discounted recently, is that it derived from Gaelic football; this theory has involved combating circumstantial evidence and backward reasoning from the present. In fact, there is scant evidence of Irish or Gaelic football influence in contemporary sources dating from the middle of the last century. The four men who had most influence on the formation of Australian football came from British universities and private schools; the first schools to play the game in Victoria were Protestant colleges; the first cup presented for challenge among senior teams was the Caledonian Cup; and the first president of the Victorian Football Association was a freemason.[21] Players with Irish names became prominent as the game expanded rather than at the outset. Rather than Gaelic football being the progenitor of the Australian game it has been argued: 'The style of play which Gaelic and Australian football share today was visible in Australian football long before it was visible in Gaelic football … Just as two games can grow apart over time, so they can grow more alike over time.'[22]

The second myth is that the game might have an Aboriginal origin. Again this in part derives from the fact that a number of the most prominent exponents of the game have been Aborigines and the high mark popularised by the Essendon stars Charlie Pearson and Albert Thurgood in the 1880s and

1890s[23] has been thought to have been influenced by a traditional Aboriginal game which involved high leaping for a possum skin. But no firm connection has been established.[24]

Thus Australian football was not a once-only invention but evolved over many decades and invented its own way of playing; devised its own rules, tactics and skills and adapted them to the Australian political, social and economic environment. Because the game was not played internationally it was also more able to change from its original rules as there was no need to confer with governing bodies from other countries.

For a long time Australian football used to carry a Latin motto *Populi Ludos Populo* — the game of the people for the people — and there is little doubt that from early on it has been played by a broad cross-section of Australian people. In addition it is interesting to note how it has found its champions among people from diverse ethnic and racial backgrounds although this should not be taken to mean that competition has always been fair and open to all. While it has been strongly supported by women, it has long promoted itself as a man's game.

The game's founders might have played for the socially select Melbourne Cricket Club but not all their pedigrees were pure merino and some of them bought their respectability. Among the first rule-makers, Rugby-educated Tom Wills' father was a rich sheepowner though his grandfather was a convicted highwayman transported to New South Wales for life; and his cousin Henry Colden Harrison who later became known as the 'father of the Australian game' and briefly attended Melbourne Grammar School, was descended on his mother's side from emancipated convicts while his father became a political radical. On the other hand William Hammersley and James Thompson were students of Trinity College, Cambridge before migrating to Victoria during the gold rushes; and Thomas Smith, a master at Scotch College, was a graduate from Trinity College, Dublin.[25] Among other early players some of the Melbourne Cricket Club cricketers were professionals like the former Surrey player Jerry Bryant, the publican of the Parade Hotel which became an early meeting place for footballers.

Australian football was quick to spread geographically and as it did so it crossed class barriers. In the 1860s it spread quickly to the Victorian gold-mining cities of Ballarat and Bendigo, and the coastal town of Warrnambool, to Hobart, Western Australia and New Zealand. In 1860 football was being played in Adelaide although initially there was some doubt that this was necessarily the Australian code. What is evident, however, is that the game moved beyond the social establishment of politicians, judiciary and the professions.[26] By the time the South Australian Football Association was formed in 1877 it should be noted that the team which filled last place on the first premiership ladder was known as Bankers,[27] and shortly afterwards trade-based teams such as ironmongers and bankers began to field teams in minor associations. South Australia's West Torrens Football Club was once called the Butchers because of the large number of abattoir workers who played for the team and the state's oldest and best known club, Port Adelaide, drew heavily on wharf labourers for a long time so that the sobriquet 'Wharfies' is still applied to the football team even though it is nearly forty years since such an employee pulled on a club guernsey.[28] In Melbourne, the Collingwood and Fitzroy clubs fielded teams comprising players who worked in manufacturing industries and the old nickname 'Shinboners' for North Melbourne derived from the practice of local butchers tying blue and white ribbons around the shin-bones of cattle as part of their shop window decorations on Saturdays during the football season.[29]

If Australian football has absorbed players from various class backgrounds it has done the same with nationalities as well. Silvagni, Ditterich, Jesaulenko, Kekovich, Schimmelbusch, Daicos, Dipierdomenico and Liberatore: the names illustrate the point but perhaps 'Jezza' is the best example of the migrant boy making good in Australian football. Growing up in Canberra in the 1950s the son of a Russian mother and Ukrainian father, Alex Jesaulenko was the butt of epithets such as 'wop' and 'dago' and regularly beaten up after school. But the long-term result was that he developed a toughness which, combined with incredible ball skills and reflexes, made him one of the most skilful players in the history of the Victorian Football League (VFL). His versatility was such that he once kicked one hundred goals in a season from full forward; in the centre he was a consistent ball winner and delivered it precisely; at half-forward he would swoop on the ball to take advantage of opportunities and was a brilliant high mark; and in defence at the end of his career he checked closely, passed soundly and

Alex Jesaulenko was a footballer who reflected the growing cultural and ethnic diversity of Australia. He became a hero in the Australian game in the 1960s and 1970s. (The *Age*).

used superb handball to set up play further afield. In 1970 he also took one of the great high marks of the modern era in the grand final against Collingwood and it was widely used to promote Australian football as the most exciting code in the country.[30]

On the one hand a 'new' Australian was being used to promote the game and nearly twenty years later VFL publicists were attempting to attract support at a football match with the catchy punchline, 'Take the kids to see some Aboriginal art tomorrow', an acknowledgement (if a patronising one) that some of the best exponents of the game are Aborigines.[31] Today it can be said that the oldest Australians receive a 'fair go' as far as representation in Australian football is concerned but this has not been so in the past and Aborigines rarely appeared in the major state leagues until the 1960s. Although Aboriginal sides from the Point Macleay and Poonindie missions played matches on the Adelaide Oval in 1885[32] and defeated strong, combined association teams, policies based on separation and restriction denied them the opportunity to play at the top level for the next seventy years. Doug Nicholls was an exception with Fitzroy in the 1930s (although he had earlier been excluded at Carlton because he was told he smelled) and it was not until 1947 that any more Aborigines ventured into the VFL. The main advance came in Western Australia where players like Ted Kilmurray, Graham Farmer, Bill Dempsey and Barry Cable began making a name, and those like Farmer, Cable and Syd Jackson took their skills to the VFL in the 1960s and paved the way for the emergence of many of the heroes of the last fifteen years such as Maurice Rioli, Jim and Phil Krakouer, Stephen Michael, Michael Graham, Derek Kickett and Gilbert McAdam.[33] By far the biggest impact of Aboriginal footballers however has been in country associations, where seemingly unfit, under-trained and undisciplined they have frequently run rings around opponents, thereby keeping alive some of the old amateur tradition of sport as play.[34]

The position of women in Australian football has been restricted to support roles. For many women and girls, their first exposure to the game was playing alongside their brothers as children. As they have reached their teenage years there has been the opportunity to join cheer squads and, from the 1970s, the brief glamour role afforded by joining the club dancing troupes which warm up the crowds for the main match. The odd part about this has been that although women seem to make up about forty per cent of football crowds, few have raised voices about sexist exploitation, so one has been forced to assume that this stage in a girl's footy graduation has won some approval.

The logical progress of making more intimate connection with the players, seen by many as the ultimate goal, has been further encouraged by football leagues and clubs which have viewed women chiefly as potential wives but also occasionally as sex objects. At the league level in the 1970s for example pretty girl supporters in South Australia could become *Football Budget* Caltex Girls of the Week, twenty-five dollars richer and in line for Girl of the Year.[35] At the club level the grooming of potential players' wives may be seen to begin with the Miss Football quests, in which the aim was both to be beautiful and to raise funds for the club. For the ardent fan, the union of football queen with the best and fairest winner probably would seem like a marriage made in heaven — although if the coach said no sex on Friday nights, the wife would be expected to camp on the sofa in the spare room. This could be just part of a pattern, in which on Saturdays would mean being smartly dressed and coiffured with other players' wives in the front of the grandstand; on Sundays washing husband's and sons' grubby guernseys, shorts and socks; then, with the passing years, serving barbecues at home games and putting on a spread for club functions at which, near the end of an evening, the president (male) would say, 'Let's hear it for the ladies' and the muttering 'Hear, hear' from the men would inevitably follow. In addition to this pattern, however, the women as whores philosophy has also been exploited, with professional strip-tease dancers proving a popular means of fund-raising at 'Men Only' nights; West Perth Football Club once attempted a membership drive using pictures of a provocatively posed model in the club guernsey declaring 'I'm hot for the Falcons in '83, come and get hot with me!'[36]

The die for women in football seems to have been hard to break, although early this century perhaps they did gain some compensations by engaging in violent acts against opposition players and umpires such as sticking hat pins into them as they left the arena and brandishing umbrellas in the heat of the moment. In more recent years women have also been more open in their admiration of male backsides in tight shorts.

During the 1980s women have begun to play a more active off-field role in the game. Some have been elected to senior committee positions on major league clubs' boards of management, some have held full-time salaried promotional positions on club staff, and many others (particularly primary school-teachers) have qualified as coaches at junior levels. The idea that Australian football was just a man's game received a severe jolt when the West Torrens Football Club employed former Olympic gold-medallist Glynis Nunn to construct their fitness programme, and women began to emerge as journalists reporting on the game and photographers capturing the action.

On field, women's contribution to the game has not been as rapid although even there they are beginning to break down barriers. The umpiring fraternity has opened its doors (even at senior level) and under equal-opportunity legislation girls have won places in junior football teams governed by modified rules. At senior levels, however, despite the formation of bodies such a the Victorian Women's Football League with clubs including the Broadmeadow Scorpions, Dingley Cobras,

Epping Hill Blues and Princes Hill Dodgers, official attitudes from male leagues have been to turn a blind eye to their efforts and for the press to report such competitions in a condescending manner.[37]

The strength of Australian football as a spectator sport has been powerful in, but also beyond Victoria. The first football games attracted only immediate friends and family but by the 1860s up to 2000 people were attending matches and the game had spread beyond participation to take in the prestige of clubs and communities. The football clubs first consisted of gentlemen who played, but the clubs were increasingly dominated by fee-paying members who took over their operations, setting the stage for the amateur-professional struggle. Much of the problem between the two groups related to moral issues. In 1874 crowds at the major Melbourne games began to top 10 000 and it was recognised early that of those who paid their sixpences to see the likes of Melbourne and Carlton play, the vast majority were intensely interested in the match.[38]

Collingwood's first association match in 1892 drew 16 000 and at the Victorian Football Association 1890 final between South Melbourne and Carlton the crowd numbered 33 000. For much of the 1890s the Depression took a heavy toll on attendances although, by the end of the decade, finals matches were again attracting crowds of over 30 000 people. At the end of the century skilled working-class players had a means of escaping their class and their supporters, taking vicarious pleasure from this, enabled Australian football to be seen as a 'positive expression of working-class life'.[39] Certainly the sense of suburban community was strong and heroes were likely to be found among the local greengrocers, plumbers and bank tellers. The big growth in spectator numbers in the Victorian Football League, however, began in the 1920s, partly as a result of relief from the First World War but also in response to a growing economy, relatively low unemployment and the greater personalising of heroes in sports journalism. The use of photographs, both in the daily press and in specialist publications such as the *Victorian Football Record* and *South Australian Football Budget*, contributed to the growth of personalities as players became more readily identifiable.

In the 1930s Depression there was never any doubt about Australian rules football's position as the game of the people. Crowd figures held firm for a number of reasons but particularly because the game offered cheap, spectacular amusement. For a shilling, football patrons had a social afternoon: ninepence for a ticket to the outer ground and threepence for a pie and sauce, whereas the only comparably-priced alternative was the matinee ticket to the cinema (the 'flicks') for one shilling and threepence. Like the cinema, the football also offered escape and outstanding deeds by the local heroes could uplift the spirit and take the mind off the day-to-day worries of life.[40]

Football attendances grew after the Second World War and total figures for minor-round matches in Melbourne topped two million for the first time in 1946;[41] but the peak years were in the 1950s and 1960s. Several interesting details have also emerged when the crowd figures of the four main football states were compared between 1964 and 1982. One is that Hobart and Perth had a higher proportional attendance at the football than Melbourne and Adelaide in the 1960s but that the Victorian Football League had a more constant drawing power over the period whereas the Tasmanian Australian National Football League showed a steep downward trend from the mid-1970s onward.[42]

The fact that football support was not keeping pace with population growth has been attributed to a number of factors: increased car ownership expanded people's horizons, loosened ties with the local community and created the opportunity to find alternative means of recreation; post-war immigration brought the challenge of alternative sports such as soccer; a more affluent public began to demand better facilities; and television coverage of sports both nationally and internationally meant loyalties could be divided so that a football fan supported not just Port Adelaide but Collingwood and perhaps Manchester United as well. The dramatic fall-off in support of the Tasmanian and Western Australian football leagues may also be explained by the professional push of the VFL and recruiting of some of those states' best players during that period.[43]

A key factor in the professional versus amateur battle during the late nineteenth and twentieth centuries was its coverage in the news media. One hundred years ago amateurism was lauded and professionalism despised: today the boot is on the other foot, with professionalism the byword for a serious and dedicated approach. In 1890 media coverage of football was found in three places: the metropolitan papers, local papers and the specialist sporting press, with the writers 'extolling the manly character-building virtues of the game' and viewing their mission as one of 'improving moral standards' rather than providing sporting information.[44]

An example of such moralising could be found in the Adelaide *Observer* of 26 April 1890: 'By virtue of being a footballer a man must be strong and active and why should a strong, healthy, young fellow lay the seeds of laziness by being paid to walk about in idleness or for playing with his comrades or against his opponents who have been working hard at their professions and trades all week.' Few reporters took the far-sighted view of the writer in the *Register* in 1891: 'True professionalism would see an equal division of funds from pooled resources and players could still be paid their due as entertainers but clubs would be of equal strength.' In practice, though, it did not work that way and professionalism was equated with degeneration, the suspicion being that if a player was paid to play well he could also be paid to play badly.

Another interesting feature of the debate on payment was the different way it was handled in Victoria and South Australia. In Melbourne the Victorian Football Association had introduced a rule in 1886 for the disqualification of players who received payment either 'directly or indirectly' for their services as a footballer but the attempt in the 1890s by the association to take over all financial control of its member clubs which would then be defined on district lines was rejected by the wealthier clubs. The split by these clubs from the VFA led to the formation of the Victorian Football League in 1897 and what has been described as a victory for running football as a 'business' and as 'entertainment for working-class supporters'.[45] In Adelaide, on the other hand, the Depression of the 1890s killed professionalism in its early forms as supporters could no longer afford to pay players a bonus for a winning game; and players were forced to buy their own boots and clothing. Such payments as existed were only for time lost from work for training and arriving at matches. In the end, the South Australian solution lay not in moralising about money or the lack of it but in the establishment of electorate football in 1897: a fair and equal competition based on players representing a specific district club. The intention of the system was to get clubs to cultivate local juniors, a point underlined several years later by the Adelaide *Observer*: 'The promotion of players from clubs' reserve grades does more for the advancement of the game than importing cartloads of cracks from Timbuctoo.'[46]

The old amateur idea began to crack later in South Australia than in Victoria, and certainly the debate by football's officialdom was one-sided and anachronistic. Overall, the labourer may well have been worthy of his hire but what difference was there between a footballer and a music hall or theatrical artist? A second argument proposed by the amateurs was that once players were paid the game would immediately deteriorate and the incidence of bribery would increase. Quite palpably this argument could not be sustained, as its opponents pointed out, since greater compensation would work as an incentive. Discussion on a third front involved bringing the truth into the open and recording payments in the club balance sheets. Club members, it was argued, had a right to know who was paid and how much.

One of the major fears was that the strongest team financially would take the best players and the game would become uninteresting to a paying clientele. In Victoria the introduction of the first salary cap, the Coulter Law, at the start of the 1930 season was an attempt to overcome this problem. It set a flat-rate match payment of three pounds in the hope of keeping clubs solvent during the Depression but, although it controlled the wage demands of the majority of players, extra money always seemed to be found for star recruits. South Melbourne was unable to pay its players in 1930 and yet three years later it bought itself a premiership on the strength of innovative fund-raising drives which secured outstanding players such as Laurie Nash, Bob Pratt and Herbie Matthews as well as more than doubling its membership.[47] One other effect of the Depression was that desperate players often became more mobile in their search for means of support and moved to the country and interstate in order to secure their futures. In 1933 Footscray advertised in the Adelaide press for five players to join them that season and South Australian interstate players George Johnston and Len Sallis both played and coached in the southeast of the state.

To some extent the amateur ethic regained ground during the 1930s although trafficking was rife, as was betting on games and the making of under-cover payments. After the Second World War match payments in the VFL under the Coulter Law rose to four pounds in 1946 and five pounds in 1950 and even in the late 1960s payments were as low as twenty-five pounds,

Finals time and young North Adelaide supporters in full war cry. (Photograph by Bernard Whimpress.)

or just under half the average weekly earnings. If the amounts sound like chicken feed it should be remembered that what was important was the principle of payment. To win a premiership meant glory and little else, and bonuses and supporters' contributions at the end of games frequently brought more money than match payments. As an illustration of the modest financial returns for players the South Australian side which defeated the Victorians in Melbourne in 1963 received only five pounds extra per man as a bonus[48] despite the fact that 8000 supporters greeted the team's return home at Adelaide Airport.

Professionalism did not begin to get a real hold in Australian football until the 1960s. Players were loyal to clubs, which gained most of their revenue from attendances and memberships. The only exceptions were those who found greater remuneration in country associations. Some have seen 1965 as a landmark year, when Carlton enticed Melbourne hero Ron Barassi to take up an appointment as captain coach — an event which caused a number of Melbourne fans to burn their number 31 guernseys in protest at his 'treachery'[49] — while others have seen 1968 as being more important,[50] when the introduction of country zoning began to tie potential VFL players to particular clubs.[51] The period when professionalism really began to increase, however, was in the early 1970s at the North Melbourne Football Club when cheque-book recruiting replaced junior development as the means to premiership success, and a wage-cost explosion began which has since been difficult to control. In four years from 1974 to 1978 player payments trebled and players became more aware of their bargaining power but the costs went beyond dollar values. As football clubs adopted business practice they began to echo marketeers' phrases that the game could be promoted as a product and in the 1980s the major leagues began to develop corporate plans.

The main problem for Australian football being run as a business is that the main emphasis of business is to make profits whereas the main purpose of football sides is to win games. Often the clubs which win grand finals end up in the red and those in financial strife then attempt to balance their books by selling off their players, their chief assets. Prior to the 1970s the main sources of football income were gate takings and memberships, and even as late as 1976 the Victorian Football League had no corporate sponsor, no marketing thrust and only a small income from television. A separation between rich and poor clubs in the VFL began to appear in the 1970s but the marketing of the game, strongly linked to television and sponsorship, has in the last fifteen years seen the spectator lose ground as a consequence.

In the 1980s the expansion of the VFL outside Victoria's borders was a major shift from its previous philosophy which placed the interests of the twelve Melbourne clubs before any other considerations. In 1990, the emergence of the Sydney Swans, Brisbane Bears and West Coast Eagles led to the attempts by the newly formed Australian Football League (AFL) to hide its disguise as a revamped VFL by stating that it was 'in existence to promote, plan and generally manage the sport of Australian football in order to achieve its full potential'[52] but some of its decisions, like those of its predecessor, have been dubious.

After South Melbourne was relocated to Sydney a lot of glamour but little profit was provided by the Sydney Swans, and the promotional endeavours centred on the flamboyant, high-flying Dr Geoffrey Edelsten (in pink helicopter), his attractive wife Leanne and a full forward in tight shorts were surely mis-guided.[53] As Bob Santamaria has described it, the marketing of Warwick Capper as a 'product' and his selection for his sex appeal was 'the most despicable perversion of the footballing ethic'. It was also right to question the validity of a game which is 'now a highly capitalised business played by professionals, not for a sporting public, composed of families, but for television audiences financed by television channels and sponsors'.[54]

There are some ironies here. Many Victorians felt their game had been hijacked and that the VFL/AFL had showed itself as arrogant as big business and big government. The links of major clubs with such entrepreneurial figures as Christopher Skase, John Elliott, Geoffrey Edelsten and Bob Ansett also underlined suspicions that Australian league football was becoming a play-thing of the rich. The expansion of the VFL meant that clubs such as Fitzroy, Richmond and Footscray, with long traditions but only local followings, began to struggle. On the surface the AFL in 1990 could boast some impressive achievements. For the first time in league history attendances topped the four million mark for the home-and-away series and finals, club memberships hit record marks, the Channel Seven network set record peak ratings and the West Coast Eagles became the first interstate team to win a finals game. The competition also confirmed its expansion into Adelaide when South Australia's premier club, Port Adelaide, deviously bid for AFL membership but lost to a hastily formed South Australian National Football League proposal which resulted in the emergence of the Ad-elaide Crows in 1991.[55]

Where the future of Australian football lies is uncertain. The season which once started on Anzac Day now begins nearer Christmas and may be killed by excessive promotion. As the Adelaide journalist Lance Campbell wrote: 'The clubs used to be bigger than the individual and the game bigger than the club. Now the promotion of the game is bigger than both of them', and added that the 'gurus of flash' were relentless in their pursuit of spending patrons' admission and membership money on 'leading-edge technology flim-flam'.[56] In the short term the Bears, Swans, Eagles and Adelaide Crows seem likely to maintain a state monopoly, although the seizure of the 1992 AFL premiership by the West Coast Eagles and the continued poor performance by the Bears and Swans could bring revised plans and second teams from South Australia and Western Australia as well as a side from Tasmania.

It is possible that football will no longer be confined to

Opportunities for disabled players to play the game are increasing. This picture was taken as a disabled spectator joins in an informal game during a break between quarters at an Adelaide league match. (Photograph by Bernard Whimpress.)

which team gathers the most kicks and scores the most goals but it is hoped that it does not just become about sponsors and marketing. Chook raffles might be behind us but perhaps corporate marketing images can be laid to rest alongside them. If there is hope for the future of the Australian game perhaps it may lie in the breasts of unsung heroes and quiet achievers. In the midst of the media extravaganza that the AFL grand finals have become it was pleasing to find that there was still room in 1991 for one of these quiet achievers, Hawthorn captain Michael Tuck, to bow out (aged thirty-eight) with seven premierships and a record 426 league games to his credit. In 1991, in the back blocks of the Central District Football Association second division, it was also heartening to discover forty-two-year-old Hughie Graham after thirty years and over 600 games of minor-grade competition still searching for his first premiership.[57]

3 Boxing

Wray Vamplew

> In the clearing stands a boxer
> And a fighter by his trade
> And he carries the reminders
> Of ev'ry glove that laid him down
>
> Simon & Garfunkel,
> 'The Boxer' (1969)

> . . . his manager took twenty-five per cent of the purse, but no punches
>
> Aboriginal boxer interviewed
> by Richard Broome (1980)

THE RECORDED history of boxing in Australia[1] began on 8 January 1814, when John Parton battered fellow convict Charles Seton into submission after fifty rounds and ninety minutes of bare-knuckle fighting.[2] In its prize-fighting form the sport faced official disapproval, and consequent police surveillance, which often forced the promoters of events to stage them in secluded venues. However, it attained popularity, particularly among the less respectable lower orders, and was much appreciated, for example, by entertainment-starved diggers during the 1850s gold rush: indeed Bendigo, one of Victoria's goldfield towns was popularly called such after a local prize-fighter who, in turn, was nicknamed after a British bare-knuckle exponent, Abednego Thompson.[3]

Further evidence that boxing was a central feature of nine-teenth-century Australian sporting life comes from another area of entertainment. Seeking similar audiences, dramatists or, more likely, theatrical producers utilised the noble art on stage. Often the boxing scenarios or a cast list which included minor boxing characters were not relevant to the plot, but, from the 1860s onwards, such sporting flavour gave way to genuine sporting narrative. Actual boxers began to appear more frequently in plays, initially providing a display which the 'real' actors watched, but later as actors themselves.[4]

Nevertheless prize-fighting went into decline from the 1860s as policing became more vigorous, corruption intensified, and ring fatalities brought adverse publicity and prosecution cul-minating in the twelve month gaoling for manslaughter of black American James Lawson after the death of Alec Agar, his opponent in a Sydney fight in 1884.[5] Most future fights were gloved boxing matches which were generally accepted by the law because they were conducted under more controlled rules. Legal tolerance coupled with propitious economic circum-stances to revive the fortunes of Australian boxing and, despite criticism from the more respectable members of society, it entered a boom period in the late nineteenth and early twen-tieth centuries only to come to grief again during the First World War. It was then that the moral outrage against boxing as a preventable evil crescendoed.[6] In contrast to many ama-teur sports bodies, the profit-oriented promoters of profes-sional boxing saw no need to abandon their activities simply because of hostilities in Europe.[7] Thus, added to the claims of brutality and moral degeneration was outrage at this unpatri-otic and disloyal behaviour which, by providing entertainment for spectators, distracted them from their duty of defending the Empire. Amongst the organisations arraigned against profes-sional boxing were the Returned Soldiers and Sailors League, the Council of Churches and the Farmers' and Settlers' Asso-ciation, but its prime opponent was the formidable Council for Civic and Moral Advancement. In vain the secretary of Stadi-ums Limited, the major promoter of boxing in Australia, pointed out that some seven hundred boxers had volunteered for the front along with numerous employees of the company and that boxing contests often raised money for patriotic funds and provided venues for recruitment appeals. The tide of criticism was overwhelming and eventually, in 1917, the Fed-eral government responded with the War Precautions Act which limited the number of boxing promotions and forced

them to share their programmes with vaudeville acts. Attendances fell away and by early 1918 major boxing stadiums in
Melbourne, Sydney and Brisbane had closed.

With peace came the return of violence to the ring as boxing
revived, though the onset of economic depression in the late
1920s and 1930s forced promoters to cater for the cheaper end
of the market and develop small, suburban venues with lower
admission prices than at the larger stadiums which held programmes less regularly than before.[8] The Second World War
presented a different picture to its predecessor and the main
venues stayed open throughout the war. This time the authorities accepted that the stadiums could assist both recruitment
and fund-raising, particularly by means of patriotic displays in
which boxers wearing their service uniforms were introduced
to the crowd.[9] Nevertheless, as post-war Australia moved into
affluence professional boxing was on a downward slope. The
rewards to fighters were less attractive relative to earnings in a
full-employment economy and audiences became attracted to
other evening entertainments such as drive-in movies, night
trotting and greyhound-racing.[10] Television, itself a competi-
tor for leisure time, provided a short-run stimulus with weekly
boxing telecasts which began in 1968 but ended in 1975
because of the over-exposure of the limited talent available.[11]

The origins of amateur boxing in Australia are hard to
discern. Organised boxing for amateurs began in England in
1867 and, like many of the developments in sport of that time,
was probably quickly transported to the Antipodes. Certainly
by the 1880s, and possibly earlier, it was being taught in the
nation's private schools in the context of muscular Christianity and manliness. Others, of a different social background, put
on gloves to compete for prizes in the 'amateur championships'
hosted by hoteliers and gym proprietors. More formally recognised titles came under the aegis of amateur athletic associations with the class connotations of the time restricting entry.[12]
In the twentieth century amateur boxing took on a social-
control aspect with Police Boys Boxing Clubs being seen as a
means to provide delinquents with self-discipline, possibly
change their lifestyle or at least keep them off the streets and
out of trouble for a while.[13]

Boxing became an Olympic sport in 1904 at St Louis, but
Australians did not compete until 1908. In medal terms success
has been very limited with no Australian golds and only a
handful of the lesser medals. Greater success has been achieved
at the Commonwealth Games with over forty medals being

won since middleweight Dudley Gallagher's silver at the inaugural Hamilton event in 1930.[14] The relationship with professionalism has been closer than in many sports, probably because amateur boxing has been a nursery in which budding professionals could exhibit their talent. Gyms have rarely been exclusive to one branch of the noble art and in the 1950s Stadiums Limited used amateur bouts as preliminary events on its professional card, thus reviving what had been common practice in the late nineteenth century.[15]

The sub-culture of professional boxing has a definite power hierarchy. At the bottom are the labourers, the fighters themselves, with status ascribed to them according to their relative abilities. Yet even champions require managers and trainers to plan their ring careers and teach them the skills of the trade, though in Australia unfortunately too many have simply acted as booking agents.[16] At the top are the promoters on whom everyone is dependent as they determine the opportunities available to any boxer.

Prize-fights were generally promoted by the backers of individual fighters, sometimes via challenges in the press, a mode of gaining opponents which continued into the early twentieth century. Another promotional strand lay with publicans who organised bouts, either outside their premises or, as demand justified the expenditure, in boxing saloons attached to them: of course public houses had always been associated with prize-fighting as the site where arrangements were made, deposits posted and victories celebrated.[17] Towards the end of the nineteenth century specialist promoters emerged utilising gymnasiums and even theatres and such entrepreneurial promotion quickly became the dominant mode, a move doubtlessly influenced by Hugh D. McIntosh's 1908 staging of a world heavyweight title fight at Rushcutters' Bay which brought in a world-record £26 000 at the gate and reputedly a further £80 000 for the film rights. Twenty thousand spectators saw the match; a further thirty thousand were locked outside.[18] A major development was the establishment of Stadiums Limited in 1913 by Reginald 'Snowy' Baker, who had boxed for Australia at the 1908 London Olympics, his younger brother, William Harald and a few other businessmen. In 1915 the sporting speculator John Wren took a controlling interest and for the next fifty years Stadiums Limited virtually monopolised boxing promotion in the east-coast capitals. With the decline in professional boxing it staged its last fight in 1975.[19]

Not all boxing took place in stadiums. At the lowest end of the promotional spectrum were the tents, tagged on to the travelling shows which took entertainment to rural Australians. Chief of these touring promoters was Jimmy Sharman. A professional fighter himself, beaten in only one of his eighty-four fights, he saw the market potential in taking boxing to the agricultural shows. This he did from 1912 with his famous catchcry of 'who'll take a glove' as locals were encouraged to challenge one of his stable.[20] His son, Jimmy Sharman Junior, took over in 1958. At this time there were still ten travelling troupes, but tent fighting was doomed. In the 1970s it was effectively outlawed in the southern states by an insistence that all fighters, including those taking up a challenge at a show, carry a medical card with a record of all their bouts and, if knocked out, not fight again for a month. Apart from a couple of mavericks who travelled out Birdsville way this was the end of the road.[21]

Boxing is an occupation in which the best are for a time irreplaceable and thus can demand high economic rents from promoters who, in turn, know that the crowd will pay to see such stars in action. This was appreciated by the managers of Australia's world champions of the late 1960s: Johnny Famechon had earned over £250 000 by the age of twenty-five and Lionel Rose some $400 000 at twenty-two. Large payouts to those at the pinnacle of their profession have existed from the days of the prize ring though here gambling provided the injection of funds rather than the gate money and television rights which pushed Jeff Fenech towards dollar millionaire status.[22] But for most boxers, especially the preliminary-bout fighters — young hopefuls aiming to make it to the top or old pugs on their way down (if they had even been up) — monetary rewards were not high. To such men the shower of coins thrown in the ring by appreciative spectators after a particularly pleasing fight would be a welcome bonus. Moreover, there was no regular wage packet: payment was by the fight not by the week. How many economically desperate men were tempted to fight too often or take one bout too many will remain an unanswerable but important question in Australian boxing history. After deductions by managers and trainers, few boxers made significant money from their activities in the ring. Even fewer appear to have been able to retain any wealth gained in this way. At least two of the three world champions cited above as examples of high earners ran into financial difficulties.[23] More generally, Ern McQuillan, a long-time Sydney trainer, reckoned that only ten per cent of boxers managed to hang on to their winnings.[24]

What of life after boxing? There was no career structure in the sport. Not even a minority of boxers could expect to become trainers or managers and challenging Stadiums Limited's promotional monopoly was unthinkable. Some retired fighters might hang around gymnasiums seeking occasional work in the trade they knew but essentially the ex-boxer had to start afresh in another occupation. Not an easy task for those who had been in the game for some time,[25] most of whom would have reiterated the view of the champion Hector Thompson that 'fighting ... is the only business I've been trained for'.[26] The employment situation would be worse for those who were forced to retire through injury as this would lessen their chances of labouring jobs, the obvious option for an uneducated but physically fit ex-sportsman.

Unfortunately this would apply to a significant number of fighters. All professional sportspeople have built-in obsolescence in that eventually experience no longer compensates for ageing muscles: physiological attrition always wins the final bout. For boxers, however, the nature of their sport meant that physical injury would end many careers even more prematurely. Their choice of occupation even cost some boxers their lives: from 1910 to 1972 eighty-five Australian ring deaths have been documented.[27] But many others carried permanent reminders of the blows they had taken. One American estimate in the 1950s was that sixty per cent of boxers were left mildly punch drunk and five per cent significantly so.[28] A study of 250 boxers registered with the British Boxing Board of Control between 1929 and 1955 revealed that seventeen per cent showed evidence of brain damage and a third of these had chronic traumatic encephalopathy.[29] There is no reason to believe that similar figures would not have applied to contemporary Australian fighters, given the then general lack of regulations to protect participants.

Under the rules of the prize ring, generally based on Broughton's (which were introduced in Britain in 1743) but sometimes modified in specific match agreements, punching with the fist was but one method of attack. Also allowed were tripping, throttling, bearhugs, throwing an opponent to the ground and, until outlawed by the New Rules of 1838, kneeing

Tom Curran, a Victorian
middleweight champion,
became a prosperous publican
from his ring earnings as a
bare-knuckle fighter
throughout the middle years
of the nineteenth century.
(Source unknown.)

and head-butting. Almost anything except eye-gouging and
hitting a man when he was down seems to have been acceptable.[30] A round lasted until one fighter was put to the floor; the
fallen combatant was then given half a minute in which to recover before planting his toe on a line scratched in the centre
of the ring. As a fight did not end till one man failed 'to come
up to scratch' bouts could be long: the longest bare-knuckled
contest documented in Australia, and indeed in the world, was
that in 1854 between James Kelly and Jonathon Smith at Fiery
Creek near Daylesford in Victoria, which took six hours and
fifteen minutes![31] Participants fought with hands protected
only by hours of pickling in brine or other toughening agents:

the damage to the hands during a fight was matched by the injuries which these same bare knuckles inflicted on the faces of opponents. There were no weight divisions: in the late 1830s ten stone Iasac Gorrick gave over two stones (nearly thirteen kilograms) advantage to Dan Chalker — even though he won, the weight differential must have hardened his task.[32]

The late nineteenth century saw the savagery of the bare-knuckle ring militated by the introduction of contests with a fixed number of limited-time rounds, by the installation of weight divisions and by the introduction of gloves. Further progress in the protection of boxers this century has involved improved ring construction so that the condition of knocked-down fighters was not aggravated, the introduction of shorter contests so that the combatants did not suffer injury simply through exhaustion, and compulsory medical examinations and ringside attendance by a doctor who can advise a referee to stop a bout. Nevertheless professional boxing remains a sport in which man's inhumanity to man is given its greatest licence. A survey of results in the early 1970s suggests that the likelihood of long-term industrial injury was not slight with 15.7 per cent of fights ending in a knockout and a further 14.6 per cent stopped because of cuts or undue punishment.[33]

Despite the danger little was done to compensate fighters or their families for injury and death until after the Second World War. The Newcastle Stadium management took the lead in 1948 by insuring boxers for £500 each against death arising from injuries sustained in a bout under their auspices. Stadiums Limited, however, continued its policy of being generous after the event in making donations to the dependants of boxers who died in its rings. After a protracted political debate, workers' compensation was extended to New South Wales boxers in 1952 and all promoters (with the significant exception of those operating the tents) were required, few of them willingly, to contribute two pounds per fighter to a fund from which compensation for boxing injuries would be paid. Nevertheless an inquiry in 1973 found that there was no uniform policy throughout Australia regarding insurance cover to persons engaged in boxing.[34]

Amateur boxers have generally been better protected than their professional counterparts with referees, less beholden to stadium proprietors, erring on the side of premature intervention. Bouts, too, have been limited to three three-minute rounds maximum for many years, though significantly when fights were reduced to four rounds in the 1890s there was some debate as to whether such short matches were a real test of manliness.[35] More recently the introduction of 'spongy' gloves, compulsory headgear, (the professional sector still does not appear to accept that the brain is as important as the testicles) and an age limitation of thirty-two have significantly increased safety aspects of the sport.[36] Indeed the greatest danger to the health of an amateur has been to turn professional without sufficient ring experience.[37]

Apart from state and colonial legal restrictions no-one has ever really controlled boxing in Australia. Promoters and matchmakers plied their trades with no regulatory body to ensure that they did not exploit the men who fought at their behest. Back in 1847 members of the Fancy, as supporters of the prize ring were labelled, attempted to establish a Pugilistic Club in Sydney to secure the integrity of the ring in New South Wales but nothing of permanence emerged.[38] A similar fate befell all further efforts over the next century and more. Calls for state or national controlling bodies intensified after the Second World War with the first serious consideration being given in New South Wales in the mid-1950s, though ultimately it was rejected by a government which had seen fit to control greyhound racing. The arguments raised in favour of a controlling body included the consequent representation on the International Boxing Board of Control and thus a greater opportunity for staking the claim of Australian boxers to challenge for world titles; the prevention of monopoly exploitation of fighters and fans; and the lessening of the possibility of corruption. Increasingly, however, the emphasis was on the protection of boxers by the prevention of mismatching and the provision of adequate medical supervision.[39]

Boxers had few within the game to protect them from economic or physical exploitation by managers or promoters though, of course, there were those outside boxing who abhorred the sport and felt that the only way to protect the participants was to prevent them fighting at all. Despite a strong Australian tradition of labour unions, such organisations did not develop to any extent in professional sport here.[40] Boxing, in particular, had almost insurmountable obstacles. There was the strong and intransigent opposition of Stadiums Limited, an organisation which, while often looking after its favoured sons, turned the unsmiling face of paternalism towards those who objected to its style of industrial relations. This in itself could have actually stimulated unionism had there been sufficient community of interest among fighters, but the monopolistic position of Stadiums Limited which enabled it almost to dictate who would and who would not gain employment served to divide the potential membership.[41] Moreover boxing is an occupation in which one man's success is inevitably another's failure: sport, unlike most more conventional businesses, has to have winners and losers. Additionally there was the geographical dispersion of boxers who trained in a myriad of small gymnasiums and rarely met — except to hit each other — at the central employment location. Nevertheless there were some attempts to unionise, especially after 1945, usually in the form of state trainers' and boxers' associations, sometimes with wrestlers included. Despite some support from trades and labour councils, these suffered a setback when it was ruled that they could not be classed as unions since boxers were essentially contract workers and not technically employed by the promoters.[42]

Two bodies, the New South Wales Professional Boxing Association and the Australian Boxing Federation, emerged in the late 1960s with the avowed intention of improving the economic position of Australia's boxers. Around the same time Stadiums Limited pushed the cause of the Australian Boxing Alliance which, while concerned for the welfare of boxers, also aimed to promote the sport of boxing. None of these gained influence in more than one or two states and their branches operated independently of each other so that control was, in the words of a government inquiry, 'fragmented and generally inadequate'.[43] That investigation, which had been set up in 1973 by the Federal Minister for Health who was concerned about the hazards of boxing, recommended the establishment of an Australian Combat Sports Commission. It was to concern itself predominantly with professional boxing and, as well as operating a licensing system for all those in the sport, was to approve all bouts, hold purses, determine rankings and nominate champions. However, this was not fully supported by the representatives from the Ministry of Health who felt that it should have a purely regulatory role and 'prevent as far as practicable the exploitation of the professional boxer'.[44] Talk of a commission remained just that.

In contrast amateur boxing gained a central controlling body in 1924. Till then the amateur athletic associations in each state were responsible for organising state and national championships, but when the 1924 Australian titles were called off virtually at the last minute, boxing administrators decided to establish their own organisation, the Amateur Boxing and

Wrestling Union of Australia.[45] Despite some opposition, most significantly from the breakaway Australian Amateur Boxing League which was set up in 1986 by trainers seeking a voice in the administration of amateur boxing in Australia, the union, now devoid of wrestling, has gained a reputation for its promotion of boxing and its protection of boxers.[46]

Sport, more than any other activity, has brought Aborigines recognition in white Australia, and none more so than boxing. When Lionel Rose travelled to Tokyo to beat Fighting Harada and win the world bantamweight title in 1968 he was greeted on his return as a great Australian not as an 'Abo'.[47] Rose's triumph epitomised the disproportionate success rate of Aborigines in boxing: from Jerry Jerome's middleweight crown in 1912 through to 1980, fifteen per cent of Australian titles have gone to these black fighters, this from a racial group comprising around one per cent of the population.[48] Aboriginal playwright, Roger Bennett (whose father Elly was Australian bantamweight champion) argues that in the 1950s boxing was *the* Aboriginal sport and Alick Jackomos, an ex-boxer who married an Aborigine, says this was equally true of the two previous decades.[49] Reasons why boxing has proved so attractive to Aborigines can only be speculative but must include the financial rewards which the ring held out to a group with high unemployment and a generally distressed economic position; boxing was also an easy sport to access with little equipment or financial outlay required; it was a mainstream Australian sport and offered a chance for acceptance in white society, or at least to join a camaraderie of fighters, black and white together; finally there was the reinforcing effect of sufficient successful role models.[50]

Promoters saw the economic value in inter-racial contests. The late nineteenth century saw many battles between 'niggers', 'darkies' and white Australians. Later these were supplemented by the importation of coloured fighters from the United States which added the spice of nationalism to the racial confrontation.[51] Pride — if that is the appropriate word — of place in such promotions must go to entrepreneur Hugh D. McIntosh who in 1908 as previously mentioned staged a world heavyweight title bout at Rushcutters' Bay between white Canadian Tommy Burns and black American Jack Johnson.[52] Whether

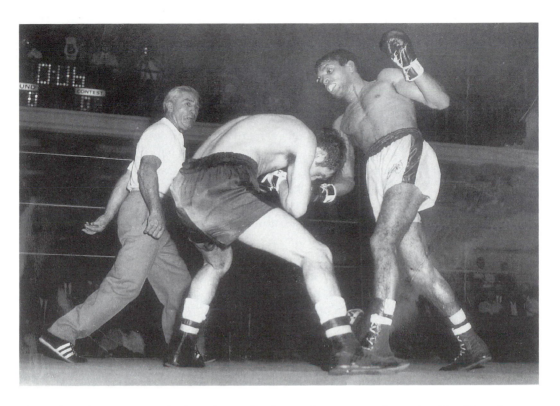

the colour line was invoked in Australia (as it often was in the United States) is not clear. A published challenge from Starlight, a native of British Guyana, intimated that one reason that he was having difficulty in securing fights may have been his skin.[53] On the other hand, although Tom Langley's biography of West Indian Peter Jackson perhaps exaggerates his non-racist treatment in Australia, it remains true that the coloured champion chose to come back to Queensland when he knew he was dying.[54]

Particularly to winners boxing brought new experiences, new environments, travel and possibly a growing self-confidence. Nevertheless few Aborigines have achieved permanent socio-economic mobility through their success in boxing.[55] Admittedly Doug Nicholls, who fought in Sharman's tents (and who also ran professionally and played in the Victorian Football League for six seasons), found that his sporting prowess underwrote his political and other activities on behalf of his people which, in turn, led to a knighthood and the governorship of South Australia. However, he was a rarity. More typical was the experience of Ron Richards, a national champion in three weight divisions and Empire middleweight titleholder, who died penniless in 1967 aged fifty-seven, a victim allegedly of poor management, alcohol and police harassment. Little

Lionel Rose fighting Tommaso Galli in Melbourne, April 1968. (Fairfax Picture Library.)

51

had changed from 1954 when an editorial in *Sport Magazine* maintained that 'without exception, each one of them [Aboriginal boxing champions] are practically dependent upon the State'.[56]

Yet it can be suggested that the failure to achieve financial security was also typical of white fighters.[57] They too were often exploited by managers and promoters and were left with little except memories and injuries. However, there were additional factors working against black Australian boxers. First, and definitely foremost, was the generally hostile societal attitudes which must have militated against Aboriginal advancement. Then there was the absence of sporting facilities: grass was not a feature of life on the reserves, let alone gymnasiums. Aborigines thus learned to box without the supervision of skilled trainers and consequently were rarely taught defensive techniques. This produced an aggressive, attacking style of fighting which was popular with spectators but left the boxers open to injury. Added to this were the claims made upon their ring earnings either by government officials or by extended kinship obligations.

Boxing is a very masculine world. For many years women were not even allowed to witness the bloody machismo of the ring, though, of course, there were those who gained entry in disguise. However, by the 1920s attitudes had changed and women spectators were being actively encouraged and the sex appeal of particular boxers was exploited to that effect.[58] Female participation is still frowned upon and indeed is illegal in most states. Nevertheless it has occurred.[59] In 1847 Annie the Nailer and Lizzy the Bullock settled their differences in a Woolloomooloo prize ring; a century later Miss Cath Thomas 'fought' Sam Smiling at a Fairfield promotion; and today occasional bouts are featured at strip clubs.[60] The exclusion of women from active participation in boxing has no solid medical foundation and was essentialy a male-based moralistic view. Whether the ban will ever be challenged legally on the grounds of gender discrimination remains to be seen.

Boxing has always had its critics, some of whom have proved powerful opposition. From its earliest days many magistrates regarded prize-fighting as illegal because of their fear that it would induce riotous assemblies. Other opponents focussed on the brutality of the ring, a publicly-condoned sadism, which they argued injured those who fought and barbarised those who watched: even the adoption of the Queensberry Rules and the use of gloves failed to stem the tide of criticism from those who saw boxing as leading to moral decay. There was also an element who took an intellectual stance epitomised in H. C. J. Lingham's verse which scorned the crowd's adoration of heavyweight boxer, Frank Slavin:

> Australian Natives are too much inclined
> To honour muscle at the expense of mind.
> They hold a Slavin is a greater hero,
> Who with shoulders, neck, and head of Nero,
> Pounds his opponents to a senseless jelly,
> Than Tadema, Leighton, Keats or Shelley.[61]

By the 1860s increasingly the law was being used against prize-fighting. Fighters were being bound over to keep the peace and, on occasion, even being jailed for engaging in contests which were, to quote Mr Justice Hargrave of the Deniliquin Circuit Court, 'breaches of the peace, got up to promote betting and drinking, and the occasion of much demoralisation and therefore punishment must follow' — in this case a year's imprisonment for George Wyse and Robert Dunbar.[62] However, it was the conviction for manslaughter of James Lawson after the ring death of Alec Agar in 1910 which focussed most attention on the legal position of boxing. Another death, of fifteen-year-old James Fogarty, clarified the issue. Initially the Melbourne coroner ruled that his opponent, Harold Walsh, should be charged with manslaughter, but later he accepted that there was a distinction between a fight to the finish and a gloved contest decided on points and which could be stopped by a referee and accordingly ruled that poor Fogarty died by misadventure.[63]

Boxing and the law appear to have come to terms. Much of what is legitimate within sport actually could bring police action if it occurred elsewhere, but generally immunity from prosecution has been enjoyed if the rules of the game concerned have sanctioned certain activities. In effect those playing sport have agreed to accept the risks of shoulder charges, short-pitched bowling and so on and the law has concurred — or turned a blind eye. However, boxing is a special case in that the protagonists do consent to physical injury being inflicted deliberately by their opponent and such consent, particularly if not fully 'informed' as to the risks involved, is not necessarily sufficient to make an activity legal if the activity can be shown to be harmful. Nevertheless there has been a willingness to modify its traditional brutality via rules which outlaw certain target areas, allow referees and doctors as well as the police to stop a contest, limit the number of rounds and use scientifically designed gloves. This may have helped its legal survival.[64] The law has also distinguished between boxing in which an element of skill is exercised and fighting in which brute force and butchery dominate.[65]

One aspect of uncivilised behaviour which critics associated with boxing was crowd disorder. The two most quoted incidents, perhaps not coincidentally, involved two of Australia's most famous fighters, Les Darcy and Larry Foley. When the latter was being thrashed by 'Professor' William Miller in a fight-to-the-finish in 1879 his supporters twice stormed the ring to give the seconds more time to revive the battered fighter, ultimately forcing the police to intervene and the referee to declare the bout a draw.[66] Thirty-five years later, rising star Darcy lost a points decision to American Fritz Holland which, although generally accepted around the ringside, caused consternation in the bleachers. When the lights were turned down to encourage the crowd to leave attempts were made to set fire to the stadium and abuse and bottles were hurled at the staff who sought to put the blaze out. In turn they used the fire hoses to douse the crowd and drive them outside. The police prevented the rioters from re-entering the building but the stadium windows were broken by a fusillade of road metal.[67] Such behaviour was probably atypical of boxing fans, though certainly in the days of the prize-fight one objective of the proposed Pugilistic Club was to 'check those rows and irregularities in the outer Ring' and, judging from comments in the contemporary sporting press, rowdyism was an issue in the 1890s.[68]

Boxing's image was also tarnished by allegations of corruption. Indeed a sport involving heavy betting, only two participants and subjective judgements by a referee almost inevitably will attract a criminal element. Fixed fights were a feature of the prize ring and one leading ring historian is convinced that gambling decided the result of many bouts in the 1930s.[69] Bribes and threats tempted or forced boxers to predetermine who would win, though the level of corruption was never such as to challenge the existence of the sport. In more recent years self-appointed controlling bodies such as the New South Wales

Professional Boxing Association have stated that they will ban any boxer who even associated with known or suspected criminals.[70]

Paradoxically, as boxing became less brutal medical opposition actually increased. This was partly attributable to new research findings on boxing injuries but was also due to the foundation in 1963 of the Australian Sports Medicine Federation (ASMF), an organisation through which medical practitioners with knowledge of sport could channel their concerns. Within two years of its establishment the national council argued that ideally boxing should be banned, but adopted a pragmatic stance in accepting that if it continued then it should be under strict safety controls enforceable by medical officers. Eventually this became the formal policy of the Australian Medical Association (AMA) and ultimately, reinforced by a report from the Victorian branch, the parliament in that state was influenced to pass legislation which regulated and accredited medical officers to attend professional boxing venues.[71] However, in 1990 the AMA resolved 'to oppose the continued existence of boxing in Australia' and currently the ASMF is polling its members to determine whether it should support the ban.[72] Medics who oppose the ban argue that it would drive the sport underground and paint a scenario of unsafe rings and a lack of medical supervision.[73] Yet it has to be questioned whether boxing is sufficiently popular to continue in an illegal form on any scale.

Boxing was an accepted part of the British heritage which had accompanied migrants on their passage from the Old Dart. *Bell's Life* saw it as central to nationalistic masculinity:

> ... the benefits resulting from the encouragement which pugilism has met with in the mother country are too familiar to every man who can boast of a descent from British blood; the tinge which pervades all classes, and gives a peculiar nobleness to our national character, is too vividly prominent as being derived from the universal determination to uphold appeals to Nature's weapons when passion impels us to resent a wrong, and the writer who will not waive the minor evils attendant upon the Prize Ring, in consideration of its numberless benefits, becomes the advocate and the partizan of the assassin.[74]

Despite its dubious legal situation and its definite non-respectability, proponents of boxing were never really forced to defend their position during the nineteenth century, particularly as the bare-knuckled prize ring transformed itself via the Marquis of Queensberry's rules. Although the *Referee* acknowledged that the bare-knuckle prize ring had had its faults, it claimed that by 1890 'those are past . . . and a contest between two skilled opponents with proper gloves is far from being in any way a degrading sight'.[75] Over time, however, under increasing pressure from social reformers and medical experts, ground had to be conceded. No longer could it simply be asserted that the manly art led to the ability to be disciplined and self-controlled in the face of pain: it had to be admitted that this manliness came at the cost of death and serious injury and that perhaps protective equipment should be worn. This opened the door to arguments that if such equipment did not prevent injury — as is possibly the case with headgear[76] — then the sport should be outlawed. Another view commonly advanced to support boxing is that it provides 'an avenue for some young men to improve their financial and personal status',[77] but given the overwhelming medical evidence, this means that such disadvantaged youths are 'exposed to the risk of further handicap in the, for most, illusory hope of advancement'.[78] At the amateur level supporters can legitimately argue that the participants believe in the sport's utility for 'physical fitness, mental alertness, disciplined work habits and a sense of fair play'.[79]

Australian governments, even those which have insisted on bicycle helmets, car seat belts and no smoking in the workplace, have been reluctant to bite the bullet on boxing's health-eroding qualities. As the Queensland Sports Minister, Peter McKenna, put it: 'If some action was taken against boxing it would set a dangerous precedent and rugby league and other contact sports might come under scrutiny'.[80] In any event it has not been established that boxing is the most dangerous sport in Australia: the last decade has seen more deaths of jockeys, motor-cyclists and hang-gliders than boxers.[81] Even the medical opposition has acknowledged that 'as a cause of injury, death, and long-term morbidity, boxing is of negligible importance compared with road accidents'.[82] What has to be assessed is what level of risk is considered acceptable by the participants and by society more generally. Certainly in the case of amateur boxing, the administration of the sport is such as to offer substantial protection to the boxer but this may be less true of the professional side where the need to entertain the audience has a powerful influence.[83]

Whether professional boxing is on the ropes is a moot point. In 1988 only fifty-three promotions took place involving 213 fighters: fourteen years before the figures were 377 promotions and 1308 boxers.[84] Yet, almost paradoxically, Australia contin-

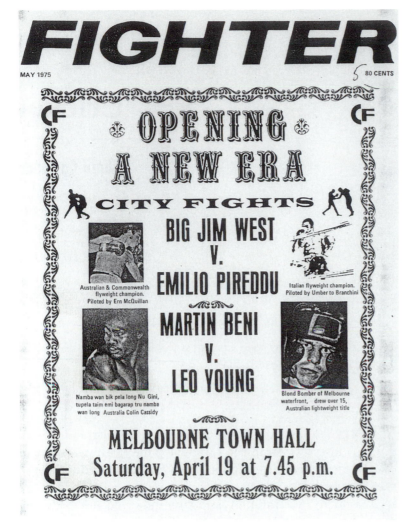

Boxing in Australia was extremely popular in the mid-1970s; in 1974 there were 377 promotions involving 1308 boxers. (*Fighter* magazine cover, May 1975.)

ues to produce world champions; most recently Jeff Fenech and Jeff Harding were added to the roll begun by 'Young Griffo' in 1890.[85] Top boxers such as these still draw large crowds and earn big purses, psychic and real income sufficient to tempt other young men to follow them through the amateur ranks into professionalism. Amateur boxing itself remains relatively healthy with around five thousand registered participants.[86] It continues as an Olympic sport, its five-ring existence threatened more by the vagaries of its judges than any challenges from medical authorities and six Australians represented their country in Barcelona.

4 Cricket

Richard Cashman

. . . the Australians were our equals, both as antagonists and as adornments to the art of cricket.

Neville Cardus, *English Cricket* (London, 1945)

CRICKET, THE first team sport played in Australia, comes closest to being the national game. Despite cycles of greater and lesser popularity, cricket has endured as a mass spectator sport. It was a British game exported lock, stock and barrel to Australia. Australians imported not only the game, its conventions and values but also bats, balls, and clothing, even the names of British clubs and their constitutions were copied word for word.

However, while Australians drew continuing inspiration from British ideals and traditions they also developed their own cricket culture, particularly during the twentieth century. The physical environment of Australia differed from that of the motherland. Harder, bouncier pitches and brighter light have long encouraged batsmen to play shots more confidently, particularly square of the wicket. Australian pitches have been kinder to bowlers of genuine pace and of leg spin than have English wickets. The great distance, cost and time of getting from one state capital to another also shaped the character of domestic competition; distance (and cost) was one reason why Australia did not have a core of professional players in the early days. Australian cricket also developed distinctive features because of the particular social and cultural environment. For much of its European history Australia has been a brash society with a fluid class structure. Unlike England the game cut across class boundaries, being equally popular in all parts of the nation, city and country and in all states. There are probably fewer private-school and coached cricketers in Australia than there are in England; many outstanding Australian cricketers, such as Bradman and O'Reilly, have been natural cricketers who taught themselves to play.

For much of the nineteenth century cricket and its administrators were certainly dominated by Anglo-Australian ideals. But during the twentieth century Australia went on to develop indigenous cultural traditions including barracking, bush cricket, larger and better-appointed ovals, bigger scoreboards, the eight-ball over and distinctive language such as guzunder, mully grubber and sundries, as well as different traditions in batting, bowling and fielding.

Cricket was played in Sydney from 1803 but reports were infrequent until 1826 when the Australian Cricket Club was formed. Cricket was played on a more regular, formal basis from the 1830s when more clubs were established, but inter-club games were occasional events played mainly on festival days and Mondays. Extensive press coverage from the 1830s onwards helped ensure that cricket became the first popular team sport of the country. The first clubs were organised in public houses and publicans were prominent as organisers, sponsors and players. Gambling was a focal point and the first games were played for large stakes. Many of the early clubs did not survive long with the notable exception of the Melbourne Cricket Club, founded in 1838, which became the most powerful Australian club, even organising national tours in the late nineteenth century. Visiting regiments contributed to the growth of cricket, too, and contests between civilian and military teams were frequent and popular.

Colonial cricket in the 1830s and 1840s was derivative and imitative of English practice. Two leading players of the 1840s, J. Rickards and W. C. Still, were linked to star British players and were known respectively as the 'colonial Lillywhite' and the 'Australian Pilch'. There was also a time lag between English innovation and colonial acceptance. Round-arm bowling emerged in English cricket in the early 1830s but was not accepted in Sydney until 1843 at the earliest.[1]

Improved communications and transportation, the growth of population and cities and a rise in real incomes led to the beginnings of inter-colonial and international competition which stimulated Australian cricket. Increased competition enhanced the popularity of cricket and created a network of colonial associations to run the game. The first match was between Tasmania and Victoria in Launceston in 1851, though it was not until 1856 when the New South Wales side defeated Victoria at the Melbourne Cricket Ground (MCG) that inter-colonials became an annual event. These matches drew large crowds partly because of the fierce rivalry which then existed between one colony and another.

The visit of H. H. Stephenson's side of English professionals in 1861–62 followed by George Parr's team in 1863–64 provided further stimulus to Australian cricket and the initial tour proved highly profitable to the promoters, the Melbourne catering firm of Spiers and Pond. The success of the visitors against local XVIIIs and XXIIs — Parr's side went through the tour undefeated — indicated a sizeable gap between British and colonial cricket standards.

Aborigines from northern Victoria, captained by English professional Charles Lawrence, were the first Australians to tour England in 1868. The team proved sufficiently popular for the scheduled ten matches to be extended to forty-seven. While reactions to the tour were mixed, the team performed creditably given their inexperience and the gruelling schedule. The tour cannot be dismissed as a 'mere speculation or stunt', although it included elements of professional exhibition cricket popular at the time.[2]

By the time of the 1873–74 English tour, captained by W. G. Grace, Australian cricket had advanced sufficiently for Victoria to play the tourists on even terms though other matches were against the odds. It was not until the visit of the professional team led by James Lillywhite in 1876–77 that Australia won what was later defined as the first test. The match featured a memorable 165 retired hurt by Charles Bannerman. The victory loomed large in colonial eyes but was not regarded so highly in England as the beaten side did not include many star English players. It was not until the tour of England in 1878 that English game authorities took Australian cricket seri-

ously. The improvement in the Australian game was evident when the tourists, spearheaded by Fred Spofforth and Harry Boyle, routed the powerful Marylebone Cricket Club side in the second match of the tour. With the success of the tour Australian cricketers profited handsomely. Each player had outlaid fifty pounds to run the tour as a limited company, and ended up with a return of over seven hundred.

Tours to and from Australia then occurred regularly. The third Australian tour of England in 1882 proved the most memorable when the side captained by William Murdoch — the strongest Australian side in the nineteenth century — secured in dramatic circumstances the first test victory in England and helped create the Ashes mythology. The hero at the Oval was Spofforth, who cemented his reputation as the greatest bowler of his era. Australian success came from colonial advances in bowling and fielding technique which, on some occasions, surprised complacent English sides. There was less colonial innovation in batting, though in the 1880s Murdoch was regarded as second only to Grace.

Many Australian cricketers were deeply committed to Anglo-Australian ideals believing that they were dual citizens, as much British as Australian. A tour to England was both a trip 'home' and a cultural pilgrimage. Five Australian test players of this era also played for England. Two star Australian players, Murdoch and Spofforth, settled in England towards the end of their playing careers to reclaim their British heritage.[3]

W. G. Grace was the main attraction at the Adelaide Oval in 1874. He was one of the England XI to play against an Australian XXII. (Mortlock Library of South Australiana.)

W. F. Mandle has argued that the organisation of an Australian XI and success off the cricket field from the late 1870s onwards helped stimulate Australian nationalism. While the Mandle argument is persuasive, it represents an optimistic assessment of the role of sport in creating nationality. David Montefiore has argued contrarily that continuing inter-colonial rivalry inhibited the emergence of an effective national controlling body.[4]

Australian cricket developed more distinctive traditions after 1900, paralleling the creation of Australian Federation in 1901 which helped stimulate greater pride in things Australian. The emergence of the tabloid press also led to the elevation of more working-class Australian heroes like Victor Trumper.[5] The ideal of returning 'home' and playing for England was far from the mind of such players.

Trumper helped create an Australian tradition of batting. He was an audacious, attacking and graceful batsman with a natural looseness and fluency who could be orthodox but had the ability to improvise on treacherous wickets. Trumper was so admired for his almost 'saintly' character — as a modest, unselfish, generous individual — that biographers have struggled to recognise the realities of the man.[6] Clem Hill was also an attacking stroke-player, a fine cutter and hooker who was the first of many outstanding left-handers. Charlie Macartney emerged in this period as another confident and courageous batsman.

The financial success of tours and the need for greater liaison between the organisers of tours and colonial cricket authorities created the need for a national controlling body. The first authority, the Australasian Cricket Council, proved ineffectual and lasted only from 1892–1901.[7] The Australian Cricket Board of Control (since 1973 the Australian Cricket Board), formed in 1905, had greater authority, which was tested in 1912 — over the question of whether the board or players should select the tour manager — when six of the leading players boycotted the 1912 tour to England. The board won this challenge to its authority.

Domestic competition had been enhanced earlier with the establishment of the Sheffield Shield, contested by New South Wales, South Australia and Victoria in the 1892–93 season. The shield was named after its donor, the Earl of Sheffield, who financed and accompanied the 1891–92 English tour to Australia. Australia toured South Africa for the first time in 1902–3 and the first home series was in 1910–11. First-class cricket was abandoned for three seasons during the First World War. Some notable cricketers, including 'Tibby' Cotter, died in action. Australian cricket was less depleted by war than English cricket and Australia, captained by Warwick Armstrong, dominated in the immediate post-war series.

The 1920s and 1930s represented the zenith of Australian cricket. The game was more popular than ever with increasing crowds at tests, at Sheffield Shield and even district games. Interest in cricket was heightened by the emergence of (Sir) Donald Bradman in the late 1920s, the controversial bodyline series of 1932–33 and the beginning of national ball-by-ball broadcasting. Bradman transformed Australian batting from an art to a science and is generally accepted as Australia's greatest batsman and greatest-ever sportsman. A self-taught batsman from the country, he dominated the game more than any previous player. An 'incurable original', he could combine grace with ferocity, playing in orthodox fashion but also often playing across the line with telling effect. He was an aggressive batsman who scored runs quickly, demoralising his opponents. The tactic of bodyline was designed to curb the phenomenal run scoring of Bradman. Bodyline, which many Australians saw as unfair, strained sporting (and even diplomatic) relations between Australia and England.[8]

Because he was so successful Bradman attracted criticism that he was an aloof, ruthless run-making machine. Debate has also continued about whether Trumper or Bradman was the greatest batsmen, though any comparison is problematic because conditions and expectations of play were so different in the two eras. Some of Bradman's detractors have lost sight of his immense popularity with the Australian public, which in the 1930s was 'Bradman mad'. Bradman was such an entertaining batsman that when he batted the crowds were almost twice as large.[9]

Bradman's success overshadowed the records and achievements of another run-accumulator, Bill Ponsford. The Bradman era was also the heyday of two fine slow bowlers, Bill O'Reilly and Clarrie Grimmett. Queensland joined the Sheffield Shield in 1926–27 but was still searching for its initial shield win in 1993. The West Indies toured for the first time in 1930–31.

Bradman was such a dominating influence that his departure left a huge gap in Australian cricket. Although Australia had some fine stroke-players in the 1950s — including left-handers Arthur Morris and Neil Harvey — gate takings declined and campaigns for 'brighter cricket' emerged. There was a yearning for another Bradman and a succession of young stars, such as Ian Craig and Norman O'Neill, each had the misfortune to be dubbed the next Bradman. Cricket also suffered competition from other sports, such as tennis, and the growth of more individualistic leisure pursuits, including surfing and surf-board-riding.

After another war-time lapse of three seasons the public was keen to watch cricket again and applauded the powerful team which beat England in Australia (1946–47) and in England (1948) — the 1948 side ranks as one of the Australian greats along with the 1902 and 1921 teams. India toured for the first time in 1947-48. Western Australia joined the shield competition in the same season. In 1953 Australia lost the Ashes which it had held for nineteen years and suffered a debacle at Manchester in 1956 when Laker took all but one wicket. On the return trip home Australia played its first tests on the sub-continent in 1956, suffering defeat at the hands of Pakistan on the melting wicket at Karachi but defeating India. In 1958–59 Australia, captained by the youthful Richie Benaud, regained the Ashes in resounding fashion. Benaud found a perfect foil for his attacking flair in West Indian skipper Frank Worrell and they created an entertaining test series in 1960–61, set up by the celebrated tie in the first test at Brisbane.

During the 1960s the future of Australian cricket seemed uncertain. There was far less attacking cricket in the four subsequent series against England with thirteen of the twenty tests drawn. This was one reason for a slide in the game's popularity.

Cricket's 1970s revival was television-related. The potential of television was first demonstrated during the 1970–71 series when national coverage of the entire test series by the Australian Broadcasting Corporation created a huge television audience of more than a million per day. Although Australia lost this series they were developing a youthful and marketable young side, which held its own against the English team in 1972 in a series which included Bob Massie's memorable sixteen wickets at Lord's. The 1974–75 and 1975–76 Australian sides which triumphed over England and the West Indies were well-bal-

anced and brimful of talent. Led by Ian Chappell, a shrewd and
attacking captain, they included the feared Dennis Lillee–Jeff
Thomson combination backed up by the tireless Max Walker,
the classical Greg Chappell, the laconic Doug Walters and the
acrobatic Rod Marsh. Remarkably New Zealand had to wait
until 1973-74 to play its first test on Australian soil: the three-
test series was won by Australia. New Zealand had been no
match for Australia in the previous encounter when one test was
played on the 1945–46 tour to New Zealand, and had hosted
Australian second teams in the intervening years.

With the revival of public interest and an expanding television audience, cricket was ripe for the picking by television
magnate Kerry Packer in 1977. Unable to gain a monopoly of
cricket broadcasting Packer signed up most leading international players to his World Series Cricket (WSC) and for two
seasons organised alternative international competition. The
WSC 'takeover' split the Australian cricket world, outraged
traditionalists and generated heated public debate. The Australian media was initially hostile, accusing Packer of reducing

The first night cricket game at
the Sydney Cricket Ground,
29 November 1978.
(Purcell/Fairfax Picture
Library.)

65

cricket to circus entertainment. It was convenient to blame Packer without recognising that the Australian Cricket Board had been slow to react to the changing character of cricket in the television age. Undoubtedly, the crisis was worsened by the incapacity of part-time, amateur-minded officials to respond to television-generated professional and commercial challenges. However, WSC promotion of one-day cricket, and particularly night cricket, was popular.

Forty-one-year-old Bob Simpson came out of retirement to lead a second or third-string side against India and the West Indies, but after he retired Australia was no match for England in season 1978–79. Cricket authorities were sufficiently worried about the future of cricket to agree to a truce with Packer by 1979. Although WSC lasted only two years it had a far-reaching impact in Australia. It led to improved player payment and provided better-quality television pictures. Programming changes, particularly the altered format of test and one-day internationals, have been more controversial. And, with the greater amount of international competition, the leading players are now full-time professionals.

Academic assessments of Packer and World Series Cricket were initially negative. Lawrence and Rowe believed that the public were the losers by the promotion of 'an increasingly aggressive spectacle manipulated by commercial television'.[10] However, in the 1980s a revisionary view of the Packer era began to emerge. Stoddart offered the striking and challenging conclusion that 'far from degrading cricket, Packer gave it new dimensions by challenging outmoded visions of the game's social position'.[11]

Australia's top cricketers, virtual professionals since the 1980s, make a good living, play all the year round and compete far more outside Australia. Cricket careers have been extended and players are less tempted to retire too early as many did in the 1950s and 1960s. Some critics fear that with the advent of greater professionalism Australians bat with more caution and calculation, as their livelihood depends on run accumulation. Cricket also became more 'globalised' in the 1980s. There are less observable differences between one national side and another. The Australian team has played so many series on the slow and turning wickets of the sub-continent that they are as used to them as Indians are to the bounce and pace of Australian wickets.

Australia took a long time to recover from World Series Cricket, with lingering feuds between establishment and WSC players. Allan Border, who became captain of the side in difficult circumstances in the mid-1980s, and who played many gritty and courageous innings, became cricket's leading test run-getter. After some lean years he led Australia to success in the 1987 World Series Cup at Calcutta and recovered the Ashes in fine fashion in 1989. In 1986 at Madras Australia participated in the second tied test in history which, like the first tied test, ended on the second-last ball.

There had been no tours of South Africa since 1969–70 when Australia met a powerful South African side. Kim Hughes captained two rebel tours to South Africa in the period 1985–87.[12] An official South African team participated in the 1992 World Series Cup in Australia and New Zealand. A team from Sri Lanka visited Australia for the first time in season 1982–83 but the first test between the two countries was not played in Australia until 1988.

Tasmania joined the Sheffield Shield competition in 1977–78 but their only real success was to win the one-day competition, the Gillette Cup, in 1978–79. The introduction of a five-day shield final in 1982–83 was a successful innovation. However, by the 1990s many were concerned about the prospects of both Sheffield Shield and test cricket.

Women have taken keen interest in cricket from its first days, but their role has been largely auxiliary, preparing afternoon tea for male players and spectating. This role was formalised by the creation of separate ladies' stands at some major ovals in the nineteenth century. While they could attend cricket matches and were admitted to cricket clubs as associate members, they did not secure membership rights at the Melbourne Cricket Ground and the Sydney Cricket Ground (SCG) until the 1980s.

Women were discouraged from playing in earlier days because the game was defined as a 'manly' one, inappropriate and unhealthy for women since it involved competition and violence. Women who trespassed on male sporting territory were regarded as unfeminine and even as closet males.[13] Yet in spite of media and public discouragement, some women did play cricket. The first recorded women's match was played at Bendigo in 1874. Club cricket dates from 1886 when the Fernleas met the Siroccos at the SCG. Although there were good crowds at some of the first women's matches, the interest was superficial. Once the novelty of women playing cricket wore off, many commentators were highly critical of, or even ridiculed, the efforts of women.

Despite persistent prejudice, women's cricket associations were formed in Victoria in 1905 and in other states in the 1920s and 1930s. The Australian Women's Cricket Council established in 1931, invited an English team to visit in 1934–35. The first ever women's test at Brisbane was well supported and publicised. Following the success of the tour the Australian women visited England in 1937.

The history of women's cricket is intertwined with the men's game. The publicity for women's cricket in the 1930s was partly a spin-off from the boom in the men's game. Women's cricket looked set to have a promising future after the Second World War when an Australian team won the Ashes for the first time and produced a star in Betty Wilson. However, by the 1960s the game was in decline and one of the state associations, Queensland, was defunct from 1963 to 1976. Tours and test matches were infrequent.

Women's cricket revived in the 1970s and the 1980s. Australian women won the second, third and fourth world cups and have dominated the world cricket scene since 1980. There were some fine achievements by Australian women in the 1980s. Denise Annetts scored a world test record for women of 193 against England in 1987, Lindsay Reeler became a prolific scorer in one-day internationals (scoring 1034 runs in twenty-three innings) and Christina Matthews achieved a world record of forty-seven dismissals behind the stumps by 1991. With more government and business support and greater co-operation between male and female cricket administrators there has been an improving environment for girls and women to play cricket. However, against 500 000 registrations in male cricket there were still only 12 281 in female cricket in 1991.

There has been a long tradition of media and public prejudice against women playing cricket. Since the onus has been on women cricketers to prove their femininity, Australian women adopted culottes (box-pleated trousers, cut to look like skirts) as their uniform as did the women cricketers of England and New Zealand. By contrast some of their international opponents, such as India, play in straighter trousers.

Aborigines were encouraged to play cricket in the second half of the nineteenth century when they were no longer

regarded as a threat in south and eastern Australia. Paternalism replaced hostility and by the 1850s and 1860s large numbers of Aborigines were playing cricket on country stations and on the missions. Missionaries believed that cricket would help civilise Aborigines. Another reason for cricket involvement was that Aborigines had become an important cog in the post-gold rush labour shortage. As useful members of many station communities they were permitted to participate in its recreational life.[14]

Aboriginal participation in station cricket in Victoria became so widespread in the 1860s that two local landowners, Thomas Hamilton and William Hayman, took an Aboriginal team to Melbourne — the first step towards the 1868 English tour. There was also considerable Aboriginal involvement in the Riverina in New South Wales in the 1860s, and later in the century at Deebing Creek, near Ipswich, Queensland and at New Norcia, Western Australia. The high point of Aboriginal cricket occurred when Aboriginal teams played before large crowds on the premier Australian cricket grounds and then toured England in 1868. Many spectators undoubtedly watched

The glamorous outfits worn by W. A. (Bert) Oldfield's Ladies' Cricket Team in 1931. *Back left to right:* Dot Edwards, Paula Krumback, D. Adair, D. McMahon, F. Adair, S. Carlton. *Middle left to right:* Katie Lang, Norma Saunders, Vacey Turner. *Front:* Maisie Mudie, Evie Carpenter. (Photograph collection of Maisie Mudie, now Lupton.)

69

the Aboriginal cricketers out of racial curiosity or interest in the sports carnivals which occurred during matches when players demonstrated their skills at weaponry, running backwards, dodging cricket balls and boomerang throwing. The team was exploited in the sense of talents being assumed as racial characteristics.[15] Aboriginal success in cricket brought some respect from Europeans and enabled Aborigines to extend 'a degree of power' in sport.[16]

Aborigines had a higher status and profile in cricket in the 1860s and 1870s than they did subsequently. Two of the 1868 tourists, Bullocky and Cuzens, played for Victoria against Tasmania in 1868 while another two tourists, Twopenny and Mullagh, played first-class cricket. In the next 110 years there have been only another five Aboriginal first-class cricketers and their careers in the game have been brief and, in three instances, controversial. Albert Henry played for Queensland from 1902 to 1905; Jack Marsh represented New South Wales from 1900 until 1902; while Eddie Gilbert played for Queensland between 1930 and 1936. Since then only two Aborigines, Ian King and Michael Mainhardt, who represented Queensland, have played first-class cricket.[17]

The 1868 tour proved a 'one-off' affair, though another one was organised in 1988 to replicate the earlier tour and to encourage Aboriginal involvement in the game. The decline of Aboriginal cricket from the 1870s was related to the replacement of paternalism by more pessimistic, institutionalised racism. With greater segregation and less contact between Aborigines and whites at work, there were fewer opportunities and incentives for Aborigines to continue playing cricket. Racial factors restricted the first-class careers of the three controversial bowlers, Gilbert, Henry and Marsh. Gilbert was one of the quickest bowlers of his time and Marsh, in the opinion of respected journalist J. C. Davis, 'could have been one of the world's greatest bowlers if he had been a white man'.[18] Various authors have suggested Marsh and Gilbert would have gone further but for 'pervasive racialism'.[19]

That Henry, Marsh and Gilbert were the victims of racism can only be inferred. To gain selection in the first place, Aborigines had to be much more skilled than the average white players and, once selected, their behaviour had to be above reproach. While playing for Queensland Eddie Gilbert lived in a tent in the backyard of a Queensland cricket official. His interstate trips were 'complicated by increasingly stringent clearance regulations and conditions' determined by state authorities who wished to curtail his freedom of movement and speech.[20] Marsh was a victim of the anti-throwing hysteria prevalent at that time. It was also difficult for players from the bush to survive in the complex and baffling world of organised cricket. After being no-balled fourteen times for throwing in his first Sheffield Shield match in Melbourne in 1901, Marsh became so frustrated that he 'deliberately threw three consecutive balls'. Marsh, like Henry, became typecast as a natural athlete who was erratic and unreliable.[21]

Racial politics have manifested themselves elsewhere in Australian cricket. There was considerable controversy about whether a Fijian cricket team should visit Australia in 1907–8, with prominent Australian Board of Control officials arguing that it would be a breach of the White Australia Policy. The tour only went ahead when Melbourne delegate Edward Mitchell was 'so incensed by the racist attitudes put forward' that he stated that if the board did not support the tour the Melbourne Cricket Club would back it. A couple of decades later the first West Indian tourists to Australia in 1930–31 were indignant to find the seven white team members booked in one hotel and the eleven black members in a separate hotel. After complaints from the tourists they were booked in the same hotel.[22]

Publicans, the first cricket administrators, viewed cricket as an extension of public-house entertainment. Drinking and gambling were an accepted part of cricket in the 1830s and 1840s. With the growth of inter-colonial and international competition, cricket became a larger enterprise with a new cadre of administrators: lawyers, politicians and men of social and professional standing, attracted by the social prestige and political potential of the game, dominated the colonial cricket associations which emerged from the 1850s.

There have been few studies, until recently, of the important role played by administrations in the politics of cricket and in shaping its agendas. While the career of élite players is frequently relatively short, some administrators have played a dominant role over the game for three and even five decades. Chris Harte, in his study of the South Australian Cricket Association, has suggested that the organisation has had some very influential and long-serving administrators such as John Creswell, Bill Jeanes and Sir Donald Bradman who have exercised great influence not only over cricket in the city and the state but also over wider sporting fields.[23] Similarly Richard Driver, a minister of lands in the New South Wales government, was instrumental in establishing the Sydney Cricket Ground Trust which provided the New South Wales Cricket Association with access to the Sydney Cricket Ground.[24]

Most administrators who ran the game from the 1850s were committed to the middle-class ideologies of amateurism, athleticism and muscular Christianity. They attempted to make cricket a moral game and campaigned successfully to remove gambling in the 1870s and 1880s. Most administrators were also part of the establishment — Anglican or Protestant in religion, Anglophile, imperialist and conservative in politics. Cricket competition was suspended during the First and Second World Wars to encourage cricketers to support the war effort.

There have been some notable conflicts between administrators and those who play and watch cricket, many of whom have not shared the conservative vision of those who run the game. There was a long-running battle between administrators from 1878 to 1912 over commercialism, professionalism and control of the game. This was a complicated battle, as David Montefiore has demonstrated, because of the rivalries between one colonial association and another.[25] The main issues were not resolved until 1912 when the newly-established Australian Board of Control exerted its authority with the result that six of the leading players withdrew from the 1912 tour.

Sectarianism reared its head in cricket in the 1930s. Test cricketer Bill O'Reilly believed that this was a factor when four of the five Roman Catholic members were hauled before the Board of Control during the 1937–38 series. The precise reason for the meeting was never made clear but the chairman of the board seemed to imply that the Irish/Catholic contingent were 'representatives of an insubordinate and disloyal team of slackers and boozers'.[26] Philip Derriman noted in the *Sydney Morning Herald* of 17 June 1993 that cricket had often been 'troubled by sectarian tensions at the administration level', and added that it was 'something of a breakthrough' when Lindsay Hassett became test captain in 1949, the first Catholic since Percy McDonnell captained the national side in 1888. Derriman also believed that there had been very few Catholic captains since 1949 and that for many decades of this century the Australian

Cricket Board (ACB) has preferred on-field leaders who were both Protestants and Masons.

The operations of the ACB, challenged by the World Series Cricket crisis of 1977–79, have become more professional from the 1980s. By placing the leading players on contracts and by establishing a cricket sub-committee, the ACB dealt constructively with the challenge of the Professional Cricketers Association of Australia which operated from 1977–82.[27]

Cricket from its very first days in Australia has attracted support from across the social spectrum. While some clubs were formed for gentlemen, such as the Melbourne Cricket Club, other clubs were formed for tradesmen and mechanics. Cricket benefited because it was the first team sport to emerge in the country and, with its extensive media coverage, it attracted broad social support, a following which it has never lost. Cricket was around and popular when suburbs and country towns were established, cities grew and colonial governments were established. By the twentieth century the leading players of the country were emerging from a variety of social backgrounds: middle-class and working-class, Anglican, Protestant and Catholic, city and country.

It is likely that Australian cricket has been more broadly based, socially and geographically, than English cricket which appears more class-restricted and stronger in some parts of the country than others. The development of large and relatively comfortable cricket grounds and facilities for spectators, including modern scoreboards, suggests that Australian administrators, unlike their English counterparts, were more comfortable with the notion of cricket as a mass spectator sport. Keith Sandiford has suggested that English administrators in the Victorian era kept admission prices relatively high in the interests of limiting cricket audiences.[28]

The broad-based support for cricket has diminished since 1945 as a more multicultural society has emerged. Since that time, cricket has suffered from its Anglicist image and has drawn few players from non-English-speaking backgrounds. Whereas Greek and Italian Australians, and many other ethnic groups, have been prominent in football codes and reached the highest levels, only a handful of non-Anglo-Celtic players have represented Australia in recent decades. These include Len Durtanovich, better known as Len Pascoe — he anglicised his name early in his career — and Mike Veletta, the first Italian-Australian to play in test ranks.

Australia has always had a strong tradition of country cricket.

Country cricket often had a distinctive social atmosphere, and one of the inducements for city teams to travel to the country for a match was the offer of good hospitality. Although the journey from Adelaide to the country town of Gawler by horse occupied half a day in the mid-nineteenth century, the outings were 'jolly affairs': 'they would play cricket all day and sup at night and in the early hours of the morning be hoisted into the six-horse bus'.[29]

Many of the greatest cricketers — Bradman, O'Reilly, McCabe, Walters, Taylor — came from the country. Brought up on hard and true surfaces — concrete, asphalt and even rolled-out ant beds — country batsmen learnt to play confident shots, particularly those across the body. Many country batsmen, uncoached natural players, have proven pragmatic and effective run-accumulators. Batsmen brought up in the more cosmopolitan and sophisticated city environment, such as Victor Trumper and Allan Kippax, have been more conscious of looking good at the crease and of adopting the latest batting fashion. The city has produced more refined and coached cricketers who are interested in playing stylish strokes such as an exquisite late cut.

Australia cricket has a rich fund of bush legends, literature and art, including the poem about McDougall's dog — who absconded with the ball to the advantage of McDougall — and the celebrated painting of Russell Drysdale. Australia has had numerous prominent cricket journalists including John Worrall, J. C. Davis, Tom Horan, Jack Fingleton, Philip Derriman, Mike Coward and its share of writers such as A. G. Moyes, Jack Pollard and Ray Robinson. The market for cricket literature and periodical material, however, has always been smaller than in England. Australia has had a succession of cricket annuals which have come out for a few years then folded. The nation has also produced some distinguished and articulate radio commentators, notably Sir Charles Moses, Michael Charlton, Alan McGilvray, Neville Olliver and Jim Maxwell. The Australian Broadcasting Corporation has developed its own tradition of commentary, favouring clear and concise service which remains close to the game itself whereas the British Broadcasting Commission has encouraged a more wide-ranging and even poetic commentary. Such was the interest in cricket in the 1930s that the ABC organised 'synthetic cricket' broadcasts during the 1938 series. Australian broadcasters, fed with scanty cable information at the end of each over, imaginatively re-created what might have occurred. These fake broadcasts were so professional that many listeners were convinced that they were real. In more recent years Australian commercial television has been at the forefront of many innovations to improve the quality and variety of second-hand spectatorship.

From the late nineteenth century onwards, school cricket became the nursery of Australian cricket and an important reason for its strength. By the twentieth century cricket was played extensively in both private and state schools and enjoyed a privileged position: educational authorities and governments supported and subsidised school cricket and there were enthusiastic teachers willing to coach cricket teams on sports days and after school hours. School cricket was at its zenith in the 1920s and 1930s when an interstate primary school competition emerged. There were many private schools as well with strong cricketing traditions. Matches between the Adelaide colleges of St Peter's and Prince Alfred were played to a finish and one match, in 1940, took seven days to complete.

The climate for school team sports and for cricket, in particular, has been less favourable since the 1960s, particularly in state schools. The changed role of physical education, criticism of élitist sport, teacher unionism, the introduction of co-education, the 'feminisation' of the teaching staff have all affected the character of school sport and led to a marked decline in school cricket. The game also suffered increased competition from other less time-consuming sports such as basketball. While there has been a consistent decline in school cricket, particularly in state schools, there has been an expansion of youth competition (from under sixteen to under nineteen) with interstate carnivals and international tours from the 1960s onwards. The slack in school cricket has been partly taken up by the Australian Cricket Board in the 1980s, backed by corporate sponsorship such as from Barclays Bank and the Australian Wool Corporation. By the 1980s the board had realised that it had to compete for the school and youth market — which had long been taken for granted — and that there was danger that cricket might disappear from junior levels. Greg McKie argues that while Australian school cricket has not declined as much as it has in England, the onus is squarely on cricket authorities to nurture school and youth sport.[30]

Cricket was the first team game established in Australia, an important reason why it appealed to all sections of colonial society. As the most British of British games the sport also appealed to an Anglo-Celtic society which largely drew its cultural and political inspiration from Britain. Initially imitative and derivative, Australian cricket developed its own forms, traditions and symbols in the twentieth century. As Australians established more of their own identity and culture, Australian cricket developed its distinctive heroes, large grounds and scoreboards, ways of broadcasting and watching cricket, humour, language and symbols of the game — its own culture of cricket.

Cricket has changed markedly during the era of television in that it has become more commercial, professional and international. Players are now almost as comfortable playing at Bombay or Lord's as they are at the Gabba. Spectator behaviour is less distinctively Australian — the ubiquitous 'Mexican wave' has crossed many spectator boundaries, national and sporting. However, the game will continue to reflect — as it always has — something about what it is to be an Australian. The Australian of the 1990s is more accepting of commercialism and professionalism in sport, of sport as entertainment, and is more part of an international community than ever before.

Although cricket remains one of the most popular sports in the country, cricket officials can no longer count automatically on its continuing popularity. With the decline of school sport since 1945 and the growth of a much wider array of alternative sports, the ACB now has to compete in the market place for the support of youth. If cricket wishes to remain a national game, it is essential that it appeal to all Australians and that it reinvent itself in a form more appropriate for women and those from non-English-speaking backgrounds. Otherwise there is a danger that, in time, cricket will become an 'ethnic' sport, the game of Anglo-Celtic male Australians.

5 Golf

Brian Stoddart

Golf destroys more dreams and lives than any other sport, because it has the capacity to make addicts out of the people who play it.

Lauren St John, *Shooting at clouds* (1991)

Daft game

Sandy Lyle in Lauren St John, *Shooting at clouds* (1991)

B Y THE early 1990s there were around 500 000 registered men and women golfers in Australia who subscribed to one or more of over 1500 organised clubs in the country. That number of players could be more than doubled by those who play on the many public courses available. In the United States it is calculated that at least ten per cent of the population plays golf at least once during the year while in Canada that calculation is as high as eighteen per cent. Based on those figures, Australian golf participation would be somewhere between 1.7 million and 2.8 million which would make it one of the most participatory sports in the country.[1]

Golf is certainly an important Australian economic factor. The industry itself puts its annual worth at over one hundred million dollars in sales alone; most metropolitan golf clubs have annual turnovers exceeding one million dollars made up mostly of fees paid by members and thousands of people are employed in manufacturing equipment or maintaining courses or providing clubhouse services; professional players compete for prize money as high as nine million dollars in recent years while club professionals make good livings in providing services to the general playing public.[2]

Seen in this light golf constitutes a distinct Australian subculture and has done so since at least the late nineteenth century. Perhaps surprisingly, then, its history and evolution in Australia have been as yet little understood. All the more so because golf encapsulates most if not all the dilemmas faced by sport in general as it has moved towards a more complex shape in the late twentieth century: social access, resource use and environmental concerns, commercialisation, administrative issues, professionalism and amateurism, internationalisation and technological advance being just some of them. This essay, then, outlines the contours of golf's important history in Australia and points the way towards the many areas begging for further analysis.

As with most Australian sports, the precise origins of the game in the country are hazy. The standard accounts have Alexander Reid playing on a course laid out on his Clyde Valley property in Tasmania during the 1820s, some Melbourne personalities hitting balls around what is now parkland in that city, with Sydneysiders following suit in the early 1850s. Other states took up the game much later and the rise of organised clubs began in the early 1880s, most notably with the original Australian in Sydney.[3] Nevertheless there must still remain the possibility of golf having been in evidence even earlier (particularly in New South Wales) given the prominence of Scots migrants and the significance of golf in their home culture.

As in Britain, though, golf boomed in Australia from the 1880s until the outbreak of the First World War.[4] In New South Wales, for example, twenty-four clubs were established between 1893 and 1901 alone, and by 1914 that figure had increased by over forty.[5] The reasons for such growth were complex, but were caught up generally in the process of community building. Given the British ancestry of almost all Australians at the time and the significance of sport in late nineteenth-century British culture, there was a predisposition

to creating sports institutions in Australia. Golf, moreover, had status connotations in the British context. While its Scottish dimensions were relatively egalitarian, that was not the case south of the border where clubs were established as exclusive environments in which the cultured society might congregate. Something of that atmosphere transferred to Australia and is most readily noticed in the creation of the 'Royal' clubs.

When what later became the Royal Sydney Golf Club was founded in 1893 it boasted several prominent members of the city's social élite — B. R. Wise was born into a legal family and became a notable politician; H. M. Hamilton was born in Australia, educated overseas including Edinburgh University (he played rugby union for Scotland) before returning to Sydney and a legal career; R. H. L. Innes was born into a legal family and went to the Supreme Court of New South Wales; C. E. Weigall's father was an influential headmaster at Sydney Grammar while Weigall himself became New South Wales Solicitor-General. Among other prominent members by the early twentieth century were names like Fairfax (of the *Sydney Morning Herald*), Knox (of the Colonial Sugar Refinery) and Arnott (of biscuit-manufacturing fame).[6]

In Melbourne a similar pattern emerged of colonial prominence and respectability. Among the founders of the Royal Melbourne Golf Club were J. M. Bruce, leading city trader and father to a later Australian prime minister; Thomas Finlay, pastoralist and director of Goldsbrough Mort and Co. Ltd;

Although golf clubs began to form in the 1880s, golfers in rural areas utilised any appropriate territory. This group is playing at Gundagai in the 1870s. (A. C. Butcher Collection, National Library of Australia.)

79

William Knox, a director of Broken Hill Proprietary; A. R. Blackwood, managing director of Dalgety & Co. Ltd; Sir William Clarke, who inherited his father's vast pastoral empire; Nicholas Fitzgerald, a director of Carlton & United Breweries; Justice H. B. Higgins, the creator of Australia's arbitration and conciliation system; David Syme, proprietor of the *Age*, one of Australia's leading newspapers; and some Melbourne University professors including Orme Masson (chemistry), Harrison Moore (Law), T. R. Lyle (natural philosophy) and T. G. Tucker (classics). This was an imposing and influential group.[7]

What these and other founders of the game in Australia did, too, was to set aside considerable tracts of land to be dedicated solely to the playing of golf. While that happened in other sports, it is arguable that only golf has done so in such a way as to have become an environmental issue. Size and site have been important here as starting points. The average golf course occupies between fifty and one hundred hectares of land so that the 1500 courses in Australia occupy up to 150 000 hectares. Given the solid development experienced in metropolitan sites before the First World War, golf courses currently occupy prime real estate. Royal Perth is now in what is the desirable suburb of South Perth; many of the famous sandbelt courses in Melbourne are located in what are now most fashionable areas; while, in the national capital, Royal Canberra and Federal are very close to each other in the sought-after inner south. Then, unlike other sports grounds, golf courses themselves were subject to intensive improvement given the tendency towards manicuring which became predominant following the First World War. Before then, it is fair to generalise, greenkeeping and course design were rudimentary arts. From the 1920s onwards, however, visits by leading international course architects like Alistair McKenzie helped develop a more scientific approach and led to more intensive upkeep.[8]

All of that was a long way from the minds of golf's Australian founders as they laid out their courses and developed their membership policies. There is little escaping the fact that metropolitan golf clubs were predominantly exclusive in outlook. That held not only for the Royal clubs but also for most of those which followed in their wake.

The group of Perth citizens who made up the first committee of the Lake Karrinyup Country Club in 1927, for example, 'drew together something of a galaxy of Western Australia's professional and entrepreneurial talent'. Dixie Clement was one of the city's leading obstetricians and helped organise the King Edward Memorial Hospital for Women, Ralph Crisp a pediatrician and superintendent of Perth Children's Hospital, H. B. Jackson a King's Counsel and director of Western Australian Newspapers, Eric Sandover an industrialist and founder of Australian rules football's Sandover Medal, Mr Justice Dwyer a leading judge and other committee members were prominent businessmen.[9] Of the 250 founding members there were at least thirty-three medical practitioners, seventeen lawyers, eight accountants, five dentists, five architects and four engineers. There was one university professor, R. G. Cameron, who held the first chair of education at the University of Western Australia. Other major groups represented were pastoralists (thirty-three), company managers (twenty), merchants (nineteen) and directors (eleven).[10] This was a distinctly upper-middle-class and socially exclusive group which set out to establish the club as a retreat for like-minded people, with wealth a large determinant of access. That was scarcely surprising because golf demanded resources in both finance (for equipment and fees to underwrite high development and maintenance costs) and time (to play required access to leisure time created largely by occupation). Lake Karrinyup was no different from many other clubs set up around the same time, with Sydney's Elanora Country Club an excellent parallel.[11]

Not surprisingly, then, with a return to peace after the First World War many enterprising entrepreneurs sought to link the social status of golf, its leisure possibilities and its economic potential. An excellent example of this came in the development of the Belvedere Golf Links Estate at Blackheath in the New South Wales Blue Mountains. Advertised for auction on Anniversary (now Australia) Day in 1920, the development provided 'the devotee of the Prince of Games with something that can challenge comparisons with the best of its sort in Australia, and as if that still needed bettering, caps it by offering an Estate in which most of the Building Sites are measured with direct frontage to the links themselves'.[12] With Blackheath likened to other imperial hill stations like Simla in India, the facilities at the golf-course estate were emphasised as being luxurious and catering specifically to the well-to-do and discerning members of society, and that was probably the overwhelming characteristic of golf's social image in Australia to that point.

Another social angle to Australian golf had begun to develop, however, and is best illustrated by the emergence of Moore Park municipal links near the Sydney Cricket Ground and what is now the Sydney Football Stadium. Moore Park was established by Duncan McMillan, a city businessman of Scottish

Club-making at Cash Bros, 52 McAuley Street, Alexandria, New South Wales, 1949. Until the 1950s, individual club-making was flourishing, but it died out because of competition from mass production techniques and imports from overseas. (Hood Collection, State Library of New South Wales.)

origin and used to a more egalitarian participation in the game as practised in Scotland.[13] He certainly tapped a responsive vein because Moore Park quickly became one of the busiest courses in the country. By the end of 1923 the course managers declared that 4600 rounds per month were being played and the following year that had increased to over 5000 per month. Averaging out to over 160 rounds per day, that also indicated the widespread interest in the game at a participatory level.[14]

Moore Park also produced a highly symbolic moment in this relative democratisation of golf. It came in 1924 when Harry Sinclair, a Moore Park member, beat Alex Russell, a Royal Melbourne member and winner of the Australian Open, for the Australian amateur title. Sinclair grew up in the working-class suburb of Redfern and learned his golf by caddying at Moore Park. He then graduated to greenkeeping which gave him time and access to develop his playing skills. While he later turned professional, in winning the 1924 title he could not have been in greater contrast to his opponent.[15] Russell was a true Victorian patrician. Born into a prominent pastoral family he was educated first at Geelong Grammar and then went to Cambridge where he was a member of Jesus College. It was while at Cambridge that he took up golf seriously and quickly became a very good player. He served as an officer during the war, won a Military Cross and then returned to Melbourne where he was Royal Melbourne champion on several occasions as well as winning higher honours.[16] To add to the symbolism, Sinclair beat Russell two and one over the patrician's home course of Royal Melbourne so that devotees of the class struggle could scarcely have a more evocative image than that of a green-keeper from a Sydney working-class suburb beating a Victorian grazier while traversing the socially hallowed fairways of Royal Melbourne.

While Sinclair took the traditional option of turning profes-sional to secure his economic future, Russell took advantage of the widening economic avenues provided by golf between the wars. He turned to course architecture by becoming an Austral-ian partner of the renowned Dr Alistair McKenzie, whose medical practice paled into insignificance as he became the first of the great designers. McKenzie made a fortune during a mid-1920s visit to Australia by charging a minimum fee of £250 to advise golf clubs on the reshaping of their layouts. Russell learned quickly, utilised his excellent social connections and was soon in demand. He implemented McKenzie's plans for the original Royal Melbourne West Course (as it is now) and designed the East Course in his own right. Lake Karrinyup founder Keith Barker knew Russell personally and so the Victo-rian was selected to design the new course there. Among his other achievements was one of New Zealand's finest courses at Paraparaumu, just outside of Wellington.

Other avenues were opening up or expanding, however, as golf became firmly established as a sub-culture during the 1920s and 1930s. In Victoria during 1928, for example, both the Golf Club Secretaries Association and the Greenkeepers Association were formed to promote the exchange of ideas, information and skills along with creating a professional ap-proach to their occupations.[17] Two years earlier the Spalding company had opened an equipment manufacturing plant to cope with the growing demand.[18] Two years before that Mel-bourne retailers had staged a golf-clothes carnival to provide the distinctive golf 'uniforms' for both men and women.[19] Machinery suppliers began to specialise in providing for golf-course maintenance as the days of horse-drawn mowers gave way to mechanical mowers and a more scientific approach to turf care. Golf magazines came and went, specialist columns appeared in newspapers, golf tourism became popular (to places like the Blue Mountains near Sydney), golfers figured along with cricketers and footballers on cigarette cards and, of course, books of instruction were legion.

It was professional golf, however, which remained in all its dimensions the most obvious and deep-seated commercial aspect of the game. When the first formalised clubs developed around the country late in the nineteenth century, many of their committees moved quickly to appoint professionals as teachers, equipment makers, sellers of golfing supplies and controllers of the playing itself. Until the First World War almost all these came from Scotland which, at that time, sent such experts all over the world.

Carnegie Clark provides, perhaps, the best example of what was possible in professional golf.[20] Born in 1881 in Carnoustie, Scotland, into a fishing family, he became a caddy at that famous course before going into the shop to learn club-making. Besides being a very fine player and teacher he became an excellent club-maker. In 1902 he left Scotland for Sydney and a sports-store contract until he joined Royal Sydney as its professional and stayed until 1930 when he shifted to Avondale. He won three Australian opens, finished second three times and won innumerable other professional events. His professional contract gave him a standard retainer, but his main income came from three sources. The club-making tradition he began in Australia turned into the Carnegie Clark golf company, which still retains his name (Clark died in 1978) but which has now passed into offshore hands. His teaching was much sought after and a full lesson book guaranteed good cash flow. He was also in demand as one of Australia's first course architects, and a large number of present-day courses all along the east coast demonstrate his skills.

In the early years, then, professionals like Clark were very much all-rounders, imported to help develop Australian golf. By the 1920s, however, two tendencies were emerging: the enhanced skills of home-grown players going into professional ranks, and the growing attraction of going overseas. These trends, in turn, would lead to the eventual division of professionals between club and touring careers. J. Victor East and Joe Kirkwood demonstrate the changes nicely. East served briefly as professional at both Royal Sydney and Royal Melbourne, then early in the 1920s went to America where he set out on a long career as a club professional, teacher and equipment adviser to both the giant Spalding and Wilson companies. On his very first trip to America he went as manager for the immensely talented Joe Kirkwood, whose earlier exploits culminated in his 1920 Australian Open victory. While his tournament skills held up well, Kirkwood made a fortune as a trick-shot artist and toured the world incessantly in the company of Walter Hagen, one of golf's most accomplished players and flamboyant characters. Kirkwood died in the United States in 1970 and his fellow traveller East in 1976 at the age of ninety.[21]

While club professionals became solidly established in Australia during the inter-war years, there was always a social distance between them and the members they served — the professional was really in a servant capacity. Cottesloe Golf Club in Perth, for example, was one of those many Australian clubs where Kirkwood and Hagen demonstrated their skills during a 1935 tour. Just a year earlier Cottesloe was one of the clubs where complaints had arisen about the professional being seen in the bar. The Western Australian Golf Association resolved to ban professionals from clubhouse bars except on such tournament occasions as they might be made honorary members.[22]

One reason for the emergence of such overt attempts at status building in an allegedly egalitarian society was the respective origins of the members and the professionals. Most of the clubs comprised memberships drawn from the social and economic élite of Australian cities. Most of the professionals who developed in Australia came from poor backgrounds, the usual path being to grow up near a golf course, become a caddy, sneak in illegal rounds on the course, become an assistant then, eventually, become a club professional. While the two groups might be joined by the game in its playing circumstances they were still separated by social attitudes and positioning. That was to last a long time with vestiges of the practice remaining in the late twentieth century, one hundred years after its formulation.

While the creators of such social policy resided in the club committees, the gatekeepers were undoubtedly the full-time secretaries (now frequently referred to as secretary-managers) who became a major feature of club life from the very early twentieth century onwards. The earliest of the full-time administrators at Royal Sydney are indicative of the directions taken by the leading clubs in their formative phases.

Ross Gore became Royal Sydney's first paid secretary after having served Royal Melbourne in an honorary capacity while in that city as an Australian Mutual Provident Society executive. A good player, he had grown up in New Zealand then come to Australia. From 1907 until his death in 1925 he steered the club towards its strong presence in Sydney. He was followed by Colonel W. R. Bertram, an Englishman whose military background prompted the introduction of uniforms for the house staff and a tough stand on industrial relations matters. Another military man, Major R. T. Coulson, then spent twenty years in the position, living at the club for all that time and guiding it through some critical developments.[23] All three men regarded the club as much as an institution as a sporting venture and all identified with the members' desire for respectability, protocol and tradition building.

In the creation and maintenance of this social space in golf, however, the gap between professionals and members was more than matched by what was for a very long time a massive gulf between members and associates. The associates were, and remain, the women members of golf clubs who by definition were 'associates' of men, invariably wives or direct relatives. The forms of discrimination were clear enough — while women were allowed to play they could do so only at times convenient to men; women paid reduced fees but in doing so had far less power over club affairs than did men; and certain areas of the clubhouse were off-limits to women. Importantly, these forms of discrimination have proved enduring. While much modification has occurred, the basic power relationships have survived. Even in the early 1970s, for example, associate members of Royal Canberra were not allowed inside the gates during the weekends.[24]

All of this was located within the prevailing social norms. The accepted patterns of society were, if anything, even more highly regarded within golf clubs than within most other social institutions and in the public at large. Women were either wives and mothers or undergoing apprenticeships for the family role. They were to schedule their activities around those of their men, hence the weekends were sacrosanct leisure time for the breadwinners who had put in a hard week. Many of those breadwinners, of course, were in professions which allowed leisure time for golf through the week — mid-week competi-

tions very quickly became the preserve of lawyers, medical practitioners, company executives and even academics.

On the playing side this had little real effect. Golf was an acceptable sport for women, in the eyes of men, given that it was not too strenuous and was reasonably decorous.[25] Women played the game very early in Australia. Indeed, the Australian Ladies' Amateur Championship was played first at Geelong, just three months before the men's equivalent and a full year before the first American women's amateur title. Given that professional golf has not been a long-time possibility for women, it is not surprising that few of the amateur champions have gone on to professional careers: Margy Masters won in 1958 before going on to an American career; Jane Lock won three times in the 1970s before turning professional; and Corrinne Dibnah won in 1981 and has become very successful on the international professional tour.

In 1986 Dale Wharton became the first woman appointed to a head club-professional's position when given the post at Royal Fremantle Golf Club in Perth. Since then a small number of women have been appointed to lesser positions and to traineeships. Yet when Dale Wharton first applied to become a trainee in the late 1970s she was prevented from doing so by the

Women players at Kensington Club, New South Wales, c. 1930s. By this time, women were beginning to fight against restrictions on their playing rights by male-dominated club committees. The golfhouse of the Kensington club is now a student cafeteria on the campus of the University of New South Wales. (Hood Collection, State Library of New South Wales.)

87

contract which specifically stipulated that candidates had to be male. The slow and late change has been related directly to the domination of the clubs by men in both numerical and power terms.[26]

That was the specific reason for the creation of Brisbane's McLeod Club which was put together in the very early 1970s by a group of businesswomen who perceived that their interests were not being met by the existing clubs. The club is run by and for women and may be regarded as a reflection in golf of the changing status of women more generally.[27]

As with many other sports, one of the main sites for the struggle over gender equity in golf has been in clothing. The earliest playing dress forms differed little from the average active-leisure clothes worn by the middle-class associates during their daily lives. Signs of challenge appeared during the 1920s with a swing towards slacks. Many associates' committees and, more especially, their overriding general (that is, male) committees held out against this change. So, too, did they hold out against the idea that women still wearing skirts might wish to discard stockings while on the course. When concessions were given grudgingly, they usually prevented the clothing revolution from reaching into the clubhouse. Similar battles were fought over the introduction of shorts and ankle socks, brightly coloured shirts and form-fitting clothes. One fashion historian has termed the consequent results as the combined worst of some very bad and ill-serving styles.[28]

Of course, the debate was not so much about the clothes as about whether or not their wearers were breaking away from established patterns of behaviour and representation as sanctioned by that section of society which carried into the formulation of golf-club traditions set ideas about how things should work.

Such ideas about convention also lay at the heart of the treatment meted out to other social minorities (at least in power terms) by golfing organisations. The treatment of Australia's Jewish population by golf clubs was scandalous. Since at least the turn of this century many golf clubs have had a policy of actively discriminating against Jewish applicants for all the mysterious reasons which characterise anti-Semitism wherever it is practised.[29] This was seen as so serious in some Jewish quarters that clubs were set up to create open playing avenues for the group. Monash Country Club in Sydney, named after Sir John Monash, is one result, created after the Second World War by people refused entry to other major clubs in the city.

Australia's Aboriginal population is rarely seen in golf circles, although an annual tournament is now held and Mark Chalker became the first of his community to become a professional. All the usual structural reasons are offered for this inequality: lack of financial resources for lessons, equipment and membership, limited access to playing facilities and the absence of role models. Those are all contributing conditions, clearly enough, but an abiding theme must also be that of rejection based on colour and cultural lines.

In this vein, golf has remained a solidly Anglo-Saxon preoccupation although the changing membership of many clubs is beginning to filter through into professional ranks. While Norman von Nida was for many years the sole prominent name of non-British stock (on his father's side, at least), in recent years Zoran Zorcic, David Diaz and Nicole Lowien represent the changing face of Australian society at last extending into golf.[30] With New Zealander Michael Campbell, a Maori, winning the 1992 Australian amateur championship, perhaps Australia itself will now have a sharper spur to wider representation.[31]

By the end of the Second World War, then, Australian golf had developed quite distinctive social patterns, one prime reason being the administrative structures created to carry on the running of the game. Curiously enough, the Australian Golf Union (AGU) was formed in 1898 before any of the formalised state bodies emerged. They all did so between 1901 (Victoria) and 1913 (Queensland). The composition of the AGU occasioned debate until the founding clubs gave up their predominent positions.[32] Until 1921 the AGU also controlled women's golf. In that year the Australian Ladies' Golf Union was formed and since then the two groups have gone their own ways.

Over the years the two national bodies have become increasingly active and, between them, control the development of amateur golf in Australia. Since the first junior amateur title was held in 1979 Steve Elkington, Grant Waite, Brett Ogle, Peter O'Malley and Robert Allenby have won then gone on to successful international professional careers. The women's junior title is an older one, beginning in 1953 when it was won by Margy Masters, and its most successful product has been Jan Stephenson.

On the professional side, 1911 marked the beginning of the Professional Golfers' Association of Australia at a meeting in Carnegie Clark's Royal Sydney shop.[33] From the outset the emphasis was on training and education for new members, then on developing the teaching of golf. The latter has become increasingly contentious in recent years as the amateur bodies have become more interested in producing good-quality junior programmes.

Both groups began to deal with quite different environments from 1945 onwards, in some measure because of changed social conditions. One interesting example involves urban shift and growing conservationist concerns. A number of urban clubs had experienced the pressure of urban drift even before 1914. As populations grew, towns spread, property prices and rates rose, many clubs moved further afield. Some of the best examples of this lie with the famous Melbourne sandbelt courses clustered around Black Rock, Sandringham, Oakleigh and Cheltenham. A number of these courses began their existence elsewhere then shifted to their present sites. They became established and the suburbs surrounded them, the golf courses eventually enhancing local property values with real-estate advertisements emphasising proximity to and/or views of the increasingly prestigious clubs as major selling points.[34]

As the care and attention of these and other like courses became more scientific and reliant upon chemical controls, major environmental questions were stored up for the future. The natural approach gave way to fertilisers, pesticides, fungicides and the rest. Later advances in automatic sprinkler systems washed chemicals more effectively into the soil. Not until many years later were the potential dangers realised.[35] This concern heightened from the 1970s onwards as the building of resort courses gathered pace in Australia. While most parts of the country have these golf and hotel facilities now, the main concentration was in Queensland and especially in the Albert Shire surrounding the Gold Coast where over thirty courses are now built or planned. Because all these resorts pushed into fragile coastal land, strict environmental safeguards have been implemented but that has not stopped the controversy. The debate now focuses on whether or not golf might actually be good for the environment.

The initially small flow of tourists attracted to golf centres now became a torrent, Japanese demands being particularly high. With Japanese developers hungry for Queensland property, as part of a Pacific Rim expansion, the environmental concern outweighed a deeper social one as the tradition of relatively cheap access to Australian golf became altered.

Another cluster of resort-type courses gathered along the Murray River on the New South Wales side of the border with Victoria. Places like Tocumwal have profited immensely from the presence of golf clubs for one simple reason — the club-houses contained poker machines which attracted daily busloads of Victorians across the border to feed the one-armed bandits (banned in Victoria itself until 1992). As a result, the clubs used the profits to build magnificent courses to attract more golf tourists to the area.

As the number of courses grew in Australia so, too, did the numbers of players. Much of the growth from the 1950s to the mid-1980s may be put down to relative prosperity linked to available leisure time. For many years now the demand for golf has outstripped the provision of facilities so that for some prestigious clubs the waiting list might be over twenty years.

Much of the popularity, however, has stemmed from Australia's international success. Peter Thomson (five times), Kel Nagle, Greg Norman and Ian Baker-Finch have all won the British Open (more correctly known as the Open Championship), David Graham won the United States Open and Wayne Grady the United States Professional Golfers' Association championship. Beyond that Australians have won a host of tournaments all over the world. Given that much of this has been relayed via television, this success has bred enthusiasm.

Australia was one of the first countries to have a full eighteen-hole coverage of golf tournaments go live to air.[36] Many of the technical advances in golf coverage have been pioneered in Australia. This built on a rich tradition of golf journalism which began very early in Australia with people like Professor E. O. G. Shann, one of Australia's foremost early economists, writing golf under a pseudonym for a Perth news-paper. Since at least the 1950s, as international success grew, media organisations have assigned specialists to cover golf in many parts of the world.

On the professional side the club/tour debate is now re-solved as, during 1992, entry to the tour was deemed to be by way of the qualifying school and not by the traineeship option. The Professional Golfers' Association has strengthened the training for those wishing to become club professionals while the tour aspirants hit balls, live cheaply and work at nights to feed their ambitions of becoming the next Greg Norman. Some now go off to the United States college circuit combining education with golf. Some succeed in getting on the tour, others are doomed to the regional pro-am circuits where, to make a few dollars, they put up with amateur partners who might have played only rarely.

Australian golf, then, has a rich and growing heritage, and occupies a solid niche in the make-up of Australian life. The game constitutes both a major social sub-culture with its own lore, tradition and customs, and has become an increasingly substantial factor in the Australian economy by providing work, manufacturing and tourism opportunities. Its future is likely to be marked by debates about social access on the one hand and the use or abuse of natural resources on the other. So long as Australians continue to be stricken by the addiction noted by Lauren St John, then golf will continue to intersect with all aspects of Australian life and social practice.

6

Horse-Racing and Trotting

John O'Hara

In their own generation the wise may sneer,
They hold our sport in derision;
Perchance to sophist, or sage or seer
Were allotted a greater vision
Yet if man, of all the Creator plann'd,
His noblest work is reckoned,
Of the work of His hand, by sea or by land,
The horse may at least rank second.

Adam Lindsay Gordon,
Hippodromania: or Whiffs from the Pipe

We have come to the conclusion that all (sportingly speaking) is
vanity. We have just returned, weary, dusty, and penniless from the
races ... We started with youth at the prow and pleasure at the helm,
but return with battered sides and sails and torn by the adverse winds
of fortune.

Marcus Clarke, *Argus*, 4 November 1867

WHEN MARCUS Clarke attended the Victoria Racing
Club's spring race meeting in November 1867 what
he witnessed, and reported in the Melbourne *Argus*,
was an occasion which involved almost the whole of Melbourne's community and which stirred the interest of people
throughout the Australian colonies.[1] The main race, the Melbourne Cup, attracted a field of twenty-seven starters from

Victoria, New South Wales, Tasmania and South Australia.[2] Interest in the event was intense, with daily trackwork at Flemington racecourse provoking regular debate in the days leading up to the race meeting. On Melbourne Cup Day the Melbourne central business district was deserted after the half-day public holiday began. Some people began walking from the city to Flemington as early as nine a.m. Those with more disposable income took the train to the course, along the new line opened just in time for the race carnival. Others chose to travel by coach or private carriage or mounted on their prize steeds.[3]

On course the racegoers were offered a range of entertainments. The race programme included a hurdle race and races for horses of all grades, from maidens to the quality performers in the cup; but race days involved more than the races themselves. Fashion-conscious ladies displayed their finery on the lawn in front of the grandstand — an area which was gently graded and bordered by flower beds. Others, more interested in entertainment than display, took up the challenges offered by the various booth operators to play Aunt Sally, forms of knock-em-down, ring the prize games, doodleembuck, red, blue, feather and star or other games of chance. Pea-and-thimble men plied their trade alongside entertainers with fiddles or others who, with their faces coated with lamp black, sang Negro songs. These last were likely to be situated outside one or other of the many publicans' booths which dotted the Flemington hill, drawing crowds and enticing holidaymakers to have a drink while watching the entertainment.[4]

For those whose interest lay in the outcome of the races, plenty of opportunities to wager on the events were available. Bookmakers, dressed in colourful clothing, wandered around the ground calling out their odds. Others sold sweepstakes tickets from betting booths and even the fashion-conscious ladies wagered pairs of gloves with each other over the relative merits of their fancied horses.[5] When post-time arrived the horses and their riders congregated around the starting position behind a flag-carrying official, whose aim was to drop his flag when all the contestants were ready. Spectators also congregated, the more fashionable in the two-storeyed grandstand opposite the winning post, the less fashionable in the shilling stand on the hill which towered above the grandstand. Those unwilling or unable to pay to watch the race stood on the hill or in the flat (inside the course opposite the grandstand). When the cup was run, about sixteen thousand pairs of eyes followed the progress of the horses around the two-mile course.[6] This was approximately 3218 metres. Australian racing changed to metric distances and weights on 1 August 1972 and the Melbourne Cup is now run over 3200 metres.

In 1867, most of those eyes searched for the colours worn by the riders of the two favoured starters, Fireworks and Tim Whiffler, both of whom had travelled from Sydney to compete. Fireworks had won the Australian Jockey Club Derby at the Sydney spring race meeting and repeated his victory in the Victoria Racing Club Derby on the first day of the Melbourne carnival. Tim Whiffler, known as Sydney Tim to distinguish him from a Ballarat-based horse of the same name, had won the other feature race in Sydney, the two-mile Metropolitan. With the two Sydney horses dominating the pre-race discussions the contest was virtually determined at the start. When George Watson dropped his flag to start the race Fireworks was facing the wrong way and was left. Meanwhile, Sydney Tim anticipated the start better and settled in mid-field. His rider, John Driscoll, took a trail behind the leader approaching the home turn and then urged his five-year-old black horse to the lead half-way down the straight. He went on to win the race by one and a half lengths from Queen of Hearts, with Exile a further three lengths behind in third place. Tim Whiffler's win gave New South Wales owner/trainer Etienne De Mestre his third win in seven years and a prize of £1790.[7]

After the cup, Sydney Tim's supporters celebrated vigorously at the publicans' booths or increased their stakes for the late races. Supporters of Fireworks speculated on what might have been and those who had backed the other runners either sought consolation from the publicans or began their search for the winner of the next race, but with the main event completed some spectators began leaving the course. The premier occasion on the Melbourne social and sporting calendar was over for another year.

This description of the day's events, with minor variations, could have been applied to virtually any city, town or village in the Australian colonies by the late nineteenth century. Horse-racing was an integral part of colonial communities and Melbourne Cup Day (or its local equivalent) a highlight of the year. In less than a century from the first European settlement, horse-racing had become a well-organised, well-regulated and highly visible sport. It was a sport where the full spectrum of the socio-economic scale met and participated to some degree. Clerks, labourers and the unemployed rubbed shoulders with gentlemen from the city. Card-sharps and pickpockets competed with bookmakers, publicans and respectable merchants for a share of the money to be made from the occasion. Both genders displayed their finery and, at race meetings like the Melbourne Cup, the whole occasion was given vice-regal approval through the patronage of the Governor of Victoria and his official party.

Nevertheless, to a careful observer class and gender differences were, perhaps, more apparent on the racecourse than elsewhere. The governor and his party in the grandstand were carefully insulated from the less acceptable elements of Melbourne society on the flat or on the hill. Ladies restricted their promenading to the lawn in front of the grandstand: those who ventured beyond the lawn immediately lost their respectability and were characterised as loose or fast women. While it was acceptable for women to bet a pair of gloves with each other (or even with their male escorts) it was unacceptable for them to wager significant sums of money or to be seen betting with bookmakers. Their expected role was to adorn the occasion; to add elegance and respectability to what was clearly intended as a male sport.[8]

Other class differences were just as apparent. Although all levels of society might meet on the course, places of refuge for the wealthy were available in the stands, with entry fees ensuring if not social homogeneity, then at least economic homogeneity. In the celebrations which followed victory class differences were emphasised further. The winning owner was invariably fêted rather than the horse's trainer or rider. Etienne De Mestre was in the happy position of being both owner and trainer of Tim Whiffler so he was the toast of Melbourne after the 1867 Melbourne Cup — but the winning jockey, John Driscoll, was simply an employee doing his job. No doubt he celebrated his victory among his peers on cup night but he was quickly forgotten by Melbourne society. The class and gender distinctions and the employer/employee relations, which at first sight appear blurred on the racecourses, in fact were heightened by the sport. Racing rejoiced in its claim to be the sport of kings and although Australian racecourses welcomed the participation of all social levels, control of the sport (and most of its spoils) was held firmly in the hands of the colonial gentry.

Even in the more isolated country districts the story was similar. At Grafton, a small village on the New South Wales north coast, more than sixteen hundred kilometres from Melbourne, virtually the entire town and most of the region's population turned out for the annual race meeting of 1867. The story of the race day's events was almost a copy of the Melbourne experience — though on a smaller scale. Perhaps the mixing of socio-economic groups was more pronounced because of the smaller population[9] but, like the Victoria Racing Club (VRC), the Clarence River Jockey Club, which conducted the Grafton race meeting, was controlled by a combination of local squatters and the main commercial centre's most prominent citizens. The successful horses were not station hacks ridden by their owners but thoroughbreds, owned by wealthy squatters. At the 1867 Grafton race carnival six of the ten races, including the two feature events, were won by horses owned by Thomas Hawkins Smith, the owner of nearby Gordon Brook station. Like De Mestre, Smith was the toast of the town after the races but his jockey was quickly forgotten.[10]

By the 1860s thoroughbred horse-racing was an established sport throughout the Australian colonies. Almost wherever a town existed races were held — at least once each year. In the more isolated outback settlements a shortage of thoroughbreds might result in races for station hacks and in some centres there was no perceived need to establish a permanent race club. The quality of the racecourses varied as much as the quality of the horses which raced on them but the sport was accepted universally, despite the occasional sermons from the pulpit about the evils of betting. Yet the sport had existed in the colonies for little more than half a century.

The first official colonial race meeting for thoroughbred racehorses was held at Hyde Park in Sydney in October 1810. It was organised by officers of the Seventy-Third Regiment, with the official sanction of Governor Lachlan Macquarie. Although this meeting was recognised as a success and plans were laid to repeat the occasion, organised racing was dependent upon the military. When the Seventy-Third Regiment was replaced in 1814 racing went into recess — to be revived briefly five years later. After another three year interval the annual races became a feature of Sydney life.[11]

Organised racing could not have begun in the colonies much earlier than it did. The initial settlements at Sydney and Hobart were established as penal outposts and racehorses were not included in the lists of essential items shipped from England. Although the First Fleet included seven horses purchased at the Cape of Good Hope, they were almost certainly working stock rather than thoroughbreds. In any case they soon strayed in the bush, along with most of the fleet's cattle, and were lost.[12]

It was not long before more horses were imported, mostly from the Cape of Good Hope. In 1798 more than one hundred horses arrived and by 1802 the horse population in New South Wales had jumped to almost three hundred.[13] Many early imports were bred for heavy farm work including the Clydesdale, the Suffolk Punch and the Shire.[14] Agriculture and survival were more important matters than recreation or entertainment, but, as the colonies in New South Wales and Van Diemen's Land became more established and as they began to change from gaols to outposts which encouraged free settlers, forms of recreation and opportunities for display increasingly became matters of great interest. The breed of imported horses also began to change as officials and settlers, both free and freed, began to use carriage- and saddle-horses to travel around the ever-expanding settlements.

One reason behind the decision to hold an official race meeting in 1810 was that unofficial races had begun to appear, and interest in them was obvious. At Parramatta a sports day which included two match races, one involving gallopers and the other involving trotters, had been held in April.[15] The road to Parramatta had also become the site of other match races, with Mr Foster's Crop establishing a reputation as the first champion over the sixteen-mile course, winning a fifty-guinea match race by more than a mile.[16] On the settlement's north-western outskirts, in the Hawkesbury district, unofficial or impromptu race meetings were held with sufficient frequency for the favoured site of contests to be known as the racecourse.

At that stage the history of Australian horse-racing was very much in the balance, at least in terms of its dominant form. Match races between standard-bred trotters were at least as common as those between thoroughbred gallopers and of course some horses, such as John Piper's Miss Kitty, were versatile enough to trot and gallop successfully. As colonial roads were improving, the demand for road horses which could maintain a solid pace over long distances, both in harness or saddled, grew proportionately and was met by the importation of greater numbers of Cleveland Bays, Norfolk Trotters and Lincoln- and Welsh-bred horses — providing a solid foundation for the development of trotting as a sport.[17] Equally however, increasing wealth, at least in some quarters of colonial society, led to an increased display of that wealth and such display included the more magnificent thoroughbred racehorse. Perhaps the most telling factors were the need for colonial society to stress its civilisation — through imitation of the preferred leisure pursuits of the English aristocracy, and the timing of the beginnings of organised horse-racing in the colonies. In England the trotter had become a favourite carriage horse by the late eighteenth century but the aristocracy and the gentry preferred hunters and thoroughbreds for sport. In North America at the time of Australian settlement, the trotter was just beginning to emerge as the favoured horse for racing.[18] In any case the Hyde Park race meeting of 1810 gave an official stamp of approval to galloping thoroughbreds, ensuring that trotters would remain second-class citizens in Australian racing.

Van Diemen's Land hosted its first organised race meeting at New Town, near Hobart in 1814 but, like Sydney, the southern outpost lacked a sufficient supply of quality horses to permit regular racing. One method used in both colonies to tackle the problem of small fields was to conduct the main races as a series of heats, usually the best of three. As the emphasis was on staying races that often meant that horses competed in three two-mile heats to earn their prizes. Often the fields for the later heats were reduced by the withdrawal of any horse which had been 'distanced' in the earlier events — that is any horse unable to finish closer to the winner than the distance pole, which was placed in the straight one furlong from the winning post.

By the mid-1820s horse numbers and colonial enthusiasm had grown sufficiently to support a more regular racing schedule and permanent race clubs began to emerge to administer the sport. The short-lived Sydney Turf Club (1825–34) and the Tasmanian Turf Club (1826) were the first, but in Sydney competition for control of the sport was contested by the Australian Racing and Jockey Club, the Parramatta Turf Club and the Agricultural Turf Club until the Australian Jockey Club (AJC) emerged as the dominant body in 1842.[19] In Van Diemen's Land the Tasmanian Turf Club and the Tasmanian Racing Club effectively divided the island between them, with racing in the smaller colony based mainly in Launceston and Hobart, the two main settlements. In New South Wales various suburban racetracks at Bellevue Hill, Grose Farm, Randwick, Homebush and Petersham were used in the 1830s and 1840s, and the beginnings of a country racing circuit was emerging at

Hawkesbury, Campbelltown, Liverpool, Penrith, Maitland, Patricks Plains, Bathurst and Yass.[20]

In the 1830s new colonies were established around the Australian continent for free settlers rather than for Britain's felons and racing began almost immediately in each of them. In Adelaide and Melbourne racing began in 1838 and in Western Australia the first meeting was held even earlier, in 1833.[21] The infrastructure of race clubs soon followed, to provide adminis-trative support and ensure permanence, although in most cases they also had teething problems before a senior body emerged to control the sport in each colony.

In the 1850s the essential elements of racing were apparent throughout Australia, but only in Sydney was the sport fully established. Even there, where the spring racing carnival held at Homebush was the feature meeting of the year, the relatively small population of both people and horses and the lack of real disposable wealth meant only one main meeting per year could be sustained. This meeting was supplemented by races in the outer suburban and country centres, by private race meetings sponsored by publicans such as Thomas Shaw at Petersham, and by city meetings organised by groups of tradesmen such as the drapers, but only the annual Homebush meeting offered significant prize money or attracted any real support from the Sydney community. It also had the advantage of support from the New South Wales Legislative Council which provided one hundred sovereigns as a prize for the annual Queen's Plate. The legislators argued that their actions provided a stimulus to improve the breed of horses in the colony, but they also gave additional meaning to racing's image as the sport of kings.[22]

Such stimulus was unnecessary by the end of the decade. Gold discoveries in New South Wales and Victoria led to dramatic changes in colonial fortunes. The rapid population growth was more than matched by the growth in disposable income. The new-found wealth was not shared evenly but those who prospered showed a propensity to display their prosperity and even those who had not succeeded on the gold fields brought a willingness to gamble and an inclination to enjoy themselves vigorously, when race meetings provided them with an excuse to take a day off from their labours. In this new context racing flourished, especially in Victoria where Bendigo, Ballarat and other gold-field centres competed with Melbourne to hold the grandest race meetings.

In New South Wales Jorrocks had emerged in the 1840s as the colony's first champion racehorse. Although he did not race until he was seven years old, by the end of his career ten years later, he had recorded at least sixty wins and collected about four thousand sovereigns in prize money.[23] He also laid claim to the title of Australia's first inter-colonial champion when he defeated Petrel, the Victorian champion, in Sydney in 1848. Petrel had earlier won match races against the two Tasmanian champions Smolenski and Paul Jones. In 1857 another New South Wales horse, Veno, defeated Melbourne's best mare Alice Hawthorne to claim £1000 and the mantle as successor to Jorrocks.[24]

These match races and the accompanying support of each colony for their local champions, led naturally to the establishment of the Australian Champion Sweepstakes race, designed to match the best horses from each colony to find the undisputed champion of the year. The race was first held at Flemington in 1859 and then moved to Randwick in 1860. Subsequent runnings were held in Ipswich, Hobart, Geelong, Ballarat, Dunedin, Wagga Wagga, Christchurch and Melbourne over the following seven years. The event held great significance and marshalled colonial pride. It also attracted the best horses available with prize money comparable to the major English races — but the Australian Champion Sweepstakes was seldom an exciting race. Its fields were small and its set-weights format meant winners were too predictable. The event probably did determine the current Australasian champion but it gradually lost its appeal as an occasion for spirited betting.[25]

This was emphasised by the growth of other regular races which attracted strong fields racing for large prize money. In Sydney the Randwick Grand Handicap had become the two-mile Metropolitan Cup by 1863. The Australian Jockey Club Derby, first run in 1861, was moved to the Randwick spring race meeting in 1865 where it joined the Metropolitan and the one-mile Epsom Handicap on the list of feature events. The equivalent races at the autumn race meeting were the St Leger Stakes (for three-year-olds), the one-mile Doncaster Handicap and (from 1866) the two-mile Sydney Gold Cup. From 1862 the autumn carnival also included a one-mile feature race for two-year olds, the Champagne Stakes.[26]

With this programme the main events of Sydney racing for the next century and beyond were established. For most races the 'sweepstakes', provided by the nomination and/or acceptance fees paid by the horse owners, was supplemented by additional prize money from the race club's coffers. The Australian Jockey Club, like its counterparts in other colonies, was

Carnival and spectacle have always been an important part of racing. This photograph shows the fashions — hats in particular — at Randwick Racecourse, New South Wales, in 1937. (Hood Collection, State Library of New South Wales.)

a non-profit organisation, which reinvested its income into facilities for spectators and prize money for the races. Traditionally its main sources of income were through the annual subscriptions of its members and the entrance fees to the grandstand.[27] But, regardless of the advances made by Sydney racing, by the late 1860s the Melbourne Cup was established as Australia's most important.

Initially the cup was little more than another feature race but a number of factors led to its rapid growth to a position of prominence. The success of the New South Wales horse Archer in the first two cups and the controversial non-acceptance of that horse's nomination in 1863 ensured that the event was publicised outside Victoria.[28] The granting of a half-holiday for the event from 1865 guaranteed large crowds and the growth of prize money — from £710 in 1861 to £1014 in 1865 — made the event financially comparable to the Australian Champion Sweepstakes.[29] But the real appeal of the race lay in its unpredictability. Unlike the Champion Sweepstakes races or the Derbys and St Legers the Melbourne Cup, as a handicap race, provided equality of opportunity to its contestants. In keeping with the spirit of the gold rush era it gave the battler a chance to win the large prize. Of course the same could be said of Sydney's Metropolitan or the Sydney Cup or of the feature handicaps of Brisbane, Adelaide, Hobart or Perth, but Melbourne's geographical position also meant that its cup race was accessible to horses from all colonies.

Because of the prize money involved the Melbourne Cup attracted champion horses as well as more moderate performers, some of which won the race despite the handicap conditions. In 1866 John Tait's three-year-old black colt The Barb which had won the Australian Jockey Club Derby a few weeks earlier, won the cup before going on to establish himself as the champion of his era with a record of sixteen wins from twenty-one starts, including the Sydney Cup twice, the Metropolitan, the Queen's Plate and the Champion Stakes. His contests with Fishhook and Tim Whiffler were highlights of racing in the late 1860s.[30] In successive eras champion horses capped their careers with wins in the Melbourne Cup but, because of the handicap conditions, only the very best were able to win the race at the height of their careers. Malua's win with 9 st. 9 lb. (over sixty-one kilograms) in 1884 and Carbine's incredible victory over thirty-eight opponents in 1890, when he carried 10 st. 5 lb. (nearly sixty-six kilograms) and the hopes of tens of thousands of small punters, were unmatched until the victories of Poitrel (1920) and Phar Lap (1930). Other champions such as Brisies (1876), Chester (1877) and Grand Flaneur (1880) won the Melbourne Cup as lightly raced three-year-olds, before confirming their rating with later victories in both set-weight and handicap races.

The success of the Melbourne Cup and the establishment of firm racing calendars in both Sydney and Melbourne disguise the fact that racing in the other colonies was less successful. In Tasmania the lack of gold discoveries led to a decline in racing, as in most other fields.[31] In South Australia racing faced a series of crises in the 1860s due to the fluctuating fortunes of the dominant South Australian Jockey Club and its inability to obtain secure tenure on a suitable racecourse. By the late 1870s most of these problems had been overcome but in the mid-1880s South Australian racing virtually collapsed, as a result of parliament's attempt to outlaw betting.[32] In Queensland, rival clubs at Ipswich and Brisbane held winter race meetings but these were more comparable with country race meetings in the established colonies than with their metropolitan counterparts. A move to spring and autumn racing and the establishment of a £500 Brisbane Cup in the late 1870s and the upgrading of Eagle Farm racecourse marked the beginnings of the expansion of Brisbane racing, but for most of the nineteenth century it remained on a level similar to racing at outlying settlements like Rockhampton, Townsville and Mackay. The introduction of totalisator betting on Queensland racecourses in the 1880s created a relative boom but did not make Queensland racing comparable with New South Wales or Victoria.[33] In Perth, the colony's isolation and its small population ensured that racing did not grow beyond the level of one annual two-day summer race meeting until the 1890s.[34]

Although the standard of racing varied around the Australian colonies its trappings were set by the late nineteenth century. In the larger colonies racing had become an industry which employed significant numbers of trainers, jockeys and stable hands but its chief function remained that of a social occasion. In country districts racing provided a rare opportunity for people of all classes to get together but, as each district grew and took on a greater sense of its own importance, the mingling of the classes was lessened and barriers between them were raised. The model for class distinction on the racecourse was provided by the Australian Jockey Club (AJC) at Randwick.

In the 1890s Randwick patrons paid one shilling for admission to the flat — the areas inside the course enclosed by the running rail. Those who paid an additional two shillings were admitted to the St Leger section, on the opposite side of the finishing straight but well before the winning post. For a further ten shillings patrons were admitted to the paddock section, an area closer to the winning post, which also enabled patrons to see the horses before they raced and to watch them being saddled. The paddock included a grandstand which gave patrons a panoramic view of the course; however the prime positions in this stand were reserved for AJC members by a wooden railing, which protected them from too close contact with the general public. Members also had the official stand which gave the best view of the course. The official stand was available, for a further one guinea fee, to those members of the public who had paid for admission to the paddock, but within that stand there were further areas restricted to 'members only' and 'men only'. In order to sit in the official stand a labourer would have had to spend the equivalent of about three days' pay.[35] If money was the basis of class distinction in the Australian colonies it was most apparent on the more developed racecourses.

Gender distinction was also obvious. Apart from the 'men only' sections in the official stand women were discriminated against through their ineligibility to join the main racing clubs. Few perhaps considered this a disadvantage, as each (male) member usually received two ladies' badges which allowed the women concerned use of (most of) the members' facilities without charge. Nevertheless women were excluded from any race club decision-making. They were also excluded from the professional side of racing — as trainers, jockeys and bookmakers. Before the senior race clubs gained control of the sport a few women had brief careers as horse trainers, notably Van Diemen's Land's Moll Smith in the 1840s and Maitland's Mary Dickson in the early 1860s.[36] But, as the 'principal clubs' gained real control and established common regulations and practices in the decades following 1880, such women disappeared from the sport.

In all colonies except Western Australia the controls on racing were tightened by the clubs themselves. Senior bodies such as the Australian Jockey Club in New South Wales, the Victoria Racing Club in Victoria and their counterparts in other states assumed responsibility for the conduct of racing in their states — and insisted that all race meetings run under their rules should be registered. In part this was a response to the growth of 'amateur' race meetings and picnic events where owners rode their own horses for minimal prize money. These meetings did not pose a threat to the major clubs but the gradual emergence of another type of racing did.

From about the mid-1880s proprietary racing threatened the position of the élite race clubs. This was conducted by profit-seeking companies (or individuals) rather than clubs. They offered smaller prizes for the winners but more entertainment to the paying public — who had access to the better sections of the racecourse for much less cost than at Randwick or Flemington. The proprietary companies usually provided more races on a programme and shorter races on a smaller course, where patrons were closer to the action. They were catering more for the working-class gambler and less for the would-be gentry of the race clubs.[37] Proprietary clubs at Canterbury in Sydney and Epsom and Sandown Park in Melbourne challenged the authority of the non-profit clubs, and their early success prompted many imitators. For about fifty years the rival groups competed for both authority and the gamblers' money. In Queensland the licensing of the totalisator on race-club courses gave them an advantage. In New South Wales a gradual imposition of control by the legislature over the maximum number of race days allowed worked against the proprietary companies. However, spurred on by potential profits, the proprietary companies usually found ways to subvert legislative intentions. One successful move was to provide pony-racing — races for horses considered too small to be successful on the thoroughbred racecourses. In part this responded to the race clubs' decision to disqualify from their courses any horses which had competed on proprietary tracks. Another result of this conflict — and of the apparent Australian willingness to attend any kind of race meetings in large numbers — was trotting.[38]

Trotting had never disappeared completely. Match races were held occasionally even at Flemington and Randwick racecourses in the 1860s and 1870s and by the late 1860s American-bred stallions were being imported to Victoria, where trotting was strongest. In that colony occasional race programmes were developed for trotters. This was taken a step further with the establishment of Elsternwick Park Trotting Club in Melbourne and its first race meeting on 1 April 1882. In the same year the United States-bred Childe Harold arrived in New South Wales to take up stud duties. Over the next twenty years his sons and daughters contributed to a relative boom in the sport.[39]

The Sydney Driving Park Club which began trotting race meetings at Moore Park in Sydney in 1885 was quickly joined by other proprietary clubs, many of which failed due to problems over track leases, bad management and wavering support from the gambling fraternity.[40] Although trotting horses were cheaper to buy and train than their thoroughbred cousins, thereby making them more available to tradesmen and others with restricted funds, the timing of the sport's development, on the eve of the 1890s Depression and the competition for the gambling dollar from the race clubs, the pony club and (at least in some colonies) sweepstakes and totalisators, meant that most trotting clubs found it difficult to survive. Gradually

however, as happened with the thoroughbred race clubs, senior clubs emerged to control the sport — providing stability and more capable management. In Sydney this role was assumed by the non-proprietary New South Wales Trotting Club from 1902 and in Melbourne the Victorian Trotting Association dominated the sport from 1910.[41]

In the early decades of the twentieth century trotting clubs proliferated, as did the conduct of trotting races at country pastoral and agricultural shows. In general the sport developed more rapidly and gained greater public support in rural areas and in the smaller states. Races involved a mixture of saddle horses and those in harness, often in the same race. Some horses trotted better when pulling a cart, but until the development of pneumatic tyres and lightweight sulkies after the turn of the century, many found the carriage a handicap. For the followers of the sport the small tracks added to the entertainment spectacle but for champion horses, who were handicapped by having to travel further than their rivals, the tightness of the often circular courses and the narrowness of the racing track sometimes imposed an impossible task.[42]

Nevertheless the growth of trotting in the early twentieth

American-bred trotting stallions were imported into Australia in the late 1860s. These two gave an exhibition at Randwick in October 1881. (*Illustrated Sydney News*, 29 October 1881, Mitchell Library, State Library of New South Wales.)

century gave Australian racing supporters even more opportunity to attend race meetings. In the main cities the rivalry between proprietary and non-proprietary thoroughbred race clubs, pony clubs and trotting clubs gave racing supporters a great deal of choice. Many die-hard supporters attended as many race meetings as possible, but the 'working classes' tended to find the excitement and accessibility of trotting and pony-racing more attractive than the staid thoroughbred galloping races, emphasising the distinction between the sport of kings and the working-man's sport.

Despite the role of the labour movement in Australian politics, from the 1890s the influence of the senior race clubs over the legislation gradually worked against the proprietary clubs, both galloping and trotting. Restrictions on the number of race days had less effect on thoroughbred race clubs than on those for the less fashionably bred horses, especially in the cities. Allegations of corruption, excess profit-taking and even rigged races lessened support for proprietary pony and trotting clubs, but it was the Second World War which finally sealed their fate.[43] Increased restrictions on racing during the war, the occupation of courses by the armed forces and the need for land for post-war housing provided the excuse for state governments to reform racing and end the dispute between proprietary and non-proprietary race clubs by removing the former. Some of their larger courses, such as Rosehill and Canterbury in Sydney and Sandown Park and Moonee Valley in Melbourne were either transferred to voluntarily become non-profit clubs, but most disappeared in the post-war building boom.[44]

Trotting survived this process but remained a minor sport. Its main problem, at least in the larger cities, was that it had either to compete with the race clubs on Saturday afternoons or race during the week, when most of the sport's supporters were at work. In Perth from 1914, and Adelaide from 1920, this problem had been lessened by the introduction of night racing under lights. Earlier experiments with night racing had proved unsuccessful but its introduction in Perth made the Western Australian city the trotting capital of Australia and the envy of trotting administrators in other states. When Perth's success was repeated in Adelaide (apart from a period when betting on night racing was prohibited) the trotting fraternity in other state capitals began to lobby their legislatures for the introduction of night trotting.[45]

In New South Wales the sport progressed in the 1920s but its

development remained slow in the face of competition between the galloping and pony-racing clubs. In Victoria trotting
was in a parlous state, under the administration of the Victorian Trotting and Racing Association, controlled by the sporting entrepreneur John Wren. Despite their efforts, the lobbyists
for night trotting found first the economic depression of the
1930s and later the Second World War used as excuses for
postponing the desired development.[46] They also had to compete against the new sport of greyhound-racing (with the
mechanical hare) which, from the early 1930s, made significant inroads into their supporters' ranks with its claims that the
greyhound was the true working-man's thoroughbred.[47] Victorian trotting enthusiasts had to wait until 1947 to witness night
trotting under lights while New South Wales waited a further
two years.[48]

As predicted by its supporters, night trotting was the saviour
of the sport, but almost as important was the closure of the pony
tracks after the war. In each metropolitan capital the weekend
was gradually divided between the galloping race clubs, which
raced on Saturday afternoons, and the trotters, which raced on
either Friday or Saturday nights.[49] In the post-war era, with night
racing as the city norm, the sport also underwent other changes.
'Trotting' became 'harness racing' in acknowledgement of the
fact that while all the horses raced in harness, only a minority
'trotted'. Most adopted the pacing gait. The name change was
also accompanied by a change of image, as the main racecourses
improved their facilities and promoted themselves as exciting
venues for an evening out, with high-class restaurants offering
extensive views of the course. Harness racing created its own
version of the Melbourne Cup, the Inter-Dominion Championship — an annual series of races which alternated between the
main cities of Australia and New Zealand. This was first run in
Perth in 1936.[50]

As many racing administrators have discovered however, no
promotion attracts supporters so much as champion horses.
Consistent winners attract punters and Australian harness racing has had its share of champions. Globe Derby, his son Walla
Walla and grandsons Uncle Joe and Ribands provided a con-
tinuous bloodline of champions from the World-War-One era
to the 1950s. Caduceus, Cardigan Bay and, more recently,
Halwes, Pure Steel and Paleface Adios were guaranteed to attract crowds to the harness-racing courses. In the 1960s television took these later champions into the nation's lounge rooms,

adding a further dimension to the sport, especially when the champions of the day met in the annual speed event, the Miracle Mile — but harness racing still remained the poor cousin of thoroughbred racing.

The deeds of the harness-racing champions were more than matched in the post-war era by gallopers such as Bernborough, Tulloch, Todman, Galilee, Gunsynd, Kingston Town, Baguette, Manikato and many others. The relationship between the two codes became institutionalised from the 1960s through the legalisation of off-course Totalisator Agency Board (TAB) betting shops. A proportion of TAB profits is returned to the racing industry, but the larger share is received by thoroughbred racing at the expense of harness racing.[51]

The TAB greatly stimulated racing in the 1970s and 1980s with clubs using their share of TAB profits to improve facilities and increase prize money — to the point where other forms of income such as gate attendance money, nomination fees and membership subscriptions now provide an almost insignificant proportion of the clubs' incomes. This is particularly so of those clubs whose meetings are broadcast by Sky Channel satellite pay-television into TAB betting shops, hotels, clubs and elsewhere, but the growth of off-course betting in this way has not been applauded universally.

In the 1990s the main racecourses are often lonely places, with expensive facilities used by ever-decreasing crowds. Most racing followers now choose to watch the events on television away from the track.[52] On country racecourses the impact is more dramatic. Those clubs unable to attract Sky Channel and TAB coverage of their events cannot offer competitive prize money — others do so at a price. In order to attract the TAB and Sky Channel, country race clubs have progressively moved their meetings from Saturdays to either Mondays or Fridays, when the metropolitan and main provincial race clubs are not operating. In doing so they attract TAB turnover, which provides the income to offer competitive prize money, but, except perhaps for local 'Cup' days, they have sacrificed the interests of their local communities as, like their city counterparts, most country racing supporters are required to work during the week.

The faces of both galloping and harness racing have changed

in the 1980s and 1990s. Gender distinctions have almost disappeared, with women members, administrators, jockeys, drivers and trainers appearing and gradually increasing their (still comparatively low) numbers. Class distinctions are further blurred with wealth remaining the sole real discriminator of privilege on the racecourse, but racing has begun to lose most of its exotic flavour. The horses continue to do their noble deeds with style and grace but colourful bookmakers are gradually being replaced by sophisticated computers and the excitement generated by large crowds of cheering spectators is being replaced by the eerieness of echoes in the almost-empty grandstands. Racing is no longer a sport of the gentry supported by the working man, providing an opportunity for communities to join together in a day of carnival festivity. In the 1990s it is a major national industry which risks losing sight of its origins in its search for ever-increasing prize money. The beneficiaries are the off-course punters. The losers are the country racing communities and the few remaining romantic followers of the sport who attend race meetings looking for something more than comfortable facilities and the opportunity to bet on their fancies.

Modern racing, with the sponsor's advertising in full view, at Canterbury, New South Wales. Horses in Race 7 on 11 October 1989 leap from the movable barrier stalls. (Lock/Fairfax Picture Library.)

7   Lawn Bowls

Louella McCarthy

THE AUSTRALIAN bowling green has many faces. It is the place where serious sportspeople participate in a high-profile sport and prize money. It is also where many thousands more enjoy their leisure and maintain their health. In Australia the bowling club is a place of social interaction and a night out for hundreds of thousands of people: its place in many rural communities, in particular, is pivotal. Bowls has had a huge impact on Australian culture, and in return, Australians have initiated changes in the way the game is played internationally.

'The bowling green' is a brief but evocative phrase, with myriad connotations throughout its life in Australia. Its nineteenth-century advocates often extolled the bowling green as a place of serenity and goodwill — a 'peaceful Eden' according to one commentator in 1900.[1] If it was also a site for competition, the rivalry was meant to be good-natured and encourage fellowship among the players. This tranquil ideal's various characteristics reflect important aspects of colonial Australia, not least because they represent particular views of nineteenth-century social life. The mid twentieth-century bowling green retained some of these connotations, albeit in a wider social context.

The bowling green in this country has flourished in its role as a quintessentially Australian institution — the club — though one where playing bowls was only one of several distractions on offer. While the club has maintained a pre-eminent place on the green, bowlers themselves have diversified. In large part, lawn bowls has changed from a pastime of the leisured classes to an organised, high-profile, mass-participation sport for both women and men. The competitive element is paramount for many Australian bowlers, who gather regularly to decide club, state and national titles. Lawn bowls has provided Australia with a number of international champions, while recent years have witnessed the emergence of professionalism, television coverage and corporate sponsorship. Thus the bowling green provides an ideal means to illustrate the changing role of sport and leisure in Australian society over the past two centuries. Questions of class, respectability, gender relations, access to public power, and the place of sport in society, are central to the history of lawn bowls in Australia.

Drawing on long-standing practice in England, the earliest recorded bowling greens in Australia were adjuncts to hotels and country estates. For the nineteenth-century British upper classes with land and labour at their disposal, the private bowling green (like the tennis court) provided both a genteel pastime and a conspicuous indicator of wealth.

Conversely, the popular form of British bowls in this period flourished around inns and taverns. As a result the game acquired connotations of seediness, a hangover from its association with the 'dissolute' habits of lower-class players who often used the greens for drinking, gambling, and other unruly activities such as cockfighting, bare-knuckle pugilism, pigeon-shooting, and dog-racing. Although evidence is scarce, these two faces of British bowls, one for the gentry and one for the masses, were both transported to Australia — but it was the gentrified form which first came to prominence in this country.[2]

There were two further dimensions to this British inheritance, however. Scottish bowls — the game most familiar to contemporary Australian bowlers — was played on well-defined rinks with an inherent orderliness, in both greens and the rules of play. The English game, by contrast, exhibited frowned-upon, even anarchic tendencies.[3] Until the late nineteenth century, the English game was played in any and all directions on the paddock, with bowls colliding and interfering with other games being played at the same time.[4] The roughness of the grounds used for English bowls provided much of the unpredictability commonly associated with the biased bowl.

While available records are scanty, it seems the first games of bowls in Australia were, like their English counterparts, played on private land or on hotel greens by the 1840s.[5] But important differences emerged in the colonial setting where Australians chose to highlight the game's upper-class forebears rather than its less respectable side.[6] It was to upper-class men that hoteliers directed their notices advertising new greens. By offering private membership at one pound per annum social selectiveness could be ensured, and the 'rough-and-tumble' element relied on by English pubs was relegated to playing bowls at times outside those reserved for members. A direct link may be seen between the Tasmanian journalist in the 1840s who was glad to see this 'manly and gentlemanly exercise introduced into our adopted country'[7] and the Petersham (New South Wales) hotelier who appealed to 'his numerous patrons, Friends and the Sporting Gentlemen of Sydney and its environs that 'Thomas Shaw, of the Woolpack Inn, Parramatta Road, has much pleasure in announcing. . . that he has just completed at great expense a full-sized, beautifully-turfed bowling green. . . [He] confidently looks forward to being honored by a large meeting of gentlemen, especially amateurs in the true old English game.'[8]

Similarly, at the Bowling Green Hotel, Sandy Bay (Tasmania) 'the officers of the 7th Regiment. . . together with the leading civilians of Hobart, were the principal patrons of the green'.[9] Towards the fringes of colonial towns' business and residential areas, land was available for bowling greens which could be patronised by men with carriages or horses. Thus bowls in Australia was transfigured into a game for gentlemen and, despite its early association with hotels, its social role was crystallised.

The period between 1860 and 1880 saw dramatic growth in Australian lawn bowls, as well as the first divergence from hotel — and privately-owned greens. Within two years, three clubs devoted primarily to bowling had opened their doors to members in Victoria — the Melbourne Club, Windsor (1864), the St Kilda Club, and the Fitzroy Club (both 1865).[10] By the mid-1870s John Young — a prominent architect, commissioner for several international exhibitions (including Sydney's in 1879), and later Lord Mayor of Sydney[11] — had bought and designed the suburb of Annandale, and laid out a green at his home, Kentville. The Annandale Bowling Club was one of five in Sydney at the time.[12] Notwithstanding the simultaneous existence throughout this period and into the 1880s of the three types of bowling green — private houses, hotels and clubs — the movement toward membership requirements was dominant.

Why did the club-based form of bowls proliferate in Australia? The emphasis by its proponents on the bowling green's value for companionship and restful recreation was certainly one important element. The class-based nature of early lawn bowls in Australia provides another clue. The first club in South Australia, Adelaide, was reportedly formed in 1897 by a group of 'gentlemen'.[13] For the most part, however, these men did not belong to the rural élite, or enjoy a leisured life derived primarily from rents, investments or inheritance. Rather, they envisaged the bowling green's 'peaceful Eden' as a respite after the day's toil.[14] The stalwarts of many prominent lawn bowls clubs in this period belonged to a distinctly urban section of the colonial upper classes, and often held positions in government, commerce and administration. In the 1870s, for instance, the short-lived Sydney Club exhibited a very select membership, including J. Barnet (Colonial Architect), E. Fosbery (Inspector-General of Police), Robert Hunt (Deputy-Master of the Royal Mint), Dr A. Leibius (Master of the Royal Mint), Professor A. Liversidge, Charles Moore (Director of the Botanic Gardens) and Christopher Rolleston (Auditor-General).[15] Many bowls clubs established in the last decades of the nineteenth century strove to maintain their social exclusiveness: besides the fees required, a black-balling rule for club membership could be invoked to ensure that only acceptable people would be admitted.[16]

Using their influence with (and even their own positions in) local government and colonial administration, leading nineteenth-century lawn bowlers sought to establish their clubs on a sound basis. The initial step involved finding suitable premises for the bowling greens. Frequently it was public land, previously parkland, which was resumed for enclosure as a private bowling club. The greens of the City Club in New South Wales were formed by alienating public land when 'a piece of ground for the purposes was secured from the Trustees of Hyde, Cook and Phillip parks, and, provided certain conditions were carried out, no rent was to be charged'.[17] Redfern, a salubrious Sydney suburb at the time, also had local government to thank for securing land for the bowling club on part of Redfern Park in 1890. Indeed, the impetus for this club seems to have stemmed from the council, or at least the mayor: the inaugural meeting of the club was held in the mayor's rooms where the offer for the land was made which the club had merely to affirm. The mayor subsequently became the inaugural president.[18] Similar trends were apparent in other colonies and states in the decades around 1900. In South Australia, at least a dozen early clubs owed their original premises to grants of public land. The Adelaide Club went so far as to boast that 'the Government granted the land on Victoria Drive. . . Bordered by the River Torrens on the north, and Palm Terraces on the south, [the greens] form one of the beauty spots of Adelaide'.[19] Thus even though their leading members could well afford to buy land, clubs tended to be built on publicly-owned parks.

It is difficult to gauge overall how the public reacted to this alienation of land, but the outcry which resulted from the approval to enclose a bowling club in a section of Victoria Park, Sydney may provide some indication. When plans for the club were mooted in 1891, a deputation called upon the Minister for Lands, whose approval was needed to alienate the land. The deputation submitted that the site 'was different to many other parks in the colony. . . It was not a municipal park. . . under the control of the [local] rate-payers and property-owners. [Rather] Victoria Park was. . . granted for the people and the children of the people who would never inherit any other land'. [20]

Despite these claims and protests, that '[i]f these gentlemen must have bowling greens let them purchase them as they are well able to do', the club was established by Act of Parliament in 1892. The minister's response may provide a clue to the privileges which bowling clubs seemed to enjoy in seeking access to public land. In 1884 Victoria Park had been brought under the provisions of the Public Parks Act, and was therefore dedicated 'for the public recreation, health and enjoyment of the inhabitants of the city of Sydney'. According to the minister's decision, enclosure of the bowling green would help in 'regulating the use and enjoyment of such land'.[21]

The nineteenth-century parks movement was initiated in part through an idealisation of Nature — trees, open air and the other benefits thought to derive from rural living. But this view was tempered by ideas about how Nature was constituted. Formal gardens were thought to be more beneficial than native plants, and 'rational recreation' would offer advantages over unplanned and unsupervised play: 'manly, organised games. . .

led naturally to self-improvement'.[22] A cynical view might place self-interest at the fore in explaining why private bowling greens were established on public land. But constant reiteration of the 'improvements' which would result from allowing bowling clubs to beautify the land they were granted seems to have provided an overriding justification for the grants.[23] Parks were perceived as offering not merely Nature's 'pleasing [and] even instructive environment', but more importantly they were portrayed as venues for 'proper sports and the means of gentle, ordered exercise'. As such, the bowling green acquired and refined the park's attributes as 'a perpetual source of good'.[24]

Initially, at least, not all Australians could enjoy these benefits. Besides the fees and membership rules promulgated by nineteenth-century bowling clubs, there were financial considerations. Starting a club required money to form the greens, build the pavilion and stock the other requisites of club life. The Waverley Club (New South Wales) provides an example of how clubhouses and greens were financed: amid the 1890s Depression, a company was formed with capital of £5000 in one-pound shares — 2248 were applied for and taken up by a membership of thirty-four, an average individual outlay of over sixty pounds.[25] Although bowlers often took pains to stress the game's camaraderie and the inherent egalitarianism of the green, in reality the early clubs were very exclusive. The salubrious sites of these nineteenth-century clubs provide one indication of the clientele.[26] Knowledge that games were played on weekdays — and that inter-colonial matches took the players away for several weeks — provides another clue about who was able to take advantage of the game.

Evocations of social exclusiveness were reinforced by the elaborate architecture of many early clubhouses and pavilions, although not everyone (even dedicated lawn bowlers) approved. James Manson, author of a monograph on bowls in Britain and the Empire, commented on the Australian scene in 1912:

> Against one serious danger the Colonials must be warned. In many places the game is pursued amidst luxurious surroundings. . . Some clubs have yielded to the temptation to build commodious and well-appointed clubhouses at an outlay of £2000 or £3000 and upwards. Lavish expenditures upon 'swagger' premises, however desirable, are not necessary. . . Every club that approves a policy which is often both wasteful and demoralising is unconsciously jeopardising the most cherished social attribute of Bowls.[27]

117

For prominent Australian bowls clubs, however, there were more pressing priorities in this period. Having established their clubs, leading lawn bowlers turned to organising and standardising the game in this country. By 1870 Victorian clubs had adopted the Scottish form and rules for play. It has been suggested that the rules drawn up by John Campbell for the Melbourne Club helped the Scottish game to conquer Australia.[28] The regularity of the Scottish rules would have appealed to those men of the urban élite who founded the colonies' early clubs. Moreover, Australian bowlers' passion for competitive matches, both inter-colonial and subsequently international, provided an impetus for the formation of the various governing bodies which came to dominate the game.

John Young's renown in bowling circles is based on his proposal for Victorian bowlers to visit his green in 1880 for the first inter-colonial bowling match. Although seemingly embraced by both sides, some umbrage was taken by one Sydney club at Young's impertinence in assuming the representative nature of his Annandale team. A public meeting was called and, in May 1880, the New South Wales Bowls Association was formed under Young's presidency. The Association's charter was to organise subsequent inter-colonial matches, and to formulate rules for the game which would be adopted by affiliated clubs. The Victorian Bowls Association was formed two months later. These associations virtually signalled the demise of all but club-based bowling greens.

The proposed roles for clubs and their overarching associations did not go unchallenged, of course. Even as it was being formulated, the image of the bowling green as a 'peaceful Eden' did not quite match the reality. A club such as Redfern in New South Wales felt obliged to include in its rules an injunction that 'no political or religious subjects or questions shall be discussed on the grounds'.[29] Internal wrangles beset the sport in Australia well into the twentieth century, while not all of the game's active participants measured up to the ideals of its nineteenth-century male organisers.

The first crack in this otherwise solid wall of masculine respectability received little publicity and even less approval. Although women may have a long history of bowls participation, the evidence is patchy. The delay between the first men's clubs in Victoria and their female counterparts was about three decades, but women's clubs appeared around the same time as men's in Western Australia and South Australia.[30] Victorian women took the lead in forming the first ladies' bowling association in 1907.[31]

The occasion of the first women's inter-colonial match between New South Wales and Victoria in 1900 provides a glimpse of male reactions. One unsympathetic journalist took the opportunity to comment.

> [F]resh interest has been lent to the matches from the fact that for the first time ladies have taken part. . . The innovation seems to have been accepted in a kindly spirit by the male bowlers, and if these most interested ones are satisfied all may be well. Nevertheless, the change is. . . another instance of women encroaching upon men's sacred preserves. . . The bowling green was wont to be. . . a spot free from the perturbations of feminine allurements. Now this peaceful Eden has been invaded, and other changes may lie ahead.[32]

Notwithstanding women's relatively early participation in the game, they were more likely, from constraints and desires of many types, to gain affiliation with established men's bowling clubs (sometimes with restrictions on available playing time and access to decision-making) than to begin their separate clubs. This tendency, as will be seen, has had ramifications on membership numbers and management practices in the latter half of the twentieth century.[33] The consequences of limited membership for women were apparent at the time. As bowls historian Gordon Sargeant remarked about the earliest New South Wales women's club with an uninterrupted history: 'Hamilton women were wise in their generation in that [in 1914] they secured a green distinct from their menfolk, which seems better than having a precarious arrangement for limited use of a men's green'.[34]

Clearly, women and men, even of the same social class, had different access to leisure facilities, and especially to the capital required for the construction of clubhouses and greens. Women's sport in the late nineteenth, and at least the first half of the twentieth century, had a different social role to that of men's. Men's sport was well grounded in the positive attributes of manliness and individuality, while women's sport, where it existed, was believed to have definite biological and demographic implications because of their roles as potential wives and mothers.[35]

In these respects, women bowlers may have been fortunate — the game did not obviously detract from feminine allure, either in the clothes necessary for play, or in the sport's degree of physical exertion. Like tennis and golf, bowls should have been quintessentially a women's game — at least by nineteenth-century standards. But bowls had an ethos from which it was difficult to dissociate: bowls was a man's game and clubs were a man's province, particularly when they cost so much to establish. The Waverley Club in New South Wales, which opened in 1894 as a socially-exclusive bowls and recreation club, became gender exclusive as well in 1899 by restricting membership to men.[36] Thus in some cases women had no choice: if they wanted to play bowls they needed their own greens, clubs and associations. Significantly the peak bodies for men's and women's bowls in Australia remain separate organisations.

Similar currents operated in regard to the game's mass appeal. Although the idea did not bear fruit in New South Wales until the 1930s, John Young had advocated the Scottish model of municipal greens.[37] With a few supporters, he envisaged the establishment of public bowling greens where membership was not a prerequisite for play. Rather, merely by paying the required sum (which varied in Scotland and England, but was commonly a shilling), the green and bowls were available to all. Such public greens, Young believed, would help to break down the social and gender exclusiveness of Australian bowls. It would expand the sport's appeal, without affecting its club-based organisational structure. In line with contemporary preoccupations, Young's arguments were predicated on bowling greens removing the working class from the streets and taverns. Instead, working people would be exposed to the landscaped orderliness of the bowling green, thereby acquiring some of the qualities believed to be inherent in bowls: good fellowship, playing the game rather than winning and the love of good health and clean living.

Yet it was not to be local and state governments which led the way in providing working-class greens, nor was the 'general good' a dominant motivation. Rather, both private industry and public enterprise, with increased productivity in mind, began providing works greens on their lands. The Locomotive Bowling Club, for instance, was established in 1909 at the South Australian Railway Workshops under the patronage of the railway commissioner.[38] This was to be merely the first of the many clubs formed as adjuncts to commercial and industrial premises.[39] Inevitably the influx of numerous working-

class bowlers led to tensions within bowling circles and forced the sport's controlling bodies to make important decisions.

After the formation of the state associations[40] and drawing on their executives as representatives, the Australian Bowls Council (ABC) was formed in November 1911 as a controlling and standardising body for the men's sport nationwide.[41] Despite the prevalence of the Scottish game, national uniformity had not immediately appeared: consequently greens (including the size of the rinks and the length of play), bowls' size and bias, and other rules of play were peculiar to each state. The ABC's formal charter was to end these discrepancies, but a side issue was to cope with the growing number of bowlers from diverse social backgrounds.

The advent of the 'composite bowl' in Australia no doubt assisted in widening bowls' sphere of interest by decreasing the cost of bowls, perhaps by as much as half.[42] William Hensell, creator of the composite bowl, also had an unenviable task as technical adviser on bowls testing in Victoria and South Australia.[43] When a ruling by the ABC required all bowls to comply with 'the formula of sizes and weights by February 1929',[44]

The transition from lignum vitae (wood) to composite (plastic) bowls was a breakthrough for an Australian company, Hensell & Co., and increased the mass appeal of bowling. This 'scientific' influence was to be reflected throughout the game in the new precision demanded from the carefully measured rinks and ditches and the need to test accurately the bias of the bowls. The bias testing table at the Henselite factory in Melbourne is shown here. In 1988 the company rolled its three millionth bowl. (Henselite Company.)

121

Hensell found himself in the firing line. 'I believe,' argued New South Wales parliamentarian Joseph Carruthers, 'that the present system of testing bowls is unsatisfactory. It is on a wrong basis, when the testers have an interest as makers of bowls and as wood turners. The tester should have no possible interest in any way conflicting with the one task of... testing.'[45]

This was not the first salvo fired in the war of words, nor was it the only topic for disagreement. The New South Wales Bowls Association was unhappy with the ABC because of their decision not to accept the New South Wales 'master bowl' as the national standard.[46] The Victorians were unhappy because the new master bowl 'would affect 5000 bowls passed by the Victorian tester'.[47] Others were simply infuriated because 'conditions under which the game must be played are being over-legislated, and that this latest proposal. . . is a source of irritation'.[48]

This standardisation did not stop at the rink however, and rulings about the clothes worn at the club and on the green created perhaps the most publicised issue for twentieth-century bowls — the uniform. Beginning with the most obvious and easily accepted proposal that slippers or soft shoes should be worn during play to protect the green, mounting legislation concerning correct dress has been accepted with varying degrees of compliance. As one bowls historian commented: 'The [nineteenth-century male] Australian bowler wore a top-hat, a swallow-tail or frock coat and stiff creased shirt, and trousers much more tightly fitted than any seen today'.[49] Although no uniform was prescribed, it is interesting that a 'type' could be seen on the greens. But attending the social diversification of Australian lawn bowls after 1900, less 'desirable' kinds of bowlers came to prominence. Complaints to the various associations about 'slovenly bowlers,' and the need to take 'drastic steps to cope with this evil',[50] led to a stream of injunctions.[51] But 'slovenly bowlers' remained. One critic in 1936 provides a clue about the perceived threat, and the persistence of socially exclusive attitudes:

> Bowlers as a class have acquired a reputation as being men of substance, and sufficiently endowed with worldly benefits to be able to spend a few shillings on their appearance. It must be admitted, however, that the dress of some players does not confirm this reputation. The oldest of clothes, the most dilapidated of hats, are good enough for bowls, seems to be the opinion of some players . . . [Yet this] game has been raised from the level of being an adjunct to a public house to a sport comparable with any national game and played by some of the state's leading citizens.[52]

Concern over proper dress highlights a period of confusion about the meaning of the bowling green for its admirers. The obvious desire to maintain gentility and respectability among a rapidly changing constituency meant that rules concerning dress became more rigorous over the next few decades. A woman bowler in 1933, wearing 'a dress with a V-cut of about six inches down the back', incurred the displeasure of the Victorian Ladies' Bowls Association. The association's secretary justified her rigid interpretation of the rules: 'If we will not allow short sleeves, even to the elbow, it is not likely that we will allow a low-backed dress'.[53] This comment suggests that seemliness, even during an Australian summer, loomed larger in the 1930s than the comfort players required to perform well.

The costs involved in acquiring the regulation uniform also operated to regularise the greens and to disadvantage the less wealthy. One Sydney clothier operating in the late 1920s offered to provide bowlers with the regulation uniform at prices ranging from three pounds ten shillings to seven pounds.[54] Not an insurmountable cost, but possibly a disincentive to joining a club.

A more pronounced disincentive arose from scheduling competition matches on weekdays. The inequity of this practice was not lost on a number of bowlers, and led to one in the 1930s calling council to account:

> Permit me space to give vent to a very genuine grievance, affecting at a very conservative estimate, at least seventy-five per cent of the bowlers in the metropolitan area. The grievance is the decision to play championship events on weekdays. . . If this is Council's idea of a broad outlook in the interests of the game, then I suggest it is time for a remodelling of Council. . . The decision. . . can only have one idea in view, and that is to force us out of the game.[55]

A related issue concerned bowls' place in the wider world of sports: should the bowling green maintain its privileged place as a 'peaceful Eden', or should the sport foster its competitive potential? From at least the 1920s a number of bowlers sought to enhance the game's acceptance as a serious sport. Uniforms, standard rules of play and equivalent greens were visible symbols of the growing desire among many Australian bowlers for recognition of their sporting skills and achievements.

Nowhere were these competing ideals more obvious than in the question of reimbursing players' travelling expenses. The first bowling team to travel was the Victorians which visited New South Wales in 1880. Of more financial consequence was the first Australian team visit to Britain in 1901. These matches, instigated by John Young (New South Wales) and Charles Wood (Victoria), meant a considerable demand on players' time and money. The Australian organisers of this inaugural international competition offered £500 as a sweetener to help smooth the travellers' path.[56] Interestingly, this financial precedent was overlooked in most subsequent debates about travelling expenses.

Australian bowlers were divided about the role of professionals on the bowling green, a question much discussed in other sports at the time. Whereas golf — a game with much the same social appeal in the early decades of the twentieth century — could provide a club 'pro' to advise members, the only professional allowed anywhere near the bowling green was the greenkeeper. Beginning in the 1920s, debates became more heated by the 1930s. Speaking at a function organised by the Victorian Bowls Association, the New South Wales patron summed up the concerns of those opposed to introducing expenses, and drew explicit parallels between lawn bowls and bodyline cricket:

> There has recently been raised the question of payment of expenses to members of interstate bowls teams... [Mr Jones] declared emphatically that any encroachment on the amateur status would not be in the best interests of the game and would be a mistake. He would sooner go away with a team of moderate players who paid their own expenses than with the finest team of experts who did not. They had seen that the inroads of professionalism into cricket had lowered the status of the game, and that reached something of a climax with the visit of the last English team when all the high traditions of the past were broken.[57]

Bolstering these arguments based on tradition and amateurism, there were claims about bowls as a spectator sport. 'There is no gate money in bowls,' claimed 'Pennant' in 1937. 'The bowler . . . has no monetary value. It is one of those things which has not been commercialised in this era of capitalisation.'[58] Only when national pride was at stake on the greens of the Commonwealth Games were the sport's controlling bodies eventually convinced that travel expenses would not undermine their ideal of lawn bowls.

Despite Australian innovations in setting up associations and standardising the rules of play, British influences remained strong among bowlers through much of the twentieth century. It may be significant that state bowls associations in Australia acquired the prefix 'Royal'. A visit to Britain by John Young

and Charles Wood to prepare for the 1901 international match resulted in the establishment of the Imperial (later English) Bowling Association. Subsequently, Australian bowlers maintained links with the Empire: reciprocal competition with New Zealand, South Africa and Canada as well as Britain dominated their international circuit. An important function of bowling clubs is suggested by the oft-mentioned idealisation of the game's fraternal spirit.[59] Members of Australian bowling clubs could be assured a welcome at any other bowling club in the world.[60] As competitors at home and abroad, Australian bowlers were plainly conscious both of their self-adopted role as advocates and ambassadors for their country, and of their country's place in the imperial order.

Whether guests or hosts, Australian bowlers were involved in more than simply the game, which added weight to the arguments for maintaining ideal standards of 'lilywhite amateurism'.[61] The honorary treasurer and assistant manager of the Australian team visiting Britain in 1922 'made no secret of the fact that they had come to boost Australia'.[62] The team was there as representative of Australian business and government interests. A recurrent theme in the speeches delivered at public occasions during the team's visit extolled British emigration to the 'golden land of Australia'. The touring party's president reportedly announced: '[Australia] wanted good men from this country; men with capital if they chose to come, and men without capital if they were willing to work.'[63] Within Australia, interstate tours were useful for 'placing the State's

Australian bowlers maintained links with the Empire. Test matches against Britain began in 1901. British bowlers playing in the 1925 tour of Australia are shown here. (Mitchell Library, State Library of New South Wales.)

125

possibilities more prominently among businessmen and citizens of this great Commonwealth'.[64] So, even if touring teams tended to comprise 'only those retired from business or in affluent circumstances',[65] it was in their own interests — and the future prosperity of Australia — to maintain 'standards'.

Playing the game had only ever been one aspect of Australian lawn bowls, of course. From their nineteenth-century origins, bowls clubs were diverse organisations which fulfilled important social functions. A number of early bowls clubs offered several sporting activites, like the Waverley Club in New South Wales where bowls was envisaged for 'the elders . . . the younger set could have their Tennis in daylight, and in the evenings a place [was available] where indoor games of cards and billiards could be enjoyed, and other social amenities'.[66]

The role of the bowling green in bringing together men of stature in business and administration was also plain. One of the first inter-club competitions initiated by Waverley provides a glimpse of these early bowlers' preoccupations. Annual matches against the Combined Banks and Insurance Bowlers started in 1895 and rapidly came to be seen as 'one of the highlights of the Club's social matches'. 'The idea, in its genesis, was to foster good fellowship with our Bank and Insurance friends, and the influence of the contact each year is felt throughout business circles of the City and Country.'[67]

In addition to business networks, the bowls club also provided a social centre. The early conjunction of bowls with hotels, and club members' desire for social interaction with people of the same social standing, led to the identification of bowling clubs with alcohol consumption.[68] Australia may have adopted the Scottish model of the bowling green itself, but it seems to have been the social dimensions of the English game which influenced clubhouse activities.

Despite early twentieth century attempts to keep the growth of Australian bowls within prescribed social and gender-specific limits, the bowling green continued to attract devotees. Between the 1920s and 1940s, the expansion of lawn-bowls clubs was most evident in country towns. In New South Wales there were thirty-five metropolitan men's clubs in 1926 and sixty-one in 1946; the number of country clubs increased from fifty to 149 during the same period.[69] Although the 1930s Depression tended to inhibit working-class participation, government-funded work schemes helped to increase rapidly the actual number of greens, most of which appeared on 'municipal parks and recreation grounds'.[70] Figures provided by the New South Wales men's association in 1936 show that of 139 affiliated clubs, 45.3 per cent were on municipal or shire land, 35.3 per cent were on club-owned property and the remainder were established on company-owned, leased or private land.[71]

Clearly, the nineteenth-century precedents by which private bowls clubs were established on public land still proved a powerful influence, even in this period of 'paternal' government concern to promote leisure facilities for working people. Nonetheless, the bowling green's somewhat muted reputation for egalitarianism took on new and more challenging connotations. Early advocates may have portrayed bowls as both 'manly and gentlemanly', but now claims were being made for the sport's classlessness. Bowls, as one participant urged in 1937, 'is no longer regarded as an old or a rich man's game. It is frequently spoken of as the most democratic game, for it knows no social distinction, and Jack is as good as his master — and probably a bit better — on the green'.[72]

One of many established during the 1940s, the Ardlethan Bowling Club in south-west New South Wales was formed in circumstances quite different from its nineteenth-century counterparts, and illustrates the changing face of the Australian bowling green. The Ardlethan Club's committee was dominated by local commercial interests: among about thirty members, fifteen could be described as small businessmen; of the rest three farmers, a dentist, two shop-assistants, one mine-foreman and a police sergeant can be identified.[73] The labour required to lay the green and build the clubhouse was undertaken by the members themselves, not an unusual practice in war-time, but one which became increasingly common after 1945.

The apparent ease with which early male bowlers created their clubs contrasts even more starkly with the struggles faced by many women bowlers. The Gold Coast Ladies' Bowling Club (Queensland) provides an example. Although the land, as with many men's clubs, was leased at a peppercorn rental from the local council, this was only the first step in creating the club. 'In the beginning there wasn't a lot of enthusiasm shown by the lady bowlers on the Coast. The general opinion was — women just wouldn't be able to handle a club alone'.[74] Nonetheless sufficient enthusiasm was engendered to ensure the club's establishment in 1965.

> Then began the drive for funds. It speaks much for the vision and imagination of the women that they had the confidence to undertake such an ambitious project without financial backing of any kind. Club members pay the ultimate tribute to Mel Ferguson that without her untiring genius for fund-raising the club might never have got off the ground. While Mrs Ferguson was getting donations of money and goods, other members were running street stalls and other money-making ventures. Dorothy Bowman and Cath Cullinane were growing pumpkins for sale on the paddock where No. 3 green now stands. Obviously, while the women had an abundance of vision and imagination, they were not short on initiative and physical effort either.[75]

By the 1930s, many competition matches were played on Saturdays rather than mid-week. But in the period of the half-day working Saturday, even this was not to everyone's liking. In 1937 vocal protest was raised against the constraints on Sunday play:

> what I am getting at is that it's about time the majority of Bowlers in New South Wales should have the privilege of entering in the competitions... [A]s it is they cannot, owing to the fact that a great many Bowlers are business and working men who do not cease work till 1 p.m. Saturday, and the competitions commence on *Saturday mornings*. If those who are fortunate enough to live without work would only stop and think for one moment what misery they cause the above, I am sure that they would not object to Sunday play.[76]

After the Second World War, however, the Australian Bowls Council (ABC) came to recognise that many players could not afford to take time off work for bowls competitions: and the increasing frequency of interstate and international matches in the more affluent post-war years brought to a head the issue of reimbursing players' travel expenses. Despite decades of dire warnings about the dangers of creeping professionalism, the ABC launched an appeal in 1954 for each state association to raise the equivalent of 'a bob [shilling] a member' in order to pay the expenses of national representatives at the forthcoming Empire Games in Vancouver. 'The cost to send seven chosen representatives totalled £3550; contributions received totalled £3535 2s 6d, leaving a sum of £14 17s 6d to be met from the funds of the ABC.'[77] The response rate to this appeal indicates that most Australian bowlers were now active supporters of (or at least reconciled to) subsidies for away play.

The overwhelming support given to this national bowls team further suggests that the movement to be recognised as a serious sport had triumphed. At the ABC's next meeting in January 1955, professionalism in bowls was given official, albeit limited, sanction when 'the new Amateur Status clause was removed from the Constitution and included in the Laws of the game. . . This validated the acceptance of payment by a "coach". . . without infringing his amateur status.' A decade later ABC capitation fees on each member of affiliated state associations was increased by fifty per cent 'on the understanding that such an increase would be used to establish a fund paying travelling and accommodation expenses of those players representing Australia in future Commonwealth games'. In the same year the New South Wales men's association ruled similarly for interstate games.[78] The major sponsorship involved when Australia hosted the first male World Bowls Championship at Kyeemagh (New South Wales) in 1966 was a symbolically powerful, public statement about the bowling green's future.

The post-war expansion of bowling clubs up to the 1960s was dramatic. Between 1946 and 1961 the number of men's clubs increased from 210 to 612 in New South Wales. Significantly, the growth was more evident in metropolitan areas than in country centres[79] — a trend which mirrored the period's rapid suburbanisation. These years were also notable for Australia's immigration influx, and for the predominance of single-earner, male-dominated households with disposable incomes. The first of these influences served to transform the ethnic face of Australian bowls by bringing to the fore many European-born migrants (like Rob Parrella[80]) whose prior experience was in other forms of the game, such as *bocce* or *boules*. The second enhanced the bowling club's role as a community social centre, and also provided both opportunities and incentives for women to participate as players and administrators. To do so, however, women bowlers still had to overcome entrenched male preconceptions about their place on the green.

Nineteenth-century attitudes saw bowls in a wide-ranging context which stressed perceived links between the game's distinctive characteristics and a number of desirable social attributes. Male dominance of the sport's organisation before 1900 was faced with the reality of women's participation. One response to this 'intrusion' was vociferous in belittling women's involvement, while attempting to reinforce masculine stereotypes of the 'feminine condition':

As a training in temperament the game of bowls should prove of excellent service to women. . . Among games, we may regard bowls as constituting the peaceful sort, and in its demure aspect find its chiefest charms. Is it then a game likely to appeal to the peculiar susceptibilities of women? The answer it is feared must be in the negative. . . Theirs is likely to prove but a dilettante fancy, and to its finer points they may remain strangers.[81]

Like the prevalence of concerns for bowls' social exclusiveness, such attitudes proved durable. In the first half of the twentieth century, as male bowlers attempted to convince an often sceptical public that the sport required skill, experience and indeed sometimes strength, they drew comparisons — in no sense confined to the bowling green — between male and female aptitudes. As one prominent male bowler remarked in 1959: 'In actual play much progress has been made by women bowlers, many of whom display fine skill in draw play and in yard-on shots. Few, however, indulge in firm shots, and fast drives appear beyond their physical strength. . . I was forced to the conclusion that the most skilful of the women would not be able to compete against the best of the men players.'[82]

Apparently undaunted by this lack of male faith in their abilities, women's bowls club membership continued to grow in Australia, consisting in 1989 of over 148 000 players in 2196 clubs.[83] This represents forty-five per cent of the world's women bowlers, and makes the game the third-largest participant sport for women in Australia.[84]

The numbers involved, however, tend to mask both women's commitment and many obstacles. Perhaps because the establishment of women's clubs proved difficult, many women's bowls clubs are formed as part of male ones; the proportion of such clubs has been estimated at between eighty-five and ninety per cent of all women's clubs in Australia.[85] The introduction of Commonwealth equal-opportunity legislation in 1984, where the two clubs are considered to be one for the sake of the legislation, makes this arrangement even more convenient.

Indeed the popularity of mixed bowling was apparent even in the nineteenth century, and it continued after 1900. Waverley (New South Wales) held a match in about 1908 'with two lady bowlers on each side'.[86] The practice persisted, and met with varying responses from the sport's governing authorities. In 1936 the Hunters Hill Club (New South Wales) formally sought association approval to hold a 'mixed-pairs' tournament, which the club seemed to regard as unremarkable and perhaps even desirable. The New South Wales Bowls

Association's executive council initially granted the permit, but then rescinded it when they 'ascertained that "mixed pairs" in this case referred to the inclusion of ladies'.[87] This episode highlights the difference in attitude between the club (who were prepared to include women, but followed approved procedures), and the association (who stuck to the letter of the constitution, and cancelled the tournament on the grounds that women were not among its members). More importantly, it suggests that in some places women bowlers were accepted as sufficiently skilled to play with the experts — the men.[88]

Perhaps surprisingly, few public expressions of bitterness seem to have resulted from actions of this sort. Mrs Sutcliffe claimed in the 1960s rather that women could 'largely thank the men for the growth of women's bowls membership'.[89] Certainly champion bowler and bowls historian Gordon Sargeant, although not convinced about women's ability to play well, conceded that 'one of bowls's most discussed problems is whether women should be admitted to men's clubs. . . The result [of their entry] has been rather startling. Mixed bowls has become so popular that clubs providing for that pastime are making it increasingly difficult for clubs who oppose mixed bowls, to get any reasonable attendance on a Sunday.'[90]

Perhaps because men and women have long played together, women's bowls has taken a similarly divided road to serious sport status and welcome leisure-time pusuit. While many women play bowls or are bowls-club members for the social and healthy side of the game, other women bowlers are now vying for international honours. The women's world championships held in Australia in 1985 saw the Australian bowlers carry off gold for both the pairs and triples.[91] Perhaps in recognition of the serious sport status women's bowls now had, the full three days of this competition were televised nationwide.

The widespread acceptance of women bowlers is reflected in their nominations as sportspeople of the year, and recognition in the Australia Day awards. Indeed, the serious side of the sport has encouraged women bowlers to expect the same degree of training that other sportspeople receive. An article by-lined 'High profile takes bowls into big prizemoney' noted:

The top [women] bowlers are dedicated athletes. . . When Australia swept all before it in the 1985 Women's World Championships, they were a fit side. Manager Jean McKinnon worked on them for months before the event. There were fitness programmes, the Australian Institute of Sport, competitions against men, and by the time they

Over the past few decades, bowls associations have been developing strategies to change the image of the game and to initiate the young into the sport. This picture shows fourteen-year-old lawn bowls prodigy Scott Taylor playing in the South Australian State Singles Championship in January 1994. (Ray Titus/the *Advertiser*, Adelaide.)

graced the greens at Reservoir. . . Dot Roche, Merle Richardson, Norma Massey and Fay Craig were not just a team of women bowlers, but a group of fit women welded into a top team.[92]

Meanwhile, this very recognition has encouraged some to reassert the perennial questions about the role of the bowler's uniform. As both men's and women's associations reported the closure of clubs and falling overall membership in the late-1980s,[93] attention has again turned to features of the game which seem to discourage participation by the young: 'strict dress rules, which exist, or exist in the minds of those young women who feel they would like to join in, act as a deterrent'.[94] Despite this recent trend, Australian lawn bowls in 1992 still claimed a total membership of over 480 000 people and almost 4500 clubs.[95]

8

Lawn Tennis

Graeme Kinross-Smith

I see no reason why a space marked off in a field or playground would not as well serve for Tennis as an elaborately furnished and covered gallery. Let players try and make a game for themselves...

> English advocate of plein-air lawn tennis, *Lawn tennis,*
> *croquet, racquets etc Illustrated* (London, 1862)

Do not think that tennis is merely a physical exercise. It is a mental cocktail of a very high kick.

> W. T. (Bill) Tilden, *The art of lawn tennis* (London, 1920)

I N THE Sydney newspaper the *Echo* on 4 July 1885 appeared an article by a member of the Rational Dress Society reprinted from the *Pall Mall Gazette*. It urged the adoption by women of the 'dual skirt' (the equivalent of the loose culottes, often reaching to the instep, worn by women today, but generally not for tennis) for the benefit of 'increased activity of limb'. The article was illustrated for colonial readers by a line drawing of the skirt's design and another of a woman clad in it reaching with a tennis racquet for a high volley.

The article gives notice that in Australian colonial society by the mid-1880s lawn tennis had become a game or recreation quite well known to a segment of the population at least, and probably still played more commonly by women than men. It had not yet become a 'sport'.

By that time also, tennis clubs had been established as adjuncts to male institutions such as the Melbourne Cricket Club (MCC) in 1878 (following the example of the United States where the first American tennis club, set up at the suggestion of a lady, became an adjunct to the Staten Island Cricket and Baseball Club as early as 1874). The MCC Tennis Club was followed by clubs that grew from the Geelong gentleman's club, the Geelong Club, in 1882 and the Sydney Cricket Club in 1885. The Australasian Lawn Tennis Association (precursor to the Lawn Tennis Association of Australia, and much later, in 1986, Tennis Australia) was founded in Sydney in 1904. These initiatives, these dates, set the scene for any social history of the pastime, recreation, game and sport of tennis in Australia.

Tennis history that is little more than details of matches, illustrated by photographs of individuals and teams with racquets crossed, palls very quickly. Any account, therefore, that seeks to ask who played and plays tennis in Australia, and how, why, when and where they played, must begin by enquiring what it meant to players and spectators to participate in those informal games of *plein-air* tennis played in Britain, perhaps for centuries, up to the late nineteenth century and in games in Australia that emulated them after 1870 or thereabouts. Then comes that strange and under-researched interregnum that followed Major Wingfield's patenting of his new game of lawn tennis in 1874 and the selling of his 'tennis kits' to interested novices. The kits consisted of racquets, balls, polished ash poles, a strong, tanned cord net, lines, rubbers, a mallet, a drill and a racquet-press. They sold in Britain and abroad and reached the Australian colonies in travellers' luggage.[1] Then came the distilling and codifying of the better features of the several games of tennis being played in Britain at the time, first by the Marylebone Cricket Club in 1875 and then again in 1877 by the All-England Croquet Club which promptly added 'Lawn Tennis' to its name and staged its first gentleman's singles championship, in effect the first Wimbledon championship. From that time devotees of tennis had an official game to which to turn for instruction — a game very close to that played today.

We can hear lawn tennis's debt to royal or 'real' tennis (strictly speaking the only game entitled to be called simply 'tennis', as the *The Times* of London has insisted in its listing of results over the years) and its enclosed court and much more complex scoring in the advocacy of the *plein-air* tennis devotee at the head of this piece. We can see that debt in artists' impressions of games played as early as the sixteenth and seventeenth centuries in Britain and France by people in the open air with no net, but using implements that resemble the racquets and the balls of the royal-tennis courts. We can follow the advent of *plein-air* or lawn tennis through innumerable permutations according to the players' whims and circum-stances, through court shapes that resembled an hour-glass, narrow at the net and running to much wider base lines, and eventually to the rectangular court used since 1877.

We can envisage colonists returning from 'home' to Aus-tralia by ship in the 1870s with Wingfield's tennis kits. We can imagine the kits deployed in the innumerable variations on Wingfield's suggested game or on the new Marylebone Cricket Club and All-England Croquet and Lawn Tennis Club rules and we can imagine these colonial games played on the lawns of Sydney and Melbourne city houses or the lawns or bare spaces of country estates and stations.

Who played? Those with the time and access to the space necessary to set out a court. And who were they? Largely the well-to-do. What balance was there between the sexes? Almost certainly a preponderence of women over men, but since we are still talking of tennis as a pastime — simply a minimally competitive and pleasant way of occupying time — whoever of either sex was available and fit at the time might play in pursuit of that uncovered India-rubber ball. The 'covered ball', at first simply bandaged with two strips of cloth and later with a more sophisticated woollen nap, appeared in the early 1890s, much to the chagrin of some players who felt it caused a decline in interest in matches, and made play in wet weather more difficult since the ball became so heavy. The earlier uncovered ball had been dried frequently with a towel or handkerchief during rain in order that play might continue.[2] The social tennis of that early period and its context is pictured in the account of the young Douglas Sladen, nephew of Sir Charles Sladen, Premier of Victoria in the 1860s. The young Sladen visited the Recreation Club in Geelong in 1880.

Life at Geelong revolved around the Recreation Ground — a sort of club, which had some good tennis courts, and rooms where people could give receptions and dances. When it was not too hot the Society girls used the tennis courts a great deal ... They played too well for me to be welcome in their games ... When they were resting, as I had met them all, and was the nephew of the principal inhabitant, they were friendly ...[3]

The story of Australian tennis is partly a story of vassalage to overseas influences, at first primarily British. Tennis, of course, was not alone in this and, like most of the popular sports, games and pastimes enjoyed by Australians before Federation — cricket and rugby being foremost among them — it followed the English model.

From this starting point in the 1870s, the social history of lawn tennis in Australia is also a story of the multi-factorial influences that affect the development of sport — technology; the roles of different social classes and their varying expectations; the relative roles of the sexes; the place of financial rewards, prize money, amateurism, professionalism and the influence of the media in the economics of the sport; the influences of history and geography; the roles of participants and spectators and so on.

Technology can be seen immediately to play a role. Lawn tennis would have been impossible without the development of the hollow India-rubber ball, since the royal-tennis ball, made of tightly-wound yards of tape with a cloth covering would bounce very little on grass.

How much was the playing of early Australian tennis governed by class? Certainly in the cities of the eastern seaboard and in Adelaide and Perth early games were the preserve of the wealthy and privileged. In the country the physical proximity of the ant-bed, clay or gravel courts of station properties might have suggested that the chance for a game had been open to a wider spectrum of men and women, including rural workers, and yet the social sanctions that applied to the mixing of social classes in other areas of life still generally applied, it seems, on the tennis court. Property owners and their families, worthy visitors, and senior employees such as station managers were the main players, albeit sometimes under pretty rudimentary conditions.

By the mid-1880s however, tennis players in the Australian colonies could be divided into those who had begun to pursue the game as a competitive sport and those who still pursued it merely as a pastime. During the 1880s and 1890s, competitive tennis reached its greatest heights in Melbourne, beginning with the Melbourne Cricket Club championships for men in 1880, and for women in 1884; the formation in 1884 of the South Yarra Tennis Club (later Royal South Yarra Tennis Club) and the institution of a men's pennant competition, the precursor of the later Lawn Tennis Association of Victoria pennant and the current Victorian Tennis Association pennant competition, from 1884. The Sydney equivalent, the men's badge competition matches, began some time later in 1890. In Sydney, the first colonial championships for New South Wales were held for both men and women in 1885 and inter-colonial championships were held there for the first time, also in 1885, and thereafter alternated between the two major capital cities. Similar inter-colonial ladies' matches began in 1908. Matches between New South Wales, Victoria and the other colonies (later states) began in the mid-1890s.[4] Because of the difficulties of travel, New South Wales commonly played against Queensland, while Victoria played against its contiguous state, South Australia, although matches against other states were also held. In Geelong, Victoria, an annual Easter tournament was begun in 1887 and by the mid-1890s had become a showcase for some of the country's best players, both men and women, drawing names like A. H. Colquhoun, Alfred Dunlop, Rodney Heath, Norman Brookes, Gerald Patterson, J. B. Hawkes and Pat O'Hara Wood who were among the country's best male players up to 1930, as well as outstanding women players of colonial and post-Federation times such as Miss Shaw (later Mrs Colquhoun), Miss Howitt (the Victorian champion from 1894 until 1900), Miss Gyton and Miss Lily Addison. The ladies' singles event of the Geelong Easter tournament was also to become officially the Ladies Singles Asphalt Championship of Victoria in 1913, the club also hosting a number of international matches.[5]

Where did this new game and sport fit into the Australian social fabric? First, it retained novelty in the eyes of its devotees, let alone those of the general public, as the possibilities of the game were explored. Witness the wording of the newspaper report of the theft in 1887 by some boys 'of the balls used in the game of lawn tennis' from the Customs House Reserve in Geelong, where the early Easter tournaments were conducted, and the air of mystery in the description of tennis's appurtenances, when set beside those of football and cricket, in the *Geelong Times* in 1889. 'The latest appliances are provided for the benefit of players. The nets are constructed of wire and the uprights are provided with a patent mechanism for increasing the tension of the nets when they become loose.'

Events in early tournaments were commonly handicaps, the tournament handicappers taking it as a matter of pride in their skill when an accomplished player was taken to three exciting sets by a tyro.[6] The dress of men and women on the courts reflected the game's origins as a polite diversion on manicured lawns. The men in long trousers or knickerbockers, wide and colourfully-striped elastic belts or cummerbunds, and perhaps

137

shirt and tie surmounted by a striped tennis blazer and straw boater hat, or coatless in shirt and striped skull-cap, had an air of social swashbuckling, all in implied contrast to the sober business suit and watch chain. The ladies wore hair upswept and gathered in a bunch, with a straw 'gem' hat pinned to it with sharp hat-pins that proved dangerous in the frenetic activity of the game. Their tennis outfits were completed by white blouses and long skirts — 'three inches off the ground, if properly cut, is sufficiently short' as one leading designer had it.

As the game became more competitive it saw modification and standardisation of all these elements. An interest developed in championship matches as well as handicaps at the highest levels of play; dress became less socially conscious and more attuned to the 'increased activity of limb' of striving players, but was always consonant with decorum and took its lead from what was acceptable at the All-England Lawn Tennis Club at Wimbledon. Similarly, through the 1880s and the 1890s the crucial differences in court surface, make of balls, racquet size and shape were brought into greater uniformity.

The ways of playing the game also changed. In early social games delicacy, gentleness and 'science' were the norm, and the volley was not *de rigueur*. But S. W. Gore in winning his first Wimbledon championship gave notice of other possible tactics that had a great deal to do with his background as a 'racquets' player not concerned with decorous self-image, but with winning. He came to the net to tap the ball away by volleying into the corners, reaching sometimes into his opponent's court to do it. Thus when a team of New South Wales visitors came south in 1883 to play two Melbourne Cricket Club Tennis Club members in an exhibition the Melbourne *Argus* was able to point the way in its report. The visitors won resoundingly, the paper noted, 'owing chiefly to the pretty and unerring manner in which one of them "volleyed". He placed the ball from above and below the net without exercising the least force or ungraceful movement and has introduced a style here which from its grace and effectiveness ought to become very popular on our courts.'[7]

From the ruck of prominent male players of the 1880s, 1890s and early 1900s — Gus Kearney, Dudley Webb, A. G. Colquhoun, 'Smasher' Bayles, H. E. Webb, W. V. Eaves,

Ben Green, Alfred Dunlop, T. Tatchell, Barney Murphy, Rodney Heath, Horrie Rice, S. N. Doust, Leslie Gaden, H. A. Parker and others — came one that would stand out in the first century of Australian tennis. Not only would Norman Brookes hold his place as Australia's outstanding player for more than a decade, but he would play a large part in ushering Australian tennis onto the international stage with his winning of the Wimbledon singles in 1907.

In 1908, during the first years of nationhood, Brookes also played a major role in changing the image of tennis in the eyes of the often scornful Australian devotees of the popular sports of cricket, racing and football. In November 1908, on a grass court specially laid down at the Warehouseman's Cricket Ground in St Kilda Road, Melbourne, the attention of Australia and the world centred on Brookes and his New Zealand team-mate, Anthony Wilding, as they strove against the Americans to retain for Australasia the Davis Cup they had won from the British at Wimbledon in the previous northern summer. The gruelling matches were played in a relentless heat-wave. The crowd saw Brookes play 102 games of world-class tennis over the first two days in temperatures over the century — an opening singles victory for Brookes, and a loss for Wilding, and then a second-day long and hard five-set doubles win, during which some spectators found the tension too great at four-all in the final set and had to leave the stands. By the time the crowd had settled for the start of the third day's play, with the thermometer at 101 degrees Fahrenheit (over thirty-eight degrees Celcius), a realisation was dawning on the sporting public. This was hardly a 'milk and water sport' as the prestigious English journal, the *Sportsman*, had disdainfully described it. The crowd, and the sporting press, were now seeing enacted in their own country contests that were both a physical and a psychological test of the players. Brookes finished in defeat in five sets, having played 159 games in the challenge round. Wilding saved the cup by winning his final singles in straight sets. Australian lawn tennis had earned a new esteem in the public mind.[8]

Brookes would go on to dominate the administration of Australian tennis, both men's and women's, until 1955. He played in a further six Davis Cup teams. He was sole Davis Cup selector for Australasia and Australia from 1907 until 1924, and continued as a member of the selection committee until 1955. He served as president of the Lawn Tennis Association of Australia (LTAA) from 1926 until 1955, and urged the establishment of Kooyong as the centre of Victorian tennis in

Australasians Norman Brookes (Australia) and Anthony Wilding (New Zealand) striding onto the court at Albert Ground, Melbourne to defend the Davis Cup against the United States in 1908. (Collection of Graeme Kinross-Smith.)

1927. He founded the Australian branch of the International Lawn Tennis Federation (ILTF) in 1951, and presided ruefully over the advent of professionalism among Australian players in the mid-1950s. Brookes died in 1968 at the age of ninety.

Many of the threads of the social history of Australian tennis seen in its most accomplished players in the period from Federation until 1930 pass through the person of Norman Brookes. For a start, he was representative of the privilege that largely determined those who reached great tennis prowess in Victoria. It is tempting to see this privilege as the main avenue to tennis success in Melbourne, while noting that the paths to accomplishment in Sydney seem to have been more varied and pluralistic. To study this 'Melbourne Club' of 1920s tennis is instructive in socio-historical terms. First we have Brookes, born in 1878, the son of a wealthy ship-owner, bridge-builder and entrepreneur in paper mills and pastoral properties. He grew up in Melbourne's Albert Park, close to the Warehouse-man's Ground (later the Albert Ground, and now the home of the Victorian Tennis Association) where he often observed inter-colonial and interstate matches while learning his tennis from the age of five on the grass court at his home, Brookwood.

From the age of eight he often played and outwitted grown men among his father's acquaintance, and took the experienced international player Dr W. H. Eaves as mentor and coach.

Brookes, described by the famous Bill Tilden as 'the greatest tennis brain of the twentieth century', was a member of the prestigious Royal South Yarra Lawn Tennis Club, frequented by the Melbourne social set. He was a member of the Melbourne Club and the Australian Club. Through these clubs and the Geelong Club, the Geelong Lawn Tennis Club and his family's business and tennis connections Norman Brookes and his family were linked to the Patterson, O'Hara Wood, Hawkes, Schlesinger, Wertheim, Dunlop, Sandral, Strachan and Blair families, among others. Brookes was a friend, fellow tennis devotee and business associate of T. A. Patterson, father of the renowned Davis Cup player, Gerald Patterson. Brookes coached the young Gerald Patterson in Melbourne and later initiated him and others like Jack Hawkes, 'Sos' Wertheim, Pat O'Hara Wood and Bob Schlesinger in forays to Wimbledon and Davis Cup venues overseas, as well as on the European and American tour, where Brookes' connections and his standing as a player after 1905 meant, as Richard Yallop demonstrates in his history of the Royal South Yarra Tennis Club, that he 'played with Counts and conversed with Kings'.[9]

This coterie of Melbourne men players, at a time when Daphne Akhurst in 1928 and Joan Hartigan in the 1930s were the only Australian women players with the resources to tour abroad, had other factors in common in their backgrounds. They had all grown to tennis skill in the Lawn Tennis Association of Victoria (LTAV) Melbourne 'A' grade pennant competition, in the Melbourne Cricket Club Autumn Championships and in the Public Schools' Championships, it being quite common then for public school boys to remain at school until the age of twenty or so. Brookes, Patterson, Hawkes and Wertheim had private courts at their homes and interacted and practised with visiting overseas players. They were all included in a social matrix that consisted of tennis in its house parties, tennis parties, jazz dances and full-dress tennis balls, self-financed international and interstate travel and travel to country tournaments. Brookes, Patterson and his father, Pat O'Hara Wood and Jack Hawkes and his father before him all filled posts important in the administration of Victorian and Australian tennis. All came from professional or business families and combined their Melbourne activities with participation in the tennis and social world of Geelong, which, through its grounding in the values of Western District pastoralism, wool-broking and business helped to cement the cosiness of the social set.

Gerald Patterson is another interesting case study. He was the grandson of David Mitchell, land developer, quarry owner of the Mitchell Estate, builder of the Melbourne Exhibition Building among many others in the city, and father of Dame Nellie Melba, Gerald Patterson's aunt. Patterson's childhood home was Rohese with its grounds and grass tennis court in Kew, Melbourne where, later, as one of the world's leading players, he appeared with Hawkes, Schlesinger, O'Hara Wood and Wertheim at Sunday tennis parties of fifty people or more. He was educated at Melbourne's Scotch College. Already an interstate player, Patterson sailed to England at the outbreak of the First World War to gain a commission in the Royal Artillery. He was awarded the Military Cross for an action at Ypres. After his 1919 Wimbledon win he returned to Australia where in 1922 he married Orme Riggall, a famous horsewoman, whose family owned large Gippsland cattle properties, and set up home in Kooyong. Patterson, who, with his wife, became a world traveller in the 1920s during the northern hemisphere's summer tennis season, taking in Wimbledon, the Riviera, the American championships and Davis Cup venues, had the urbanity of Brookes in mixing with influential society. He was on the board of Hawkes Brothers, hardware merchants and mild steel importers, Geelong, and often visited the Hawkes beach house and tennis court at Barwon Heads. He also played royal tennis at the Melbourne court that fronted onto the Exhibition Gardens. At the suggestion of the great tennis devotee, Robert Gordon Menzies, Patterson entered conservative politics and stood as a candidate for Menzies' United Australia Party in the Federal seat of Corio in Victoria in 1940, but was defeated. In 1946 he toured overseas as non-playing captain of the Australian Davis Cup team with John Bromwich, Dinny Pails and Adrian Quist. Patterson's tennis prowess took him to victory in the Wimbledon singles in 1919 — at the age of twenty-four he defeated his forty-one-year-old mentor, Norman Brookes, and again in 1922. He played in the Australian Davis Cup teams of 1919, 1920, 1922, 1924, 1925 and 1928, and won many other Australian and international tournaments.

The team-mates of Brookes in his three Davis Cup appearances after the First World War and of Patterson in his six Davis Cup appearances were, in the main, Victorians drawn from this social group. In 1919 R. V. Thomas of South Australia and J. O. Anderson of New South Wales joined Brookes and Patterson in the Australian team. The 1920 team was composed of Victorians. In 1921 Norman Peach and Clarrie Todd of New South Wales joined Hawkes and J. O. Anderson in the team. In 1922 Anderson accompanied Wertheim, Patterson and O'Hara Wood. In 1923 he again joined three Victorians — this time Hawkes, I. D. McInnes and Bob Schlesinger. In 1924 Fred Kalms, a wheat and sheep farmer from West Wyalong in New South Wales, as the sole representative from country tennis in the Australian Davis Cup team, stood at the ship's rail with Patterson, O'Hara Wood and Bob Schlesinger as SS *Sonoma* left Sydney for Honolulu and the United States. Australia mounted no Davis Cup teams in 1926 or 1927 and when it did again in 1928 the selections signalled not only the advent of the Crawford era in Australian tennis (Patterson was selected with Jack Crawford and Harry Hopman) but the coming of a greater pluralism — modelled on the Sydney receptivity towards all comers, rather than on Melbourne exclusivity — in the opportunity for a wider range of players to gain experience and to reach their full potential.[10]

What of the place of social class among ordinary weekend and spare-time Australian tennis players up to this time? Clearly this varied from place to place, community to community. And yet there is strong evidence that until technological and social factors came together to open tennis as a sport to a wider spectrum of the Australian population in the 1950s and 1960s, social clout and financial standing still played considerable roles among club players, even though among tennis devotees this sometimes remained unacknowledged or unrecognised. 'Austral', the tennis writer of the sporting journal, the *Referee*, in his idiosyncratic book *Lawn Tennis in Australia* presents us with a picture of tennis for the ordinary player in the country in 1912. Tennis, he wrote, brought together 'in a friendly, and in this case, wholly unimportant rivalry, those who wish to gain social intercourse at the same time as they find opportunity for moderate exertion in the open air'. 'Austral' paints for us the getting up of a game on a station property, with telephone calls to neighbours, so that young men might come the intervening eight miles on horseback, while the car is sent twenty miles to bring the McPhillamy girls to the court. These players, he stresses, are not champions, the finer points of stroke-making are lost upon them. They are 'get the balls over or bust' players, from among whom, as he says, might nevertheless come a Crossman or a Windeyer (naming two of the crack country players of New South Wales of the 1890s), or a Clarrie Todd, who became in 1921 the first country player to be selected in an Australian Davis Cup team. 'Every country town', he writes, 'has its local club, where, in the cooler winter (the inland summer being often too hot for tennis and the young men being called to cricket) the local dentist and one or two solicitors set out for a game. Out here in Australia we luckily have no class distinctions,' and he remains unaware of the ironic contradiction between his examples and his generalisation.[11]

Tennis at club level in the capital cities and larger provincial towns was still probably primarily a Protestant pursuit, surrounded by the business ethic and the concomitants of the Masonic Lodge, with due concern for decorum, appropriate dress (in which the All-England Lawn Tennis Club at Wimbledon provided the lead) and social acceptability — so that a club president in the Victorian provinces could deplore the specially bestowed membership of a promising teenager in the 1940s because she travelled to and from the courts by tram, her parents not having a car to collect her.[12]

Sydney and places further to the west and north were more relaxed and accepting of such things, more welcoming of a wide spectrum of society in their club memberships. If social privilege, exclusivity and private means tended to be the Melbourne pattern until 1930 or thereabouts, in enabling players to reach the heights, Sydney seemed to exemplify other ways of coming to recognition. Sydney had a stronger tradition of tennis prowess developed through country tennis, on the one hand, and on the other, support of promising players through employment by sporting firms when they had been drawn to the capitals.[13] J. O. Anderson was raised in Strathfield, Sydney, while Jack Crawford had his grounding on the station court of his family at Urangeleine, near Albury, coming to Sydney in 1926 when he was seventeen. Later, in Sydney, Anderson worked as a sporting sales representative and subsequently ran his own small business and Crawford worked for a sporting firm. Room could be found at the top for players of great ability but of dubious social standing — as in the case of the country-reared Davis Cup players Clarrie Todd and Fred Kalms, for example — but perhaps not without cost to them socially. Fred Kalms felt considerable loneliness and ostracism on his overseas tour in 1924, having so little in common socially or in education, cultural background and urbanity with Patterson, O'Hara Wood and Schlesinger and the accompanying Brookes.[14]

Australia's success as a tennis nation, despite its remarkably small population, owes debts to country tennis and to climate — the two go together. Robert Gordon Menzies, at pains to explain that success in the 1950s, when the country's population was a mere nine million, put it thus: 'Australia, for tennis purposes, is one large California. The varying climates of the six states have this in common: they favour outdoor sport and outdoor living. Material standards of life are high; leisure is abundant ... Most dwelling houses stand in their own grounds and gardens. For all these reasons our inbred love of sport finds opportunity and expression ...'.[15] It was that climate and opportunity that allowed so many country people to play on ant-bed, gravel and asphalt courts in country New South Wales and then to come to Sydney when Country Week was inaugurated in 1909 to play on the immaculate grass courts at Double Bay and from 1923 at White City, off Rushcutters' Bay, there to battle first for the country championship and then to play against the city-nurtured players in the City-Country match. And similar traditions of country competition developed in other states. The players of great ability delivered to Australian tennis through this tradition in New South Wales, Victoria and Queensland, despite being distanced in their formative years from coaching and regular top-level competition, are legion: among the women are Louise Bickerton, Edie Butcherine, Esme Ashford, Marjorie Cox (Crawford), Margaret Smith (Court), Cynthia Sieler (Doerner), Evonne Goolagong (Cawley), Jan Lehane and Diane Fromholz (Ballestrat): among the men, Gus Kearney, Jim Bayley, Jim Willard, Clarrie Todd, Fred Kalms, 'Gar' Moon, Cliff Sproule, Vic McGrath, Jack Crawford, Jim Matthews, Rex Hartwig, Geoff Brown, Jack Arkinstall, Bob Howe, Bob Mark, Tony Roche, Mark Edmondson, Mal Anderson, Roy Emerson and Rod Laver. Part of the input of country tennis in New South Wales also consisted of the 'Dubbo Hardcourts': from 1915 until the early 1950s the New South Wales Hardcourt Championships were played at Dubbo in the central west pastoral country of the state, drawing crowds of two to three thousand people in the stands during June in earlier years and later each September.

Most people are familiar with the chief actors in Australian tennis from the 1930s on. Crawford's smooth-stroked and relaxed genius dominated much of the 1930s until players who had striven in his shadow began to emerge — Hopman, Bromwich, Quist and others. Nancy Wynne (Bolton) became a force in Australian women's tennis to be compared with the earlier Brookes in male ranks or with Margaret Smith (Court), who was to come to prominence in the 1960s. Wynne was six times winner of the Australian women's singles championship from 1937 until 1951. Australian and state championships, as well as Australia's account of itself in Davis Cup competition, were centred around John Bromwich and Adrian Quist during the 1940s, their careers interrupted, as so many were, by military service during the Second World War. The pair nevertheless won the Australian doubles championship eight times between 1938 and 1950 and, playing all rubbers between them, won the Davis Cup from the United States in 1939, figuring also in several other challenge rounds after the war.

The 1950s saw a major change in tennis both in Australia and overseas — a change that ushered in Australia's greatest hour among the tennis-playing nations. It was an hour which can never come again, considering the popularity of the game world-wide in the 1990s, the incentives for players to dedicate themselves to the game from their early teens, and the great depth of talent among both women and men players represented in the first 200 names on world computer rankings. That 1950s change was generated primarily in America by Jack Kramer's insistence first on the superiority of the serve-and-volley game — powerful serve; then speed to a killing volley or smash — when set against the longer and more patient rallies, placement and tactics of the Crawford-Bromwich-Quist era, and also on his undaunted orchestration of professional tennis, against the conservatism of the world's tennis administrations.

It was around the young and talented Frank Sedgman that these changes were enacted in Melbourne, Australia. Harry Hopman played his last tennis at international level as playing manager of the 1938 Davis Cup team and in the 1939 team, and then began his run as Australian Davis Cup captain in 1950. When he retired from that role in 1969 he had seen Australia, now playing in the American Zone, to fifteen Davis Cup victories, principally against the Americans. Sedgman was Hopman's first protégé, and spearheaded the Davis Cup victories of 1950, 1951 and 1952. In 1952 he won the Wimbledon singles, doubles and mixed doubles titles and then repeated the triple feat at the United States national championships. Within two days of the end of the 1952 challenge round, Sedgman signed as a professional with Jack Kramer's tennis troupe, and was soon followed by Ken McGregor. After their exploits under Hopman's tutorship in the Davis Cup in 1953, 1954 and 1955, Ken Rosewall (in 1956) and Lew Hoad (in 1957) also turned professional. They were to be followed in this golden hour of Australian tennis by Ashley Cooper and Mal Anderson in 1958, Rod Laver in 1963, and Roy Emerson, John Newcombe and Tony Roche in 1966-67. In the eighteen years from 1950 to 1968 these players had ensured that an Australian won the Wimbledon men's singles titles eleven times, the French singles nine times and the American twelve times. Australians also won the Wimbledon men's doubles thirteen times. Of them all, Laver was perhaps the most accomplished, winning the Wimbledon singles title four times and the Grand Slam (the French, Wimbledon, American and Australian titles) not once, but twice, a feat never equalled and scarcely likely to be, given today's multitude of talent. It was not until 1968 that an International Lawn Tennis Federation decision allowed professionals to enter the Wimbledon championships and other international events, and from that time the Australian national and state championships have been open to both professional and amateur, bringing back to the general fold all the champions lost in the interim as competition for rising players.

In the period from 1960 until 1973 Australia produced its greatest woman player in Margaret Smith (Court). As well as numerous other titles, Court won the Australian women's singles championship eleven times, Wimbledon three times, six United States singles titles and the Australian women's doubles on nine occasions, as well as winning the Grand Slam in 1970, and playing for Australia in many Federation Cup matches. She made two successful comebacks to top-level tennis after having children.

The path to success for Australian male players has required a great deal of dedication and courage of each individual. The way to comparable success for women has been even more difficult in a sport that has been male-administered and in which males receive more attention for their physical strength. From the beginnings of tennis in Australia and elsewhere, the mounting of events for women has lagged behind the initiation

147

of men's titles. The chances for men to make overseas tours either privately, or with the support of the LTAA for Davis Cup tours began earlier and have been much greater than those for women over the years. The New South Wales player Mrs Mall Molesworth was able to tour overseas in the 1920s and play at Wimbledon because her husband gained a fellowship to Oxford University.[16] In 1922 a New South Wales women's team toured New Zealand where they won all their matches and were prominent in the national championships. In 1925 the first Australian women's tennis team sailed for Europe — Daphne Ackhurst, Esna Boyd, Mrs Harper and Mrs Utz. In 1928 Louise Bickerton and Daphne Ackhurst toured overseas. But these were sporadic opportunities. In the 1930s Joan Hartigan was fortunate to be able to tour overseas during the Depression years of the 1930s. She toured with the Davis Cup team in 1934 and was beaten by Helen Jacobs in the Wimbledon semi-finals that year and by Helen Wills Moody in 1935. In the opinion of some of those knowledgeable about Australian tennis, Nancye Wynne (Bolton) might have become the world's leading woman player if she had been nurtured with overseas experience earlier in her career, but the interruption of the war years and the death of her husband on active air-crew service in Europe combined with the lack of opportunity for women players to prevent it.[17]

The challenges issued by women players to male decision-makers at the top level — indeed at all levels — of Australian tennis had been a steady necessity since the game's inception. It became more forthright and public in the 1950s, but became more intense again after the advent of professionalism. In 1956 Mary Carter (Reitano) and Daphne Seeney objected to being moved from centre court at Milton, Brisbane, during the progress of their Australian championships semi-final to make way for a men's match, and went on strike by locking themselves in the dressing room until a compromise was reached. Again in 1961 women players locked themselves in the Kooyong dressing rooms until granted a more equitable share of the centre court for their matches.[18] Margaret Smith (Court) protested vehemently at the inadequate conditions provided for the women's teams on tour under the management of Nell Hopman in the early 1960s,[19] and other players also complained of the inadequate living expenses paid by the Lawn Tennis Association of Australia for women players living in London for the weeks of the Queen's Club tournament and Wimbledon. It was not until 1963 that an international competition for women (the Federation Cup) to rival that of the Davis Cup for men was established, partly due to the efforts of Nell Hopman. The third year's round of Federation Cup matches were held at Kooyong, Melbourne, bringing teams from all over the world.

In 1970 the Australians Kerry Melville (Reid) and Judy Tegart (Dalton), playing as professionals, joined six other international players including Billie-Jean King and Julie Heldman to boycott the Pacific South-West tournament promoted by Jack Kramer, for which the women's prize money was little more than half that for the men.[20] With the aid of Gladys Heldman, editor of *World Tennis*, the women players went on to establish the first tournament for women on the professional circuit — the Virginia Slims tournament.[21] In Australia, the first tournament to offer equal prize money for women players was the South Australian Open in 1973. In 1974 the Australian Women's Tennis Association (AWTA) was founded. It conducted its first sponsored women's tournament in Sydney. In 1990 the AWTA became the Australian Federation Cup Foundation.

By 1982 the venue of the Australian Open championships was firmly established at Kooyong and the Australian women's championships were re-integrated with those of the men to meet the standards set by the International Lawn Tennis Federation for a Grand Slam event. In 1983 the total prize money for the Australian Open exceeded one million dollars for the first time, and planning began for a new tennis centre in Melbourne that would host it as part of the Grand Slam. Since the opening of the National Tennis Centre in 1988, the Australian Open has drawn the best women and men players of the world to Australia in January each year.

Where does tennis stand now as a sport in comparison with earlier decades? Melbourne still perhaps holds an edge in the concentration of the administration and staging of Australian tennis, but in some ways that is a hollow claim in the final decade of the century, when Australian tennis is so closely integrated with the international circuit.

It is probable that in the 1990s in Australia, a greater proportion of tennis's devotees than in earlier decades actually play the game at one level or another as well as watch it, although

The National Tennis Centre at Flinders Park, Melbourne, has been the home of the Australian Open championship since 1988. (Photograph by Graeme Kinross-Smith.)

this is not necessarily the case in other countries where availability of courts is low. Tennis world-wide continues its rise in popularity. In this — as in other aspects of the game such as its organisation and policing, prize money, the Davis Cup commitment of professionals, the nature of galleries, the public image of players — technology has played an important part and binds Australian tennis more firmly than ever to overseas trends. The distinctive image of Australian players that was possible in the 1950s, 1960s and 1970s has been blurred by the sheer plethora of events on the professional circuit, and by the homogenisation of the sport brought about by the availability of rapid travel, large purses, computerisation and the role played by the media and, in particular, television. The passionate interest shown across the nation in the radio descriptions of the 1953 Davis Cup match between Lew Hoad and Tony Trabert at Kooyong is unlikely to occur in the televised and computer-ranked 1990s — tennis is no longer so closely linked to the national psyche.

Technology's first contribution to lawn tennis was, as we have noted, the India-rubber ball that made the game possible. Later came the possibility of air travel, enabling Australian players to avoid the long sea voyages to the metropoles of the sport in the northern hemisphere. As Jack Hawkes has said of his overseas travel in the 1920s: 'Even to reach America for the

Davis Cup matches meant nearly a month aboard ship. We didn't train very seriously. We arrived pretty flabby and then relied on the American tournaments before the Cup ties to get physically fit again.'[22]

Meanwhile, racquet construction had followed a steady improvement in materials and strength, and court surfaces other than asphalt, ant-bed, grass and gravel became possible, particularly in the capitals. Air travel facilitated the early professional tours, and although tennis players had always been aware of playing to the gallery, these tours were the beginning of tennis as show business, a trend taken up and refined when tennis became a television sport, and therefore a sport inextricably bound to advertising. In the 1990s, the timing of end changes in matches is geared to the time taken to show television commercials, and top players earn much of their money from endorsements of products that might be represented by a logo glimpsed in the heat of action on television or that are advertised in print or television by the player's face or name. Today, technology's development of the powerful, wide-bodied racquet has prompted discussion of changes to the rules to accommodate the added advantage it gives the server, and there is experimentation with electronic means of determining when those bullet-like services are faults.

The welter of events with prize money today and the competition for those prizes means that gym work and the use of sports psychology and specialised coaching are standard for top players. National training for promising juniors is partly institutionalised through such bodies as the Australian Sports Commission, Tennis Australia and the Australian Institute of Sport and partly sponsored by companies whose image in association with tennis can boost sales. In the debate about our perceived need to create a player in the top fifty of the Association of Tennis Professionals computer rankings lurk the old yearnings for something equivalent to the Hopman era of the 1950s and 1960s — and the same complaints of inequity in favour of males in apportioning of funds, coaching assistance, assistance with travel, and in the ratios of male and female in administrative and coaching positions emerge again.[23]

In all this increase in monetary rewards, speed, variety of event, televising of matches and upgrading through technology of equipment, the nature of the tennis gallery in Australia has changed, as it has world-wide. Watchers, especially those who are non-players, are more partisan today in a sport that once prided itself on non-partisan applause. Players and umpires

Pat Cash, the last Australian to win a Wimbledon singles championship (in 1987) is pictured playing in the 1991 Kooyong CML Classic with his doubles partner, John Fitzgerald. (Photograph by Graeme Kinross-Smith.)

tolerate it for the benefits to the sport and to the coffers of sponsors, tournament organisers, television channels and individuals in a game in which since 1973 in Australia we have seen the advent of corporate boxes at court side, in which business and professional employees wine and dine, while watching a game that often they do not understand in any depth.

Much of this is endemic to tennis world-wide and is not specific to Australia, and is preoccupied with winning, with success. But if we look into the picture that represents the midpoint of the experience of tennis to Australians in the mid-1990s — those local suburban courts on weekends and in the evenings, with the traffic flowing past scarcely out of hearing but almost out of mind, and four kids just about to become teenagers (one of them is named Milisovic and another Tan Toh Lim) vying on one court while two middle-aged couples battle it out in a mixed doubles on the other — it seems that the game is accessible these days to people from a greater range of socio-economic circumstances and cultural backgrounds than ever before. They play as release, as experiment, as laughing competition. And yet, from the way Milisovic is pounding down those double faults, we could swear that he has been watching television and that he is trying to be a young man called Ivanisevic.

9   Netball

Ian F. Jobling

It is not everyone that can avail themselves of the advantages and pleasures of the many games, few of them are of such a nature that women and children can participate.

W. F. Morrison, *Aldine history of South Australia* (1890)

Men and women go their own ways, but men get the best of the bargains because they have more ways to go.

Donald Horne, *The lucky country* (1965)

Girls will know that they can play their own sports, and often excel in them, but that generally women's sports — as with all recreational activities — are denied the status accorded to men's.

Anne Summers, *Damned whores and God's police: the colonization of women in Australia* (1975)

NETBALL[1] IS a relatively modern sport, a derivation of the basketball game devised by James Naismith. It was called 'basketball' because the aim of the game was to place a soccer ball into either of the two peach baskets Naismith nailed up in his Springfield, Massachusetts gymnasium, and it arrived in Britain in 1895 when Dr Toll, an American, visited Martina Bergman-Osterberg's Physical Training College at Hampstead. Since there were no printed rules, the game was passed on by word of mouth. In this early indoor version, there were no lines, circles or boundaries on the court and the goals were two waste-paper baskets attached to walls at each end of the hall; as the walls formed the boundaries to the court, the ball was never out of play. In 1897 an American woman visited the college, by then relocated to Dartford, and taught the game as then played by women in America. Metal rings were now used instead of baskets, there was a larger ball and the court was divided into three sections. The game was also played outdoors on grass and by 1899 the Spalding rules for women had been adopted. After completing their studies at the college, many women teachers took the game to schools, so the need for uniform rules became imperative. The Ling Association (now known as the Physical Education Association of Great Britain and Northern Ireland) had been founded in 1899, and in 1901 this association established a sub-committee to revise and publish the first rules. The goal rings were reduced to their present size (fifteen inches or 380 mm in diameter) with nets added, and posts raised to their present height of ten feet (3.05 metres). The name of the English game was changed to netball at that time because baskets had been replaced by rings and nets.[2] *The game of netball and how to play it*, written by B.H. Grieve and published by the Ling Association, produced the flexible rules which would later create considerable difficulty in spreading netball nationally and internationally.[3]

The early history of netball in Australia is poorly documented. It was played in primary and secondary schools at the beginning of the twentieth century and was most likely introduced by teachers from England. Hyland has stated: 'In Victoria it is on record that an Inter-School seven-a-side basket ball competition was conducted in Victorian Primary Schools in 1913. The game was played in Secondary Schools too, and in 1915, two male teachers are said to have put rules on paper for State Schools.' All over Australia, netball flourished in the schoolyards.[4]

In 1920 there was a sports ground which included outdoor courts at the Young Women's Christian Association (YWCA) Hostel in the Melbourne suburb of Richmond, and teams representing YWCA clubs played there.[5] Girls' clubs and churches played against each other and in 1922 Louise Mills

Aboriginal girls playing 'basketball' in the Moree District, 1963. This photograph was taken during the Chief Secretary's Department's tour of south and western New South Wales, on behalf of the Aborigines Welfare Board. (Government Printing Office, State Library of New South Wales.)

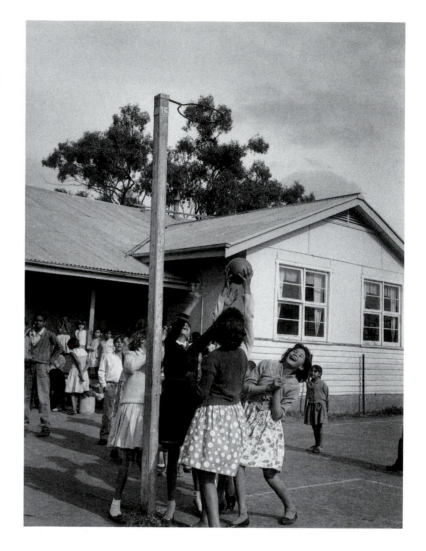

and Nonie Hardie, both of the YWCA, called a meeting for those interested in playing competitively. The outcome was the Melbourne Girls' Basket Ball Association with five affiliated clubs. Competition games commenced in May 1923 with six teams and by the following year there were twelve teams in the Association.[6]

Well before the formation of the All-Australia Women's Basket Ball Association (AAWBBA) in 1927 there were active city, regional and state associations. Nine-a-side basketball was played in Queensland from 1920 until the late 1930s under the auspices of the Queensland Ladies' Basket Ball Association (QLBBA).[7] During the 1929–30 season there was a breakaway from the QLBBA — the Queensland Women's Basket Ball Association (QWBBA) formed to introduce seven-a-side basketball. At Ithaca State School in Brisbane, the game was played on a rough, sloping playground with white ground markings. At one end the goal was on a post, at the other it was attached to a very large ironbark tree. There were lots of washouts and gutters in the ground, so at the ironbark tree end, the goal 'got higher and higher' after any rain.[8] The Ithaca State School Basket Ball team wore white blouses and school ties, navy bandannas with the school form embroidered on the front, navy-blue bloomers, black stockings, and white sand-shoes. It was the teaching and coaching given to young players in primary and secondary schools throughout the nation that helped produce the skills and enthusiasm to continue playing netball after leaving school, thereby forming the nucleus of the community clubs and associations.

The first interstate match occurred when a team representing the Melbourne Girls' Basket Ball Association travelled to Sydney in 1926. This led to the formation in 1927 of the All-Australia Women's Basket Ball Association (AAWBBA). Foundation members of the Association were New South Wales (City Girls' Amateur Sports Association — changed in 1929 to the New South Wales Women's Basket Ball Association), Queensland (Australian Ladies' Basket Ball Association — changed in 1931 to the Queensland Women's Basket Ball Association), South Australia (the South Australian Women's Basket Ball Association), Victoria (Melbourne Girls' Basket Ball Association — changed in 1928 to the Victorian Women's Basket Ball Association) and Western Australia (Basket Ball Association of Perth — later changed to the Western Australian Women's Basket Ball Association).[9]

The AAWBBA held its first tournament in 1928. Its constitution and rules and details of the basketball rules appeared in the minutes of the AAWBBA meeting of 1927 and May 22, 1928, respectively. The programme of the first AAWBBA competition in Melbourne from September 1–8, 1928 is worthy of note because the social aspects of the competition were as important as the actual games.[10] The report of the AAWBBA in 1929 noted that all states had been represented at the carnival and that 'one of the most important factors about the Association is that it is helping to bring about uniformity, which is very desirable, as regards Basket Ball rules, and we hope that the date is not far distant when we can welcome Tasmania as one of our affiliated States'.[11] A request that Victoria and Tasmania 'be asked to come into line with the other States and call themselves WBBA' was recorded in the minutes of the fourth annual general meeting in 1931,[12] but it was not until 1933 that Tasmania participated in the interstate carnivals.

Some of the media comments, attitudes and platitudes during the early years of the AAWBBA interstate carnivals highlight the significance of this game for women. The following extracts, appearing under the headline 'Women out of doors' by Beetec, are from the Adelaide press during the 1933 Adelaide carnival:

> When James Naismith invented the game of basketball 42 years ago ... he little dreamed that ... it would come to be one of the most popular sports for girls. It has a cosmopolitan interest in that the players are to be found among both industrial workers and academic students ... Each day there has been a barracking partisanship from spectators at the court ropes ... It is a tribute to the girls that they play the game with sufficient skill and seriousness to attract men and women of all ages to their matches ... As in all team games, character building is an important feature born of important requirements. In basketball, coolness and self-control, endurance and accuracy, quickness of movement, and strong, immediate judgment, are the first essentials. Quick turns and eager anticipation are necessary ... accurate judgment and coolness are required ... Although there are many tumbles and bumps, there is not the slightest element of roughness; unintentionally, there may be a foul.[13]

In 1934 the AAWBBA carnival was held at New Farm Park in Brisbane. The teams arrived by the Kyogle Mail and gathered for a civic reception given by the lady mayoress and broadcast by radio 4BC. The media were most supportive, captains of each state team were interviewed on 4BC on the morning of the first day of play and several matches were broadcast.[14]

In Sydney, the City Girls' Amateur Sports Association was actively associated with netball as were banks, shops, offices and industrial establishments. A newspaper article reported: 'The basket ball season has now come to a close, after a successful season, in which forty-three clubs competed in four grade competitions .... We feel that the standard of our play has greatly improved this year, due to the fact that several weeks of compulsory coaching was held on Wednesday evenings at Rushcutters' Bay Oval (electrically lit) and regular practices were offered throughout the winter nights on Mick Simmons' roof'.[15]

An interesting commentary about clothing was recorded, with an accompanying photograph, during the 1929–30 Queensland Ladies' Basket Ball Association nine-a-side season:

> There is a likelihood that the Basket Ball Association may be troubled with a variation of the 'shorts' problem which caused a stir in athletic circles last year. The athletic shorts were considered to be too short but length does not constitute the objection to the Romantique team's nether garments. It is the tightness of the shorts which is causing uneasiness. Quite apart from the daring appearance of the players, there is a feeling that one day the strain will be too much, and, as on the football field, players may be asked to 'gather round' while a necessary change, perhaps, repair, is effected.[16]

From the earliest days of the AAWBBA, a prime objective was 'to organise interstate and international matches'.[17] The association approached both England and the United States in 1932 to establish international basketball links. These efforts were unsuccessful. Contact was made with New Zealand in 1935 and Australia's earliest international matches were with that country.[18] There were no standardised international rules, several countries played different games or variations of the same game. Within Australia there were varying forms of 'netball' played — there were even rival associations to the state bodies of the AAWBBA.[19]

A significant move, establishing international links, occurred in 1937 when Edith Hull, the president of the AAWBBA, visited New Zealand following the cancellation of the Australian interstate carnival after an outbreak of infantile paralysis (polio).[20] She went to New Zealand to investigate that country's game and to invite a representative New Zealand squad to attend the 1938 AAWBBA interstate carnival. It was hoped that this would 'lead to the adoption by New Zealand of the Australian seven-a-side game and a regular interchange of visits.'[21] But the New Zealanders were not to be dominated by the netballers from across the Tasman. Their initial reaction was to refuse the invitation to the tournament because it coincided with their own. They rejected the idea of adopting the Australian game completely, but were more amenable to compromise on the rules. Hull was informed that if agreement was not reached by the end of 1938 the New Zealand association would not pursue the matter further.[22] Facing this resistance, Hull stepped outside her allotted representative powers and became more conciliatory. Australian netballers should appreciate Hull's handling of this situation because it helped establish international netball in Australia. At the next meeting of the New Zealand Basket Ball Association the invitation from the AAWBBA to attend the 1938 tournament was accepted. 'It was not a matter of which game they preferred but which would be in the best interests in the long run for International Basketball.'[23]

The New Zealanders imposed some conditions: that Australians be given a demonstration of the New Zealand nine-a-side game, that the touring party be increased from twelve to fifteen and that an agreement on uniform rules be negotiated for internationals and be 'as near as possible to the English rules'.[24] Edith Hull believed that by the end of her visit she had convinced New Zealanders about the advantages of the seven-a-side game. One problem she saw was in the method of starting and re-starting a game. The Australian game used a centre bounce considered potentially dangerous by New Zealand administrators. The nine-a-side version used a centre pass — a coin toss determining which team started — and from then on the centre pass was taken by the team which had the goal scored against them.

The differences in rules helped evolve two distinct styles of play. An obvious one was the 'guarding' rule in the New Zealand game where the defending player was allowed to spoil an attacker's pass by jumping in a vertical plane extending the arms sideways or upwards without actually making physical contact. This meant that New Zealand passing differed from the Australian style because it required two-handed passes from behind the head or from the chest. In fact, the New Zealand style of goal shooting was also two-handed from behind the head.[25] The Australian style of throwing tended to be one-handed from the shoulder.[26] Hull noticed that New Zealand players passed the ball quickly with the ball rarely held for any length of time by any one player.[27] Perhaps this was because of the rule which allowed them up to two bounces of the ball, with no bounce being used to gain territory. Other minor rule differences had to be negotiated for the forthcoming tour, such as re-shooting for a goal if the first attempt was unsuccessful.

The New Zealand team arrived in Australia in 1938 primarily to participate in the interstate tournament in Melbourne. The team also played an all-Australian team on August 20 — Australia's first international match. The final score (Australia forty to New Zealand eleven) was not indicative of the closeness of the match nor of the 'splendid teamwork' displayed by the New Zealanders. A press report stated: 'Time and again the New Zealand team's system outwitted the Australian players but faulty goaling lost it chances of victory'.[28] The *Sporting Globe* of 20 August 1938 concluded: 'Brilliant play by Australia's defenders, Merle Leabon and Jean Wood kept New Zealand subdued in the early stages of the Women's International Basketball match at Royal Park today. With a lead of fourteen goals at half-time Australia went on to win forty-eleven.' The New Zealand game utilised a larger goal ring placed directly adjacent to the pole rather than six inches from it as in Australia, which might account for the inaccurate shooting in this match. The New Zealanders also had problems with the 'foot rule'.[29]

Rule modifications were trialled in the Australia–New Zealand match and in a practice match between Victoria and Tasmania.[30] In all other matches New Zealand played according to the seven-a-side rules, apart from the 'demonstration' nine-a-side match which was one of the conditions of the tour. The international rules drawn up were a mixture of the New Zealand, Australian and English codes.[31] New Zealand made major sacrifices by allowing the reduction of team members from nine to seven and also the elimination of guarding, which suggests they were eager to establish an international code.[32] The major differences between the international rules and the Australian code were:

(a) commencement of game by pass instead of centre bounce, then alternate pass throughout the game
(b) difference in size of court
(c) tightening up of body-foul rule to eliminate all personal contact
(d) throw-up instead of a bounce for a 'tie-ball'
(e) time limit of five seconds for goal shooting
(f) a more liberal interpretation of the progression rule
(g) players to stand anywhere within their own playing areas
(h) elimination of 'off the court' play (outside boundaries)
(i) opponent of player taking a penalty pass may not take part in the game until the ball is touched by another player.[33]

The 'new rules' were accepted by the AAWBBA and the various state associations were urged to adopt them.

The AAWBBA proposed that an international body be established comprising delegates from Australia, England and New Zealand to control international netball. A constitution for the International Women's Basket Ball Council, with aims to further international basket ball and standardise the rules,[34] was submitted by the AAWBBA in 1939. This council was to consist of two delegates from each affiliated national association, business to be conducted by mail. The tour by New Zealand generated much enthusiasm in Australia for further international competition. A reciprocal tour to New Zealand in 1940 was arranged, selected players to be responsible for their own expenses.[35] The team would be truly representative of the federation and, if possible, at least one player from each state would be in the team. The *Sydney Morning Herald* of 4 September 1939 named the players stating it was 'the first representative all Australia women's basketball team to tour New Zealand': B. Douglas-Ballen, L. M. Conchie, D. Middleton, J. Wood, M. Linton (Victoria); R. Good, M. Wester (South Australia); E. Metcalf (New South Wales); D. Basley (Western Australia); P. Ferricks (Queensland); N. Reardon (Tasmania); D. Rooney (Manager) and A. Clark (Umpire). Team members were to be more than good players, they were to be 'promoters' of the 'new outdoor basketball' as an international game! Players were required to pass an examination on the new rules prior to the tour. Additionally, 'the Council requires that you will take an active part in umpiring and general basketball matters in your state on your return'.[36] The proposed 1940 tour was as much dissemination of the international rules to the states as it was a sporting tour. However, the Second World War intervened, the tour was cancelled and there was no consideration of any international basketball for the next five years.

The strength of netball was assured, however, because it had taken hold at the grassroots and much of its post-war success sprang from this. In 1932, for example, the tiny Victorian town of Mitiamo saw its netball club formed with players enduring primitive facilities but enjoying great friendships. By 1989 Mitiamo had declined to thirty-six houses, post office, general store, hotel, hall, school, two churches, eighty people — and four netball teams.[37]

Regional women were attracted to a game which offered them a choice to socialise on their own (away from the men for whom they normally provided the catering at football matches), which was not greatly time-consuming, which had a supportive atmosphere for children (especially girls) and which, as a game, was 'quick, spectacular and exciting'.[38] Given these conditions, regional growth was assured.

The Second World War was a significant time for Australian women. Their contribution to economic, social and political life increased markedly given their involvement in the war effort. While the economic and political benefits may have been diluted in the immediate post-war era, women gained in collective self-confidence. In many respects this attitude can be seen in Australian netball. One example of self-confidence in the abilities of women was that male umpires were excluded by AAWBBA in 1947 'in the best interest of our game'.[39]

The role of men in the development of netball has always been a complex one. Many local associations gained impetus in their early days from men with influence. Brandon Collins, for example (after whom the Port Augusta netball complex is named), got caught up in netball when his daughters began to play in the early 1940s. He put old car seats in his earthmoving trucks, covered them with canopies and jolted teams throughout the Port Augusta region. Later he began the drive to provide better facilities.[40] Other men throughout Australia ended up as coaches, again drawn in by family involvement. In country areas netball and football teams often travelled together for away fixtures (often in the kind of rudimentary transport provided by Brandon Collins), and there is some evidence to suggest that the same awkwardness of gender relations that marked Australian society generally was present on these specific occasions.[41]

If women took increasing control as umpires, coaches and administrators however, the ironical impact of social change would catch up. In 1986 in Port Augusta the creation of a 'mixed' club was mooted, to create more of a family atmosphere, and in 1991 the international federation lifted the ban on male players so that the all-Australian body could report that full gender equity was present.[42] That was some way off in the late 1940s.

The All-Australia Women's Basket Ball Association declined an invitation to tour New Zealand in 1947, probably for financial reasons, but it did advise New Zealand that its team could attend the 1948 carnival.[43] Again, mostly the players themselves would finance the tour costs to New Zealand. The playing uniform comprised of a tunic, two shirt blouses, one pair of playing shoes and two pairs of briefs per player. With the exception of the tunics (purchased by the AAWBBA for future use) and the playing blouses (donated by Pelaco, the shirt manufacturers, possibly the first sponsorship of Australian netball), players were responsible for acquiring their own uniform. It is possible that stockings also had to be acquired because the New Zealand association originally required that players wear them on the court. However, the AAWBBA approached the NZBBA to allow the Australian team to wear 'sockettes', as was the practice in Australia, and photographs of the tour show the Australian players without stockings.[44] Players had to pay their own insurance coverage and medical examination costs. The AAWBBA's contribution was minimal — the purchase of the team ball and a minor part of the playing uniform. Accommodation was the responsibility of the NZWBBA and this was mostly through billeting.

Most players selected for the 1948 tour were from Victoria and South Australia, with five and three representatives respectively. The remaining four players were from each of the other state associations,[45] thereby upholding the policy of all-Australia teams comprising at least one representative from each state. This was consistent with the AAWBBA view that such international tours should ensure the greatest benefit to the game throughout Australia. It was also made obvious to the players that they were representing their country as they were instructed either to paint green and gold stripes on their luggage or to use green and gold straps.[46] All were to receive instruction in speech-making. At the presentation of the selected team, the president of the AAWBBA, Mrs Calvert 'drew attention to the excellent training for public life afforded by such tours and hoped the players would take a prominent part, not only in basketball matters but in community affairs on their return.'[47]

The touring party travelled by flying-boat from Sydney to Timaru where they played two matches against a combined South Canterbury, Temuka and Ashburton side. The match played in the morning under the Australian seven-a-side rules was won easily by the Australians, fifty-two goals to eight.[48] However, the match played in the afternoon under the New Zealand nine-a-side rules was won by the home team, twenty-nine goals to twenty-one. The Australians won the three 'test' matches against a representative New Zealand team under seven-a-side rules and all other matches played either under seven-a-side or nine-a-side rules.

The tour aroused considerable interest in New Zealand and crowds exceeded two thousand at some matches. The Australians' skill level and their novel play influenced their popularity. The mobility of the Australians surprised the New Zealanders as nine-a-side rules restricted player movement. In addition, the New Zealanders were not used to the three-second rule and often held onto the ball too long in the seven-a- side game, which meant that their passes were not nearly as quick as those of the Australian team. The Australians shot the ball at goal more accurately.[49] Both the AAWBBA and NZBBA considered the 1948 tour a success and the AAWBBA invited a New Zealand team to tour in 1951.[50] However, the tour did not eventuate and a proposed tour by New Zealand in 1955 was cancelled by the NZWBBA at 'the eleventh hour'[51] because the New Zealanders had decided to continue playing the nine-a-side code rather than the seven-a-side code worked out in 1938.[52]

There was now a new sense of urgency in establishing contacts with England. When news was received about the New Zealand cancellation of the 1955 tour, the AAWBBA secretary was directed to write to the All England Netball Association (AENA) to invite an English team to tour in 1956 or, failing that, to determine whether the English association would host a team from Australia.[53] The reply from AENA proposed that AAWBBA send a team to England in 1956 to play under AENA rules:

> We (AENA) too, feel it would be very good to have mutual matches but impossible for us to send a team to Australia as soon as 1956. But if some of your players could come here we will do our best to give them some matches, and entertain them in various parts of England.
> As you say, the rules of netball are not too much different from your BB rules and we probably could have a little time training your players so that matches could be played under AEA rules.[54]

The AAWBBA accepted eagerly. A team of ten players and two officials would be sent with a representative player from each state, provided a player was suitable for selection.[55] English netball was very different from the seven-a-side game played in Australia so the Australian team spent many hours on board ship learning the new game.[56] One of the differences was the increased amount of court movement allowed to players

'Basketball' teams march through the streets of Newcastle, New South Wales, during the Floral March, 5 September 1953. (Hood Collection, State Library of New South Wales.)

in the English game. As a result, the English game lasted only thirty minutes while Australian basketball went for an hour. One of the problems encountered by the Australian team was that it took them about half the game to 'get into stride'.[57] The tour was a long one, from the end of February to the end of May and, as was the case for the New Zealand tour eight years earlier, was expensive for the individual player. Each team member had to pay up to £350 to cover tour expenses,[58] roughly the equivalent of one year's wages for most players. Some had to resign from their jobs.

The British press reported how the Australians had learnt the 'new game' on the voyage. As one columnist stated: 'Netball possesses no Ashes — yet! But I can't help remembering that we once taught the Australians how to play another ball game. And look what they did with it!'[59]

Early in the tour the team was regarded as a curiosity by the media, an Australian representative team being sent to learn a new game. Some reporters possibly found it difficult to regard it a fully-fledged sporting tour (such as men's cricket and football tours from Australia which had been occurring for decades) and concentrated on the human interest angle. For example, one newspaper described the team as 'ten pretty girls in green blazers and berets' and reported social activities while in Ipswich: 'this afternoon, they played a team from Cowles at the Convent, ... and tonight they will visit the Ipswich Arts Theatre to see the "Dashing White Sergeant"'.[60] As the tour progressed and the Australian team demonstrated superiority at the game, this attitude altered accordingly. The outcome of matches on the tour was sixty-four wins and only three losses, and the media reflected surprise and a closer examination of the style of play which produced this success.

It is important to recall the grassroots growth and development which made such prominence and success possible. In Victorian country towns like Boort, during the 1940s and into the 1950s, games were still played on dirt which often turned into mud, local volunteers held the sport together at their own expense financially and timewise, and much of the objective was social spirit.[61]

Port Augusta provides an excellent example of this mass background.[62] In sheer numbers of teams alone the history is remarkable:

1942	3 teams	
1944	9 teams	
1952	18 teams	
1956	18 teams	200 players
1969	88 teams	800 players
1986	88 teams	1000 players

By 1986, one woman in four under the age of twenty-five in Port Augusta was playing netball on Saturday afternoons in the winter. Beyond the playing arena, netball was clearly a networking institution and also allowed for other social circumstances to be worked out. In 1960, for example, a team from Umeewarra won the C grade competition which, superficially, seems an unremarkable social event — the photograph, however, reveals an all-Aboriginal team whose players might well be regarded as the forerunners for Marcia Ella and Sharon Finnan who, thirty years or so later, would be prominent nationally. For many white women in the region, netball might well have provided one of the very few moments in which they would encounter Aborigines in a social sense.

As an offshoot about the debate on men's roles, too, netball opened other possibilities. In 1973 Port Augusta saw the creation of a Married Ladies Association with four teams in the inaugural Wednesday competition. Women's lives were accommodated in this game, but sometimes controlled, too — in 1984 Port Augusta enacted a new rule which required pregnant women to get a medical clearance three months into their term, to have the medical practitioner name a date at which they could play their last match before delivery, and to absolve the Association from any responsibility at any time during the pregnancy.

Meanwhile, the regional game continued to grow through such events as the Poinsettia Week Carnival which, in 1959, saw teams competing from Port Augusta, Whyalla, Mt Gambier, Alice Springs, Barossa and Light, Eastern Eyre Peninsula, Kimba, Iron Knob, Flinders, Woomera and Quorn. It was all a long way from the Dashing White Sergeant at the Ipswich Arts Centre, but it was what provided the growth of Australian netball.

At the time of the 1956 tour the AAWBBA was considering affiliating with the AENA and possibly even adopting netball rules for the sake of future international competition. Some players sought to practise umpiring while on tour.[63] However, Australians wanted to maintain an 'Australian game', so when the possibility of forming an international code arose the Australians responded willingly. Representatives from Australia, England, Wales, South Africa, New Zealand, the United States and Northern Ireland attended a 1957 conference in London to discuss a standard code of 'basketball' rules. At this international conference in 1957 an international federation of basketball and netball federations (IFNA) was formed. The first meeting was held in Ceylon in August, 1960, Gwen Benzie and Lorna McConchie were the Australian delegates. It was proposed that international netball tournaments be held every four years, the first to be held in either England or Adelaide in 1963.[64] It was the beginning of a new era for international netball. The first matches played under the new international rules were the Australia–New Zealand matches played throughout Australia in 1960. Three 'tests' were played, the Australian team emerging victorious, two to one.

All Australia netball teams have won six of the eight World Netball Championships held quadrennially since the inaugural competition in 1963. Australia beat New Zealand in the first IFNA World Tournament played at Chelsea, England with nine other countries competing (England, Ceylon, Jamaica, Northern Ireland, Scotland, South Africa, Trinidad-Tobago, Wales and West Indies). Subsequent host cities and winners of world tournaments were: 1967 Perth (New Zealand

— Australia was second); 1971 Kingston (Australia); 1975 Auckland (Australia); 1979 Port of Spain (Trinidad-Tobago — Australia was second); 1983 Singapore (Australia); 1987 Glasgow (Australia) and 1991 Sydney (Australia).

Much of the recent Australian success has been an outcome of the Super League Series which began with Esso as sponsors in 1985 and from the development of young players at the Australian Institute of Sport (AIS). Netball was a foundation sport at the AIS and former Australian player Wilma Shakespear was appointed inaugural head coach. The AIS programme in Canberra, along with more recent netball programmes at many state sports institutes, has provided Australia with competent young players with international experience. In the last decade there have been many international netball competitions in addition to the quadrennial world championships, including several test and tri-test series at both the under-twenty-one years and open levels. Since the advent of the AIS unit the age of players representing Australia has decreased from an average of twenty-six years to twenty-two years.

Netball is currently the largest participation game for girls and women in Australia. The total number of players registered with AANA is approximately 400 000: that number exceeds 750 000 when netballers playing with churches, social, business, school and tertiary institutions and the Combined Australian Netball Association (CANA) are included. 'Indoor netball' is a development of the last decade. The rules are basically the same, but because the game is played in special indoor centres the ball is never out-of-bounds because it bounces off nets placed around the courts. This modification increases 'court action' and eliminates the stop-start problem usually experienced in traditional netball. Mixed netball is another popular form which has enhanced the social nature of the game.

As with many sports played by women, sponsorship and publicity, especially by the electronic media, have been difficult to attract. There has been the usual circular problem: netball did not have the support of the media because it did not encourage a great number of spectators, especially males, and therefore sponsorship was meagre. However, this trend is

Ann Sargeant represented New South Wales and Australia for eleven consecutive years before retiring in 1988. She captained Australia for the final six years, during which time the team won three world championships. (*Manly Daily.*)

changing, especially following the recent introduction of national competitions. The high standard of play and presentation of matches has attracted a large number of spectators and television viewers.

Yet, the real success of netball as a sport in Australia rests with what it offers women as participants and administrators. In Australia women have continually challenged patriarchal structures, but they have not occupied positions of power or become stake-holders in Australian sport. As McKay has stated, sport has tended to reproduce hegemonic structures by keeping women 'in their place' through denying or restricting experiences which most men take for granted.[65] Netball is the antithesis of this. It has enabled girls and women to become both highly-skilled athletes and to manage and control their sport at local, state, national and international levels. Netball has retained and extended those many positive characteristics postulated in the first decade of this century: 'Like all organised games, Net-ball is essentially character building. The selfish player has little or no chance ... the rough player is penalised ... Good temper, pluck, determination, extreme agility of mind and body, are traits universally found among Net-ball players, and best of all perhaps, that inexpressibly happy attribute, *esprit de corps*.'[66]

10 Rowing and Sculling

Daryl Adair

The pair couldn't pull a cigar.

(Brisbane) *Chronicle*, 11 November 1894

The banks of the river were fairly well dotted with spectators of both sexes and of all ages, and the colors of the competing crews floated, and were waved from many points along the course.

Report on the inter-colonial eight-oar rowing championship, *Referee*, 3 December 1890

IN THE early 1800s impromptu rowing matches were contested on Sydney Harbour by the crews of visiting ships, and Tasmania's Derwent River hosted informal challenges between the crews of whaling boats and shore stations, who vied for the 'championship of the industry'.[1] Pride may have been at stake, but money often was as well.[2] The inauguration of regattas in 1827 suggested that rowing would also become popular as a sport conducted on a regular, more formal basis. These events began on the waters of the principal coastal cities, Hobart and Sydney, and by the late 1830s regattas were also being organised as part of annual festivities to celebrate European discovery and British settlement of the colonies.[3] Expressions of imperial loyalty became characteristic of early regattas: events were held to celebrate the British monarch's birthday, and when the Duke of Edinburgh visited Australia in

1867, a regatta was organised as part of Melbourne's welcoming reception.[4] Therefore, as with other sports imported from England, rowing began not only as a recreational activity, but as an aspect of civic ceremonial.

Sculling races also featured in aquatic contests from the 1830s. Amateur scullers competed for trophies or prize money, whether as part of organised rowing regattas,[5] or extempore match races.[6] At this time the term amateur did not infer an absence of pecuniary interest in sport, for competitors often competed for prizes or stakes, although these differed greatly in scale. In addition to the nominal offerings of essentially chivalrous amateur contests,[7] wager boat-racing was a popular pastime for sculling enthusiasts and backers alike, with large stake money and side bets a feature of match races in the mid nineteenth century.[8]

In the 1850s wager boat-racing was formalised in a new way with the inauguration of professional sculling championships in Australia.[9] Although extempore match races continued, there was also a title to be claimed. Scullers assumed the label 'professional' not simply because they competed for money, but as a consequence of their employment status. The best professional scullers were invariably sponsored by backers, which enabled them to be relatively free of the time and monetary constraints of regular employment, and thus they could concentrate on improving technique and physical endurance.[10] Australian scullers first competed in world professional sculling championships on the Thames in 1863,[11] and from 1877 to 1907 world title races, attended by tens of thousands of spectators, were regularly staged in Australia, and more specifically in New South Wales.[12] Winning was vital as backers put up large amounts of stake money in expectation of success and they also looked to make money from side bets.[13] With professional bagmen on river banks, the spectating public also had opportunities to risk cash and wagering was popular during championship races.

Crowds were also attracted to major sculling contests because of the unprecedented international successes of Australian professional scullers between 1876 and 1907, when seven Australians held the world title for twenty-two of those thirty-one years.

The sculling match in Sydney for the Championship of the World in 1877. Seven Australians held the world title between 1876 and 1907. (*Australasian Sketcher,* 4 August 1877, Mitchell Library, State Library of New South Wales.)

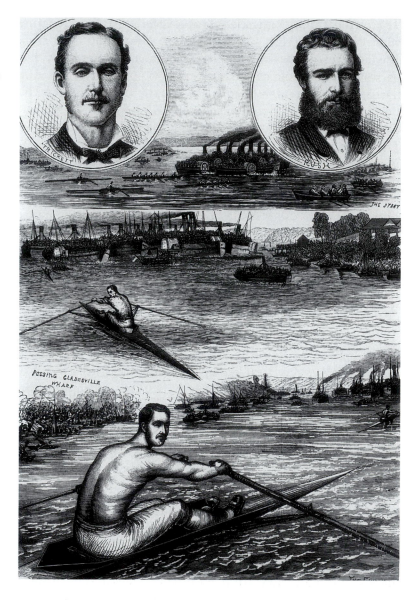

Others came because of the carnival atmosphere of the occasion, which involved brass bands, side-show entertainment, and food-and-drink stalls. It was a day out in an era of infrequently organised mass entertainment. Moreover, the presence of official dignitaries at championships, including mayors and aldermen, heightened the social and political importance of the occasion. These civic leaders typically booked a passage on a steamer to watch the race and they were joined by Sydney socialites parading the latest fashions.[14]

Victorious professional scullers were lauded publicly. Ned

Trickett became Australia's first sporting world champion when he defeated the English title-holder on the Thames in 1867. He returned to a triumphal welcome in Sydney and was paraded through the streets. As one newspaper put it, 'such a [large] crowd rarely, if ever, has been seen in Sydney'.[15] Bill Beach, who captured the world title in 1885 from the visiting Canadian champion, Edward Hanlan, was similarly revered. The Victorian Rowing Association invited the New South Wales sculler to appear in Melbourne, and when he trained on the Yarra 'thousands lined the banks to watch him'.[16] The greatest display of public adulation was offered to Henry Searle, who retained his world title on the Thames in 1889. But this time the crowds which gathered were in mourning, for the sculler had contracted typhoid while abroad and died upon his return to Australia. Searle's body was transferred from Melbourne to Sydney and the funeral cortège was solemnly observed by thousands of people along the train route. In Sydney an estimated 170 000 assembled to witness the funeral procession, which took two and a half hours to reach St Andrew's Cathedral.[17]

While professional scullers were often patriotically described as heroes of colony and nation, they were also committed to earning an income.[18] This was not simply a case of avarice, for a sculler's success could be temporary and, therefore, a monetary return needed to be maximised. The Canadian visitor Edward Hanlan was particularly entrepreneurial. He often received challenges from competitors but only agreed to race them if they were prepared to match the enormous stake he was prepared to risk. Hanlan also earned income as a showman. He gave exhibitions on rowing machines in theatres and town halls and, on the water, 'Hanlan Regattas' regularly attracted between three and ten thousand paying spectators. The Canadian performed various tricks for his audiences and concluded the spectacle 'by walking on the surface of the water with the aid of large galvanized iron coffin-shaped shoes, measuring 4 feet 6 inches'.[19] This was not simply mixing sport with business. Sculling *was* Hanlan's business.

In the early 1900s, Australian professional sculling declined as a mass spectacle. Part of the problem was that contests were held spasmodically. Other major spectator sports, notably horse-racing and cricket, were conducted on a regular basis, so attendance became a routine part of many people's lives. It was not only the fact that world-championship events were few and far between by the 1890s,[20] match races between New South

Wales professionals had declined in popularity. The *Referee* argued that a shift to mid-week competition was a principal cause of this and that huge crowds could be expected if races were again scheduled on Saturdays. The problem was that bookmakers were an integral part of professional rowing and on Saturdays they were being drawn to horse-racing.[21]

There were additional financial problems. Although promoters earned revenue from steamer passages, entry to enclosures and grandstand seating, many spectators were content to watch races from vantage points which required no payment.[22] Moreover, the 1890s Depression reduced the amount of money backers and promoters were prepared to risk,[23] and accusations of irregular conduct in contests did little to inspire the confidence of punters.[24] With less money from vendors and sponsors, the festive atmosphere of sculling championships began to decline. This carnival culture had, in the past, even managed to attract people with only a passing interest in the sport itself.[25] But, in addition to organisational and economic factors, interest in professional sculling also declined in the early 1900s because Australians no longer dominated world championships and title races were held in other countries from 1907 to 1919.[26] Although Australians held the title in the 1920s and 1930s, the sport never reached the heights of colonial years. Part of the problem again was distance. Bobby Pearce won the world championship in 1933, but was a resident of Canada and, although he held the title until 1943, he did not defend it in Australia. The last effort to restore interest in the professional game was in 1946, with the formation of the Parramatta River Sculling League. But support was lacklustre, 'and the League soon died'.[27]

The genesis of crew rowing in Australia lay in the organisation of regattas during the early years of settlement. Regattas remained central to competitive rowing in the mid-nineteenth century and they were typically social, as well as sporting occasions, as individuals of high community status, notably civic leaders and merchants, offered patronage and sponsorship of regattas.[28] However, these occasions were not, at this early stage, socially exclusive. As in England they involved vocational rowers, the watermen, who continued their workplace competition in sporting rivalries.[29] There were also races for amateurs, 'all comers' and young rowers. Novelty events were popular and a few programmes included races for Aborigines.[30] Regattas were characterised by a carnival atmosphere and they often drew large crowds of spectators. While many people only had a passing interest in aquatic sports, the events offered a day out, a good time to be had and an opportunity to rub shoulders with others or poke fun at them.[31]

Amateur rowing and sculling were formally organised from the 1860s through the formation of clubs. The origin of many of these clubs lay not only in enthusiasm for rowing, but in a common group interest outside of the sport. In late nineteenth-century Victoria, for example, the names of clubs such as Electric Telegraph Rowing Club, Mercantile Rowing Club, Harbour Trust Rowing Club and Banks Rowing Club reveal that members were drawn from these vocations.[32] Even the Victorian Early Closing Association, which achieved a free Saturday afternoon for workers at Melbourne drapers' shops in 1871, organised a rowing club, demonstrating that its members would make good use of extended leisure time. Other club names reflected region or community, such as the Ballarat, Rutherglen and Richmond rowing clubs.[33]

In their formative years amateur rowing clubs were diverse in character. This is illustrated by the membership philosophies of two very different clubs. On the one hand, the I Zingari Rowing Club, which began in 1882 in Adelaide, took its name from the socially-select amateur British cricket club and adopted similar policies of exclusion and hierarchy. The club was formed by a number of Adelaide's leading citizens and the Governor of South Australia became its patron for many years. The name of a proposed member was placed on the club notice-board and, after several weeks, members of the club committee were given an opportunity to apply the 'black ball' test. These were deliberate strategies to make the club a preserve for gentlemen of high social status.[34] On the other hand, the Leichhardt Rowing Club adopted a liberal view of membership. Henry Parkes, Premier of New South Wales, declared the club open on 24 September 1887, and announced: 'The club has been formed without any regard to the condition of life of those who become members of it — and, as the address presented to me expresses it, the manual labourer and the brainworker row side by side in the same boat. Well, that is exactly how it should be — not only on these bright waters but on shore.'[35]

This co-operative view of club rowing was stimulated by an association with the adjacent Balmain Working Men's Rowing Club which had assisted in the formation of Leichhardt. But, although the club was not intended to be an enclave of privilege like I Zingari, it nevertheless had the usual trappings of social respectability. The governor agreed to be chief patron, other honorary positions were accepted by the mayors of Leichhardt and Sydney and several council aldermen competed at club regattas.[36]

The newly formed rowing clubs comprised men who described themselves as amateur, thereby distinguishing themselves from professional competitors and watermen. But, in terms of monetary reward from rowing, it was a rather tenuous distinction, for many amateurs — whether manual labourers or gentlemen — competed for cash prizes. For example, the 1872 Anniversary Day Regatta in Hobart featured an 'inter-colonial gig race for bona fide amateurs with a prize of one-hundred pounds'. A similar contest followed in New South Wales for £130 first prize and there was considerable speculation about the outcome, both in terms of crews' ability and moneys wagered.[37]

While many amateurs as well as professionals had a pecuniary interest in rowing and sculling, distinctions between the two groups were essentially social. Professionals were invariably sponsored by backers, so they were paid to train. Also, as some of them were former watermen, they had developed their sporting skills while at work. In contrast, amateurs were essentially part-time rowers and their sport was clearly separated from their work. They might have competed for nominal or sizeable cash prizes, and even gambled on the outcome, but they relied on so-called 'natural' ability to win. The status of amateur was, however, complicated by the emergence of distinctions between bona fide amateurs and manual labour amateurs from the 1870s. Again the differences were social rather than financial. Both groups had traditionally competed for cash prizes as well as honour, but bona fide amateurs argued that manual labourers had an unfair competitive edge because their work enabled them to be physically fit. In contrast, bona fide amateurs were typically office workers or from the professions, so they were denied such opportunities.[38]

In the colonial period there was no national rowing association and the colonies adopted their own interpretations of amateur status. This was the cause of bitter conflict in several instances, the most notable between rowers representing New

South Wales and Victoria in the 1870s. When a highly fancied Sydney crew was beaten into third place behind the Melbourne and Ballarat clubs on the Yarra in 1873, a Sydney spokesman stressed that its crew 'contained bona fide amateurs only, whereas the Victorian crew, under Victorian rules, included several manual labourers'. This appeared an imbalanced contest, he suggested, for 'people confined in an office had no show against men who worked with their arms, or their hands, or in the sun all day'.[39] At a subsequent inter-colonial regatta organised by Sydney, amateurs who earned their living by manual labour were ineligible to compete. Victorian clubs, however, refused to send their crews and Sydney finally relented. The ill-feeling of this episode generated considerable publicity and a crowd of 15 000 spectators saw Sydney post a decisive victory, with 'news of the result . . . despatched to the city immediately by carrier pigeon'.[40] The Sydney gentlemen were triumphant as they proved they could still compete on even terms with blue-collar rowers. But they continued to push for a demarcation between bona fide and manual-labour amateurs and they had success. The New South Wales Rowing Association (NSWRA) was formed in 1878 and although it later allowed clubs such as Balmain and Leichhardt to accept manual labourers they were not allowed to contest races against bona fide amateurs.[41]

Several inter-colonial conferences during the 1880s and 1890s failed to bring about a uniform definition of amateur status. The NSWRA adopted an élitist position similar to England's Amateur Rowing Association (ARA) and argued that a separation of classes was desirable both on and off the water. But in 1892, after considerable pressure from the other colonies, the NSWRA agreed to accept that manual labourers who competed for 'honour and trophies', and not cash prizes, could be classified as bona fide amateurs.[42] The demise of the 'cash amateur' was accepted by all the colonies and this followed similar moves in England and the United States, where middle-class proponents of 'rational' recreation had fostered a utilitarian view of athleticism in the public schools.[43] Increasingly sport was promoted as an exercise to improve the mind as well as the body and it was to be played for its own sake rather than for monetary reward. Wagering, in particular, was seen as a shady practice which undermined values of fair play and chivalry. Consequently, it was no longer acceptable for gentlemen rowers to profit from their sport, whether through monetary prizes or wagering on the outcome.[44] In addition, manual-labour amateurs were expected to follow the notion that sport was not work and that only at work was money respectably earned. Watermen, though, were not regarded as manual-labour amateurs because they were employed for wages 'in or about boats'.[45]

Manual labourers were finally accepted as full amateurs in Australian rowing, with even the recalcitrant NSWRA agreeing to the reform in 1903.[46] But, as this position was not held by the ARA in England, it complicated Australian involvement in international rowing. Subsequently some Australian competitors were barred from competing in English championships.[47] Even the great sculler Bobby Pearce, who won a gold medal at the 1928 Olympics, was disqualified after winning the Henley Diamond Sculls in 1930 because he was a carpenter by trade. Ironically he returned the next year as a whisky salesman and won convincingly — and legitimately.[48] Amidst protracted debates from the late 1930s on, the English amateur definition eventually focused upon pecuniary considerations in rowing, rather than class prejudice.[49] Australian rowing was again more liberal than its English counterparts. In 1934 the clause barring men who worked in or about boats for wages was deleted.[50]

In accordance with their amateur ethos, rowing clubs and associations have been profit takers not profit makers, for their revenue was generated to improve club facilities and to hold regattas. Finances were raised principally through members' subscriptions, social evenings and the sale of liquor for members on premises.[51] Gate money from spectators was a less common form of income, as it was difficult to enclose river banks for such a purpose, though Albert Park lake proved to be suitable and in 1887 some 3000 spectators paid for admission to a reserved section around the lake and 'large numbers' occupied seats in the grandstand to witness the Victorian Rowing Association's inaugural Melbourne Regatta.[52]

Although competitors at inter-colonial regattas were not entitled as amateurs to earn money from their sport, the events themselves were subsidised by rowing associations and their members. For example, in preparing for an inter-colonial contest in 1890, the NSWRA reported that '[c]ontributions towards paying expenses are coming in very well . . . and the race is sure to be a financial and aquatic success'. The New South Wales rowers, while not expecting to take a share of any surplus revenue, nevertheless received other privileges. The New South Wales crew was 'quartered on the river for the last week of training', no doubt to enhance their preparation, but not at the rowers' expense. As amateur bodies, the rowing associations were not, however, always flush with money. The option of commercial sponsorship of events was complicated, as the amateur ideal emphasised that sport was distinct from business. But the Victorian Rowing Association (VRA) was unperturbed, accepting the 'Lorne Whisky Trophy' from the distillers Farrar Brothers in 1890. The *Referee* defended the decision, arguing, '[w]hatever objection there may be to the acceptance of advertising trophies . . . it will give a good race for oarsmen and so foster rowing'.[53]

Amateur rowing and sculling were principally fostered by colonial and imperial rivalries. Intercolonial competition began with four-oared events in 1863 and the amateur sculling championship of Australia was started in 1868. By 1878 an inter-colonial event for eights was introduced and went on to become the premier amateur contest.[54] This was particularly so after 1920 when the event became the prestigious King's Cup, a trophy awarded by George V in recognition of the victory by an Australian Imperial Force (AIF) eight at the Henley Peace Regatta in 1919.[55] Imperial links were also important in the popularisation of rowing and sculling in the leading Australian universities and public schools. Several of these recruited tutors and schoolmasters from England who were rowing enthusiasts.[56] The first inter-university race was held in 1870, but interest increased from 1896 with the presentation of the Universities' Cup to Australian colleges by 'old competitors in the Oxford-Cambridge Boat Race'.[57] The major nursery for rowing, however, has been the schools. The first Head of the River began in Victoria in 1868 and the English rowing ritual eventually became nationwide, with thousands of students cheering on their peers, a tradition that continues today.[58]

Imperial links in rowing were also apparent in the annual Henley-on-Yarra, beginning in 1904. It was developed by prominent Victorian rowing identities to be a showpiece for their sport and was intended to be a glamorous, ostentatious social occasion in the tradition of Henley-on-Thames. Consequently it was more formal than its colonial forebears, both in terms of participation and attendance. The trappings of the English carnival regatta were on display in the guise of houseboats, marquees, fireworks, illuminations and guests in formal attire. Even more derivative was that winning rowers received 'trophies made as facsimiles of the English originals, for races of the same name'.[59]

Although other Australian Henleys were organised, the

Henley-on-Yarra remained the premier social event on the rowing calendar.[60] Indeed, for many spectators the glamour of the occasion was central to their day, not the boats on the water, and one of the most popular Henley contests had nothing to do with athleticism. The title of 'Miss Henley', contested annually from 1933, was awarded to 'girls who were particularly attractive and well dressed'. This inspired eligible young ladies of sufficient means to adorn themselves in the latest fashions and to engage in a promenade which, although considered respectable, was nonetheless a source of titillation. During the war, however, the Henley-on-Yarra went into decline, and never fully recovered its carnival features in the 1950s. In 1955 it became part of the new Moomba festival, and although Miss Henley was crowned Queen of Moomba, the regatta and its social significance have since been subsumed by the popularity of Moomba itself. Indeed, the results of rowing races are now given little attention during the celebrations.[61]

In the colonial period, women were generally considered to be recreational rowers who steered boats for pleasure. Rowing began as a leisurely pursuit for ladies and, because women from prosperous families tended to have access to river craft, it was also a pastime which suggested privilege.[62] But some women began to take a different view of rowing, seeing it as an athletic pursuit rather than as a promenade, and these women chose to race each other in earnest.[63] They did not fit stereotypes of casual and genteel recreational behaviour, principally because they aimed to win. For these women rowers, competing had become an extension of participation, as it had for men. They were, nevertheless, expected to appear 'lady-like', as indicated by their rowing dress and demeanour. Rickards explains that: 'a women's crew consisted of six members, one girl being required to gather the long black skirts which covered great bloomers as each girl sat down into the boat, and then to be ready to quickly hand the skirts back before they stepped ashore after each race or training row'.[64]

An early example of competitive rowing by women occurred at the May 1901 Federation Regatta on Albert Park Lake, Victoria. The occasion celebrated the visit of the Duke and Duchess of York to Australia and, amid a variety of aquatic events for males, a sculling race for women was included. Miss Cassie Woolley of Victoria defeated her New South Wales rival Miss E. Messenger and the victor was presented with a ruby-and-pearl bracelet by the Royal visitors.[65] It soon became common for women to stage their own regattas and match races, such as on the Parramatta River in 1906, when ten crews contested a ladies' championship and a prize of twenty pounds. In the following year the Ladies' Sculling Championship of Australia began and, in addition to a title, the winner received twenty-five pounds.[66] Several rowing clubs and boatsheds for women were established before the First World War and interstate club challenges soon began.[67] Some women also competed against each other in professional sculling events and two professional clubs for ladies were formed in New South Wales from 1913; these survived some ten years.[68]

Some of the male clubs supported women's rowing by including races for the ladies' clubs on their regatta programmes. Leichhardt began doing this from 1914 and the 1920 regatta included a mixed fours event, which was open to ladies from the Western Suburbs and Sydney clubs, as well as the men from Leichhardt.[69] The inclusion of an interstate four-oared event for women at the 1920 King's Cup in Brisbane suggested that women's rowing had earned some respect from the men. This was symbolised by the presentation of a sterling silver trophy to the winning South Australian team. It was donated by the Licensed Victuallers Association of Queensland and, fittingly, it was in the shape of a woman dressed in rowing attire, holding an oar. In the same year the Australian Women's Rowing Council was formed and the Women's Four-Oared Championship of Australia became an annual event.[70]

But while women's rowing had made progress, in comparison with men's rowing it remained very much a poor relation. Women rowers were few in number and had limited access to rowing equipment and facilities compared with men, who had their own boats and clubhouses and did not allow female members. Still, there was some co-operation between women's and men's rowing clubs. Races organised by the Victorian Ladies' Rowing Association (VLRA) in the 1920s were contested in practice clinkers once used by men. Similarly, when the Essendon Ladies' Rowing Club began in 1923, '[t]he girls rowed in an old four-oared boat passed down by the Essendon men's club', and their clubhouse was a small shed lent to them by a Mr Fitzsimmons.[71] While the women may have been grateful for the offers of such equipment, these arrangements nevertheless reflected their subordinate status as rowers. But the Essendon ladies were resourceful, and in 1932 they built their own two-storeyed clubhouse at a cost of £380. It was important for ladies' clubs to become self-sufficient for they functioned independently of the men despite occasionally rowing on the same regatta programmes.

However, while events for ladies had been included in many male club regattas from 1914, the practice appears to have declined during the 1930s. This was largely a response to assertions of separate spheres of participation for males and females in organised sport generally. In school sport, games between boys and girls had been played on occasions but were generally phased out after the war. The mixed games had essentially been 'friendly' contests but, as organised competitive sport had become accepted in schools, girls and boys were separated. While the young ladies had tended to row 'gently' in the early days, they were increasingly oriented towards performance, and particularly winning, as goals of participation.[72] This transition had also occurred in club rowing. Although Young Women's Christian Association (YWCA) girls began rowing on Albert Park Lake from 1911, they 'did not encourage competition'. But in 1927 they joined the VLRA and participated in regattas. The YWCA nevertheless remained a conservative force in women's rowing. In 1929 the club lodged a complaint with the VLRA, objecting to 'girls racing in mixed combination with the men'. A consequence of the debate which followed was that increasingly, many women were confined to rowing in their club regattas, although it was expected that they could still participate in the various Henley carnivals.[73] However, the male rowing fraternity, which had once supported women's rowing, was increasingly indifferent, or even hostile, to the participation of female rowers in carnival regattas. For example, at the 1939 Henley-on-Yarra, the Victorian (Men's) Rowing Council enforced 'an "almost forgotten" rule that prevented women rowing on the same programme as men'. They defended their decision by pointing to the large number of events at the regatta which, they claimed, 'was enough to handle without additional women's races'.[74] This was an arbitrary decision which symbolised the inferior status accorded to women's rowing by men.

There were, however, further obstacles to women's competitive rowing. As the females practised on most days, not only to improve technique but to build up stamina, some critics produced articles in the press suggesting that rowing may be 'too strenuous', or even 'harmful', to women.[75] They were not only considering the physiological capacity of women to train and compete, they were arguing that rowing challenged prevailing norms of femininity and domesticity. The *Australian Women's Weekly*, although depicting state rowing crews in 1936 as 'strong but dainty', nevertheless described them as unusually tall and heavy: 'some of them ate steak three times a day, which is not surprising as they practised twice daily'.[76] The emphasis here was on the strong rather than the dainty. Moreover, as there was a significant time commitment required by these women, this was seen to compromise their domestic duties, particularly if they combined work as well. As Stell puts it, the upshot was that '[W]omen rowers faced a great deal more criticism than other sportswomen.'[77]

Despite opposition, Australian women's rowing had resilient characteristics. Unlike English women's rowing, where universities were the foundation of female competition, most Australian women rowed in clubs. Therefore, a greater diversity of women could be involved in Australian rowing, as they were not explicitly excluded on the basis of class or education. This is illustrated by the 1936 women's four-oared rowing championships, which involved women from an array of occupations — domestic service, factory work, clerical and retail.[78]

During the 1940s and 1950s, however, women's rowing stagnated. In New South Wales, for example, Sydney Ladies' was the only club to survive, struggling on with a tiny number of members. The war years had interrupted competition and clubs found it difficult to continue, both in terms of members and finance. Sydney remained the only New South Wales ladies' club until the mid-1950s, when the Leichhardt and Mosman ladies' clubs were formed. However, although the Leichhardt ladies rowed with success, they were unable to field a team in the 1960s. Similarly, in Victoria, only three women's clubs existed, including the YWCA which re-formed in 1965.[79]

There was, at that stage, no hint of a resurgence in women's rowing. But the Melbourne and Sydney clubs resumed interstate contests and Kath Bennett (née Suhr), one of the leading female rowers, claims that 'there was a great revival nationally in women's rowing' as a consequence of the staging of the Australian women's rowing titles on the Port River in Adelaide in 1968 and 1969.[80] Interest in rowing was also stimulated by competition against New Zealand women crews in 1966 and

185

1970, and there was talk that women's rowing might soon become an Olympic sport.[81] On the other hand, Bennett, who rowed for the Victorian YWCA club from 1965, recalled that in her early days 'women rowers were regarded as freaks by men'.[82] The Victorian Rowing Association had typically adopted a patronising attitude towards the women, whom they did not allow to compete at official regattas until 1970. But this concession proved to be a major turning point in the development of women's rowing, for women competed at the 1970 King's Cup regatta at Murray Bridge in South Australia: this was the first time since the 1920s that women crews competed at a national level on the same programme as men's rowing events. Women's events were also programmed at Henley regattas during the 1970s and some of the men's rowing clubs began to accept women as full members.[83]

Concurrently, women's regattas had become more popular and several new ladies' clubs were formed around Australia.[84] Women's rowing was also boosted by participation in world championships and at the Olympic and Commonwealth games from 1980 and 1986 respectively.[85] Several medal-winning performances in the 1980s suggested that Australian women rowers could be competitive at this level.[86] In the same period, women's and men's rowing associations around Australia were affiliated. Today, gender-specific inequities in participation, equipment and decision-making are less pronounced.[87] Thankfully, women rowers are no longer considered freaks. Indeed a few of them, such as Adair Ferguson, have become sporting celebrities.[88]

The sport of rowing has relied heavily upon the introduction of young people into school and club competition. Concurrently, rowing has needed veteran rowers to coach young enthusiasts. In addition to this advisory role, many veterans have not lost the urge to compete. But it was not until the 1970s that veteran racing was accepted into regattas on a regular basis.[89] The inauguration of the Australia Day Veterans' Regatta by the New South Wales Rowing Association in 1981 suggested that racing among older rowers was being taken more seriously. Part of the reason for this was that officially sanctioned veterans'

championships and masters games were being conducted overseas and, increasingly, Australians were becoming involved. Many of them subsequently brought home medals, which impressed their clubs and associations.[90] Veterans had become successful competitors in their own right.

Rowing has become popular among disabled athletes. The Australian Rowing Council, in accordance with international trends, has encouraged this and events for disabled rowers were scheduled as part of the King's Cup Regatta at Penrith, New South Wales in May 1988. Categories of competition were introduced to accommodate different types of impairment, whether paraplegia, spina bifida, amputee, and so on.[91] The sport has provided enjoyment and confidence to many participants. As one of them explained: 'Rowing has given me . . . the freedom to get out of my wheelchair and onto the river . . . and renewed vigour for more independence.'[92]

To some people, rowing is principally about having a good time and 'fun' regattas have become popular during the last twenty years. One of the most imaginative has been the Henley-on-Todd in Alice Springs. The event is staged on a dry river bed — deliberately so — for the Todd rarely flows. Crews 'run' the course inside makeshift craft and those who fall end up in the dirt rather than the drink, although there is plenty of that on offer. The Darwin Beer Can Regatta is similarly convivial but more scientific, for the boats (comprised of beer cans) need to float and remain intact during the race — otherwise the rowers end up as swimmers. A new sport in Australia is dragon-boat racing, involving crews of twenty paddlers, a drummer to keep time and a 'sweep' to steer the course. While spectators find the dragon-boat festivals a lot of fun, many of the crews are serious competitors. Indeed, Australia has been represented at international dragon festivals since 1980.[93] More conventionally, the Margaret River Regatta in Western Australia, introduced in 1976, has been described as a 'country picnic-style regatta', with brass bands, pony rides for kids, plenty of food and drink and — oh! some rowing! [94]

In regattas, events are contested over set distances. Unlike athletic meets there is no marathon event, so long-distance oarsmen and women have tended to compete separately from other rowers. The courses vary considerably in length, from as little as the ten-kilometre annual Canberra marathon, to the 275-kilometre River Run on the Murray in South Australia. In some cases a handicap system is used, so novices and experienced rowers are drawn closer together.[95] In addition to organised competition, some rowers have fancied breaking long-distance performances and several Australian rowers and scullers have since been recognised by the *Guinness Book of Records*.[96]

In the early colonial period, rowing matches were contested by crews with little training, in the development of either technique or stamina. But as rowing clubs and competitions were formalised, rowers practised more regularly. There was also more incentive to train because, with the presentation of an array of cups and prizes, the prestige associated with winning had risen. On the other hand, some rowers and scullers were already in athletic condition as a consequence of a life of physical labour, whether on land or water. This was true not only of manual-labour amateurs, but professional competitors as well.[97]

The sporting press regularly reported on the training of professional scullers and tips were offered about their chances in coming challenges. Significantly, a champion's loss was often ascribed to poor preparation or inappropriate diet. When Trickett was defeated by Hanlan for the world championship in 1880 he 'had gone through an agonizing weight reduction programme' to meet the challenger. Four years later, when Beach defeated Hanlan, *Melbourne Punch* explained the loss as a consequence of the Canadian's lavish training diet, which consisted of generous servings of 'roast mutton, roast turkey, plum pudding, champagne and porter'.[98]

In amateur ranks there was a more ambivalent attitude towards training. 'Pure' amateurs considered that rowing was, in essence, a contest of style and so-called 'natural' ability. Training to improve stamina contravened this urbane sporting ethos, reminiscent of the pastimes of English gentlemen.[99] But with the organisation of competitive school and club rowing, pride in performance necessitated practice. Increasingly, amateur rowers in both England and Australia saw winning, not simply participation, as an end in itself.[100] Consequently, many amateur rowers embraced a solid training regimen and coaching manuals on style and fitness became popular.[101] Nevertheless, amateurs remained critical of what they saw as 'contrived' means of athletic prowess, such as that of professional rowers, who were paid to practise, and manual labourers, who were physically fit to row because of their work.[102] All rowers who were serious about winning nevertheless had at least one further thing in common — an increasing awareness of the importance of physical condition to achieve success. Among these was the amateur Charles Donald, whose stamina was said to derive from 'strict training and total abstinence from liquor and smoking, a rule to which he ceaselessly adhered'.[103]

While athleticism and team sports were encouraged by many educators and religious leaders, particularly during the period 1880–1920,[104] there were also critics, who complained that fondness for sport had become obsessive. One critic observed that a youth was considered 'nothing if not a cricketer, a footballer, or a rowing man'.[105] Another argued that 'cricket and boat-pulling being the grand objects of all human effort . . . will ultimately yield . . . a population of idle youths without aim or object, incapable of any useful effort'.[106] Even the heroic reception given to the deceased Henry Searle was seen as cause for concern in the mind of one critic: 'what is the lesson conveyed to the Australian youth if not that the development of biceps, not brains, is most desirable, and that the achievements of Searle are more worthy of emulation than those of a Gordon or an Edison'.[107] But although sceptics of sport were sometimes vocal, in comparison with supporters of physical culture, they have been few and far between.

The incipient modernisation of rowing and sculling owed much to ongoing improvements in boating equipment and innovations in style. The early racing boats were clinker-built, wide and heavy, with a fixed seat. But leaner, lighter, and hence swifter craft were being designed for British competition during the 1830s and the outrigger and sliding seat soon followed.[108] A variety of innovations influenced builders in Australia and rowers who ignored them found themselves at a disadvantage.[109] As one rowing committee put it when considering the use of swivel rowlocks to replace fixed pins in 1924: 'we must progress with the world, and as the majority of rowing countries had adopted swivels, particularly at the last Olympiad, we should be ruled by such a decision'.[110]

There were also variations in rowing style. In the 1880s derivations of the English orthodox style emerged. Victorian rowers used a 'vigorous beginning', while New South Welshmen attempted 'to pull with the same even strength from beginning to the end of the stroke'.[111] But the most serious challenge to orthodox styles began during the early 1900s with the influence of Australian Steve Fairbairn as a rowing coach in England. The Fairbairn style, which emphasised 'a swing of

189

An indoor rowing machine designed and produced in Australia in the 1970s . This equipment was used by the Australian eight in training for the Munich Olympic Games. (Australian Information Service, National Library of Australia.)

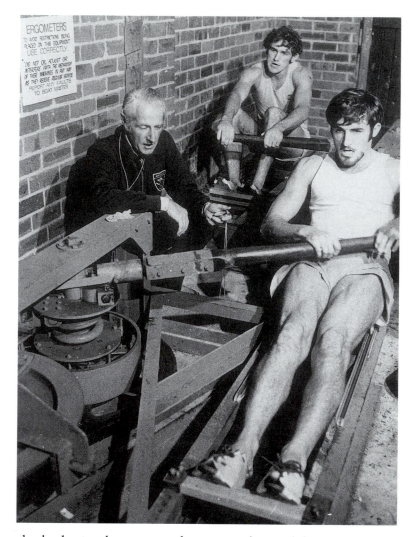

the body simultaneous with an even drive of the legs through the stroke', caused controversy among traditionalists, who advocated 'holding the body straight'.[112] By the early 1930s the 'Fairbairn' style had become popular in Australia, with few clubs persisting with 'the distinct shoulder lift'. But there were a variety of modifications to the new style and, in New South Wales, there were criticisms of 'a system of chaotic individualism in coaching', together with 'calls to return to the standard style of previous years'.[113]

During the last forty years, in particular, the sport of rowing has been influenced by scientific methods and technological advances. Photo-finish and video coverage of races has assisted judges to assess close finishes.[114] Training equipment has improved; for example, the indoor rowing machine — the ergometer — has been installed at many clubs.[115] Streamlined lycra rowing suits have made for minimal wind resistance, while retaining comfort.[116] A recent innovation has been electronic training and racing aids for coxswains and coxless shells; these display stroke rate, count and time.[117] Rowing coaches now draw upon scientific experts to advise on strength training, diet, gearing ratios and equipment for rowers.[118] Not surprisingly, therefore, the demands made upon today's top rowers are enormous. As Mike McKay, a member of the Oarsome Foursome rowing team put it, '[w]e are not professional by price-tag, but we certainly are by dedication and hours logged'. However, as the crew have all signed a contract with the sports promoter International Management Group, this suggests they anticipate an indirect return from success in their sport.[119] Also, a more routine form of financial assistance has come in the way of sponsorship. In 1985 rowing was accepted into the Australian Institute of Sport in Canberra and scholarships have since been awarded to several promising young rowers.[120]

As in sailing, experiments in boat design, construction and materials have yielded improvements in shell-weight, handling and aerodynamics.[121] A notable introduction was the winged keel, pioneered by an Australian company, Sargent and Burton, in 1984. As with their sailing counterparts quick success resulted, with winged-keel boats breaking world records.[122] Rowers of international standard have been particularly alert to the adoption of technical improvements to maximise performance. A good example of this was when the previously undefeated Oarsome Foursome suffered a loss to arch-rival the United States in 1992, which convinced them to change to American-designed cleaver blades. Using them in training the team concluded, 'we've been quicker than ever before', and went on to win gold at the Barcelona Olympics.[123]

Performance technology has become an integral part of international rowing competition. But it has detractors. When a company offered the Australian Rowing Council (ARC) the use of a 'drag-reduction film', the ARC was left with little choice but to purchase the material, because they expected that other leading rowing countries would do the same. But rowing's international governing body chose to ban the film because 'it is unfair to the poorer racing nations who already have a hard enough time purchasing decent equipment to be competitive'.[124] Subsequently, there have been calls to standardise boats. In the meantime, Australian Rowing reports, 'rowers are continually looking for ways to make their boats go faster and will try almost anything to be the first across the line'.[125] Within limits, of course, for some scientific innovations,

191

After the 'Oarsome Foursome's' Olympic victory in Barcelona, 1992. (Reuters International.)

such as performance-enhancing drugs, have been made illegal for rowers. To monitor this, the ARC introduced random testing of competitors from April 1988, with severe penalties for transgressions.[126]

Although many rowers and scullers have competed with different motives — whether fun, fame, money or national pride — they have had at least one thing in common, a passion for their sport. What could it have been like to pull oars in a dash to the finish line, with crowds cheering noisily? How tortuous or rewarding was the training that went into performance? And to the uninitiated, how did it feel to glide across the water through balanced self-propulsion? We get an insight into the love of rowing from an early member of Leichhardt Rowing Club, who with fondness recalled: 'We used to rattle home in the cool of the evening when the window panes of Balmain were all turned to gold by the setting sun, with a cool nor' easter chasing us from behind . . . Ye Gods! It was great!'[127]

11 Rugby

Murray G. Phillips

The soldiers of the Sydney barracks amused themselves with a game called football.

Sydney Monitor, 25 July 1829

The worst punishment that can befall a Rugby footballer is to be dismissed from the field but in Australia at least it does not carry the shame lawmakers intended.

Jack Pollard, *Australian rugby union* (1984)

WHILE IT was played in early colonial Australia, football was mentioned sparingly in social commentary. What emerges from the incomplete record is that football was not as popular as horse-racing or cricket, matches were often organised in conjunction with other activities or as part of holiday sports meetings and, as a consequence of the situation in England where there were numerous types of football, games were played by a variety of rules.[1] It was not until the second half of the nineteenth century that rugby, as a distinct form of football, emerged in Australia.

At least three clubs — University of Sydney (1863), Sydney (1865) and Wallaroo (1870) — have staked credible claims for having initiated rugby in Australia. The University of Sydney Club is often cited as playing rugby games against visiting British warships from 1863 but the latest research places more credence with the Sydney Football Club. It was formed by members of the Albert Cricket Club and the first recorded game was played on 17 June 1865 in Hyde Park.[2]

The origins debate highlights two important issues regarding early rugby in Australia. First, union emerged in Sydney not long after the unique features of the game — an oval ball, running with the ball in hand, H-shaped goals, scoring above the cross bar and points for tries and goals — had evolved in the second quarter of the nineteenth century at Rugby School in England.[3] Second, the early institutions provide an insight into the social make-up of the game. The Wallaroo Club, for example, largely comprised ex-students from Sydney's early private schools. Two of the founding members, the Arnold brothers, are illustrative. From a wealthy pastoralist family, Richard Arnold attended Rugby School in England in the 1860s while Montague Arnold placed advertisements in Sydney newspapers that resulted in the formation of the club.[4] In Sydney, rugby union was organised and played amongst men of the wealthier classes. The social pattern was no different in Queensland. When the game gained popularity there in the early 1880s, its organisers and participants were also from the upper echelons of society.[5]

The exclusiveness of rugby union in the early years was perpetuated by the private-school education system which was crucial in the development and diffusion of the game. The schools not only employed teachers from Britain who promoted the game as the premier winter sport, but in Sydney the schools played occasional matches against international teams, were an integral component of the senior club competition and school officials were instrumental in establishing the Southern Rugby Football Union (SRU) in 1874. Furthermore, after the students finished their education they continued the game learned at their schools. In the 1870s and 1880s, graduates of the private schools and Sydney University founded new rugby clubs in the city, while those who returned to rural properties established the game in country New South Wales areas including Orange, Bathurst, Mudgee, Goulburn, Maitland, New England and the districts that were later to form the Australian Capital Territory.[6] Union also found advocates in Victoria and Western Australia but encountered major resistance from Victorian (later Australian) rules football.

While new clubs were formed and the game spread from its narrow geographical base in Sydney it did not, as sociologists Dunning and Sheard have argued, exhibit many of the structural properties that characterise modern sport.[7] Early rugby in Australia displayed many traits attributed to folk games: high levels of socially tolerated violence that resulted in some clubs changing to Victorian or Australian rules football, informal social control as many games were played without referees, and regional variation of rules that required teams to agree on scoring systems and infringements before and during matches.[8]

These inconsistencies led to the formation of the Southern Rugby Football Union (SRU) (1874) and the adoption of the existing English rules. The SRU was formed only three years after the Rugby Football Union (RFU) in England in 1871 and preceded the unions of New Zealand, Wales, Ireland and South Africa.[9] The first rugby union administrative authority in Australia, like the RFU, was a turning point in the modernisation of the game. It provided a central focus for organisation and a set of rules that settled many aspects of play, made disputes easier to decide, reduced on-field violence with the abolition of 'hacking' — the deliberate kicking of an opponent's shins — and organised competitions played by the five founding clubs.

Following the formation of the SRU, and particularly in the last two decades of the nineteenth century, larger numbers of men and boys flocked to the game. In Sydney, while there were five clubs with one team each in 1874, twenty-five years later, there was a senior and four junior competitions — a total of seventy-nine clubs.[10] This growth necessitated the formation of a new administrative body in 1897, the Metropolitan Rugby Union (MRU), that was affiliated to the New South Wales Rugby Union (NSWRU — the SRU until 1892), to organise the game exclusively in Sydney.[11] The boom was matched in Queensland. In the season following the tour of Queensland to New South Wales in 1882 — this provided the impetus for union in the northern colony — there were two clubs; nine years later there were seventy-two in Brisbane.[12] The establishment of the Central Queensland Rugby Union in 1886 illustrated that union had spread quickly from the capital city to the provincial areas of Queensland.[13] Other colonies also played the code and there were humble beginnings in both Victoria and Western Australia in the 1880s.[14]

The game's following was promoted further by inter-colonial competitions that began in 1882 and by international tours which commenced two years later, but union did not become a mass spectator sport until the later years of the nineteenth century. In 1899, Australia witnessed the first official test against Great Britain, and victories by the national side as well as by the Queensland team over the tourists provided a great fillip. Shortly after, attendances at matches, although not as numerous as Australian rules football crowds in Melbourne, reached previously unattained levels. Sydney games attracted up to fifteen thousand spectators. Interest was further boosted in Sydney in 1900 by the replacement of the club system by a district system based on residential qualifications which ensured a more entertaining competition by preventing players gravitating to successful clubs.[15] Between 1902 and 1907, gate receipts from matches controlled by the MRU increased threefold from £1336 to £4078.[16] Also in 1907, the record crowd attendances set at cricket matches in the 1890s were rewritten when 52 000 — one-tenth of the population of Sydney — went to the Sydney Cricket Ground to watch New South Wales play New Zealand at rugby. While it was not directly competing with cricket, rugby union was challenging the summer game for the largest following in Sydney.[17]

The increased patronage of the game reflected its appeal to different levels of society. From union's beginnings in the middle- and upper-class educational institutions and clubs drawn from similar social groups, it diffused to the working class.[18] The mushrooming of clubs prior to the turn of the century had opened the game to a larger cross-section of the male community. Furthermore, in 1888 union was adopted in the state schools, the educational system available to those who could not afford the fees of the private schools.[19] The game's foothold in the education system and the growth in clubs for both seniors and juniors ensured participants from a variety of backgrounds.

While union's following was growing, it was also coming under increasing criticism. The NSWRU was castigated for its total reliance on English authorities for rules and regulations and its inability to make the game more appealing to spectators. Additional pressure was coming from the working class. The administration, which remained firmly in the control of the privileged classes,[20] displayed a very inflexible approach to the needs of a game which, through the process of downward social diffusion, catered for men from all walks of life. The major bone of contention, which resulted in a breakaway movement, was the financial hardship imposed on working-class participants. Players, if injured, incurred medical fees and lost working time and wages. For many people it was difficult to reconcile that the NSWRU was in the financial position to purchase the Epping Racecourse for £15 000 in 1907, yet withdrew its medical-aid assistance and transferred the responsibility for injured players to the clubs in the previous season.[21]

Several cases involving injured players inflamed the situation. The most prominent was Alec Burdon, a barber, who missed work for ten weeks as a result of an injury suffered in a representative game in 1907. He sought compensation for time lost and medical expenses but his request was rejected.[22] The treatment of Burdon was discussed by a group of men who met at the sports store of Australian cricketer, Victor Trumper. At the same time a tour by the All Golds, a professional New Zealand team, to play against the National Rugby Union (NRU) in England was announced.[23] The All Golds were also invited to play in Australia by those who met at Trumper's sports store, and the visit was the catalyst that stimulated a rebel football organisation.

Interested people met on 8 August 1907 at Bateman's Crystal Hotel, George Street, Sydney where it was resolved to form the New South Wales Rugby Football League (NSWRL). The key figures were H. C. Hoyle, a railway employee and future Labor Party politician, who was appointed president; J. J. Giltinan, whose occupations have been described as a draftsman, commercial traveller, salesman and a manufacturer's agent, was secretary and V. Trumper was treasurer.[24] In subsequent meetings, a team was picked to play the professional rugby players from New Zealand and a constitution was drafted in which the rules of the English NRU were accepted.[25] This constitution was not concerned with switching to a new code so much as adopting new rules to protect the financial security of players. The emphasis on the new code came later.

The organisers were keenly aware of the need to attract the best footballers from union to help launch the new game. Their target was H. H. 'Dally' Messenger, the most talented and well-known player of the period. He left the decision to his mother who, after a visit from Giltinan and Trumper, approved her son playing against the touring team.[26] There is some debate as to the date of this meeting but it is likely that Messenger's decision was made before he played his last union test on 10 August 1907.

The New Zealand All Golds played three games in Sydney

in August against a New South Wales team, referred to as the All Blues, under rugby-union rules as the NRU's constitution had not yet arrived in the country. Attendances were well below equivalent games in union but were enough to ensure financial success. Following the games in Sydney, Dally Messenger, the star player of the series, joined the All Gold team bound for England. This tour promoted Messenger as a world-class player and in Australia it helped focus public attention on rugby league.[27]

While Messenger was in England, the league game was taking shape in Australia. In Brisbane, the Queensland Rugby Association was formed on 28 March 1908 and organised matches against the returning All Golds.[28] In Sydney, eight clubs — Glebe, Newtown, South Sydney, Balmain, Eastern Suburbs, North Sydney, Western Suburbs and Newcastle — were formed. Cumberland joined later in the year and the first season started on 20 April 1908.[29] But even though league had begun in both states, union was still dominant as it drew larger crowds, more press coverage and had the choice of the best grounds.

At the end of the 1908 season the first Australian league team, known as the Kangaroos, toured Britain. The tour organised by Giltinan was a failure. More games were lost than won and poor crowds resulted in a financial disaster.[30] In contrast the union team, the Wallabies, touring England and Wales at the same time, won twenty-five of their thirty-one matches, beat England at Twickenham and won the Olympic gold medal. The Wallabies triumphantly travelled home first class; the bankrupted Kangaroos had their fares paid by the NRU.[31]

The news did not improve for the fledgling code when the Kangaroos arrived back in Australia. The game seemed more secure when official club competition began in Brisbane on 9 May 1909, but there was controversy in the New South Wales Rugby League. The original triumvirate of Hoyle, Giltinan and Trumper were removed from office as a result of allegations of financial mismanagement. Furthermore, spectator numbers were down at club matches and other fixtures.[32] The biggest crowd to attend the games of the returning Kangaroos was 2000; a similar Wallabies match attracted 22 000 spectators.[33] Rugby union was still the most popular code.

Then a scheme was devised that proved to be the turning point in the struggle between union and league. A series of games between the Kangaroos and many Wallabies who had been converted to play league was concocted by some members of the NSWRL and financed by J. J. Smith, an entrepreneur who later became Lord Mayor of Sydney and was well known through the journal bearing his name, *Smith's Weekly*.[34] The Wallabies were paid sums that ranged from fifty to two hundred pounds and were expelled from the amateur game. These games caused controversy within the Kangaroo team because the original league players received less money for their efforts than did the converts. Some league officials were also unhappy as it was considered unwise to give an entrepreneur control over the fixtures. The struggling code, however, undoubtedly benefited.[35]

With this new crop of talented players and the first tour of the English NRU, league attracted unprecedented interest in 1910. Even though the NSWRU planned interstate matches and a large international programme of games against the New Zealand All Blacks, a Maori team and a combined side from California and Stanford universities, the game's appeal was significantly reduced by the defections to league. The trend was evident early in the season as 16 000 watched a league club game at the Agricultural Ground, while nearby 12 000 watched the interstate union match at the Sydney Cricket Ground.[36] International matches reflected the same trend. The best crowd attracted to an international union game was 15 000 for the contest between the All Blacks and the Wallabies, while 39 000 went to watch the league game between the Australians and the English.[37] Rugby league had gained the ascendancy.

One major advantage of rugby league was that it was a superior spectacle. Union could be a slow, closed and stagnant game; league, following changes made in England around the turn of the century, was played with a reduced number of players, no lineouts and a more efficient clearing of the ball from the ruck. It provided better entertainment.

Union was in trouble. Money was lost on the heavy international programme and union authorities relinquished their tenure on the major grounds and sold Epping Racecourse in 1911.[38] At the same time, league continued to grow. In Sydney, the number of teams increased to a point where divisions were necessary in the lower grades, the best sporting venue — the Sydney Cricket Ground — was secured for matches and large crowds attended major games. Just as importantly, league was extending beyond its original bases in Sydney and Brisbane as it spread along the north-eastern coastline of Australia and into inland country areas. City versus country matches were inaugurated in New South Wales and inter-city contests commenced in Queensland. The game was further promoted in the country centres with touring teams playing matches outside the capital cities.[39] The decentralised nature of the game in Queensland was reflected in the number of country players in the state team: over half played their football outside Brisbane in Ipswich and Toowoomba.[40] In under a decade since its beginning, league had displaced union as the major winter spectator sport in New South Wales and Queensland.

The differences in the game symbolised the divergent social traits of the codes. Three interrelated issues — political affiliations, social class and sporting ethos — epitomised two games that increasingly catered for different social groups. Union was overloaded by conservative politicians from its inception.[41] In contrast, league had strong links with the political movement established to represent the working class, the Labor Party. The contributions of Labor politicians including H. V. Evatt, J. Fihelly, F. Flowers, H. C. Hoyle, J. Lamaro, J. Larcombe, E. R. Larkin, W. McKell, T. D. Mutch, E. W. O'Sullivan, R. E. Savage, J. J. Smith and J. C. Watson, to name but a few, were significant in the organisation of the game.[42] Since the 1950s the Labor Party, while still a supporter, has not been as directly involved in the game's management. The major exception to this trend was Senator Ron McAuliffe, a key figure in Queensland's league and an instigator of the very popular State of Origin matches started in 1980.[43]

The role of the Labor Party epitomised the working-class support for league. Early players, where it has been possible to identify them, were from the non-professional section of society. The occupations of the All Blues, the first league team in Australia, include 'four labourers, two painters, two carpenters, one storeman, one waterside worker, one boat builder, one "athlete" (later a fireman), one cleaner, one compositor, one clerk, one dealer (in fish), one boilermaker, one journalist, one draper, one tailor and two unknown'.[44] Furthermore, the game was established and thrived in working-class suburbs of Sydney and when these social groups moved from the inner suburbs to the west and south-west, clubs from areas like Parramatta, Canterbury-Bankstown and Penrith have succeeded. The rise

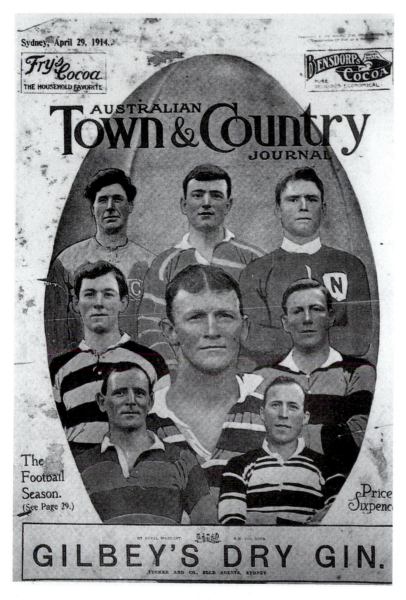

Sydney, April 29, 1914.

Fry's Cocoa
THE HOUSEHOLD FAVORITE.

BENSDORP'S COCOA
PURE DELICIOUS ECONOMICAL·

AUSTRALIAN
Town & Country
JOURNAL

The
Football
Season.
(See Page 29.)

Price
Sixpence

GILBEY'S DRY GIN.
TUCKER AND CO., SOLE AGENTS, SYDNEY.

In 1914 the New South Wales Rugby League conducted three competitions with eight Sydney metropolitan teams in first grade, fourteen in second and twenty in third. This is reflected in the cover of the *Australian Town and Country Journal*, 29 April 1914. (Collection of Ian Jobling.)

and fall of some clubs has been explained by the changing social composition of surrounding areas. According to one authority, the lack of success since 1922 of the North Sydney Club, one of the founding clubs of the NSWRL, has been attributed to the disintegration of the local working-class community. The district has become a middle-class commercial area and it is argued that there is a reduced talent pool of players available to the club.[45]

In contrast rugby union, while played by a wide spectrum of the population prior to the split, became increasingly dominated by the middle class. This was partly a result of the attraction of league to the working class, but also because of exclusionist practices adopted by union administrators. The initial response of the older and more powerful sporting organisation was to banish all players and officials involved in the new code. This aggressive and antagonistic response of the NSWRU was understandable because union was, without doubt, the more popular football code and by taking such a hard line with dissidents it hoped to deter further defections and to destroy the new sport. Amateurism was the issue of dissent. Rugby union officials, from privileged private-school backgrounds, believed that sport not only had physical benefits but promoted desirable moral, educational and social traits. Financial rewards corrupted the perceived benefits of sporting participation. This view was ratified in 1908 by the Amateur Sports Federation of New South Wales when, in response to the establishment of the league, it refined the laws of Australian amateurism: any pecuniary gain from sport would disqualify the athlete as an amateur. League, even though administrators worked on a voluntary basis and not all players were paid, was decried as a professional sport.[46]

The differences between the two games were highlighted during the First World War as Australia was divided by sectarian issues, industrial conflict and the vitriolic referenda campaigns. The controversial issue of the continuance of sport added to the social turmoil. Union authorities promoted the middle-class, Anglo-Protestant view of patriotism which did not include sporting competitions. Games alternated with military drill in 1915 and then the premiership programme was cancelled for the remainder of the war. Rugby league, aligned with the working-class, Irish-Catholic faction, adopted a more pragmatic aproach. In keeping with sports established on more professional lines such as Australian rules football, boxing and horse-racing, league continued its programme to assist recruiting and to contribute to patriotic funds by arranging special benefits. Interstate and international games ceased but the public, despite poor press coverage, turned out in large numbers to see club games in both states. Gate takings in Brisbane, for example, increased sixfold as many people showed the need for some relief from the tragedy of war.[47]

The respective decisions taken during the war had lasting effects in the following decade: union suffered; league boomed. The amateur game was re-started in Sydney in 1919 but there were few available venues, only a small number of competing clubs and no district competition.[48] In Brisbane the situation was worse as the Queensland Rugby Union was not re-formed until 1929 and several teams were forced to change codes.[49] League prospered as radio broadcasts started, a number of long-lasting competitions such as the Maher, Cowley and Bulimba cups were established, Australia won the rugby ashes for the first time on Australian soil and the Australian Board of Control was established on 4 December 1924 to manage international matches.[50]

One of the most far-reaching achievements for league after the First World War was the introduction of the game into the New South Wales state schools. It was adopted by Sydney's Marist Brothers Schools in 1913, through the efforts of the secretary of the NSWRL and future Labor member for Willoughby, E. R. Larkin, and seven years later other Catholic schools started playing the game — but union was the dominant code for schoolboys. The amateur code was played in primary and secondary state schools as well as in the majority of the private educational institutions. Under the direction of the Labor Minister for Public Instruction, T. D. Mutch, the New South Wales Public Schools Amateur Sports Association (PSASA) was instructed in 1920 to include league in the schools.[51] League finally had a nursery in the largest educational system in New South Wales and it quickly outstripped union. By 1930, there were 115 school league teams as opposed to forty union equivalents registered with the PSASA.[52] The dominance of league in state and many Catholic schools, and its exclusion from the private schooling system in both New South Wales and Queensland, have added further to the division of the games along class lines.

During the third decade of the twentieth century women began their playing association with rugby. Neither of the codes was a mainstream female sport because of the physiological and social-psychological myths that have limited women's participation in sport. Football threatened the twin tenets of fertility and feminity. Union historians do not record females playing the game, but women participated in league in the 1920s. There were some short-lived competitions in Sydney and in country areas of New South Wales, as well as a number of special events. Female football, however, was never considered as serious, important or meaningful as its male equivalent. Most female matches were organised sporadically and conducted specifically for fund-raising purposes rather than to exhibit sporting prowess.[53] The more obvious role of women was as spectators. Even though they were rarely mentioned in this capacity, special admission categories and early photographs confirm their presence in the crowds.

The token nature of female football participation continued in the Depression of the 1930s with several charity matches organised to benefit unemployed women. The hardships of the Depression, which began in the late 1920s and at their worst resulted in almost one-third of the work force unemployed,[54] had few adverse effects on the codes. After the Queensland Rugby Union was revived in 1929, interstate union games began again and an Australian team toured South Africa for the first time in 1933.[55] International league games continued throughout these economically troubled times and a record crowd for test matches of 70 204 crammed into the Sydney Cricket Ground to witness the 'Ashes' contest in 1931. Interstate matches were attracting between 30 000 and 50 000 spectators while South Sydney, the most successful club of the period, regularly had crowds of 20 000 spectators.[56] Support was not limited to Sydney. League prospered in Newcastle, known for its mining and steel industries and a strong working-class culture. Even though one of the largest employers, Broken Hill Proprietary Limited, retrenched half of its workers, which resulted in the description of Newcastle as a ghost town, the local competition experienced its best seasons in 1931 and 1932. It has been argued that 'as a close knit working-class community, Newcastle and its surrounding townships used sport as a social cement. It bound people together at a time when capitalism was rending society apart. For the worker and miner support of a football club was a bulwark against the vagaries of life.'[57]

As in the Depression, football did not suffer during the Second World War. The question of whether sport should be played during war-time was not considered as important as three decades earlier. This made less contentious the decision by the codes to continue. The only exception was the Queensland Rugby Union, which ceased operations. Both games were affected by military restrictions, but union's continuation of its domestic competition in New South Wales enabled one of the most successful Australian teams to tour England in 1947 and 1948.[58] Similarly, league benefited by continuing its programme.

In Brisbane, the popularity of the game fluctuated during the war,[59] but in Sydney league was very well patronised. Total crowds at Sydney matches, with the exception of a decline in 1944, steadily increased from 414 000 (1940) to 777 000 (1945). This was quite remarkable considering the game was subjected to an entertainment tax and that the standard of play suffered from limited training opportunities and a shortage of personnel as players enlisted or were required for military work. Moreover, people flocked to the game even though an enemy force had attacked the Australian mainland for the first time.[60] With government approval and press support, rugby league, the mass spectator sport, maintained its popularity in Brisbane, and in Sydney its following grew as people needed respite and entertainment during the world calamity.

Once hostilities ceased both games were promoted internationally. In 1946 the Wallabies toured New Zealand and the English rugby-league team travelled to Australia. Two years later, Australia was a founding member of the International Board of Rugby League (IBRL) formed in Bordeaux, France[61] and, in 1949, the formation of the Australian Rugby Football Union (ARFU) gave rugby in the Antipodes a voice on the International Rugby Board (IRB). The ARFU assumed responsibility for organising tours by international teams, previously the duty of state unions.[62]

In Australia, the 1950s were years of unrivalled growth for both union and league at the international level. For union enthusiasts there were games against the Fijians for the first time, matches against traditional rival nations as well as a two-test series against the South Africans. League followers were equally entertained. The first World Cup was held in 1954, no less than five Australian teams travelled overseas and nine international teams played in Australia.[63] In addition, there were unsuccessful attempts to sell the game to the Americans and the South Africans.

There was a corresponding domestic expansion of league. It had gained small footholds in Victoria in the 1920s and a decade later in the Northern Territory, but it was after the Second World War that the game was started in South Australia, Western Australia and Tasmania. By 1957, league authorities could boast that their game — albeit with differing degrees of popularity — was played in every state and territory. Union could claim the same after the official establishment of union in Tasmania in the 1920s, in South Australia in 1930 and in the Northern Territory in the 1970s.[64] Both games, however, have never challenged Australian rules football as the major code outside Queensland, New South Wales and the Australian Capital Territory. Many commentators argue that the rivalry between New South Wales and Queensland in both sports has, until recently, been at the expense of national development.

While geographical expansion of the games has suffered there has been a diffusion to different ethnic and racial groups. League, and to a lesser extent union, provides social acceptance and integration for many players and supporters of non-British heritage. League teams formed in areas with large migrant populations like the Illawarra District of New South Wales, and many of Australia's immediate past and presently successful players — Conescu, Daly, Elias, Ettingshausen, Gasnier, Grothe, Krilich, Lazarus, Peponis, Raudonikis and Ribot — are the succeeding generations of the mass European resettlement of the late 1940s and early 1950s.[65]

Equally evident has been the Aboriginal contribution to football, more so in league than union. Aborigines play union and there have been some Australian representatives, notably the Ella brothers, but the middle-class nature of the game and its promotion in the private schooling system works against their participation. Because it is played in state schools, in country areas and on the reserves, league is more popular with male Aborigines and since the 1960s greater numbers of Aborigines have been lured to major competitions in Sydney and Brisbane. In the 1987 Sydney competition Aboriginal footballers constituted nearly nine per cent of the players in the top two divisions, yet Aborigines only represent between one and two per cent of the New South Wales population.[66] For Australia's native people, however, league represents a paradox. On the one hand, Aborigines are over-represented in the sport when compared with the population in general and, therefore, league is perceived to be more accessible than other sports. On the other hand, they play in positions characterised by speed and lack of leadership that support the popular stereotype and few Aborigines go on to coaching or administrative roles.[67] There are some obvious exceptions with respect to coaching and leadership, for example Arthur Beetson and Mal Meninga, but overall league has done little for the social plight of Australia's Aborigines.

One of the biggest attractions of league to Aborigines has been the chance to improve their economic position. Player payments, previously determined by income from gate receipts,[68] dramatically improved with the introduction of licensed clubs in New South Wales. These social clubs were

Mark Ella playing in the third test between Australia and New Zealand at the Sydney Cricket Ground in July 1984. Ella was awarded an OAM in this year, as was his sister Marcia for services to netball. (Mathews/Fairfax Picture Library.)

formed in the late 1950s to foster football and, with the introduction of poker machines, greatly increased the revenue available. In Queensland, until recently, government legislation prevented such gambling and league clubs have not been as financially important. For league, the additional revenue increased the power of Sydney clubs to attract the best players from country areas, from Brisbane and more recently from England and New Zealand, and to provide the strongest competition in Australia. For union, it permitted clubs to establish a financial independence from the organising authorities and to fund overseas trips for players.

While Sydney union clubs grew financially there was frustration at their limited power within the NSWRU. As a result, the Sydney Rugby Union (SRU) was formed in 1965 to give the metropolitan clubs control of their destinies.[69] Union in Queensland, despite no financial assistance from poker machines, continued to develop after the stagnant period of the previous twenty years. In the 1960s, the Queensland Junior Rugby Union and Queensland sub-districts competition were formed, the Queensland Country Rugby Union was re-constituted and rugby authorities acquired land at Ballymore. Membership of the Queensland Rugby Club grew from 200 to over 2000 after a permanent site was established.[70]

During this period rugby was drawn into the growing international trend to sever ties with South African sport. South Africa lost the right to compete in Commonwealth Games in 1961, had not competed in the Olympic Games since Rome, was expelled from the Olympic movement in 1970 and was banned from many international sporting federations.[71] Rugby was significant because South Africa retained full member status on the International Rugby Board and, like cricket, rugby competition continued against other nations.[72] Australia became embroiled in the anti-apartheid movement during the 1971 Springbok tour. There were several violent demonstrations. In Brisbane, for example, a state of emergency was declared and the game switched from Ballymore to the Brisbane Exhibition Ground to enable more effective security.[73] This tour ended official matches between the two countries until an Australian team travelled to South Africa in 1992.

Rugby league had troubles of a different kind. Gate attendances were falling: total crowds in 1971 were down 200 000 compared to three years earlier. To rectify this situation league instituted many modifications to make the competition more entertaining for spectators. Home-and-away matches, a five-team semi-final series, changes in scoring, and the six-tackle rule were introduced. The last innovation was an extension of the four-tackle rule adopted a decade earlier, and it revolutionised the game.[74] By the end of the 1970s these changes had partially restored the sport's following.[75]

Implicit in the growth of union and the changes in league in the 1970s was their commercialisation. Previously both sports were almost exclusively funded by gate receipts but, since the 1960s, they have been financed by sponsorship, television rights and licensed clubs. Corporate involvement in union started in the mid-1970s when the Australian Rugby Football Union first accepted sponsorship from a sportswear company.[76] Since that early assistance, sponsorship has grown steadily at the top level. In the 1980s, corporate assistance to the Queensland Rugby Union was a mere $20 000 and in the following decade it had swelled to $2.1 million, sixty-seven per cent of the organisation's income.[77]

In league, sponsorship of player awards, competitions and championships began in the 1960s, while advertising on club jerseys was initiated in 1976 when Eastern Suburbs signed a deal for $150 000 over three years.[78] Because of the popularity of the game and its perceived value to corporations, some clubs are presently signing sponsorship deals exceeding one million dollars annually.[79] The largest financial package, reported to be between twelve and thirteen million dollars over five years, was signed by the New South Wales Rugby League in 1989 with the Winfield cigarette company.[80] The financial commitment outlaid by sponsors ensures that capitalism saturates rugby league. Companies have naming rights to competitions and their logos adorn football fields, players' jerseys and even changing rooms. Recently, the NSWRL was forced not only to defend its sponsorship from objectors within its own ranks and in the face of mounting public criticism, but to look for alternatives, as the Federal government legislated against advertised funding of sport by cigarette companies.

Corporate sector interest has been directly related to television coverage. The broadcast media began its association with radio coverage of league matches in 1924 but the major commercial catalyst, television, was first involved in the early 1960s. Unlike sponsorship, there was much debate about the viability of televising games as administrators were concerned about the effect on attendances. Initially television coverage was sporadic and did not provide a major source of funds. For example, in 1976 the NSWRL received only $15 000 to telecast the grand final.[81] Presently, there is regular television coverage and, until the recent problems of the television industry, competing networks have ensured maximum fees were exacted by the league administration. In 1990, the Channel Ten network paid $45 million for three seasons to televise the game.[82] These financial commitments have not been without demands and game schedules are now organised to maximise television exposure at the expense of clubs' or players' needs. What was predominantly a Saturday afternoon activity is now played mid-week and Friday and Saturday nights.

Rugby Union heroes Nick Farr-Jones and Michael Lynagh in the ticker tape parade through Sydney streets to honour the Wallabies' World Cup win in 1991. (Golding/Fairfax Picture Library.)

Because of a more restricted audience union has not received the same television exposure. International and interstate matches are regularly televised, but not club competitions. The fillip in the game's profile was the inauguration of the rugby World Cup in 1987. Four years later the second tournament produced an income of $85 million for organisers and affiliated bodies. Shortly after, the IRB announced alterations to the game to make it more appealing to a wider group of spectators.[83] The success of the World Cup resulted in increased sponsorship for Australian rugby union, and in more television coverage as the game was moved to a commercial network in 1992. Commercial interests in rugby union continue to be well served by a southern-hemisphere competition, initiated in 1993, that includes teams from Australia, New Zealand, South Africa and Western Samoa.[84]

Not only have union and league changed aspects of their games but there have been major transformations in organisational structures. Administrations in both codes now resemble large-scale business enterprises rather than traditional sporting organisations. The New South Wales Rugby League epitomises this process. By 1983 crowd attendances had dropped below the slump a decade earlier, the president resigned amidst controversial circumstances and most of the thirteen clubs were technically insolvent. A general manager was appointed and a board of nine directors replaced an unwieldy committee of club delegates. The policy to expand the competition, initiated in 1982 with the inclusion of teams from Canberra and Illawarra, was continued in 1988 when Brisbane, Newcastle and the Gold Coast-Tweed joined the NSWRL.[85] This strategy, which has decimated local competitions, enabled the NSWRL to obtain larger fees from television networks and commercial sponsors. Revenue is likely to increase as current plans for the 1995 season include teams from Perth, North Queensland, Auckland and another from Brisbane. One feature of the expansion has been the employment of a marketing company to promote the game.[86] Rock stars Tina Turner and, more recently, Jimmy Barnes have transformed the traditional image of rugby league from a tough and violent game to an exciting spectacle played by professional male athletes. As a result, league has maintained its traditional blue-collar supporter base and increased the number of females and middle class who follow the game. The overall result of the strategies adopted by the business-like NSWRL was a growth in gross income from $3 million in 1983 to $16 million in 1991.[87]

While new administrative structures, television and marketing have popularised league and union to a wider cross-section of the population, there is little evidence that a similar process is operating in the playing ranks. There is no empirical research on the socio-economic backgrounds of contemporary union and league footballers. However, a survey of 1992 Australian representative players indicates the social stratification in the codes. In union seventy-six per cent (nineteen) of all test players were educated at fee-paying schools, sixteen per cent (four) at state schools and eight per cent (two) at both.[88] In league, twenty-nine per cent (five) of test players attended fee-paying schools, fifty-seven per cent (eleven) state schools and fourteen per cent (three) both.[89] In addition, there are some subtle differences in the fee-paying schools category: élite and exclusive private schools of Queensland and New South Wales play union; Catholic schools, which cater for students from different levels of society, predominantly play league. The educational history of this limited sample of players suggests that there is still a strong relationship between socio-economic background and the codes.

The period of commercialisation also highlights the extent to which both league and union have strayed from the tenets on which their games were founded. When the NSWRL was formed in 1907, one of its prime ideals was to cater for the needs of working-class players — to enable them to play without incurring any financial loss. Over the years, league authorities have imposed a series of restrictions on players to cater for the commercial needs of the game in a competitive leisure market. There are now limitations on wages of footballers in the form of salary caps, restrictions on their terms for playing overseas, and financial penalties imposed for publicly criticising the game. In addition, players are subjected to random drug testing and, for a short period, till the courts decided otherwise, also to a draft system that dictated the club for which they would play. Early administrators, many of whom had players' interests at heart, would be surprised and probably dismayed at the fundamental changes in the game.

Rugby union, like league, has strayed from its founding ethos. Union has always prided itself on being a game played by amateurs. It was on the issue of amateurism that union expelled players who adopted the rival code and it is the lack of financial gratification that administrators, participants and supporters claim is responsible for the special components of the game — its utilitarian benefits and its social flavour. Since the last World Cup in 1991, the definition of an amateur, which has been adhered to in differing degrees, has been modified to allow players to earn an income from writing books, making advertisements and guest appearances. Union, at the top level, is very similar to league in its management, promotion and relationship with the media and commercial sponsors, and only technically different in respect to financial rewards to players. It also appears that the final bastion of amateurism, player payments, is under threat and, as Australian coach Bob Dwyer predicts, union could be professional by the end of this decade.[90] If this comes to fruition, the major differences between the codes will be their playing patterns and the social composition of the participants.

12

Soccer

Philip Mosely and Bill Murray

The way an Aussie kid thinks about his football [soccer] is still certainly a long way from how the English, Italian or Brazilian kids see it. Aussie kids won't die for it, whereas the others live it and breathe it every single day.

Craig Johnston, Australian-produced Liverpool star (1991)

wogball, n. Colloq. — soccer

Macquarie dictionary (Sydney, 1982)

ONE OF the greatest achievements of the British Empire was to spread association football (to give the game its official English title) around the world. Today it is the world's most popular sport — with the notable exceptions of the English-speaking members of the old empire. As in the United States, Canada, New Zealand and white South Africa, soccer in Australia enjoys only secondary status in the shadow of a local brand of football. In New South Wales and Queensland, rugby is the dominant football code, union to begin with, then league after the split. In all the other states the ruling passion is the indigenous Australian game, first known as Victorian rules, later Australian rules. Ironically soccer, still seen as a foreign game, is the only football code with a genuinely national dimension: it is the second most popular football code in every state in Australia. Unlike Australian football and rugby, however, it has not entered the Australian soul and despite its immense progress in recent years it has laboured under the slur of being foreign. In the early days the dominance of British migrants saw it branded as a 'pommie' game and then with the massive influx of European immigrants after the Second World War it was equally denounced as a 'wog' game.

The dominance of immigrants has been soccer's blessing and its curse: without the migrants it would lose most of its following, with them it is dismissed as un-Australian. This could change with the wider acceptance of multiculturalism in Australia and, above all, with the recent successes of the youth teams in international competitions. The frequently voiced claims that soccer was about to become the number-one Australian code and the equally shallow fears of the game's enemies who thought there was ground for such claims date from the 1880s. For the first time, however, there is sound reason to believe that Australian soccer might be making significant progress on the world scene.

A form of football was being played in Australia as early as 1829 when soldiers in Sydney's Hyde Park barracks were 'in the habit of amusing themselves with the game of "football"'.[1] The first officially recorded game was in Melbourne in 1858 under what became Australian rules, for which the first set of rules was actually published in 1866, less than three years after the formulation of the rules of association football in London. 'Football' was played before increasingly large crowds from the 1860s, particularly in Victoria and before the association game had taken hold in Britain the main football codes in Australia already involved significant handling and heavy tackling. The first official game of soccer had to wait until 1880 when the Wanderers played King's School in Sydney.[2]

In pre-1880s Britain football, of any code, was essentially a middle-class game controlled by former private schoolboys. Australia was no different. Four of the six original committeemen of the Wanderers were graduates of the English private-school system with John Walter Fletcher, the club's first secretary, the key official. Born in London, the son of a barrister, he was educated at Cheltenham College and Oxford before arriving in Australia late in 1875. Fletcher established his own private school, Coreen College, and introduced soccer

1 8 5 0.

NEW YEAR'S DAY !!!
OLD WHITE HART INN,
GREAT BOURKE STREET.

THE Lovers of the good old English merriment are invited to witness the different sports opposite the
Inn on

TUESDAY NEXT,
consisting of
GOAT RACING—PRIZE, A SUIT OF CLOTHES.
CLIMBING THE GREASY POLE—PRIZE, HAT AND GUN.
A PIG RACE WITH GREASY TAILS.
QUOITING AND SKITTLES.

The whole to conclude with a
GRAND MATCH
at the old English Game of
FOOTBALL.

Luncheon will be provided.

there in 1881, playing along with the Arcadians formed out of St Paul's Church of England based in the then affluent suburb of Redfern. It was the Wanderers, Coreen College and the Arcadians who established the English Football Association (of New South Wales) in 1882, and together with that in Natal, it became one of the first football associations formed outside the United Kingdom.[3]

Football was less popular in New South Wales and Queensland than in Victoria in the 1880s, with Australian rules and rugby competing to be the main code. Soccer was never a serious contender. The abundance of space, grassy pitches and comparative wealth posed no restrictions on the more violent rugby code or the free-ranging Australian game, while the dominant figures from the English private-school system who took sport to the Australian schools were more often rugby, rather than soccer men. Also, by the late 1880s when soccer had swept all before it in much of Britain, it was being seen as a working-class game. This did not enhance its reputation in Australia.

In New South Wales, too, soccer was played mainly by working-class enthusiasts: and, unlike their counterparts in Britain, they also took over organisation of the game. The three areas in Sydney which became identified with soccer (Pyrmont, Balmain and Granville) were centres of industry and working-class employment. Outside Sydney the game thrived in the coal- and shale-mining districts that ring the County of Cumberland. To the north, the Newcastle and South Maitland coal fields populations began playing in 1884 when some Scots established the Minmi Rangers. To the south,

A handbill advertising New Year's Day sports in Melbourne in 1850. (Reproduced from 'Garryowen', *The Chronicles of Early Melbourne*, Fergusson and Mitchell, Melbourne, 1988.)

215

the Wollongong collieries began their long involvement with soccer by establishing the North Illawarra Rovers in 1886. The shale miners of Joadja in the south-west followed suit in 1887 with their Southern Cross Football Club which played nearby southern highland clubs during the next decade. To the west, Lithgow's coal miners and iron workers set up their first club in 1889. Finally, to the north-west and completing the ring around Sydney, clubs sprouted up among the shale miners in the Capertee and Wolgan valleys early in the twentieth century.[4]

New South Wales remained the most powerful soccer state with Queensland its only serious rival. The southern and western states rapidly took up the Australian game, usually under the influence of Victorian expatriates. Soccer was spread by working-class enthusiasts. In Victoria, the game began in Melbourne in 1883 and centred around the inner working-class suburbs of the city; the development of the La Trobe Valley brown coal field produced further teams and associations. Queensland's first club formed in Brisbane in 1883, but the game's real strength there came from the mining district of Ipswich. Western Australian soccer began in Perth in 1892. Local leagues drew strength from the port of Fremantle and annual clashes with gold fields clubs at Kalgoorlie, Coolgardie and Boulder City. In South Australia, workers at a Norwood pottery in Adelaide established the game in 1893. Port Pirie's smelting works provided early and regular competition. The game emerged in Tasmania in 1908 thanks to the involvement of visiting sailors, while soccer in what is today the Australian Capital Territory began in 1914 when construction workers organised some games to play in their leisure time.

At a time when Australian football and rugby were in the hands of locally-born organisers, soccer was generally run by British, especially Scottish, migrants often reflected in the plethora of Caledonians, Rangers and other teams of obviously Scottish inspiration. The Welsh and Irish influence was less pronounced, but this is hardly surprising in that soccer developed much later in those countries than it did in England or Scotland.

Despite its minority status, soccer was still feared by the established football codes and often evoked hostility. In New South Wales, soccer enjoyed a few surges of popularity, usually related to periods of large migrant intakes: the 1880s, 1910–14 and, above all, the 1920s. The greatest boom came with the immigration after the Second World War, dominated not so much by British as by European immigrants. As after all its periods of expansion, soccer would self-destruct given the tensions between the new arrivals and the more conservative local custodians.

One of the early Australian soccer pioneers (like many others, native born) was Jack Logan. The son of a Scot, Logan was a central figure at the turn of the century. He was treasurer (1892–95) and secretary (1896–1900) of the Southern British Football Association that replaced the (New South Wales) English Football Association in 1884. At the end of 1900 he moved to Queensland whence he emerged as the Queensland delegate to the 1911 Australasian Association Football Conference. It was at this conference that soccer's first national body was formed, the Commonwealth Football Association (Australia). Logan was elected its first president.[5]

No sooner had soccer's first national body been established than a split appeared in New South Wales. The issue concerned the peculiarly Australian organisation of sport whereby major teams are allocated a region and have first playing claim on all people resident in that district. There was no promotion or relegation in the district leagues, which were recognised as the premier competitions in rules, rugby and cricket. For British migrants, reared on a tradition of local clubs with promotion and relegation determining the top teams, the district system posed problems. When they established their own teams, based on ethnic bias rather than a district, they found their route to the top competition perennially barred. A breakaway group was formed in 1914 and the fight was won by 1916. However, by the early 1920s the district system was back to last until the 1950s. The issue would erupt more severely in 1957.[6]

The Commonwealth Football Association (Australia) disbanded during the First World War but re-emerged in 1921 when it changed its title to the Australian Soccer Football Association (ASFA). The game was led by Sydney A. Storey, who became a New South Wales state politician and long-time president of the ASFA. From 1913 soccer's national body organised interstate carnivals but they merely revealed the imbalance in the popularity of the game: in terms of players, spectators, grounds, finance and organisation, New South Wales dwarfed all others. New South Wales and Queensland were the only states which fielded representative teams filled by locally-born players. In the Australian-rules states soccer was a poor relation, relying on migrant players. In 1913 Victoria fielded a representative side with all Britons — they did, however, find one Australian for the 1914 team. This situation changed little over the next two decades and whatever growth soccer enjoyed in the 1920s ended with the 1930s cessation of immigration. The Victorian Soccer Football Association could not even acquire sufficient grounds to host the 1934 interstate carnival. The South Australian British Football Association successfully promoted the game at school level but by 1939 had only thirty-two teams. In Western Australia, soccer struggled along in Perth, the surrounding ports and mining centres while Tasmanian soccer was non-existent by the end of the 1930s. The dominance of New South Wales, and to a lesser degree Queensland, was obvious when the English Amateurs toured in 1937. During the three tests played, only three places were not filled by New South Welshmen. Of the tour's £11 371 total income, £7884 (seventy per cent) was raised in New South Wales, £2286 (twenty per cent) in Queensland. Most of the games were played in these two states but that in itself indicated where the strength lay.[7]

The popularity of soccer in New South Wales was due largely to the emergence of progressive officials in the 1920s, who built on the competitions established in mining and industrial areas. They developed schoolboy programmes, particularly in Sydney, and took advantage of the immigrants who flooded into the state after the First World War. They used first-rate enclosed grounds, gaining income from gate receipts, while several clubs purchased or attempted to purchase their own grounds. The game was also boosted by various international matches and tours abroad.

There had been plans to tour 'the old country' as early as 1882. The English Football Association in London agreed to play host at the end of the 1882–83 season. The Scottish, Irish and Welsh football associations gave their blessing in December 1882 and this led to the first New South Wales versus Victoria inter-colonial matches in 1883, which served as pre-tour trials. But despite great optimism and the promise of a large subsidy from Dr James G. Beaney, a Victorian surgeon and generous patron of the game, the tour never eventuated.

Neither did the proposed tour of 1885 when it was planned to include two or three Aborigines as in the 1868 cricket tour. Invitations to tour New Zealand in 1895 and the United States in 1896 were also declined. The problem lay in Australia's isolated geographical position: it was too expensive to make the trip. Followers had to wait until 1922 before an Australian team went on an overseas tour to New Zealand, establishing the tradition of cross-Tasman encounters. Later, other teams went to the Dutch East Indies (1928), New Zealand again (1936, 1948, 1958) and South Africa and Rhodesia (1950) before Australia embarked on its first world cup campaign in 1965. In the years between 1927 and 1935 Australia was also invited to send teams to tour Yugoslavia, Spain, Portugal, France, Belgium, Hungary, Czechoslovakia, Canada and South Africa. Unfortunately the Australian authorities could not accept these invitations.[8]

Elsewhere in the world there were soccer teams that had the time and the money to make the trip to Australia, and in the inter-war period Australia entertained many visiting sides. These tours boosted the game, attracting large crowds, but they also showed up Australia's lack of playing ability.

The popularity of the New South Wales game in the 1920s can be seen in the immense crowds attracted to the international tours organised between 1923 and 1927. In 1923 New Zealand returned Australia's visit of the previous year and drew a record crowd of 12 000 in the match versus Australia in Sydney. Later that year the record was broken when a game against a Chinese team made up of university students attracted 47 500 spectators crammed into the Sydney Cricket Ground for the game against New South Wales. The novelty factor had much to do with this: 16 000 saw the Chinese in Newcastle and 12 000 in Brisbane a week later. A Canadian team toured in 1924 and, though less of an attraction, pulled in 20 000 to their first match in Sydney and 15 000 the following Saturday. The most popular visitors, however, were the English in 1925. Denied the Sydney Cricket Ground by a wary New South Wales Rugby Football League, the tourists played before a full house at the Sydney Show Ground: 44 500 paid to watch with an additional 5000 members seeing the game for nothing. Gate receipts totalled £3692. Elsewhere the England team attracted 10 000 in Fremantle, 7000 in Adelaide and more than 10 000 in Melbourne. A record-breaking 25 000 watched the tourists at the Brisbane Exhibition Ground.

The Chinese returned in 1927. They paid their own way but

couldn't recover their costs: their standard of play was not good enough and the novelty factor had worn off. They also had to compete for attention with the touring Czechoslovakian team, AFK Vrsovice, known today as Bohemians Prague but retaining their nickname, the Roos. The kangaroo was adopted as the club emblem during the tour. The Czechs drew 18 000 in both Sydney and Brisbane, reasonable crowds in view of the small Czech population in Australia at that time.[9]

Of the touring teams, only England won all their games. The Australian successes against the visitors were almost entirely due to the New South Wales presence. Queensland performed creditably but all other states were beaten soundly, scores sometimes reaching double figures. Politeness often made the visitors ease up but, when provoked, they could turn on the pressure with startling results — no more so than when Australia was humbled by an England XI by seventeen goals to nil in 1951.[10]

The visits from foreign teams were a mixed blessing. The revenue allowed New South Wales and Queensland to consolidate their foundations but for the other states, labouring already under the dominance of Australian rules football, the easy victories by touring sides revealed a massive gap in quality. The native born had turned their backs on the game while for British migrants the comparison with the game 'back home' was derisory. Unless personally involved, they gave up interest in the local game. Even in New South Wales success brought the familiar problem of richer clubs wanting to keep the money and power to themselves.

In 1928 the strongest teams in Sydney, Newcastle and Wollongong challenged the state body and seceded when their demands were not met. They formed the New South Wales State Soccer League (NSWSSL) — what would be called a super league today. The split was complicated by ethnic elements: on the one hand, long-standing state officials were committed to the district system and what they saw as the interests of the game as a whole, on the other the self-interest of the newer clubs based on recently-arrived British migrants. By the end of 1929 whole district associations had transferred to the breakaway body. The Australian Soccer Football Association, whose officials were sympathetic to the old New South Wales administration, refused to acknowledge the NSWSSL initially but capitulated by late 1931.[11]

Queensland, too, was afflicted by administrative strife between Brisbane and Ipswich over the distribution of gate money. It began in 1929, with separate competitions for the

two districts, blew up into full-scale conflict in 1931 and was only resolved at the year's end.[12]

These splits in the two major states came before the full severity of the 1930s Depression. Unemployment and under-employment on the coal fields, the power bases for soccer, was by then widespread. Buoyed by the success of previous seasons and unaware that the recession was the beginning of the Great Depression, breakaway officials and supporters launched their schemes at the very time that soccer could least afford to divide its efforts. The negativism of division was exacerbated by the economic climate. A partial recovery was made in the late 1930s, aided mostly by the English amateur tour in 1937, but by then larger events were on the horizon. The conflicts of this time, however, were mere tiffs compared to that which rent the game in 1957.

England vs. Australia at the Sydney Cricket Ground, 3 July 1937. (Hood Collection, State Library of New South Wales.)

The first immigrants to arrive after the Second World War were 'displaced persons' from Europe. They were followed by other refugees and then by those assisted or unassisted by the Australian government. Excluding Australian returnees, over six million immigrants came to Australia between 1945 and 1990. From Europe the major groups were the Italians (411 000), Greeks (247 000), Yugoslavs (217 000), Dutch (187 000), Germans (171 000) and Poles (113 000). Only the United Kingdom/Ireland and New Zealand provided more immigrants than Italy over the same time. Between 1945 and 1965, the chief period of refugee immigration, the six major European nationalities dominated all others. They totalled 799 000 compared to the total of 340 000 from the United Kingdom/ Ireland. The figures were reversed from 1965 to 1975 with the United Kingdom/Ireland dominating. After 1975, and especially from 1980, Asia took over from all others: so far the Asian contribution to soccer has been minimal.[13]

Italians were the dominant immigrant group from 1945 to 1965, and they produced many of the best soccer teams. Between 1965 and 1970 Italy still provided the largest number of immigrants, closely followed by Yugoslavia and Greece; thereafter Yugoslavs and Greeks outnumbered the Italians. Whether for numerical reasons, or because they integrated better, Italian teams then suffered a comparative decline, while Greek and Yugoslav teams came into their own.

Before the Second World War, however, there had been a few teams obviously not Anglo-Australian. The Maltese in north Queensland established a club at Mackay in 1926, and others played in Adelaide in 1929. Greeks were involved in Melbourne as early as 1932, though they seem not to have had their own club. Melbourne's Jewish-based Hakoah were playing from 1933 at the latest, their Sydney namesakes emerging six years later. Club Italia played in Sydney during 1937 and 1938, and an Italian club surfaced in Broken Hill in 1939. Its opponents included local Yugoslavs playing under the name Napredak. An Italian-based club, Savoia, named after the reigning royal house, made an inauspicious debut in Adelaide in 1940. It only lasted a season, but did re-form in 1946 as Juventus and is known today as Adelaide City, national champions for 1991–92, 1993–94, and runners-up for 1992–93.[14]

Within a few years of the Second World War the influx of European migrants was reflected in teams representing the countries from which they had come. By 1948 there were many former refugees attending first-grade games, and in the following year Italian, Maltese, Dutch, Yugoslav, Greek and Macedonian clubs began emerging in minor competitions. In 1950 Jewish, Hungarian and Czechoslovakian clubs were formed.

Thereafter Polish, Serbian, Croatian, Ukrainian and a host of other ethnic clubs proliferated, with rival Hungarian teams emerging as a result of the exodus after the Hungarian revolution of 1956. Within just a few years Australian soccer had become a league of nations. In migrant camps at places like Greta, Uranquinty, Bathurst and Bonegilla there were teams with representatives from just about every nationality.

British immigrants were as eager to play and watch soccer as the Europeans but were generally happy to join existing district clubs. There were not enough to cater for the influx, however, so new Anglo-Australian teams were formed. However, numerous British migrants turned their backs on the game, put off by the poor play and by what they saw as the temperamental volatility of the 'Latins'. There were not the same pressures on the British to seek shelter in a club of their own language and culture. The best British players, too, soon found out that there was much more money to be made playing for clubs of continental origin. Not only that, they were treated like stars, both on and off the field. By the mid-1960s some of the major ethnic teams were made up of Britons, with only a token representative of their own nationality. The clubs run by Anglo-Australians were still restrained by residual notions of amateurism, a distaste for treating players like stars and the thought that money made from the game should go back into junior levels rather than into players' pockets.

Soccer grew in every state in the 1950s and 1960s. In New South Wales the long-established local junior associations ensured that the game had a strong Australian base which the arrival of 'new' Australians complemented. The Australian element was reinforced by the post-war baby boom that peaked in 1961, by efforts to promote the game at all levels of schooling and by lowering the age for children playing the game. European migrants boosted the crowds. In Sydney in 1953 match attendances for first-grade fixtures totalled 132 000; three years later they were 346 000, rising to 450 000 in 1959 and 835 000 in 1962. The next year's first-grade final achieved a record of 30 158 in club attendance. The 1962 and 1963 seasons were the peak years for post-war soccer in New South Wales.[15]

In the other states, the overall numbers were less but the pattern similar. In 1958 record crowds for tourist matches in Perth (12 140), Adelaide (23 000) and Melbourne (31 000) were attracted by Stanley Matthews' Blackpool. In 1959 Italian fans helped post record attendances for club games in Perth (3340) and Adelaide (4200) and in 1960 in Brisbane (6500) and Melbourne (10 600). The average for Melbourne's Sunday matches at Olympic Park reached between six and seven thousand in 1960. The growth continued up to 1962 and 1963, prompting talk of a national league by Italian and Greek clubs in particular. Limited by local and lesser lights, they sought interstate competitors in their chase for greater glory and money. When crowds fell in all states in 1964 there was even more reason for the top clubs to seek each other out. Plans for a national league were begun in 1965 for a projected start in 1967.[16]

Soccer's growth was watched with fear by some Australians who thought the game might take over from their own. In the Australian-rules states, some schools and even education departments banned soccer, and in 1951 in Tasmania glass was scattered on the ground where the visiting England soccer XI was due to play. In 1952 the Victorian Football League moved to secure its monopoly on sporting fields in Melbourne in order to prevent soccer being played on them. In Sydney the crowd of 30 158 who came to see the 1963 soccer grand final drew anguished comment from the New South Wales rugby league's president, Bill Buckley, that rugby league could be displaced as the state's premier code. Television's Channel Nine even televised live the second half of the game, and coverage in the press was in marked contrast to the usual contempt with which the game was treated.[17]

Public contempt was particularly strong in Victoria. When in 1958 a Melbourne soccer club sought to lease a council ground usually used by an Australian-rules club, one alderman replied with a sneer, 'let them play . . . in the gutter'.[18] In 1965 youths daubed anti-soccer slogans over fences at the Middle Park ground, chopped the goal posts down and tried to set fire to the grandstand. Victoria was not alone. Adelaide's Polonia met pernicious opposition from Australian-football elements who coveted the Polish club's home ground. And in all major cities the term 'wogball', extensively used in schoolyards by the early 1960s, revealed many a bigot's heart.[19]

The prevailing policy regarding migrants in the 1950s and early 1960s was assimilation, not integration or multiculturalism and those groups which more easily fitted into the 'Australian way of life' were more easily accepted. Others, who resented or could not accept the cultural coldness or hostility of Australians, turned to their ethnic communities where they could speak their own language, enjoy their own culture and make friends among those they understood and who understood them. Soccer was a haven for non-English speaking migrants;

for men and for women, too, who joined community clubs where soccer was only one activity, although usually the dominant one. These clubs were a reasonably private part of the new migrant's culture but soccer was very public. It was also un-Australian and this was played up in the media. Unfortunately the media had much on which to feed their prejudices, with pitch invasions to attack players or the referee, all-in brawls among players and spectators and unwillingness to play by the rules.[20]

Underlying the reporting was a cynical amusement on the one hand, prejudice stretching to racism on the other. Of several Aborigines who made names for themselves through soccer, Charles Perkins financed his way through Sydney University with the money he made out of the game, and claimed that only in soccer could he escape the racism of Australian society. But there was also a more rational dislike for European enmities being replayed on Australian soil. It was rational, because no-one liked to see Greeks fighting Macedonians and Croats fighting Serbs, yet it was also unrealistic for Australians to believe it possible for centuries-old conflict to be forgotten, especially when it had been exacerbated by the Second World War, merely because immigrants had removed themselves from their birthplaces. There was also a cultural gulf in the way soccer was played between Anglo-Australians and Europeans, the former favouring a more physical, hard-tackling game, the latter a more cultured artistic approach dismissed by Australians as a 'pansy' style, nowhere more obvious than in attitudes towards the goalkeeper: fair game for the Australians, sacrosanct to the continentals. Off the field there was an equally wide cultural gap in how the game should be administered, the more conservative Anglo-Australians wanted the money to be spread around; those clubs which actually generated most money (always European) wanted to keep the money to themselves. The result was a series of breakaways from state associations and the formation of those federations that govern soccer in Australia today.[21]

By the end of 1956, resentment among migrant clubs in Sydney against state association officials came to a head when Jewish club Hakoah's application for first-division status was rejected.

The district system was still in place and though it allowed promotion and relegation, this was not automatic. Migrant clubs Prague and Sydney Austral gained promotion at the end of 1955, but promotion and relegation were kept selective, to ensure each district in Sydney was always represented in first division. In the rapidly expanding game of that time this was an outdated system so the ambitious and progressive clubs, nearly all migrant, formed the breakaway New South Wales Federation of Soccer Clubs (NSWFSC) in January 1957. Crowds and gate takings settled the administrative wrangle in favour of the federation, but what soccer gained in new dynamism it lost in the self-interest of clubs that put ethnicity before the game.[22]

Club control was considered crucial by clubs like Prague, Sydney Austral and Hakoah. Their followers bankrolled the game through increased gate revenue, yet little was returned to them. The money flowed into grounds, juniors and promotions, including the association's licensed club, Soccer House. The migrants had little interest in these activities. Their aim was full professionalism, their emphasis unashamedly on soccer's top players. Where the British-Australians who ran the Australian Soccer Football Association (ASFA) frowned on paying players, the migrants spent freely on club transfers, signing-on fees, player payments and bonuses. Often the financial demands outstripped resources but the migrant clubs were intent on football success. It was satisfying by itself, but it also enhanced a migrant community's status.

The breakaway NSWFSC was officially recognised by the ASFA in 1959, and this example spread to other states. The clubs drawing the largest crowds seized control in Victoria in 1959 though a federation did not form till later: Western Australia established a New South Wales-styled federation in 1960, South Australia in early 1961 and Queensland in late 1961. All states provided delegates to the ASFA and, eventually, federation officials outmanoeuvred the federal body's established executive. Led by New South Wales the state federations came together in a new Australian Soccer Federation (ASF) in November 1961. The ASFA collapsed and, although some old-guard Australian officials stayed on, the post-war European migrants were now in charge.[23]

The principal headache for the newly formed ASF was of the New South Wales Federation's making. From 1958 it had allowed its leading club, Prague, to entice overseas players to the club without obtaining clearances from or paying transfers to several Austrian and Dutch clubs. The combined transfer fees totalled £46 000 and when these were not paid the federation of International Football Associations (FIFA), the world-governing body, suspended Australia from April 1960. This ban prevented Australian club or national teams from playing anyone affiliated with FIFA. Overseas tours, so necessary for the game's national well-being, were out. The revenue which tourists brought to the local game was lost.

Negotiations began in 1962. Ampol Petroleum reportedly would underwrite a settlement of up to £20 000 with FIFA. The ASF president from 1962 to 1968 was William G. Walkley CBE, managing director of Ampol. The large number of new arrivals in Australia included some leading ex-officials from European soccer. Advised by such contacts, an agreement was reached when £18 500 was paid over. FIFA lifted its ban in July 1963 and Australia re-entered world competition.[24]

For most soccer lovers in Australia, the big annual event was the visit of a professional team from the home country. They came regularly in the 1950s and 1960s, once relations with FIFA were restored. Most games were picnic matches for the visitors, with the local team in the anomalous position of having the opposition cheered to the echo, while *their* every mistake was jeered. Success for state or national teams was a low-scoring defeat. However, touring sides faced increasingly competent opposition from the 1970s onwards. Australia gained its first victory over stiffer opposition when it defeated Greece in 1969 and although there were few other wins, victories over Uruguay and Yugoslavia stunned the world press in 1988.[25]

Australia had more consistent success against Asian teams. It was Australia's entry into the World Cup competition of 1966 that began a series of regular encounters with Asian opposition. That first 1965 entry ended with a thrashing by a remarkable North Korean team that went on to humiliate Italy and almost cause an upset against Portugal. In the preliminary rounds for the 1970 World Cup in Mexico, Australia was eliminated by Israel, who were to provide considerable opposition in years to come. In 1974 Australia negotiated eleven matches before qualifying for the finals in West Germany and the team's success was embraced by the Australian media which, for the first time, treated soccer as a serious game. There

Australia vs. Germany in the World Cup series in Hamburg, 18 June 1974. Berti Vogts, West German defence player, counter-attacks Australian striker Peter Ollerton in the second half of the game. Germany won three goals to nil. This is the only World Cup Final in which Australia has played. (Australian Associated Press, photo supplied by Fairfax Picture Library.)

is no success like international success, and Australians, like everyone else, like to see winners. The Australians acquitted themselves honourably in West Germany, holding at bay the eventual winners, West Germany (nil to three goals), and East Germany (nil to two goals) and drawing with Chile (nil-all).

The successes of the 1974 national team led to the formation of a national league in 1977. The first national club competition of any major sport in Australia, it helped to raise playing standards, organisation and public profile. Yet teams from the west have never participated, Tasmania had no team strong enough to participate, and the part-time teams of Brisbane, Melbourne, Adelaide and Canberra, as well as Sydney and other New South Wales soccer hotbeds like Newcastle and Wollongong, found the travel irksome and expensive. The national league has undergone several changes of format, most recently into a summer game often played in the evening, but the original concept of a truly national league rivalling the other football codes has not materialised.

Despite a troubled national league and the inability of the national team to qualify for another World Cup final, the game has undergone steady progress.[26] The media has grown less hostile and the game received help from an unexpected quarter when the new Special Broadcasting Service's television chan-

nel 0-28, set up to appeal to Australia's ever-increasing multi-national community in October 1980, adopted soccer as its main sport and gave the game unprecedented coverage. At the Australian Institute for Sport, established in Canberra after Australia's poor performance at the Montreal Olympics in 1976, soccer was one of the sports to benefit most, with incalculable benefits for the game at youth level.

Sponsorship, both the bane and the lifeline of some sports in the 1980s, has proved a problem. It was believed only Anglo-Australian aspects of the game would appeal to the sponsors, so one solution was to ban ethnic names. Adelaide City was then still known as Juventus, South Melbourne as Hellas and Sydney CSC (from 1993 called the Sydney Knights) as Croatia. Attempts to hide the affiliation of major soccer teams is an anomaly given the all-party approach to multiculturalism in contemporary Australia. Most ethnic groups are encouraged to

Australia plays Argentina in the World Cup qualifier in front of a capacity crowd at the Sydney Football Stadium in October 1993. This photograph shows Australian player Jason van Blerk being tackled by the Argentinian defender Sergio Vásquez. This match, a draw, was part of a two-leg qualifying series. Australia went on to lose the second match in Buenos Aires. (Clayton/Fairfax Picture Library.)

flaunt their ethnicity, soccer clubs are expected to hide it. The aspects of multiculturalism soccer has presented to the public occasionally have not been desirable — and there have been elements in the media only too anxious to denigrate the ethnic game, if not the ethnic communities they represent.

The ethnicity conundrum remains, but the game's future looks bright and its problems solvable. In Portugal in 1991 Australia won the bronze medal in the world youth tournament and, as the host nation in 1993, was beaten for third place by a professional England team. To qualify for the Barcelona Olympics in 1992 the under-twenty-three team played against favourites Holland in Utrecht and won with a unique blend of continental skill, Aussie guts and a miraculous Ned Zelic goal. In Barcelona itself a failure of nerve gave Ghana third place, but the likes of Zelic have become heroes, with the fan mail and adulation that go with it. With these youths lies the key to the acceptance of soccer by Australians: they are local heroes who despite their names speak with broad Australian accents. Zelic has gone the way of all great soccer talent, to Europe, in his case to play for Borussia Dortmund. In doing so he joined an ever-growing band from Eddie Krencvic, one of the first to make it in the European professional leagues, to fellow youth-stars like Paul Okon and Mark Bosnich, youngsters of potential international class. Australian soccer just may be coming of age.

13 Swimming, Surfing and Surf-Lifesaving

Douglas Booth

. . . the body is the most potent metaphor of society.

Bryan Turner, *The body and society* (1984)

O N EASTER Monday 1902 two swimmers stood on the wharf at Gosford, New South Wales, at the start of a race. Trudge, swimming correspondent for the Sydney *Sportsman*, called the pair 'a typical cornstalk — long thin and bony' and 'a nuggety champion'. According to Trudge, 'the sapling' wore 'an ordinary pair of swimming drawers and showed so much of his anatomy' that a swimming association official turned away from the 'most hideous sight'. The champion 'appeared in full Association rig, but the trunks were of cloth, not stockinette, in accordance with the regulation of the governing body of swimming.'[1]

In 1990 swimmer Janelle Elford led the Australian team at the opening ceremony of the Commonwealth Games in Auckland wearing a green one-piece swimsuit, covered by a flowing multi-coloured silk and chiffon coat. Compatriot and flag bearer Lisa Curry-Kenny declared her support for the costume saying, 'Janelle has a great body to go in it ... Anyone who has a great body should flaunt it if they [sic] want to.'[2]

We have here two bodies in public view. One repulses, the other attracts. Yet, less than a century separates them. The cultural production of the ideal middle-class body — slim,

231

tanned, athletic and self-disciplined — is the history of disciplined permissiveness and the transformation of repressive
bodily regimens. Swimming, lifesaving and surfing (surfboard-
riding) were integral elements of this change.

Surf-bathing, swimming and surfing in public view were
legitimised and legalised in Australia early this century. This
was a critical moment in the creation of public attitudes
towards the revealed body, for the three sports helped pacify
the social hysteria that generally accompanied such display.
Sportspeople were by definition disciplined, lifesavers symbolised selfless humanitarianism, swimmers fed nationalist pride
— all three activities confirmed the therapeutic benefits of active lifestyles and all fuelled new consumer desires and markets.

The reproduction of the ideal body is a feature of modern
consumerism that creates and satisfies desires for new experiences and personal fulfilment. Satisfying new desires meant
new tolerances, especially of hedonistic practices, but it also
meant a new system of control. The uniform normality of mass
consumerism encouraged people to work meticulously on their
bodies through diet and exercise and extended the public gaze
of surveillance and discipline. Although the initial shift to
permissive consumerism occurred in the 1920s, it became more
visible after the Second World War. In the mid-1960s, technological, social and political changes coalesced in the counter-
culture phenomenon. Surfing exemplifies a paradox of
counter-culture: on the one hand, its style (dress, music, argot
and ritual) marked a countervailing lifestyle; on the other, it
provided a new activity to be commodified by capitalism. Professional surfing, lifesaving and swimming emerged at this con-
juncture and like most sports, they exploited what Bryan Turner
calls the 'ethics of managerial athleticism' — the creation and
conveyance of acceptable body images.

Medical practitioners alerted the European aristocracy to the
therapeutic properties of cold-water bathing in the sixteenth
century. But until the rapid growth of industrial cities in the
eighteenth century and spreading awareness of pollution, dis-
ease and public health, the burgeoning middle classes did not
acknowledge the healthy benefits of bathing. Both sexes had
bathed together in pre-industrial times but middle-class con-

cerns ended this practice.[3] Puritanical morality located social stability in the renunciation and repression of hedonism: civilisation was synonymous with an asceticism and temperance that demanded 'denial of the flesh and the control of emotion'.[4] Puritans and evangelists believed that immodest public displays corrupted morality so they confined public bathing to segregated enclosed baths (fresh and sea-water) and horse-drawn bathing machines (sea-water). Like prisons, schools, hospitals and factories, bathing enclosures put citizens under surveillance to maintain social order.[5]

Bathing was popular in early colonial Australia. In 1834 the *Sydney Gazette* described it as the town's 'favourite recreation'.[6] Baths and space initially shielded unclothed bodies from public view. The marines constructed a swimming enclosure on Sydney Harbour during the first year of settlement. Forty years later the government subsidised the Fig Tree Baths at Woolloomooloo Bay for males. Mrs Bigges opened baths at the Domain shortly after to cater for men and women — at separate times.[7] 'Licentious' males, however, continued to bathe naked within the built environment, prompting official intervention. Governor Macquarie objected to this 'indecent and improper custom' and banned bathing at the government wharf and dockyard.[8] In 1838 the government prohibited bathing in all waters exposed to public view between six a.m. and eight p.m.[9]

New ideas about 'correct' character and the interrelated institutionalisation of physical activity reinforced the social relations of bathing during the nineteenth century. Social Darwinism and the Victorian middle class's fetish with physical and mental health produced specific notions of 'correct' character. The desired gentleman displayed 'true manliness' which resided in the 'harmonious growth' of physique and character. A true male was 'strong of body and pure of heart', loyal, brave and active, a leader and self-reliant.[10] The desired lady was gentle, graceful, frail, modest, nurturing and dependent. These characteristics complemented her primary function — reproduction. The medical profession theorised that women's biological functions and physiological structure mitigated against strenuous physical activity although it recommended light, non-serious exercise, such as dancing and strolling, to stimulate the constitution. Later it encouraged social games such as croquet and tennis. However, most viewed these games as 'matrimonial services' rather than expressions of sporting ability. Thus they merely reinforced the supportive and ornamental social functions of women.[11]

Evangelical groups saw physical activity as a way of teaching 'correct' character — morality, discipline, moderation and sobriety.[12] But this required the rationalisation and institutionalisation of sport. English swimmers conducted the first carnival in the western world in 1837. Australian men followed nine years later at Robinson's (formerly Mrs Bigges's) Baths and the Adelaide City Baths hosted women's events in the mid-1870s.[13] The formal organisation of Australian swimming began in the 1880s as swimmers established clubs at newly built baths and pools. Inspired and motivated by financial gains, an obsession with good health, and a garbled ideology of social Darwinism, imperial duty and fierce individualism,[14] municipal councils and entrepreneurs constructed pools and baths across the country. The 'Natatorium' (Pitt Street, Sydney) hosted the first New South Wales championships in 1889 and three years later six clubs formed the New South Wales Amateur Swimming Association (NSWASA) to codify men's swimming.[15]

These conditions affected the public display of the body. In the 1830s and 1840s males swam naked while women wore pants, skirts, hats and shoes.[16] Segregated enclosures, however, allowed women to remove burdensome costumes. By the 1870s they were wearing short-legged cotton costumes without pants — essentially the same as male swimmers who had covered up under social pressure. By comparison, open sports such as athletics, cricket and cycling imposed strict constraints on women's public appearance. The aquatic medium also removed an 'ideological impediment' to women's swimming — effort: 'no matter how hard the competitors pushed themselves, the watery medium minimised the outward appearance of effort and exertion'. Segregation, enclosure and the medium of participation legitimised women's swimming by creating the impression of a socially non-threatening sport.[17]

Ideas about 'correct' character and moral behaviour were widespread. American Calvinist missionaries in the Pacific condemned surfing as immoral. Ancient Polynesians, especially the Hawaiians, developed and mastered surfing — the art of standing on and manoeuvring a board across the face of a breaking wave. Early European explorers, travellers and sailors expressed surprise and amazement at the surfers' skills.[18] But the missionaries believed that Christianity demanded the 'reformation' of Hawaiians' private lives.[19] They denounced surfing as evil and immoral: the courtship rituals associated with the sport led to 'constant intermingling, without any restraint, of persons of both sexes and of all ages, at all times of the day at at all hours of the night.'[20] By the mid-nineteenth century, few Hawaiians surfed.

The middle-class obsession with health fostered what Christopher Lasch calls a 'therapeutic outlook': the body became exposed to endless private and public examination 'for tell tale symptons of psychic stress, for blemishes and flaws' and 'for reassuring indications that ... life is proceeding according to schedule'.[21] The therapeutic outlook legitimised the re-vealed body, which supplanted the reserved, modest, restrained and hidden Victorian body. It also engendered hysteria amongst moralists disgusted by the revealed body and led to struggles over public bathing and costumes.

Among the bourgeoisie, self-assured and indifferent to the gaze of others,[22] promenading and bathing were simple hedon-istic pastimes. The economically and socially ambitious middle classes, including health faddists, physicians, physical educa-tors, utopians and propertied elements, endorsed these pursuits for their own financial and social interests. On the other hand, moralists, whom Freud called the agents of disgust[23] (and known colloquially as 'Mrs Grundy'), argued that daylight bathing threatened public decency and order.

In New South Wales the Local Authorities Act empowered municipal councils to pass by-laws controlling bathers. Manly and Randwick imposed an eight a.m. curfew, however Waverley permitted bathing at Clovelly at all hours provided bathers were 'properly and becomingly clad',[24] although the police continued to prosecute bathers under Section 77 of the Police Offences Act.[25] In October 1902 William Gocher, proprietor and editor of the *Manly and North Sydney Daily*, forced the issue by defying the law and bathing during daylight hours at Manly. He bathed at midday on three consecutive Sundays, wearing a neck-to-knee costume along with a mackintosh while ap-proaching and leaving the ocean. Police Inspector-General Fosbery declined to prosecute Gocher. A similar well-docu-mented incident the following month explains Fosbery's dis-cretion. Waverley Council requested Fosbery prosecute naked bathers who ran along the beach and 'appear to take great delight in this somewhat disgusting habit'.[26] At Bondi Beach two constables recorded the names and addresses of fifteen bathers, two of whom wore neck-to-knee bathing costumes and the remainder 'small trunks'.

The police recorded that the bathers were 'respectable men and residents of the district' and that they had not observed any bathers naked or undressing in public view. Further investigation revealed that the complaints emanated from Mr Farmer, the lessee of Bondi Baths. Farmer paid the council £150 per annum and according to the police was 'annoyed at seeing so many people enjoying a free bath'.[27] Fosbery thus concluded that if 'bathers wear suitable costume and public decency is not outraged, I am unable to see that a practice permitted for so many years should be stopped. Indeed, I do not suppose that the magistrates would inflict penalties for any breach of the Act ... therefore ... I do not see my way to take action beyond instructing the police that decency is to be observed.'[28] But daylight bathing was only one battle in the public presentation of the revealed body.

Social reformers advocated surf-bathing and sun-bathing as essential for the production of healthy, attractive and youthful bodies. The *Australian Star* suggested that 'the brown skinned specimens of manhood' who spend their weekends at the beach are 'a sight worth looking at'.[29] A 'science' of surf-bathing, part of the scientific intervention into literally every point of social life, lent credence to the therapeutic benefits.

> Sand, surf, sunshine and the free winds of heaven make up the prescription which is confidently recommended as a sort of universal medicine ... This, if not the elixir of life, must surely be part of it, and is certain to tone up the system and lengthen the life. It is plain that he who wishes for a royal road to health and happiness should take the first step to it by getting sunburnt, it is well understood that a well-browned skin is much healthier than a white one. So the sun-worshipper looks with pity upon his pallid brother as one who stupidly neglects a most evident good.[30]

Moralists warned that immodest bodies undermined decency and threatened public order. They insisted on preserving 'the common standards of propriety that prevail amongst civilised nations'[31] and focussed attention on bathers' costumes, sun-bathing and mixed bathing. Complaints inundated newspapers. 'A mother of girls' claimed that the 'heaps of sprawling men and lads, naked, but for a nondescript rag around the middle' had forced her to leave Balmoral beach. She said that the so-called bathing costumes 'might put an Aboriginal to

Miss E. Robinson (winner) and Miss G. Phillips (runner-up) congratulate each other after the Ladies 75 yard swimming race at the New South Wales Championships held at Manly Beach in Sydney, 6 March 1926. Bathing costume regulations for women in the early twentieth century required them to wear 'combinations' which comprised a neck-to-knee costume over which was worn a tunic, as is shown here. (Australian Consolidated Press.)

shame' and recommended punishment by flogging.[32] 'Daily dipper' said that sun-bathers 'put themselves on the same level as dogs'.[33]

Local councils passed by-laws regulating bathing costumes. Bathers initially had to cover their bodies from neck to knee. Later, men had to wear an additional pair of trunks of dark material and women a tunic, also of dark material, to the knee. Reformers decried the restrictions, claiming they thwarted the therapeutic benefits of surf-bathing. R. D. Meagher, a member of the Legislative Council, said if surf-bathing was to have a 'salutary effect on skin, nerves, and tissue', salt water and sunlight must strike the body. He accused moralists of undermining the new woman: 'Where is Mrs Grundy going to stop? Our Australian girls no longer consider it good to wear pale and uninteresting complexions like the heroine of the *Young Ladies' Journal*, but are devotees to Old Sol and Neptune — these bronze Venuses, with Ozone in their nostrils, and vitality in their constitutions'.[34] It was very different from when firm muscles and tanned faces symbolised lower-class women.[35]

Manly, Randwick and Waverley councils and the government drafted a new set of beach ordinances in October 1907. The costume would 'cover the body from the neck to the bend of the knee; and be of such material as not to disclose the colour of the skin [and] ... shall consist of complete combinations, together with a tunic worn over the combinations, both covering the body from the neck to the knee, and the tunic shall have sleeves reaching to at least half way from the shoulder to the elbow'.[36] Bathers interpreted the tunic as a 'skirt' and protested at Manly, Coogee and Bondi beaches where some males donned women's skirts.[37] The new beach ordinances, promulgated seven months later, contained no reference to a tunic.[38]

Much of the pressure sprang from economic interests. Property owners, land speculators and a myriad of small business people such as food, transport, souvenir and entertainment vendors eyed the commercial opportunities afforded by surf-bathing. As one newspaper correspondent wrote, 'but for prudishness and false modesty the waves breaking on the sands might have been rolling sovereigns into the pockets'.[39] Frank Donovan, founding president of the Manly Surf Club (MSC), attributed population growth and increases in property values, housing rents and rates in the Manly area to surf-bathing.[40]

Lack of facilities such as dressing rooms and safety equipment led surf-bathers to form clubs. On the argument that they were providing a public service, councils permitted these clubs to build club accommodation. Bathers sought membership, not specifically for any humanitarian desire to serve the public but more for access to the facilities. According to one early member of the MSC the club 'was run by ... old men, who were primarily concerned with having a decent dressing place and showers'.[41] Not surprisingly, bathers called the first clubs 'dressing-shed syndicates'.[42] The formal constitution of surf-bathing clubs was several years away. At a public meeting to launch the MSC in July 1907, Donovan urged surf-bathers to 'get up and do something to put upon a first-rate footing a glorious form of sport'. Poor conditions, he said, derived from lack of organisation.[43]

In October 1907 the surf-bathing clubs formed the umbrella Surf Bathing Association of New South Wales (SBANSW) to lobby for official recognition of the sport. The class structure and aims of SBANSW ensured that its members were equally as conservative as the moralists whom they opposed.[44] At the formation of the MSC, for example, Donovan recommended that the 'officers and committee should be men of some standing'. Of the initial 600 members, half were 'leading citizens' and the remainder young men trained as lifesavers.[45]

In 1911 the New South Wales government appointed a Surf Bathing Committee (SBC) to report on the sport. John Lord, President of SBANSW, chaired the investigation team which included Charles Paterson, a foundation member of North Steyne Surf Club and Lord's successor in surf-bathing. The SBC concluded that surf-bathing was a 'clean and healthful pastime' with considerable commercial benefits. But it warned that growth depended upon proper controls and policing, recommending that councils appoint club members as beach inspectors. 'By choosing the older and more responsible members [the councils] will secure the aid of men who will use their authority with moderation and discretion for the good of the public, and for the advancement of surf-bathing.'

The Surf Bathing Committee supported existing by-laws against 'loitering on the beach clad only in bathing costume'. It objected to persons in bathing costumes mixing with the public and recommended that bathers walk from the dressing pavilions to the water by the most direct route.[46] The government accepted nearly all the SBC's recommendations.[47]

In March 1902, at the close of the 1901–2 swimming season, Sydney women competed in their first major carnival — in the presence of male spectators. The New South Wales State Ladies' Swimming Championships drew no adverse public reaction. Enclosed venues meant that swimming did not undermine morality. The medical profession expounded the 'scientific' benefits of swimming. The popular press, courting readers and advertisers, enthusiastically reported swimming affairs. Female swimming had been part of the educational curriculum since the late 1890s and a 'whole generation' believed that competitive swimming for women was normal.[48]

But, like Gocher's protests against restrictions on daylight surf-bathing seven months later, the championships were the beginning of a long struggle. Integration of 'scantily clad athletic young men' and 'breathless young women dressed in wet skimpy costumes' at the pool concerned the agents of disgust. As 'Trudge' put it: 'That venerable dame, Mrs Grundy, has got a dead set on affairs of this character, and holds up her hands in holy horror at the mere mention of ladies swimming in the presence of the trousered sex.'[49]

The following season the New South Wales Amateur Swimming Association (NSWASA) approved the recently established Sydney Ladies' Swimming Club's affiliation, although it refused the club representation on the executive.[50] By 1906 the NSWASA included six women's clubs. However, NSWASA officials considered women's swimming an administrative burden and, rather than expand the bureaucracy and executive to include women, the men's association created a separate and subordinate women's controlling body. The New South Wales Ladies' Amateur Swimming Association (NSWLASA) was formed in February 1906.

Conservatives in the swimming establishment argued that 'improperly clad' competitors threatened the ideal 'images of middle class femininity — the modest and impeccably moral angel'. To 'restore decorum' and enforce its authority, the NSWLASA instructed competitors to wear cloaks before and after events, banned male spectators from women's carnivals and forbade women to compete in front of men.[51]

Resegrated women's swimming was shortlived. Men contributed to sociability and raised the number and quality of prizes, while women rebelled against the exclusion of male relations, friends and members of the press. In November 1910 influential women competitors formed the New South Wales League of Swimmers to integrate the sport and offer money prizes. More than three-quarters of NSWLASA members defected to the league.[52] It too, had a brief life. The NSWLASA revoked its 'no-men' regulation during the 1911–12 season amid controversy over the selection of Sarah Durack and Wilhelmina Wylie in the Australian team for the 1912 Olympic Games.

The fifth Olympic Games included women's swimming events for the first time. Before Durack (the fastest female swimmer in the world) and Wylie could compete in Stock-holm, the ladies' association had to rescind its rule forbidding women from swimming in public and the men's association had to approve their selections. The ladies' association considered the motion at a meeting in mid-March 1912. Miss Rose Scott, president of the NSWLASA and a prominent figure in the history of women's rights, and A. C. W. Hill, secretary of the NSWLASA, opposed the desegregation motion saying that 'immodest behaviour' at mixed carnivals would undermine femininity.[53] Sections of the press also expressed doubts. 'The well-shaped girl might easily get over her qualms, no matter how modest she may be, but her less-favoured sister is alto-gether differently placed. Men who have attended swimming shows where the other sex took part, could not help but notice the quizzing and guying girl contestants were frequently sub-jected to.'[54] Interestingly, the *Bulletin* considered Durack a 'favoured sister'. It described her as 'a fine, understanding miss, with the clear eye of perfect health, and a figure that shows no symptoms of ropes and athletic muscles, abnormal develop-ment, or any other nightmare'.[55]

Delegates ignored the negative sentiments and voted to send the pair to Stockholm. Hill's warning to the ladies' association that the men's body would not ratify the decision proved wrong. The NSWASA confirmed the selection of Durack and Wylie subject to them paying £150 each to cover the association's expenses and to the appointment of respect-able chaperones.

Australians hailed Durack and Wylie as national heroines after they won gold and silver respectively in the 100 metres freestyle at the 1912 Games. The pair swelled nationalist pride and legitimised the public presentation of the athletic female.

Lifesaving and swimming illustrate the struggle over public representation and presentation of the body in the first decade of this century. Before conservative middle-class groups ac-cepted the new body image, officials had to show that the activities over which they presided were morally sound and would not incite unruly passions. Ironically, given the expan-sive nature of the beach, which logically should have hindered surveillance, the Surf Bathing Association appears to have achieved legitimacy before the swimming association. In 1912 'Natator' of the *Referee* wrote, 'I believe in the mingling of the sexes on our beaches and under proper supervision; but the cad is much more in evidence at a swimming meeting where women figure than he is in the surf.'[56]

The commercialisation of bourgeois culture and the spread of mass consumption in the 1920s and 1930s radically altered control over the body. Mass consumption propagated a new culture of pleasure and a new tolerance of the revealed body: it 'required a new lifestyle embodied in the ethic of a calculating hedonism, and a new personality type, the narcissistic person'.[57] The beach became the most visible site of hedonist culture in Australia — a place where the attractive sons and daughters of the middle classes 'displayed their bodies with cheerful eroticism'.[58] While the new culture liberated the body from repressive regimens, through advertising it advanced a new method of discipline. Increasingly sophisticated advertising created the desires it promised to satisfy, including the desire for (and loathing of any deviation from) the mesomorphic sporting body.[59] It manipulated people to adopt rigorous self-imposed regimens (diet and exercise) to achieve their 'desires'. The standardisation of commodities, a characteristic of mass consumer culture, imposed a further social conformity on populations through the public surveillance that compels individuals to seek 'normality'.[60]

The Surf Bathing Association of New South Wales was formed 'to advance the sport and pastime of surf-bathing' and it did not automatically appeal to the public. One young Novocastrian woman in the 1930s described lifesavers as 'a whole lot of rude, beer-drinking, swearing, womanising lads'.[61] Fearful of jeopardising its precarious tenure at the beach, the SBANSW emphasised its rescue service and redefined its 'sole aim' as 'the promotion of lifesaving in the surf'.[62] It also displayed its discipline and the seriousness of its function by 'dramatising the beach as a military parade ground' and adopting an athleticism based on military-style drills.[63] The SBANSW reinforced its humanitarian role by changing names in 1920 to the Surf Life Saving Association of New South Wales. In 1923 the New South Wales association became a national body, the Surf Life Saving Association of Australia (SLSAA).

Within a couple of years, the SLSAA became the guardian of public morality at the beach. In 1927 the association executive recommended that male bathers wear a one-piece costume and municipal and shire councils passed by-laws to this effect. However, neither the public nor the clubs accepted the regulation, which was essentially unenforceable.[64] George Philip, president of Tamarama Surf Life Saving Club and Randwick alderman, recounted an incident when a man 'had the audacity to lower his costume off his shoulders':

I went over to tell him it was not allowed. I was told where to go, reinforced by language containing all the colours of the rainbow. I just walked away in the lordly way I thought an Alderman should, to the clubhouse. It was not long before I had a deputation ... from the beach asking me to overlook the incident, which I most magnanimously did, particularly as I did not know where I stood in the matter.[65]

Less than a decade later, the SLSAA advised the government that shorts are 'sufficient costume for men'.[66] Expounding an ideology of therapeutic benefit and self-discipline, the SLSAA declared that 'it should be our aim to encourage young men to take pride in their physique. This cannot be better encouraged than by the opportunity to expose their rippling muscles to sunshine, fresh air and public eye.'[67] Changing social attitudes resolved the debate over men's topless bathing. The Adelaide *Advertiser* provided a perceptive insight into this process: 'it has become increasingly clear that most people, even if they are not personally enthusiastic about trunks, see nothing seriously objectionable in the wearing of them, and, for this reason are not prepared to support a general ban on their use. The conversion of one council after another in the topless bather crusade, has been the reflection of the trend in public thought and taste.'[68] Similar trends followed the bikini and, later, topless bathing for women.

Beach beauty contests, which began after the First World War, exemplify growing tolerance of the revealed female body. John Rickard describes them as a 'local adaption of glamorous Hollywood images' for 'an audience of suburban voyeurs'.[69] Yet, exhibitionism contains its own method of self-discipline. Contest promoter and organiser, the *Sunday Times*, said that 'many surfer girls do not realise the need of general physical culture and care of the body'. This, it suggested, requires self-discipline:

The girlish beauty that has charm is an effect of a wise discretion in all ways of life. It does not go with late nights and general dissipation, however innocent. The girl who wants to look charming in a surfing costume must be fastidious in all her habits and wise in all her exercises. She must dance and walk well. She must eat sensibly. She must avoid all excess. Otherwise, sooner or later, come all the enemies of beauty.[70]

The sports clothing and advertising industries were essential to this self-discipline. As Marion Stell points out, briefer clothes, while promising new freedoms, enticed women to reveal more

Ronnie Anderson at Bondi, January 1935, demonstrating the 'statue' style of riding typical of the pre-Second World War era. The board was 2.7 metres long. (Hood Collection, State Library of New South Wales.)

of their bodies.[71] Self-discipline (exercise and dieting), combined with the use of an expanding range of toiletries and accessories, ensured they conformed to the 'correct' shape.

The Surf Life Saving Association of Australia approved and encouraged surfer girl contests.[72] The sole entry criterion — 'modest charm' — was consistent with the association's notion of femininity. Women served in lifesaving clubs only as domestic and decorative labour. The SLSAA banned them from rescue work and competition until the early 1980s because they were 'not strong enough physically to carry a heavy belt and line or to swim competitively in surf races'.[73]

The culture of pleasure penetrated the lifesaving movement in different forms despite its philosophy of sober moderation and utilitarianism. This included surfing. Young *haoles* (European-Americans) at Waikiki 'rediscovered' Polynesian surfing on boards around the beginning of the twentieth century, and the activity reached Australia during the following decade. Charles Paterson brought the first Hawaiian *alaia* (longboard) to Australia in 1912. Although surf-bathers at North Steyne could not master it, several Manly youths persevered, riding broken white water on locally designed and built craft. They included Claude West and Esma Amor. The popularisation of surfing followed the international travels of Olympic swimmer and Waikiki surfer Duke Kahanamoku. He won the gold medal and broke the world record for the 100 metres freestyle at Stockholm and the New South Wales Amateur Surfing Association invited him to Sydney. During his 1915 stay in Australia, Kahanamoku demonstrated surfing at Freshwater and taught West the principles of manoeuvring the board to stay ahead of the white water. Lew Whyte, a Geelong businessman, also watched Kahanamoku's demonstration at Freshwater. Four years later he visited Hawaii and purchased several boards which his friends used around Anglesea and Lorne.[74]

Oversized, heavy and cumbersome, the *alaia* boards posed a hazard to both their riders and the surf-bathing public. Sydney councils called them 'instruments of destruction' and in the early 1920s initiated the first of many 'ban the boards' campaigns. Some lifesavers, including Claude West, used boards as rescue craft which lent them some official support, but even as early as the mid-1920s the surfboard symbolised excessive permissiveness. Paterson visited Hawaii in 1927 and recorded his disgust at the degenerate nature of undisciplined hedonism at Waikiki:

> Hawaiian beach boys spend their whole time on the beach, giving exhibitions on the board or taking out bathers on board or outrigger ... Many visiting women make fools of themselves over these lazy boys. They are utterly spoiled. The beach is a riot of colour in costumes, dressing gowns and coolie coats. There are no restrictions as to costume. People wear what they like. Some roll them down to the waist (men and girls both) and revel in the sun. Nothing is done in the way of teaching life saving, nor are there any life saving appliances.[75]

Individual lifesaving clubs in Australia organised surfing 'displays' and others conducted paddling races at carnivals although both were 'expedient' if time was short.[76] Surfboard-riding thrived, however, especially after the introduction from California of the hollow, finned board in the mid-1930s. In 1941 surfers sought permission from Waverley Council to form their own club at Bondi. Some Surf Life Saving Association officials supported the idea believing it would give the association more control over boards and more power to police 'irresponsibles'.[77] After the Second World War, the association recognised the longboard as rescue equipment and included it in national championships.

The culture of beach pleasure strained the relationship

between swimmers and lifesavers. Both traditionally competed in the other's carnivals. So close was the relationship, that before the formation of the Federation of International Swimming Associations in 1908, the secretary of the Lifesaving Society in London proposed an international union of swimmers and lifesavers.[78] Many of Australia's best swimmers in the first decades of the twentieth century, such as Harold Hardwick and Andrew 'Boy' Charlton, were lifesavers. Australia's early pre-eminence in swimming declined after the 1924 Olympics and officials blamed the glamour and allure of the beach for enticing competitors away from the pool. In the words of former NSWASA official Syd Grange, swimmers were content to 'lounge on the beaches' and 'reflect upon past achievements'.[79]

Swimming subsequently adopted a new persona. In the 1940s professional swimming coaches, including Forbes Carlyle, Frank Guthrie, Harry Gallagher and Sam Herford, espoused small clubs and scientific methods. Their objective was to produce human machines: 'fluent stroke makers' and 'efficient technicians'.[80] While they coached heroes such as John Devitt, Murray Rose, Dawn Fraser, Jon Henricks, Lorraine Crapp and Shane Gould, their methods often complemented the mean and petty authoritarianism of too many amateur swimming officials. As Dennis Phillips unhappily reminds us, swimming officials destroyed the careers of some of Australia's champions.[81]

The culture of pleasure expanded beyond sober moderation after the Second World War. Advances in technology (cheap, effective and simple-to-use durables), and changes in retailing (standardisation of commodities), distribution (department stores and supermarkets) and communication (advertising and television) created and appeased an insatiable appetite for new goods, new experiences and personal fulfilment. The car and the malibu surfboard[82] embodied the growing culture of pleasure and symbolised freedom and self-expression.

Hawaiian and Californian lifesavers brought malibus to Australia for an international carnival coinciding with Melbourne's Olympic Games. They demonstrated the new boards to enthralled crowds at Avalon and Manly (Sydney) and Torquay (Victoria). Films such as *Big Surf* (1957) produced by

American Bud Browne, Bernard 'Midget' Farrelly's win in the unofficial world surfing championship at Makaha (Hawaii) in 1963 and his victory in front of an estimated crowd of 65 000 in the first official World Surfing Championships at Manly in 1964 increased the sport's local popularity. However, it was Hollywood's discovery of surfing, as portrayed in the 'commercial monster' Gidget (1959), that propelled it 'into a state of mass consciousness'.[83]

According to orthodox cultural history, the lightweight malibu board freed surfers from the fetters of body-surfing and lifesaving and they formed an anti-social 'surfie' sub-culture based on rivalry with 'clubbies'.[84] It is a grossly simplistic account. As surfing gained popularity the danger of surfboards washing into bathing areas increased. This initiated a spatial reorganisation of the beach and the physical separation of board-riders and surf-bathers. The Surf Life Saving Association of Australia had assumed the mantle of duty of care at the beach and was the logical body to organise and enforce the separation. The process raised tensions between lifesavers and surfers and led to 'incidents', but it is incorrect to paint the SLSAA as an over-zealous policeman.[85] Contrary to popular myth, surfers did not leave the lifesaving movement en masse.[86] The SLSAA relied for recruits upon young people with an affinity for the beach, and it introduced surfing as a national title in 1965–66. And as late as 1964, specialist surfing magazines such as Surfing World carried reports of lifesaving sport. Municipal councils were also ambivalent. While suspicious of surfing's lifestyle they eyed its commercial potential.

The leg-rope largely resolved the spatial reorganisation of the beach in the 1970s. It dramatically reduced the number of riderless boards washing through bathers and opened areas of the beach to surfers which remained inaccessible to surf-bathers.

Surfing's anti-social face emerged in the late 1960s. This must be analysed within the context of broader socio-economic and political shifts. Tolerance is a double-edged sword. When 'new social impulses are set free', John Clarke and his colleagues explain, 'they are impossible to fully contain':

> Open the door to 'permissiveness' and a more profound sexual liberation may follow. Raise the slogan of 'freedom' and some people will give it an unexpectedly revolutionary accent and content. Invest in the technical means for expanding consciousness, and consciousness may expand beyond predictable limits. Develop the means of communication, and people will gain access to print and audiences for which the web-offset litho press were never intended.[87]

In the mid-1960s tolerance, freedom and choice intersected with other changes. The extension of secondary and tertiary education to cater for the population bulge and the technological requirements of industrial production encouraged youth to probe, question and challenge. If education promised individual fulfilment, it also exposed new fears about nuclear annihilation, ecological catastrophe and social alienation. These contributed to growing social anxiety and pessimism. The social conditions of modern production fragmented the extended family, thus further weakening traditional moral authority. De-colonisation and Third World liberation informed the social conscience of the educated middle classes about women's rights, Aboriginal rights and the Vietnam War. Collectively these changes engendered a radical cultural disaffiliation among broad sectors of the educated middle-class youth who resolved to 'invert' bourgeois society.[88]

Counter-culture disciples transposed the work-leisure dichotomy into a work-is-play philosophy, rejecting high consumption, materialism and competition. They expounded a 'fraternal' individualism that extolled creativity and self-expression within a co-operative milieu.[89] Strategically, counter-culture was an amalgam of alternate, typically utopian lifestyles, and political activism.

Soul-surfing epitomised the counter-culture and was the dominant mode of surfing in the late 1960s and early 1970s. The 1966 world champion, Robert 'Nat' Young, described soul-surfing as a 'reaction' against competition which 'helped restore ... balance' to the sport.[90] Young's claim that 'by simply surfing we are supporting the revolution' was the maxim of an era.[91]

Soul-surfers scorned the establishment. 'Clubbies' were a prime target. The cartoon character Captain Goodvibes (a variously disguised pig) who appeared in *Tracks*, an alternative monthly newspaper for surfers, ridiculed the conservatism of lifesavers and condemned their 'fascist' behaviour. Yet, the letters pages in *Tracks* suggest many soul-surfers shared Captain Goodvibes' disdain of women and his homophobia — in common with the clubbies whom they despised.

Counter-culture's transgression of the moderate limits of middle-class tolerance led to its condemnation: surfers were undisciplined, indulgent and decadent; they were rotten, long-haired, unwashed, drug addicts. But the end came from within: counter-culture was simply unsustainable. Yippy leader Jerry Rubin's immortal words, 'people should do whatever the f*** they want',[92] may have been psychologically comforting, but it could not reconcile the contradiction of alternative independence in an inter-dependent society. Moreover, the young aged, lost energy and gained new priorities and commitments, particularly after the resolution of major political rallying points, notably the withdrawal of troops from Vietnam and the abolition of conscription.

Counter-culture's discourse of awareness, its 'philosophical' environmentalism and Eastern mysticism, were incoherent. Statements such as surfing is 'the ultimate liberating factor on the planet. You're working with nature in the raw in surfing' and, 'when I surf, I dance for Krishna' are pure gibberish.[93] Drugs, a key source of counter-culture's enlightenment, compounded the babble. They may have given prominent surfer Ted Spencer 'an insight and an appreciation of the energy of . . . underlying things', but as David Caute points out, 'the claimed journeys to "inner truth" degenerate, on inspection, into puddles of vomit'.[94] If drug taking was revolutionary praxis, it also paradoxically affirmed the culture of indulgent consumption and the demand for instant gratification. Lastly, a more dynamic capitalism simply subsumed counter-culture, including soul-surfing.

Counter-culture performed a valuable role for advanced capitalism by 'pioneering' new commodity forms, particularly in music and leisure. Entrepreneurially-minded surfers, mostly seeking pleasurable and playful lifestyles, began commodifying surfing's style in the early 1960s producing new fashions, magazines, films and music. Counter-culture did not diminish these experiments. On the contrary it gave capitalism 'greater flexibility'.

> In many aspects, the revolutions in 'lifestyle' were a pure, simple, raging, commercial success. In clothes, and styles, the counter-culture explored, in its small scale 'artisan' and vanguard capitalist forms of production and distribution, shifts in taste which the mass consumption chain-stores were too cumbersome, inflexible and over-capitalised to exploit. When the trends settled down, the big commercial battalions moved in and mopped up.[95]

Even at the height of counter-culture, progressive businesses boosted, incorporated and exploited surfing's clean, refreshing and sporting images. Surfing complemented products concerned with the body, health and lifestyle. Advertising agencies inverted negative images, such as casual indifference, portrayed by soul-surfing. In the early 1970s, for example, surfer 'Jimmy Peterson' (*Bio-Clear* medicated cream) symbolised

249

the now-ideal middle-class Australian youth. His tanned skin, lengthy blond-streaked hair and casual form (nestling with his girlfriend) conveyed an image of simplicity and innocence instead of scruffy untidy indifference.

Today, swimming, lifesaving and surfing are commodities, the viability of which depends heavily upon 'managerial athleticism' — the creation and conveyance of acceptable body images. Successful sportspeople are today 'trained, disciplined and orchestrated to enhance [their] personal value'.[96] But while the three sports largely survive as products, their respective paths to this existence (that is, professionalism) were vastly different, and in the case of the last two unique.

Swimming became a professional sport in the 1980s. Commercial pressures, government and popular demands for international success, the need for sponsorship and demands by swimmers for financial rewards transformed swimming and other Olympic sports. Although there are good accounts of the development of professionalism within the Olympic movement,[97] the precise details of the Australian experience require further study.

Professional sport became a part of Surf Life Saving Association of Australia's structure in the early 1980s. This followed *Coolangatta Gold*, a film based on a forty-two-kilometre Ironman event. The producers organised an actual competition for the film using lifesavers. The event drew excited media and public attention and alerted lifesavers and entrepreneurs to a new commodity. The SLSAA feared that entrepreneurs would organise events outside its control and, with its sponsor Kellogg (Australia) Pty Ltd, established a grand-prix circuit in 1986. However, the National Council of the Surf Life Saving Association could not reconcile professional sport with a humanitarian and voluntary association and refused to develop the circuit to its full potential. Dissatisfied with the management, administration and structure of the circuit, leading ironmen teamed with the International Management Group in 1989 and formed a rebel competition — the Ironman Super Series. The ironman event remains a site of struggle within the SLSAA between professional sportspeople and the national council.[98]

Amateurism never encumbered surfing. Early surfers endorsed and advertised products, wrote newspaper and magazine columns, and made their living from associated industries. Competitions in the early 1960s offered prizes and money became widely available in the mid-1960s in the United States. (In 1965 US officials declared swimmer John Anderson ineligible for the Olympics after he won a sports car in a surfing competition.) The anti-competition ethic of soul-surfing undoubtedly delayed the onset of a professional circuit but it did not totally subsume surfing. Not all surfers embraced its alternate philosophies, the disjointed tenets of which made absolute subscription impossible anyway. Many pursued competitive surfing which, as Midget Farrelly put it, 'sure beat being arrested at customs with heroin up your arse'.[99] Nonetheless, in some respects, counter-culture had a positive influence on the development of professional surfing. Its work-is-play philosophy opened new social and economic spaces. Perspicacious and resolute surfers recognised that professionalism offered competitors, administrators and a plethora of small businesspeople a viable avenue to eternal hedonism.

Professional surfing, like all developing sports, confronted problems associated with governance and codification. Attempts to resolve these during the 1970s resulted in uncertainty within the sport and engendered bitter personal rivalries and jealousies. The International Professional Surfing Association (IPSA), formed in 1969 in Hawaii, represented the first attempt to govern professional surfing. CBS television producer Larry Lindberg proposed the idea to surfers during the Duke Kahanamoku Surfing Classic.[100] In 1970, the IPSA conducted the initial Smirnoff contest (considered the unofficial world championship until 1976). Fred Hemmings, winner of the 1968 world title, directed the Smirnoff contest and with Randy Rarick and Barnie Baker organised the inaugural Pipeline Masters in 1971. But the IPSA tournaments suffered from poor direction and administration. Invitations were issued by reputation, the rules varied between contests, judging appeared inconsistent and judges seemed biased

In 1975 surfers Terry Fitzgerald, Mark Warren, Ian Cairns and Peter Townend, with Graham Cassidy (promoter of Surfabout — one of Australia's first professional tournaments) and Doug Warbrick (proprietor of Rip Curl — surfboards and surfing accessories) established the Australian Professional Surfers Association (APSA).[101] Simultaneously, Hemmings, Rarick and Jack Shipley formed International Professional

Surfers (IPS). Both bodies introduced a ratings system (the APSA allocated points based on placings, the IPS on prize money), by-laws and contest rules to develop a grand-prix circuit. There was little immediate progress and in 1977 Cairns and Townend formed the Association of Surfing Professionals (ASP) with the same aims. Hemmings claimed that the IPS was not a surfers' association but a co-operative marketing effort and changed the name to International Professional Surfing. Hemmings, in one sense, outmanoeuvred Cairns and Townend by recreating the grand-prix concept in 1978. After securing sponsorship from Pan-Am he enticed many surfers back to the IPS.[102] However, Cairns and Townend's brazen attempt in 1976 to advance professional surfing through an ostentatious marketing venture known as the Bronzed Aussies had lost them much support. Cairns later revived the ASP and with funding from Ocean Pacific (clothing) wrested administrative control of professional surfing from Hemmings in 1982.

'Managerial athleticism' has been an essential ingredient in professional surfing. Hemmings asserted that professional 'surfers will have to be clean and healthy athletes; there will be no room for drugs'.[103] Pioneer surfer manager Mike Hurst said the professionalism would depend upon surfers' appearance and intellect, their ability to articulate, project and be colourful, and, he added, they must be photogenic.[104] Cassidy insisted surfers 'put their old ... ways aside and come up with a character . . . acceptable to the public'.[105] The APSA's constitution included a 'code of conduct' compelling members to 'forward a good image' to sponsors and the public.[106] Recent world champion Kelly Slater (United States) is the quintessential 'new' surfer: 'I always want to portray a good image, "Don't do drugs, stay in school." . . . it's really important for me to say that in every interview.'[107] Yet, surfing retains a peculiar style, combining unparalleled hedonism with the fatuousness of counter-culture. As one professional recently described his feelings, 'I surf for the same reason I perpetually flog myself to the heights of orgasmic pleasure — because it feels good.'[108]

Most social theories emphasise the development of mass consumption and ignore the role played in sport in the transformation of the production of the middle-class body. Repressive

Guy Leech, covered in sand and looking exhausted, has a television camera pushed in front of his face after winning the Ironman contest at Harbord Beach in Sydney, 28 January 1985. (Miller/Fairfax Picture Library.)

regimes controlled the presentation of the body in public for most of the nineteenth century. New representations of the body first emerged in isolated social spaces, such as enclosed swimming pools and the beach. By pointing to economic advantages, improvements in health, and moral virtue, swimmers and surf-bathers expanded these spaces early this century and showed that hedonism was not incompatible with discipline. Mass consumerism further spread the new leisure lifestyle and its hedonistic practices. Mass consumerism permitted the unashamed display of the body by subjugating it through self-disciplinary maintenance routines.[109] Freud offers an interesting psychological explanation of this condition by pointing out that 'repression is often achieved by means of excessive reinforcement of the thought contrary to the one which is to be repressed'.[110] This raises questions such as how liberated is the sportswoman who must continually validate her sexuality? In a long battle against sexual innuendo, Dawn Fraser had to constantly deny that she was masculine.[111]

Today, Australia's national swimmers, professional surfers, ironmen and ironwomen (lifesavers) present themselves, and are presented by governments, sports officials, managing agents, sponsors and advertisers, as models of acceptable appearance and exemplars of the body's expressive capacity.[112] These images are not self-perpetuating; there are definite limits. First, marketing is essential. The fading popularity of the 'official' Surf Life Saving Association of Australia ironman circuit in favour of the Ironman Super Series is testimony to the power of marketing. Second, the agents of disgust remain vigilant. Manly Council's 're-dressing' of bathers at Reef Beach, after sixteen years of officially-sanctioned unclad sunbathing and swimming, reflects Mrs Grundy's determination. Lastly, the influence of science cannot be dismissed. For most of this century science proclaimed the benefits of the exposed body; today it warns of the dangers. There has been a noticeable decline in the revealed body at the beach. One teenager recently described the situation as follows: 'You lie around the beach, you get burned. You go in the water, you stink. So your skin is pink and your hair stinks. You might as well have smooth white skin and fresh smelling hair.'[113]

Fifty years ago, George Ryley Scott observed that the revealed body is a *fashion* that waxes and wanes. History, he correctly reminds us, warns against making any assumption about the future of the revealed body in public. It is a serious lesson for many sports.

14   Track and Field

John A. Daly

When we think about Australians who have done well at the Olympics, the names that come most readily to mind are those of women ...

Dennis Phillips, *Australian women at the Olympic Games* (Sydney, 1992)

The formation in the early 1980s of the Australian Institute of Sport and since then institutes of sport in each State have ... enabled Australia's élite athletes to perform at a higher level than ever before.

Athletics Australia, *The Landy Report*, 1992

I N THE early days of British settlement in Australia, as we have already observed, such fashionable English sports as steeplechasing, polo, hunting and horse-racing were the preserve of the colonial élite (or those who aspired to gentry status), who used these symbolic but exclusive display activities to indicate their position in the new society. The sports of the lower orders, however, were those of low organisation requiring only energy or physical strength but little or no equipment. Athletic activities like boxing or foot-races (walking or running) were organised by entrepreneurial colonial tavern keepers. In keeping with British traditions, these activities offered impromptu sporting entertainment for a drinking and gambling clientele wherever groups of ordinary folk were congregated. Old English sports like the high leap, putting-the-stone, wrestling, running over varying distances (and sometimes over sheep hurdles) allowed members of a community to identify with a local champion and gamble on the result. There were other tavern sports like quoits and skittles but 'athletic sports' could cater for family groups and were deemed respectable, whereas the quoits and skittles were usually tavern-yard activities and were considered not appropriate for women or children.

Foot-running, or pedestrianism as it was then known, was a feature of the earliest sports meetings in colonial Australia. Matches of ability attracted much attention and large crowds. Often head-to-head contests, they were sometimes made more complex and amusing by conditional rules (for example, each pedestrian to carry a jockey). The extraordinary pedestrian William Francis King, or 'the Flying Pieman' as he became popularly known in Sydney in the 1840s, carried animals across his shoulders when he walked from Campbelltown to Sydney in eight and a half hours and from Sydney to Parramatta in just under seven hours.[1] Usually, however, the contests simply matched two 'peds'. A typical challenge was that put forward by W. G. Lambert in 1845.

A CHALLENGE

The advertiser challenges to run any person in the Colony for any distance being not less than a mile for the sum of 20 pounds at the Adelaide Races in January next.[2]

Lambert, licensee of the Club House Hotel in Hindley Street, had been a well-known pedestrian in England before emigrating to South Australia. Widespread interest in 'locomotives' like Lambert and King encouraged the sport, and prize money attracted famous peds from all over the world — Tom Malone and Frank 'Scurry' Hewitt from Ireland, Harry Hutchens and Albert Bird from England, and Lou Myers from America. These 'champions of the world' came to Australia in the nineteenth century to compete against local athletes. When public enthusiasm for such contests was at its peak in the 1870s the winners could earn substantial sums.

Robert Watson of Scone in New South Wales 'better known than any pedestrian in Australia' contested a 200-yard race (about 183 metres) for a purse of £400 against Charles Carver of Moree. The race attracted 3000 spectators to the Maitland racecourse in May 1878. The *Sydney Morning Herald* described the race thus:

William Francis King, 'the Flying Pieman', was an innovative 'pedestrian' in his athletic challenges. (National Library of Australia.)

when about 160 yards had been traversed, the favourite [Watson], who was fully six yards in front looked back and beckoned to his opponent who was struggling gamely but hopelessly. Watson then folded his arms and ran the remainder of the distance at his ease, winning without an effort by seven or eight yards. It was a popular victory and Watson was escorted back to town by a large crowd cheering enthusiastically. The same evening the stakes were paid over.[3]

Prize money was impressive in colonial Australia and attracted a wide variety of peds of all classes including local Aborigines who contested many races. The 1889 Carrington Sheffield offered a prize of 500 guineas and was won by an Aboriginal lad, Billy Williams. This race, run at Moore Park, was named after the popular sporting governor, Lord Carrington, indicating upper-class patronage.[4]

The chance to bet on a runner like Billy Williams and win up to £10 000 from the bookmakers at the ground meant that large crowds were common at the venues, which were often lit

257

by gas lights for evening meetings. In Sydney the Sir Joseph Banks Hotel at Botany was the popular venue for the peds, especially from 1884 when Frank Smith, a theatrical entrepreneur became proprietor. Smith engaged runners from overseas, encouraged Aboriginal athletes to compete to give added interest and uncertainty to races and placed no limits on betting. Prizes of up to 800 guineas attracted star athletes and hence large audiences so much so that suburban horse-racing clubs in Sydney postponed meetings rather than risk heavy losses by trying to compete with Smith's sports.[5]

The success of these athletics meetings (and the rich rewards, either in prize money or gambling wins) was responsible ultimately for their decline. Press reports of the 1880s deplored the suspicious events surrounding the conduct and organisation of some meets. Athletes competed under assumed names, 'ran dead' (did not try) or teamed up to make a killing from the bookmakers. Deception became commonplace and included mismeasuring of distances and regular instances of visiting athletes being paid appearance money and then deliberately running dead against local champions whilst betting on the result. Such sharp practices gradually reduced the popularity of professional athletics in Australia.

In their place amateur athletics were advocated as healthy, manly and moral activities and were sponsored by prominent influential citizens who sought to counteract the appeal of the professionals to an easily distracted working class. In Adelaide it was a group of the colonial gentry (Messrs Morphett, Kingston, Hawker, Bundey and Ayres) who formed the Adelaide Amateur Club in 1864 (the first such club in Australia)) and who encouraged the working class to do likewise in Port Adelaide where the Port Adelaide Club was established in 1870.[6] The pattern was similar in other colonies.

H. C. A. Harrison was the amateur sprint champion of Victoria from 1859 to 1866 and in his autobiography states that 'we [a committee of gentlemen] formed the Amateur Athletic Club in 1866'.[7] The Sydney Amateur Athletic Club was established in July 1872 and members were 'elected by ballot, so that there [was] no chance of the professional element creeping in'. The State Governor, Sir Hercules

Robinson, was patron and the club boasted nearly one hundred muscular Christians.[8]

The combination of sport and religious ideals was nowhere more in evidence than in denominational boys colleges. The private schools had always included athletics of the amateur kind in their sport offerings: King's School and Sydney Grammar, St Peter's College in Adelaide and Melbourne Church of England Grammar School all encouraged athletics in the English tradition. A similar pattern emerged in the other capital cities — Hobart, Brisbane and Perth. When senior students completed their schooling they continued their sport at university, either in Australia or at Oxford or Cambridge in England. England in fact was always the reference point in terms of standards and rules. In June 1870 a 'lover of sport' wrote to the *Register* in Adelaide drawing attention to the fact that current performances by members of the Adelaide Amateur Athletic Club were comparable to Oxford and Cambridge records: for example, Adelaide Amateur Athletic Club recorded 10 seconds for the 100 yards, against Oxbridge's 10.2 seconds; 20 feet for the long jump, against 20 feet 3 $3/4$ inches; and 5 feet 4 inches for the high jump against 5 feet $4^1/2$ inches.[9] Indeed the winner of the hurdles race in the English inter-varsity match in that year was a South Australian, John Lancelot Stirling, who, after completing his schooling at St Peter's College in Adelaide, attended Trinity College, Cambridge.[10]

The first meeting of the Sydney Amateur Athletic Club was attended by the Governor and Sir James Ferguson, visiting Governor of South Australia, who could report on the success of amateur athletics in Adelaide and its influence on the working class. However, while South Australia witnessed the establishment of the first amateur club in Australia, it was New South Wales which first organised clubs into an interactive and supporting association under the guidance of Richard Coombes. Victoria followed in 1891, Queensland in 1895, Tasmania in 1902 and South Australia in 1905. Western Australia formed an association in 1905 but it was disbanded in 1908 and did not re-form until 1928.

The Amateur Athletic Association of New South Wales was formed in 1887. Richard Coombes, 'an English pedestrian of some note', was one of a group who met in Sydney to 'take over management of amateur athletic sports in [the] colony in an effort to counteract the "moral endangering" influence of the professionals'.[11] Coombes was to be president of the New South Wales association for over forty years (1894–1935) but became

259

even better known for his efforts in promoting the Olympic movement in Australia and for establishing the Amateur Athletic Union of Australia. He was an ardent supporter of the Olympic movement and had been one of the senior sports officials responsible for the establishment of the Australian Olympic Federation in 1895.[12] His espoused philosophy of 'sport for sport's sake' was the basis of a strong amateur ethos that defined the operation of the Amateur Athletic Union well beyond his lifetime. Indeed, even before his death in 1935, his unyielding attitude to amateurism in sport prompted the description of him as 'a living fossil — a Corinthian'.[13] The influence of Richard Coombes on Australian sport and the ideals one should possess in playing extended beyond athletics but he is quite rightly regarded as 'the father of amateur athletics in Australia'.

The first Australasian Track and Field Championships were held in Melbourne in November 1893. New South Wales, Victoria and New Zealand were the only teams competing but the event was reported widely throughout Australia. After the third Australasian championships were conducted at Sydney Cricket Ground in October 1897 an inter-colonial athletic conference, chaired by Coombes, took place and a committee was formed to draw up rules for an Amateur Athletic Union of Australasia. Coombes was elected president and Edward S. Marks honorary secretary/treasurer. Both held these positions until 1934. New Zealand withdrew from the Union in 1927.

Pierre de Coubertin had made it quite clear that 'the Olympics must be reserved for men'. He was, of course, a man of his time, dismissing women's wish to participate in athletic contests as inappropriate 'Amazonian ambition'.[14] Eventually, however, a decision was taken to include athletic events for women in the Olympics in Amsterdam in 1928. This prompted the New South Wales athletic association to provide races for women in their championships from 1926. Edith (Edie) Robinson won the sprints in that year and repeated her success in the two following years. She was selected as Australia's first female Olympic track athlete in 1928 and was placed third in the semi-final of the women's 100 metres.

At the time of the 1928 Games there were three women's

athletic clubs in New South Wales (Botany, Kensington and St George) affiliated with and supervised by the Amateur Athletic Association of New South Wales. The first inter-club competition for women was held at the Shepherd's Bush Coursing Track at Mascot in New South Wales in 1929 and news of the success of that meet encouraged women in other states to organise their own activities. In the 1920s however, women's competitions in all states of Australia were determined by the men and their sporting organisations until the women took control of their own associations. Victoria and Queensland did this in 1929, South Australia in 1931, New South Wales in 1932, Western Australia in 1936 and Tasmania in 1937. The Australian Women's Amateur Athletic Union was formed in 1932 although the first national championships for women were conducted in Melbourne in January 1930.[15]

The need to organise their own activities was evidenced by the fact that national representation, range and even conduct of events was determined by the whim of male officials. For many years men determined the range of events available for women at athletic meets; often women were only allowed a restricted number of tries in a field event (for example, two attempts rather than three in a high or long jump), ostensibly to save time.

Women athletes were excluded from the first two Empire Games teams in 1930 and 1934. It was regarded as 'basic prejudice against women's track and field'.[16] Even in 1938, when the Empire and Commonwealth Games were to be held on home soil in Sydney, the secretary of the Australian Amateur Athletic Union (with Richard Coombes' approval) announced that 'no more than six women' would be endorsed in the Australian team.[17] Doris Magee, the first secretary of the AWAAU, argued the absurdity (and unfairness) of such a decision and the Empire and Commonwealth Games Association agreed to intervene and raise the quota of female athletes to fourteen. In the eight events available to women at those games in 1938, Australian women won ten medals — five gold, three silver and two bronze! It is now well known that women athletes have continued that impressive record for Australia, winning seventy-five per cent of all Australian gold medals in the Olympic track and field events.[18] The names of Shirley Strickland, Marjorie Jackson, Betty Cuthbert, Maureen Caird, Glynis Nunn and Debbie Flintoff-King are now enshrined in Australian sporting folklore because of their success in the athletic arena.

For fifty years the two men's and women's athletics groups operated separately, but in the early 1980s, under pressure from the Federal Government, they combined to form one single association. That organisation operates today as Athletics Australia with branches in each state. An inter-club system of competition exists in each of these states with the best athletes graduating through state championships to the nationals. Successful athletes at the national level are selected to represent Australia in overseas competition, notably the Olympics and the Commonwealth Games. While the combining of the men's and women's associations has been welcomed by the athletes, has rationalised facilities and equalised financial support, opportunities for women in administrative leadership positions have once again been restricted and many of the talented women leaders of the 1980s left the scene when the senior positions in Athletics Australia and the state branches were assumed by men.

While men's and women's athletics (formerly 'amateur athletics') have combined to conduct events, the professionals have preserved their own Athletic League with each state conducting its own programme of events. Major meets like the Easter Stawell Gift are still considered significant Australian sporting events with a wide section of the community taking a special interest in the conduct (and winning!) of the event each year. The Stawell Gift, the world's oldest and Australia's most prestigious professional foot-race, was first run in 1878 before an audience of 2000 spectators. The race, run over 130 yards (now 120 metres), was won by a twenty-four-year-old farmer, W. J. Millard, who received 'a purse of twenty pounds'. The current value of a win at Stawell is $25 000.

In the professional ranks two athletes are still revered — Arthur Postle, 'the Crimson Flash', and Jack Donaldson, 'the Blue Streak'. Postle set world records for sprint events from fifty yards (5.1 seconds) to 200 yards (19 seconds). He was reputed to be the fastest human alive in 1906 when he defeated R. B. Day of Ireland on the Kalgoorlie gold fields. Record crowds were attracted to all his races. Jack Donaldson rivalled Postle in events over 100 yards but in South Africa in 1910 he defeated Postle and American champion Charles Holway in

the 100 yards in 9.38 seconds — a new world record. It was not until 1948 that this record was beaten. Donaldson was called 'the Carbine of Running' and assumed legendary hero status. His 130-yard world record lasted until 1951. At Stawell Donaldson is still spoken of as the greatest of all professional athletes, however, he really does have to share that title with Arthur Postle.[19] Elimination of the competition ban between amateurs and professionals and the introduction of open athletics occurred in Australia in 1985; athletes from both ranks now compete against each other.

There have been few Aboriginal athletes in amateur ranks but the professionals always welcomed their involvement. The prize money available was enough incentive to compete, particularly in the bush, and some Aboriginal athletes attained legendary status in their time. Bobby Kinnear was the first Aborigine to win the Stawell Gift in 1883 while Charlie Samuels, 'the prince of black pedestrians', was regarded as the greatest runner in the world in the 1870s. He beat the English champion Harry Hutchens over 150 yards in 1877 and in the same year he defeated Irish champion Tom Malone. He was reputed to have run the 100 yards in 9.1 seconds at a time when

Golden Girl Betty Cuthbert wins the 200 metres final at the 1956 Olympic Games in Melbourne. (Burke/Fairfax Picture Library.)

the recognised world record was 9.8 seconds![20] Few Aboriginal athletes were encouraged to compete as amateurs; consequently their names have been missing at national representative level. However, in the 1992 Olympic Games in Barcelona a young Aboriginal woman, Cathy Freeman, represented Australia and her people with distinction.

The first modern Olympic Games were held in Athens in 1896. Australia had one representative, Edwin Flack.[21] 'Teddy', as he was known, attended Melbourne Church of England Grammar School. He never became the school athletic champion but in 1893, after joining the Old Melburnians, he won the Victorian and Australasian one-mile championship. He repeated this success a year later. Flack left Australia in 1895 to study accountancy with Price, Waterhouse and Company in London and joined the London Athletic Club. He travelled with members of that club to Athens to contest the middle-distance events in the Olympic Games. He won both the 800 metres (2 minutes 11 seconds) and the 1500 metres (4 minutes 33.2 seconds), competed in the tennis (with Englishman George Robertson) and entered the marathon. When Flack won his track events an Austrian flag was hoisted to announce his success as the organisers could not locate an Australian flag! Prior to his going to Athens the English journal *Sporting Life* had written of Flack: 'Though not up to the best English form, Flack has, however, shown sufficient pace and stamina to earn for himself a distinct and meritorious place as a cross-country runner at home.'[22] Indeed he led the Olympic marathon for the latter part of the race and dropped out just three kilometres from the finish.

Flack is perhaps the greatest of Australia's Olympic representatives but there have been many other success stories. Gold-medal athletes at the Games have been Flack (1896), Nick Winter (1924), Jack Metcalfe (1936), John Winter (1948), Marjorie Jackson (1952), Shirley Strickland (1952 and 1956), Betty Cuthbert (1956 and 1964), Herb Elliott (1960), Maureen Caird (1968), Ralph Doubell (1968), Glynis Nunn (1984) and Debbie Flintoff-King (1988). Of course there have been some near misses — athletes of great talent and world fame who did not win gold at the Olympics but are notable nevertheless:

Gold! Silver! Bronze! Decima Norman on the winner's dais after the 220 yard sprint event at the 1938 Empire Games in Sydney. Her Australian team-mates J. Coleman and E. Wearne came second and third. (Hood Collection, State Library of New South Wales.)

John Landy, Ron Clarke, Judy Pollock, Raelene Boyle, Lisa Martin, Ric Mitchell, Decima Norman, John Treloar, Pam Ryan, Peter Norman, Marlene Mathews and Gary Honey to mention but a few of these. John Treloar, Decima Norman and Raelene Boyle each won the sprint double at a Commonwealth Games. Others have won significant events. Rob de Castella became a national hero after wins in world marathon events like the world championships in Helsinki in 1983 whilst Lisa Ondieki (Martin) and Steve Moneghetti are both world-ranked marathon runners with significant victories in major races.

Australian athletics received a real fillip when the Olympic Games were held in Melbourne in 1956. Australia was quite diffident about this international exposure but 'the friendly Games' in Melbourne raised public awareness of the strength of athletics in this country in comparison with other more populous nations, established a number of heroes and heroines in the sport and gave valuable training (and confidence) to the country's administrators and officials in the conduct of an international event.

Australia selected a team of seventy-six athletes — fifty-five men and twenty-one women. The team included John Landy, who had attracted national and international attention in his quest to be the first athlete to run the mile in less than four minutes. Shirley Strickland de la Hunty, world-record holder and gold medallist in the 80 metres hurdles in Helsinki four years earlier was also in the team. She repeated her success in Melbourne while Landy finished a gallant third in the 1500 metres. The women athletes were the strength of the team and captured the hearts of the nation who witnessed their efforts (and the Games themselves) on television for the first time. 'Golden Girl', Betty Cuthbert won both the 100 and 200 metres and Marlene Mathews, another Australian girl, was third. The women's 4 x 100 metres relay team (Cuthbert, de la Hunty, Fleur Mellor and Norma Croker) won the gold medal in 44.5 seconds and in doing so broke the world record.

The presence of twenty-four men and sixteen women in finals coupled with the success of the 'golden girls' captured the imagination of the Australian sporting public and assured a continuing interest in track and field athletics. The 1950s and 1960s were the halcyon days of athletics in Australia. There had been some notable successes prior to Melbourne — Nick Winter who won the triple jump in Paris in 1924 and John Winter, winner of the high jump in the London Olympics of 1948 — but it was the successes of the 1950s that established the sport in Australia.

The 1950s began with impressive wins to two women at the Empire Games in Auckland, New Zealand — Marjorie Jackson and Shirley Strickland. Jackson had attracted attention when she defeated Olympic champion Fanny Blankers-Koen of Holland over 100 yards in Sydney in 1949. She set four world records in 1950 and won the sprint double at the Olympic Games in Helsinki in 1952. She was the first Australian woman to win an Olympic gold in athletics and was adored by the Australian sporting public as much for her modesty as for her sporting prowess. She was affectionately known as 'our Marj' and 'the Lithgow Flash'. Strickland had run third behind Blankers-Koen in the hurdles in the 1948 Olympics but won the event in Helsinki in the world record time of 10.9 seconds.

Herb Elliott who won the 1500 metres in Rome in 1960 and Ralph Doubell, winner of the 800 metres in Mexico in 1968, were significant achievers in the 1960s but Betty Cuthbert in

Tokyo in 1964 and Maureen Caird in the 80 metres hurdles in Mexico in 1968 continued the impressive record for Australia's women athletes. Raelene Boyle came close to emulating Cuthbert in Munich in 1972, when she won two silver medals in the 100 and 200 metres. Her near success there and in Mexico four years earlier, when as a seventeen-year-old she equalled the world record for the 200 metres, coupled with gold medal wins in the sprints and 400 metres at the Commonwealth Games have earned her a place in Australian sporting history. Ron Clarke excited Australians in the 1960s with his record-breaking runs (in 1967 and 1968 he equalled Paavo Nurmi's record of seventeen world records) but never captured their hearts because of his inability to win an Olympic gold — a fact which says much about the national preoccupation with winning.

The Olympic Games in Montreal (1976) and Moscow (1980) witnessed little success for Australian sportsmen and women, particularly in athletics. Concern in the country that the sporting success which characterised Australians was declining prompted the establishment of the Australian Institute of Sport in Canberra in 1981. Athletics was one of the first 'nation-building' sports to be included in the Institute which sought to develop the potential of Australia's top sportspeople.

There has been a decline in numbers of competing athletes in Australia over the last two decades, but this is not dissimilar to other sports in the country. The sport is not yet unified — Athletics Australia is the parent body nominating representative teams for international events and catering for community sport; Little Athletics caters for youngsters under the age of twelve and the Athletic League represents professional athletes. All these organisations have branches in each state and their own administration. Attempts are currently underway to group them into a National Athletics Council.

The sport, especially the amateur section, still looks back to its proud performance history, particularly in the 1950s and 1960s, while trying to re-establish a reputation for excellence through the efforts of current top athletes. Athletics Australia has responded to an in-depth study of the sport (*The Landy Report*, 1992) by encouraging junior development; by reorganising itself into 'commissions', each with a specific responsibility for advancing the sport; and by supporting the efforts of the Australian Track and Field Coaches Association which has a system of coach education and accreditation to ensure that ability, when discovered, will be nurtured. A grand-prix circuit of special competitions, one in each capital city, with prize money for selected events mirrors the successful European circuit and is a national showcase for current talent in the country.

Athletics Australia is aware that its status as a significant sport depends on the international success of its élite performers. The days of Jackson and Cuthbert, Elliott and Doubell are past but not forgotten. The task for Athletics Australia, it would seem, is to provide contemporary heroes and heroines for a nation which identifies with and applauds only success.[23]

15 Reflections Past and Present

Brian Stoddart

W HILE IT is now almost automatic for academics to acknowledge the interconnections between sport and modern culture, nonetheless it is worth noting how much these essays on Australia reinforce the point. Indeed, Australia emerges as a major site in which sports underwent the transformation from pre-modern to post-modern circumstances under the pressure of full-scale social re-ordering.[1] If the rudimentary sports activities which arrived from Britain with the late eighteenth-century convict ships (to challenge activities displayed by the first nation peoples) resembled a host's cultural practice, then the sports of two centuries later suggest an independent practice well down the road towards a genuine cultural independence sought so desperately by late twentieth-century Australian political leaders.[2]

If the pioneers in the social history of Australian sport largely set out to show, first, that sport reflected the same trends as other areas of social life and, second, that sport might even have played an important role in building the cultural framework, these essays go beyond that — even locating sport at the core of debate about Australia evolving as a distinct and distinctive society.[3] Furthermore, sport has moved increasingly to the forefront as an issue in discussions about where Australia goes from here.

At the risk of making a gross generalisation, we can say that the essays collectively develop two overriding themes:

Spectator sport in December 1936. Watching the second day's play in the second test, England vs. Australia at the Sydney Cricket Ground. Australia retained the Ashes, having regained them in England in 1934 with Don Bradman as captain, after losing them in the 'Bodyline' series in 1932–33. (Hood Collection, State Library of New South Wales.)

persistence and change. Australian sport has been sometimes reluctant to shift from entrenched positions, sometimes adept at taking on new possibilities. The 1977 'Packer Revolution' in cricket demonstrated both tendencies: the Australian Cricket Board was loath to adapt to new social conditions while its leading players embraced a new option most enthusiastically.[4] It is in this juxtaposition of conservatism and progress that lies much of Australian sport's volatility both on and off the field. From there it is easy to turn to some recurring themes and to make some sense of them.

One constant criticism about the academic analysis of sport is that it concentrates upon élite activity, upon professional and mediated sport which is more about entertainment and business than 'true' sport.[5] Louella McCarthy and Bernard Whimpress, in particular, argue that sport is a popular Australian activity because Australians *enjoy* playing and/or watching sport. From the earliest days, sport provided a welcome break

from workaday drudgery whether in early nineteenth-century convict circumstances or those of the late twentieth-century capitalist economy. If sport did replace religion as the opiate of the masses then it did so with one important distinction — a vast array of people not only drew solace and reassurance from sport but also found unbridled pleasure and delight as well.[6]

Louella McCarthy added an important dimension. In explaining the rise of bowling clubs she emphasised an Australian penchant for competition. That desire is mentioned throughout the essays and is an important consideration when analysing the relationship between big-business entrepreneurs and sport which reached its heights in the 1980s: Alan Bond (Bond Corporation and the America's Cup), John Elliott (Carlton United Breweries and Carlton Football Club), Kerry Packer (Australian Consolidated Press, Channel Nine and cricket, polo and the rest) and, *par excellence*, Geoffrey Edelsten (private medicine and the Sydney Swans Football Club) all reflected, successfully or unsuccessfully, the idea that business competitiveness had its counterpoint in sports.[7] It is an area which warrants greater attention.

So, too, do those persistent themes of mass participation (of a playing or non-playing kind) and social enjoyment. They

This scoreboard showing England's first innings in the second day's play in the second test in 1936 has been replaced with an electronic scoreboard. The legendary 'Hill', also shown here, had changed dramatically by the late 1980s, part of it becoming the Doug Walters Stand and the rest covered with seating and now known as 'Yabba's Hill'. (Government Printing Office, State Library of New South Wales.)

might underlie Australia's sporting preoccupation but they are as yet little understood. Such understanding is important not just for intellectual satisfaction, either. The Australian Sports Commission is now anxious about the continued availability of volunteers who make up eighty per cent of sport's machine but who are now showing signs of dissidence.[8] Could it be that the traditional commitment is being undercut by dwindling pleasure in or even love for the activity? If that is the case, it will be a seminal change in the Australian sports complex.

The issue of social access to sport in Australia is a major theme here and may be divided into the constituencies of gender, race, ethnicity and wealth.

Given the work of the contributors, and taken in conjunction with that of others elsewhere, it is now patently obvious that sport has been one of the major sites for structured and ongoing inequality for women.[9] Indeed, along with the issues of equal work and equal pay opportunities, sport might well be *the* locus for such inequality in Australia. Women began by being unable to join sports organisations, bet, or ride or own horses, as John O'Hara indicates. When they did get joining rights they frequently were given unequal status, as in golf and bowls. Then came the struggle to participate in certain sports (but not in boxing) or in particular events, as within athletics. Even if those battles were overcome, gaining equal funding and/or media coverage in the late twentieth century proved just as difficult as did the initial access in the late nineteenth.[10] Women have given Australia vast success in athletics and swimming, vast numbers in netball and bowls and vast service in administration yet their playing field is still uneven. This is one area in which old practice remains persistently pronounced and symbolic of a deeper social stubbornness in the Australian cultural psyche.

No less sad has been the experience of Australia's first nation people.[11] True, the mythical 'average' Australian has lionised Lionel Rose, Evonne Goolagong, Mark and Marcia Ella, Arthur Beetson, Polly Farmer and Cathy Freeman but they might well be regarded as the standard exceptions to point up the rule that Aboriginal people have been massively discriminated against in sport. As Wray Vamplew suggests here,

Australians became more aware of the links between sport, politics and racial identity in 1968 when Australian Peter Norman won the silver medal in the 200 metres sprint at the Mexico Olympics. He is shown here with Americans Tommy Smith, gold medallist, and John Carlos, bronze medallist, who stare downward during the playing of the *Star Spangled Banner* and, with black-gloved hands, make the Black Power salute in protest. (Associated Press/Fairfax Picture Library.)

economic imperatives probably determined the over-achievement in organised professional boxing, and did so undeniably in the rural boxing tents where the deliberate and unedifying spectacle of blacks and whites being pitted against each other physically occurred in a sanitised version of the murderous clashes of the nineteenth century. In most if not all sporting codes Aboriginal people have experienced short-term adulation, long-term vilification and unsustained support in their post-playing careers. Little wonder, then, that the Australian government's much-vaunted 'reconciliation' of the 1980s and 1990s is glaringly absent in sport.

The story is a little better and rather more complex in the broader-scale multicultural Australia. Put crudely, a largely monocultural Australian society evolved a set of sporting codes and practices from the mid-to-late nineteenth century onwards leading to a sport/culture synchronicity which prevailed

273

until the 1940s. Since the post-war succession of mass immigration programmes, those original codes and practices have struggled to accommodate new developments or to reflect fully the new cultural diversity.[12]

This is most clear in the soccer case as delineated by Bill Murray and Phil Mosely. Despite its long Australian heritage, soccer became a major game only after 1945 in the wake of mass European migration. The power of cultural and sporting tradition and prejudice became manifest as 'newcomers' either rejected or could not penetrate 'Australian' sporting institutions, creating instead their own microcultural environments based on soccer clubs. Much of the revolutionary aspect, of course, lies as much with the history of the wider cultural and sporting reaction as with the history of soccer itself. The key question, clearly, is whether sport is to be seen as a cohesive or divisive force in Australian cultural evolution.[13] In many respects soccer has been more the latter than the former.

Australian rules football and, to a lesser degree, rugby league have been more culturally integrative. The reasons are obscure and require more analysis but have their roots in community structures and attitudes, access to particular sports forms in the education systems, the approaches taken by individual sporting organisations and the very histories of the individual migrant communities themselves. Whatever the cause, ethnic names are far more predominant in the Australian Football League and the Australian Rugby League than in cricket circles (although the recent arrival of New South Wales batsman Richard Chee Quee might be the harbinger of change) or in tennis, golf, swimming or rowing. Migrant women, needless to say, are doubly or trebly marginalised.

Wealth, or the lack of it, has long been one determinant of access to Australian sports.[14] Obviously, the more capital intensive the sport the more the possession of wealth becomes a prerequisite for participation: offshore yacht racing, motor racing, polo and golf are cases in point. Inevitably, social exclusivity becomes built into those sports by way of stringent entry requirements (often invoking access to appropriate social networks) and high fees to add to the basic equipment costs. John O'Hara acknowledges this in his account of thoroughbred and standard-bred racing with the latter involving social groups unable to capitalise the more expensive form. Interestingly enough, many such exclusive sports institutions were keen to gain the 'Royal' prefix, thereby tying themselves, symbolically at least, to an imported rather than an evolving national tradition.

Again, this area of economic stratification and social status is much under-researched in Australian sports history, but collective biography emerges from these essays as one potential way forward.[15] As Graeme Kinross-Smith shows, for example, leading tennis figures were significant in other areas of life. Sir Norman Brookes was not only a tennis supremo but also a good golfer (member of Royal Melbourne and, as a left-hander, member of a minority group — he is also said to have invented the golf trundler) as well as a leading industrialist. His sporting and business connections overlapped constantly as interchangeable social attributes. These characteristics provide the clues for finding the multi-dimensional movers and shakers in Australian society at any given point. An analysis of any edition of *Who's Who in Australia*, paying attention to sporting and private-club membership soon locates the source of male power networks. Sports clubs are too frequently overlooked as the homes of real social power in Australia.

On social access, then, these writers have shown the continuity of practice rather than massive change: women, Aborigines, ethnics and the poor are still marginalised in Australian sport, frequently despite the valiant work of government groups established to correct the deficiencies.[16] Sport demonstrates the ease with which change can be legislated (as in the area of equal opportunity) and the enormous difficulty in turning that change into practice.

Sport has had a leading Australian role in what Norbert Elias termed the 'civilizing process'.[17] That is not to say that Australia relentlessly became a 'better' place, but that sport was an important tool in producing what the dominant cultural group considered to be appropriate modes of behaviour. The attack on uncontrolled gambling in a number of sports during the late nineteenth century was part of that, as was the constant theme of eliminating *undue* violence in sport. Each era produced its own form of acceptability, sometimes turning previous predilections upside down. Elias would have appreciated the accounts here of battles waged over clothing in sports — it was not just a matter of determining utilitarian wear, it was a battle for social control as Douglas Booth illustrates in the swimming and surfing case.

Such deep concern for social stability should assure sport a central place in any subsequent debate about social change. Control has been a vital issue in Australian sport, a theme put most provocatively (and debatably) by Jim McKay in another quarter.[18] Every sport studied here reveals battles between participants and administrators, entrepreneurs and associations, state and federal organisers along with struggles over selection policies, administrative change, sponsorship arrangements and media cover. It was about who had the ideological 'right' to direct the sport in any given social context. Sport is ultimately about power, but few analysts have understood the real meaning and significance of that power for the protagonists.[19]

As Richard Cashman hints, the battle over the composition of the 1912 Australian cricket side to tour England was more than just a spat sparked by personality conflict (although that helped fuel the fight as it did in many similar incidents across many other sports before or since). It was a struggle for the control of resources. So, too, was rugby's bifurcation into union and league codes as outlined here by Murray Phillips. A study of Australia's sports history, therefore, is a simple way to destroy any residual beliefs in Australia as a sharing, egalitarian society.

This switches the focus to the administrative history and practice of Australian sport. These essays are replete with stories about tussles inside clubs, associations and national bodies. Many of those bodies have undergone substantial change during their histories but such change has usually been hard-won, complete with winners and losers. Australian football has had its share of alteration during the twentieth century on the way, first, to becoming the Victorian Football League itself then, in the late 1980s, the Australian Football League. The composition of its rules and protocols has occasioned great debate amongst other football states, most notably South and Western Australia. The transmogrification of the Australasian Cricket Council into the Australian Cricket Board of Control (that word again, significantly) then in 1973 the Australian Cricket Board bears the same story about struggles for representation and recognition (despite being in the national seat of government, the Australian Capital Territory Cricket Association has sought vainly for years to gain representation on the board).

It is fair to note that although these administrative issues are now well recognised by social historians of Australian sport, they are not yet fully understood. There is much interesting

Australian Paralympic swimmer Tracy Barrell in Sydney. (Clayton/Fairfax Picture Library.)

work to be done, work which will unlock greater understanding of the role of sport in the Australian social environment.

A similar point may be made about economic history — the issue is touched upon by most contributors here, but we are not close to matching Wray Vamplew's seminal work on Britain.[20] One way forward is via a thorough-going analysis of the amateur/professional debate because the issue of money (or, more precisely, the problem of who *is* getting it versus who *should* get it) is a persistent refrain in that argument.

Golf and tennis have had relatively well-defined roles for professionals (in golf for both coaches and players from the start, in tennis for coaches initially and players much later) but other sports have stumbled at the waterjumps of professionalism. (This analogy immediately raises horse-racing but, as John O'Hara indicates, the controlled presence of trainers and jockeys and bookmakers from the mid-nineteenth century onwards resulted from the 'sport' being considered as an industry, a business more than a sport. It should be placed in a different category.)

Daryl Adair, Murray Phillips and John Daly posit the close relationship between perceptions of professionalism and perceptions of social status in the Australian context with some of it, at least, taken directly from the British model.[21] Richard Cashman suggests more prosaic reasons for the stunted growth of professionalism, smallness of population and vastness of geography combining to render paid sportspeople economically unviable. Bernard Whimpress and Bill Murray with Phil Mosely repeat this in their accounts of sports which have moved towards semi-professionalism. Much the same story emerges from rugby league and cricket where surprisingly few top players even now admit to being fully professional.

Some answers to the puzzle might be found in sports like lawn bowls and netball where, until very recently indeed, the emphasis has been upon participation rather than mass spectating which, obviously, is one necessary prerequisite for flourishing professionalism. This is why, for example, Australia's leading athletes complain constantly about having to go overseas in search of recognition, for which read money. Athletics in Australia has rarely been watched by enough people to produce sufficient revenue to support highly-paid performers: at least, not since the late nineteenth century when professional athletics was wiped out by the civilising movement and the crowds went elsewhere.

One avenue worth exploring for answers here, then, concerns the neglected philosophy of Australian sport. The amateurism issue, or the professional problem, has swung about the question of what it was or is that Australians want their sport to do in and for their society. What role is it to fulfil? This is not a merely academic question, either, because it relates directly to public debate about sizeable chunks of public funds devoted to sport development in the midst of economic recession and ballooning public debt.[22] The issue of sport's social relevance is never far away.

A crowd of 33 000 fun runners in William Street, Sydney, at the start of the City to Surf race, 13 August 1989. (Towle/Fairfax Picture Library.)

The clear connection here is to national representation. These essays mention many international stars: Fanny Durack, Margaret Court, 'The Demon' Spofforth, 'the Great White Shark' Norman, Don Bradman, Decima Norman and Betty Wilson. Some have lasted a long time and others much less so, but the common issue is what have they *really* symbolised of Australia overseas? There have been and continue to be countless assertions about what sporting success does for Australia's image, yet these essays reveal little extant research into the matter — we will need to interrogate American and British sources before we know what the citizens of those nations have divined about Australia from the sporting and social performances of Australians in their countries.[23]

It is a worthy question given the amount of public money allocated to coaching and scientific development, the latest examples of what has been a long and consistent Australian interaction between science, technology and sport. Many of these essays show Australia to have been a 'clever country' (the late twentieth-century government objective for national economic growth) for a long time. The Henselite lawn bowl, made in Melbourne, has long dominated the world market. Australia was a major manufacturer of tennis and golf equipment but much of that has gone offshore in the face of economic uncertainty, as demonstrated by Tom Crow's now vastly successful, American-based Cobra golf equipment company. Dennis Lillee's aluminium bat did not last long, but Australian cricket balls and other equipment have been recognised as world class for a long time.

The most significant relationship between Australian sport and technology, however, is unquestionably that concerning the media and, most particularly, television. Every sport examined here has had at least some of its history shaped by media coverage. The Melbourne Cup gained much of its national status by way of a national telegraph system which concentrated public attention on results. Colonial newspapers reported the late nineteenth-century overseas triumphs of scullers and cricketers and boxers. The rise of sports-specific press coverage made players into stars and readers into spectators. Radio turned racing into a Saturday preoccupation for thousands, perhaps millions of Australians and transformed race callers into national institutions (not incidentally, radio coverage of racing arguably had a direct line influence on betting habits and so helped create the Totalisator Agency Board). Then came television.

Many critics regard television as the greatest of all change agents in twentieth-century sport.[24] There is a growing and complex literature devoted to the subject overseas, yet it is ironic that in Australia the detailed analysis has scarcely begun. Ironic on two principal counts: that Australia is still widely believed to be sports mad, and that it has been a world leader in the technical innovations of sport on television. Either directly or indirectly the television industry has revolutionised the playing form, conditions and rules of international cricket, made players and associations in several sports much wealthier than they used to be, created a new industry of sports marketing and management, altered (for better or worse) the strategic thinking of almost every sports association in the country, changed the sporting-menu tastes for millions of fans by the globalising of sports programming, and perpetuated the public discrimination against women's sports.

The overwhelming thrust of academic analysis of all this has been gloomy, to wit, that television has ruined sport.[25] These findings represent a misshapen view of what sport was like BT (before television), and an assumption that Australian society (and its foreign counterparts) had produced a sports form in syncromesh with its broad social patterns. Those assumptions are flawed seriously and will be redressed only by a full-scale analysis of Australian sport's historical interaction with the media.

This is just the latest of several comments here about 'What Is To Be Done', so the point has been reached where such lines of development should be sketched out because, if nothing else, all these essays highlight fascinating and crucial areas in which further investigation is required if the full contours of Australian sport are to be understood.[26]

The relationship between sports practices and educational institutions is a most significant one.[27] As Murray Phillips shows, the choice of codes by public, state and denominational institutions determined the histories of rugby union and rugby league. Associated questions concern the changing shape and emphasis of physical-education programmes over the past century, and the rise of sport as issues for analysis in physical and social sciences.[28]

Sporting patterns differ in rural and urban Australia with the latter largely neglected so far. Louella McCarthy indicates the pivotal role of the bowling green as social focal point in country towns, Richard Cashman and Graeme Kinross-Smith comment in passing on patterns of representative honours from rural areas, John O'Hara emphasises the social significance of country racing (much of it now altered by television coverage). Again, specific case studies of rural regions or towns will be revealing.

There are still surprisingly few good biographies of players.[29] Perhaps that is a legacy of the overwhelmingly one-dimensional, socially segmented view adopted towards sport by most writers to date. It might be time now to place some of the great stars in social context: Sir Donald Bradman, for example, as player, administrator, pioneer professional, businessman, almost-recluse and exemplar of Australia's twentieth-century experience.

If there are gaps in this collection concerning long-time favoured and successful sports (hockey, squash, cycling, sailing, motor sports) then there is still even more to be covered in the rise of either new sports or formerly sleeping ones. American football is now played in Australia, baseball is exporting players to American major and minor leagues, basketball is one of the fastest growing sports in Australia, triathlon and ultramarathon activities attract thousands of participant devotees, and various adventure/leisure sports flourish. While the circumstances of their current success are more the stuff of sociology, their collective rise emanates from history and will affect the future shape of Australian sport. In sport, at least, we are far from 'the end of history'.[30]

For all the talk about the 'politics' of or in sport, there is little detailed analysis yet of the ways in which sport as an institution has resonated with the national and state legislative and political process. Politicians identify with sport, conduct much of their business in sporting terminology, celebrate successes and ignore failures, allocate funds and expect results, hitch national futures to national sporting endeavours and affect the common touch through association with sport, yet we still do not know clearly why they do that. It is well worth a history of its own.

All readers will have their individual additions to make to this list but there is a last point to be added here if only because it helps further break down the stereotyped prejudice of sport as an unflinchingly, unquestioningly physical preoccupation with no reference to the more cerebral aspects of life. The art and literature of Australian sport have been much neglected yet have plenty to say about our sporting predilections, heritage, expectations and loyalties.[31] From Nat Gould onwards writers as varied as Dal Stivens, Barrie Dickins, Frank Hardy, David Williamson and Brian Matthews have been shrewd on sport as have artists like Pro Hart, Russell Drysdale and Noel Counihan. An assessment of their contributions would help ensure that the study of sport becomes an even more important factor in unravelling the mysteries of modern Australia.

That point sums up this collection. The writers set out to illuminate some aspects of modern Australian sports history, to open avenues for further research. An important corollary, however, was to shift the location of sports analysis further into the main framework of the study of Australian culture. By raising issues like gender, race, economics, media, politics, religion, education, the arts and more, the writers hope to have succeeded in those ambitions. If nothing else, these essays indicate firmly that investigation into the social history of Australian sport now has not only established an honourable and distinguished base from which to work, but also has a substantial and intriguing future.

Notes and References

Chapter 1: Australians and Sport

1 For a study of this cultural transfer *see* John O'Hara, 'An approach to colonial sports history' in Wray Vamplew, *Sport and colonialism in nineteenth century Australasia*, Australian Society for Sports History, *Studies in Sports History 1* (Adelaide, 1986), pp. 3-18

2 Wray Vamplew, 'Sport: more than fun and games' in Eric Richards, *The Flinders history of South Australia* (Adelaide, 1986), pp. 433-65; Reet A. Howell and Maxwell L. Howell, *The genesis of sport in Queensland: from the dreamtime to Federation* (Brisbane, 1992).

3 *Bell's Life in Victoria and Sporting Chronicle*, 8 January 1858.

4 *Sydney Morning Herald*, 24 January 1874; *Australasian*, 17 January 1874.

5 *Australasian*, 2 September 1882.

6 *Australasian*, 5 March 1898.

7 Gerald Crawford, 'Griffiths, Albert' and Scott Bennett, 'Trickett, Edward' in Wray Vamplew, Katharine Moore, John O'Hara, Richard Cashman and Ian F. Jobling (eds), *The Oxford companion to Australian sport* (Melbourne, 1992), p. 169; p. 360.

8 Scott Bennett, 'Rowing and Sculling' in Vamplew et al., *The Oxford companion to Australian sport*, pp. 291-92.

9 The first test between the two countries saw New Zealand bowled out for forty-two in the first innings and fifty-four in the second. No more tests were played till 1973.

10 John A. Daly, *Quest for excellence: the AIS [Australian Institute of*

Sport] in Canberra (Canberra, 1991).

11 Quoted in Jeff Wells, 'Sorry Ros, these figures don't add up to a world power', *Australian*, 10 September 1992.

12 W. F. Mandle, 'Cricket and Australian nationalism', *Journal of the Royal Australian Historical Society*, 59.4 (1973), pp. 225-46.

13 For a discussion on this *see* the contributions to John O'Hara, *Ethnicity and soccer in Australia*, Australian Society for Sports History, *Studies in Sports History*, no. 10 (forthcoming).

14 B. James, 'We are playing soccer not politics', *Sports Magazine*, 16.1 (June 1963), pp. 36-7.

15 *Australian*, 17 March 1992.

16 *See* Roy Hay, 'British football, wogball or the world game? Towards a social history of Victorian soccer' in O'Hara, *Ethnicity and soccer in Australia*.

17 Ray Crawford, 'Athleticism, gentlemen and Empire in Australian public schools: L. A. Adamson and Wesley College, Melbourne' in Vamplew, *Sport and colonialism in nineteenth-century Australia*, pp. 42-64.

18 Richard Stremski, 'Australian rules football' in Vamplew et al., *The Oxford companion to Australian sport*, p. 35.

19 John O'Hara, 'Melbourne Cup' in Vamplew et al., *The Oxford companion to Australian sport*, p. 242.

20 Andrew Lemon, 'Horse-racing' in Vamplew et al., *The Oxford companion to Australian sport*, pp. 181-87; Wray Vamplew, 'From sport to business: the first seventy-five years of horse-racing in South Australia', *Journal of the Historical Society of South Australia* (1983), pp. 15-33.

21 For a discussion of the development of electorate sport in Sydney, *see* Martin Sharp, 'Sporting spectacles: cricket and football in Sydney, 1890-1912', PhD thesis, Australian National University (Canberra, 1986).

22 Harold Freeman and Andrew Lemon, *The history of Australian thoroughbred racing*, vol. 1 (Melbourne, 1987), p. 240.

23 John Blanch, *Ampol's Sporting Records* (Sydney, 1978).

24 For information on these true-blue Aussie sports see the entries in Vamplew et al., *The Oxford companion to Australian sport*

25 Barry Andrews, 'Tugging four bits off the deck at the WACA: Australian sport and Australian English' in Richard Cashman and Michael McKernan, *Sport: money, morality and the media* (Sydney, 1981), p. 145.

26 For a run through the conventional approach see Ian F. Jobling, 'Australian sporting heroes' in Wray Vamplew, *Sport: nationalism and internationalism*, Australian Society for Sports History, *Studies in Sports History*, 2 (Adelaide, 1987), pp. 91-2 and Richard Cashman, 'The Australian sporting obsession', *Sporting Traditions* 4.1 (1987), pp. 47-55.

27 Keith Dunstan, *Sports* (Melbourne, 1973).

28 Cashman, 'The Australian sporting obsession', pp. 47-55.

29 Wray Vamplew, *Australians: historical statistics* (Sydney, 1987), p. 383. This volume also has figures for cricket and horse-racing.

30 Roy Hay, 'Soccer and social control in Scotland 1873-1978' in Cashman and McKernan, *Sport: money, morality and the media*, p. 233.

31 Scott Bennett, *The Clarence Comet* (Sydney, 1973), p. 83.

32 Gerald Crawford, 'Corrigan's funeral', in Vamplew et al., *The Oxford companion to Australian sport*, p. 97

33 Murray G. Phillips, 'Australian sport and World War One', PhD thesis, University of Queensland (1991), pp. 71-81.

34 On this *see* Daryl Adair's forthcoming Flinders University PhD thesis, 'On parade: ceremonial spectacles, crowds, and collective identities in Australia, 1901-1938'.

35 Commonwealth Department of Sport, Recreation and Tourism, *Australian physical activity surveys, 1984-1987* (Canberra, 1987); Commonwealth Department of the Arts, Sport, the Environment and Territories, *Summary of the pilot survey of the fitness of Australians* (Canberra, 1992). To be rated 'highly physically active' necessitated undertaking sufficient exercise to make one sweaty or breathless at least three times a week for a minimum of twenty minutes each time.

36 William Bundey, *Reminiscences of twenty-five years yachting in Australia* (Adelaide, 1888), p. 138.

37 Bundey, p. 147; *South Australian Parliamentary Debates* (1872), p. 515.

38 *South Australian Register*, 8 November 1875.

39 John A. Daly, *Elysian fields: sport, class and community in colonial South Australia* (Adelaide, 1982), pp. 112-42.

40 Bundey, p. 140; Daly, pp. 60-5.

41 The seminal contribution here is Lois Bryson, 'Sport and the oppression of women', *Australian and New Zealand Journal of Sociology* (1983), pp. 413-20. *See also* Helen King's pioneering work, 'The sexual politics of sport: an Australian perspective' in Richard Cashman and Michael McKernan, *Sport in history* (Queensland, 1979) and the recent major historical survey of women in Australian sport by Marion K. Stell, *Half the race* (Sydney, 1991).

42 Vamplew, 'Sport: more than fun and games', p. 451.

43 *See* the contributions to *Equity for women in sport*, the proceedings of a joint seminar held by the House of Representatives Standing Committee on Legal and Constitutional Affairs and the Australian Sports Commission, 27-28 February 1991 (Canberra, 1991).

44 A study of capital city daily newspapers in 1980 showed that 96.2 per cent of sports reporting dealt with male sport. When the study was repeated in 1988 the proportion had fallen: to

95.8 per cent! (Figures quoted in Lois Bryson, 'Gender' in Vamplew et al., *The Oxford companion to Australian sport*, p. 154.) A sampling of the Adelaide daily press revealed that the percentage devoted to women's sport in 1850, 1875 and 1900 was nil, 2.3 per cent in 1925 and 1975, and 6.2 per cent in 1950. (Vamplew, 'Sport: more than fun and games', p. 435.)

45 What follows is based on Colin Tatz, *Aborigines in sport* (Adelaide, 1987) and his similarly titled contribution to Vamplew et al., *The Oxford companion to Australian sport*, pp. 1-4.

46 John Mulvaney and Rex Harcourt, *Cricket walkabout: the Australian Aborigines in England* (Melbourne, 1988).

47 Reasons for this are being analysed by Bernard Whimpress, a postgraduate student at Flinders University.

48 Brian Stoddart, 'Ethnic influences' in Vamplew et al., *The Oxford companion to Australian sport*, pp. 131-33; Andrew Dettre, 'New Australians boost our sport', *Sport*, February 1956, 17-19.

49 *See* the contributions to O'Hara, *Ethnicity and Soccer*.

50 [South Australian] *Register*, 29 January 1885; Bundey, p. 44.

Chapter 2: Australian Football

1 Figures taken from *Australian sports directory* (Canberra, 1992), p. 68. The total figure was 477 988 but only 400 for women.

2 Sophie Arnold, 'Grassroots footy', *Age Weekender*, 3 May 1985.

3 Allen Aylett, *National Football League handbook* (Melbourne, 1984), p. 3.

4 This body was previously known as the Australian Football Council, the Australian National Football Council and more recently as the National Football League.

5 Geoffrey Blainey, *A game of our own* (Melbourne, 1990), p. 87.

6 [Adelaide] *Observer*, 13 October 1888.

7 John Stanley James (Michael Cannon (ed.), *The Vagabond Papers* (Melbourne, 1969), pp. 207–9.

8 The first rugby union test between Australia and England was not played until 1899 and the first Wallabies tour was not until 1908. Australia did not play its first soccer tests until 1922 against New Zealand and did not enter international competition until the 1956 Olympics.

9 Bernard Whimpress, *The South Australian football story* (Adelaide, 1983), p. 98.

10 [Adelaide] *Observer*, 3 June 1905. Such calls were often accompanied by the cry of 'One flag, one destiny, one football game: the Australian'.

11 Ian Turner and Leonie Sandercock, *Up where Cazaly?* (Adelaide, 1981), p. 67.

12 B. W. O'Dwyer, 'The shaping of Victorian rules football', *Victorian Historical Journal*, 60.1 (1989), p. 27.

13 O'Dwyer, 'The shaping of Victorian rules football', p. 34.
14 O'Dwyer, 'The shaping of Victorian rules football', pp. 34-5.
15 O'Dwyer, 'The shaping of Victorian rules football', p. 37.
16 Blainey, p. 38.
17 *Australasian*, 30 July 1870.
18 *Mullens' footballers' Australian almanack* (Melbourne, 1951), p. 57.
19 O'Dwyer, 'The shaping of Victorian rules football', pp. 32-3.
20 Henry Harrison, *The story of an athlete* (Melbourne, 1923), incorporated in A. Mancini and G. M. Hibbins, *Running with the ball* (Melbourne, 1987), p. 125.
21 Blainey, pp. 88-92.
22 Blainey, p. 92.
23 C. C. Mullens, 'A.J. Thurgood, champion of champions' in Gary Hutchinson, *Great Australian footy stories* (1983), p. 89.
24 Blainey, p. 96.
25 Blainey, p. 33.
26 [Adelaide] *Register*, 28 May 1860.
27 Whimpress, p. 14.
28 Personal conversation with Port Adelaide Football Club historian John Wood. The last wharf labourer to play for Port Adelaide was Jim Sawford in 1957 and he worked on the ship or what is known as 'down under'.
29 Turner and Sandercock, p. 51.
30 Malcolm M. Conn, *Aussie rules Top 40 1976-1985* (Melbourne, 1986) p. 25.
31 Alan Atwood, 'Black artistry in big leagues', *Time*, 2 October 1989.
32 [Adelaide] *Observer*, 6 June 1885, 11 July 1885.
33 Colin Tatz, *Aborigines in sport* (Adelaide 1987) consolidates most of this information, pp. 68-74.
34 Personal conversation with Peter Baker, a schoolteacher who played in six successive grand finals in the Ceduna district of South Australia in the early 1960s.
35 The author was editor of the South Australian *Football Budget* at the time and took photographs of the girls for the award.
36 West Perth Football Club membership recruiting brochure 1983.
37 Bernard Whimpress, 'Strictly for the Girls', *South Australian Football Budget*, 3 September 1983.
38 R. E. N. Twopeny, *Town life in Australia* (London, 1883) p. 207. It may be of interest to point out that apart from being a journalist, editor, entrepreneur and commentator on colonial manners, Twopeny was also an early exponent of the Australian game, captain of the Adelaide Football Club and secretary of the South Australian Football Association in its first season.
39 Turner and Sandercock, p. 115.

40 Turner and Sandercock, pp. 109-15.
41 Wray Vamplew (ed.), *Australians: historical statistics* (Sydney, 1988) p. 383.
42 Michelangelo Rucci, 'National and SANFL [South Australian National Football League] attendances 1964-82', in *Football Times yearbook 1983* (Adelaide, 1983), p. 63.
43 During this period Graham Farmer and Barry Cable were recruited from Western Australia; and Darrel Baldock, Ian Stewart, Peter Hudson and Royce Hart from Tasmania.
44 Robin Grow, 'Nineteenth century football and the Melbourne press'. Paper presented to the Australian Society for Sports History's fifth biennial conference, *Sporting Traditions V* (Adelaide, August 1985), p. 3.
45 Turner and Sandercock, pp. 45, 53.
46 [Adelaide] *Observer*, 14 May 1910.
47 Turner and Sandercock, p. 106.
48 [Adelaide] *Advertiser*, 3 August 1963.
49 Cited in Graeme Atkinson and Michael Hanlon, *3AW book of footy records* (Melbourne, 1989), p. 209.
50 Bob Stewart, *The football business* (Melbourne, 1983), p. 118.
51 Country zoning was introduced into South Australia in 1972.
52 *Australian Football League annual report 1990*.
53 *Bulletin*, 17 July 1986.
54 Bob Santamaria, 'Is commercialism killing football?', *IPA [Institute of Public Affairs] Review* (1990) pp. 50-1.
55 *Australian Football League annual report 1990*.
56 [Adelaide] *City Messenger*, 13 May 1992.
57 [Adelaide] *Advertiser*, 31 August 1991.

Chapter 3: Boxing

1 Thanks go to the Australian Research Council and Flinders University for financial help, to Janice Cameron, Robyn Day and Robin Ordynski for research assistance, and to Marilyn Chandler for her word-processing expertise. Although references will be given for specific incidents and events, generalisations are drawn from a variety of sources including — Peter Corris, *Lords of the ring* (Sydney, 1980); W. J. Doherty, *In the days of the giants: memories of a champion of the prize-ring* (Sydney, 1931); Johnny Famechon, *Fammo* (Melbourne, 1971); Rocky Gattellari, *The rocky road* (Melbourne, 1989); Grantlee Kieza, *Australian boxing: the illustrated history* (Sydney, 1990); Grantlee Kieza and Peter Muszkat, *Fenech: the official biography* (Sydney, 1988); Ray Mitchell, *Great Australian fights* (Sydney, 1965); Ray Mitchell, *The fighting Sands* (Sydney, 1965); Kenneth Roberts, *Captain of the push: when a larrikin chief ruled the Rocks* (Melbourne, 1963); Lionel Rose, *Lionel Rose: Australian*

(Sydney, 1969); Raymond Swanwick, *Les Darcy: Australia's golden boy of boxing* (Sydney, 1965). Use was also made of *Australian Ring Digest, Australian Sportsfan, Fighter Magazine, Referee, Sporting Globe* and *Sports Magazine.*

2 Richard Broome, 'Boxing' in Wray Vamplew, Katharine Moore, John O'Hara, Richard Cashman and Ian F. Jobling (eds) *The Oxford companion to Australian sport* (Melbourne, 1992), p. 64.

3 Graeme Aplin, S. G. Foster and Michael McKernan, *Australians: events and places* (Sydney, 1987), p. 383.

4 Richard Fotheringham, *Sport in Australian drama* (Cambridge, 1992), p. 18, p. 39.

5 Corris, pp. 38-48.

6 Much of what follows is based on chapter 2 of Murray G. Phillips, 'Australian sport and World War One', PhD Thesis, University of Queensland (1992).

7 Less is known about the reaction of amateur boxing. Certainly the Victorian Amateur Athletics Association, which controlled amateur athletics, boxing and cycling in that state, abandoned its championships. However, bouts between servicemen were utilised as a distraction and a morale-boosting entertainment both *en route* to Europe and, particularly, in the post-Armistice wait for demobilisation.

8 Corris, p. 119.

9 Corris, pp. 146-47.

10 Corris, p. 164.

11 Department of Tourism and Recreation, *Report of the interdepartmental committee inquiry into boxing and other combat sports* (Canberra, 1974), p. 28; Michael Sutherland, 'The bell stilled on ringside: end of an era' *Fighter* (October 1975), p. 36.

12 Stan Shipley, 'Boxing' in Tony Mason (ed.), *Sport in Britain: a social history* (Cambridge, 1989), p. 178; 'Boxing at public schools', *Referee*, 11 April 1894; *Referee*, 6 July, 1 August 1894.

13 Joe Lynch, 'Where are our Australian boxing prospects?', *Sport* (August 1954), p. 36.

14 Reet and Max Howell, *Aussie gold: the story of Australia at the Olympics* (Melbourne 1988).

15 *Sport* (December 1954).

16 Bill Henneberry, 'Is your manager an asset or a liability?', *Sport*, 2.11 (April 1956), pp. 57-8.

17 Daryl Adair, 'Public house sports' in Vamplew et al., *The Oxford companion to Australian sport*, pp. 282-83.

18 Richard Broome, 'Burns-Johnson fight' in Vamplew et al., *The Oxford companion to Australian sport*, p. 35; Fotheringham, p. 46.

19 Richard Broome, 'Stadiums Limited' in Vamplew et al., *The Oxford companion to Australian sport*, p. 334; Gerald Crawford, 'Baker, Reginald Leslie' in Vamplew et al., *The Oxford companion to Australian sport*, p. 49; Andrew Lemon, 'Wren, John' in

Vamplew et al., p. 385. In late 1953 Art Mawson, who had promoted small fights around Sydney for some time, established the Australian Boxing Club in a direct challenge to Stadiums Limited. However, the refusal of Stadiums Limited to offer matches to boxers who fought for Mawson, its purchase of Mawson's Leichhardt stadium lease and some poor business decisions by Mawson himself doomed the venture. 'Gloves off', *Sport Magazine*, 1.12 (May 1955), pp. 46-8. In the 1960s some of the New South Wales licensed clubs featured boxing promotions.

20 Gary Parker, 'Sharman, Jimmy' in Vamplew et al., *The Oxford companion to Australian sport*, pp. 310-11.

21 John Carlisle, 'Who'll take a glove', *Australian Sportsfan*, 1.2 (May 1972), pp. 4-6; *Advertiser*, 10 February 1990. 'A current affair' (Channel Nine, 15 June 1992) featured Fred Brophy's boxing tent which he had run for twenty-five years and his family before him for much of the century. Stockmen and drovers came from up to 500 kilometres away to the Queensland country town of Boulia for a weekend dedicated to the outback culture of drinking, horse-racing, gambling and boxing. No medical assistance was in evidence. Brophy reckoned the popularity of his tent, with Aborigines and whites, was one in the eye for the anti-boxing fraternity!

22 Nicholas Fox, 'Facing the choice — the money or the box-on', *Bulletin*, 27 June 1970, p. 22; Derril Farrar, 'Jeff Fenech slugs his way toward millionaire class', *Bulletin*, 25 March 1986.

23 [Adelaide] *Advertiser*, 9 June 1987; Bret Harris, *The proud champions: Australia's Aboriginal sporting heroes* (Sydney, 1989), p. 87.

24 Richard Broome, 'Professional Aboriginal boxers in eastern Australia 1930-1979', *Aboriginal History*, 4.1 (1980), p. 50.

25 Broome, 'Aboriginal boxers', p. 51, estimates that the average retirement age would be twenty-five to thirty years.

26 Ron Saw, 'People', *Bulletin*, 12 June 1976.

27 *Report of the interdepartmental committee inquiry into boxing*, p. 50

28 S.K. Weinberg and H. Arond, 'The occupational culture of the boxer', *American Journal of Sociology*, 57 (1952), p. 468.

29 A. H. Roberts, *Brain damage in boxers* (London, 1969).

30 Dennis Brailsford, *Bareknuckles: a social history of prize-fighting* (Cambridge, 1988), pp. 8-9, 97; *Bell's Life in Sydney*, 10 April 1847.

31 Kieza, *Australian Boxing*, p. 8.

32 Corris, pp. 11-12.

33 Based on 7187 bouts traced in *Fighter* (July 1970-August 1976).

34 *Sporting Globe*, 3 March 1948; Corris, p. 159; *Report of the interdepartmental committee inquiry into boxing*, p. 24.

35 *Referee*, 17 September 1890.

36 Lou Lewis, 'Safety in boxing', *Think* (June/July 1992), p. 16.

37 Lynch, 'Where are our Australian boxing prospects?', *Sport*, (August 1954), p. 37; Adrian McGregor, 'Amateur fighters get hurt too', *Bulletin*, 27 October 1973.

38 *Bell's Life in Sydney*, 12 June 1847.

39 *Sport Magazine*, 2.2 (July 1955), p. 67; Bill Henneberry, 'Should we have boxing control?', *Sport Magazine*, 2.5 (October 1955), pp. 34-5; Barry Ward, 'We must have a boxing board', *Australian Sport and Surfriding*, 18.1 (June 1964), pp. 52-3; Ward McNally, 'Australia badly needs a boxing commission', *Australian Sportsfan*, 1.9 (1972/73), pp. 44-5.

40 Braham Dabscheck, 'Unionism' in Vamplew et al., *The Oxford companion to Australian sport*, pp. 362-64.

41 Lynch, 'Boxing prospects', p. 37; Discus, 'Gattellari v Algieri', *Bulletin*, 15 December 1962.

42 Corris, pp. 157-58.

43 *Report of the interdepartmental committee into boxing*, p. 34.

44 *Report of the interdepartmental committee into boxing*, p. 10.

45 *Referee*, 30 August 1924.

46 [Adelaide] *Advertiser*, 4 January 1988, 26 July 1991; *Report of the interdepartmental committee into boxing*, p. 12, p. 34.

47 He was voted Australian of the Year in 1968.

48 Broome, 'Aboriginal boxers', p. 53.

49 [Adelaide] *Advertiser*, 10 February 1990.

50 Some whites, of course, suggested that Aborigines had genetic advantages with their speed of punch and quickness of eye being 'attributes handed down from their forebears, whose existence depended on the speed, accuracy and force with which they threw a spear or wielded a nulla nulla'. Similarly their 'toughness about the head' was deemed hereditary. M. Williams, 'Abo boxers are lifting the crowns', *Sporting Globe*, 23 April 1948.

51 The post-Second World War migration also led to 'ethnics' being similarly utilised. 'The invasion is on', *Sport*, November 1954, pp. 44-5.

52 For details see Richard Broome, 'The Australian reaction to Jack Johnson, black pugilist, 1907-9' in Richard Cashman and Michael McKernan (eds), *Sport in history* (Brisbane, 1979), pp. 343-63.

53 *Referee*, 12 November 1890.

54 Tom Langley, *The life of Peter Jackson: champion of Australia* (Leicester, 1974).

55 Much of what follows on Aboriginal boxers is based on information in Harris, Broome, *The proud champions*; 'Aboriginal boxers', and Colin Tatz, *Aborigines in sport* (Adelaide, 1987), though the interpretation of the evidence is not necessarily theirs.

56 *Sport Magazine*, 1.3 (1954), p. 67.

57 Based on a survey of 250 traced boxers for which more than

minimal information can be obtained. Clearly the sample was biassed towards the more successful, that is, they either won titles or stayed in the sport for several years.

58 Corris, pp. 102-3.

59 *Report of the interdepartmental committee into boxing*, p. 93.

60 *Bell's Life in Sydney*, 11 September 1847; *Sporting Globe*, 15 December 1948. Some other bouts are detailed in Marion K. Stell, *Half the race* (Sydney 1991), pp. 18-19.

61 Quoted in Fotheringham, p. 2.

62 *Bell's Life in Victoria*, 2 February 1867.

63 *Referee*, 23 November 1910.

64 Wray Vamplew, *Sports violence in Australia : its extent and control* (Canberra, 1991), p. 10.

65 Pallante v Stadiums Pty. Ltd., 3-4, 7-9 April 1975, Supreme Court of Victoria. For many years the *Police manual* in Queensland contained specific instructions for police supervision of boxing matches including using the authority to stop a contest in the case of brutality, a mismatch, exhaustion or serious injury. *Report of the interdepartmental committee into boxing*, p. 11.

66 *Sporting Globe*, 24 August 1935.

67 *Sporting Globe*, 2 November 1935.

68 *Bell's Life in Sydney*, 12 June 1847. Isolated incidents of crowd riot are recorded throughout the twentieth century, but more research is needed on crowd behaviour in Australian boxing, in particular on the effects of racism, nationalism, betting, alcohol and the institution of points decisions.

69 Corris, p. 32, p. 121.

70 *Report of the interdepartmental committee into boxing*, p. 146.

71 Wray Vamplew, *A healthy body* (Canberra, 1989), p. 70.

72 Jak Carroll, 'Boxing debate rages', *Sport Report* (Spring 1991), p. 7; 'President's message', *Sport Health*, 10.2 (June 1992), p. 4.

73 Lewis, 'Safety in boxing', p. 16.

74 *Bell's Life in Sydney*, 17 April 1847.

75 *Referee*, 26 November 1890.

76 It is suggested that the headgear impairs a boxer's vision, that a false confidence is created; and that the brain still gets shaken up. Soren Schmidt-Olsen, Soren Kaalund Jensen and Vagner Mortensen, 'Amateur boxing in Denmark: The effect of some preventive measures', *American Journal of Sports Medicine*, 18.1 (1990), pp. 98-100.

77 *Report of the interdepartmental committee into boxing*, p. 9.

78 National Committee on Violence, p. 250.

79 Bruce Kidd, 'Boxing and the law of assault', in J. Barnes, *Sports violence and law reform* (Ontario, 1984). *See* arguments advanced in 'Why every Australian schoolboy should be taught to box', *Sporting Globe*, 29 March 1924.

80 *Australian*, 7 June 1986.

81 Data collected by author.

82 National Health and Medical Research Council, *Health aspects of boxing* (Canberra, 1975), p. 1.

83 A study in Ontario showed that less than one per cent of amateur bouts ended in a knockout compared to twenty-nine per cent of professional fights. 'Boxing and the law', p. 35.

84 [Adelaide] *Advertiser*, 25 April 1989; Ray Mitchell, 'Figuring the year', *Fighter Magazine*, January 1974.

85 On 2 September 1890 Albert Griffiths defeated New Zealander Billy Murphy in Sydney to claim the world featherweight title, although the Americans have never officially recognised this as a title bout. Gerald Crawford, 'Griffiths, Albert' in Vamplew et al., *The Oxford companion to Australian sport*, p. 169.

86 Nigel Hopkins, 'Ring of fire', [Adelaide] *Advertiser Magazine*, 19 January 1991.

Chapter 4: Cricket

1 Jas Scott, *Early cricket in Sydney 1803 to 1856*, edited by R. Cashman and S. Gibbs, (Sydney, 1991); Richard Cashman, 'The rise and fall of the Australian Cricket Club 1826-1868', *Sporting Traditions*, 5.1 (1988), pp. 112-30.

2 John Mulvaney and Rex Harcourt, *Cricket walkabout: the Australian Aborigines in England* (Melbourne, 1988).

3 Richard Cashman, 'Symbols of unity: Anglo-Australian cricketers, 1877-1900', *International Journal of the History of Sport*, 7.1 (May 1990), pp. 97-110.

4 W. F. Mandle, 'Cricket and Australian nationalism in the nineteenth century', *Journal of the Royal Australian Historical Society*, 59.4 (December 1973), pp. 225-45; David Montefiore, 'Cricket in the doldrums: the struggle between private and public control in Australian cricket in the 1880s', Australian Society for Sports History, *Studies in Sports History*, 8 (Campbelltown, 1992).

5 Chris Cunneen, 'Elevating and recording the people's pastimes: Sydney sporting journalism 1886-1939', in R. Cashman and M. McKernan (eds), *Sport: money, morality and the media* (Kensington, 1981), pp. 162-76.

6 Maxwell Howell, 'Will the Real Victor Trumper stand up?', Conference paper, Australian Society for Sports History, 1985.

7 Radcliffe Grace, 'The Rise and fall of the Australasian Cricket Council 1892-1900', *Sporting Traditions*, 2.1 (1985), pp. 37-46.

8 Ric Sissons and Brian Stoddart, *Cricket and Empire: the 1932-33 bodyline tour of Australia* (Sydney, 1984).

9 *See* 'The Bradman factor' in R. Cashman, *'Ave a go, yer mug!* (Sydney, 1984), p. 92.

10 Geoffrey Lawrence and David Rowe (eds), *Power play: the commercialisation of Australian sport* (Sydney, 1986), p. 164.

11 Brian Stoddart, 'Sport and television', unpublished paper, pp. 13-14. *See also* R. Cashman, 'Sport, big business and the spectator', *Current Affairs Bulletin* (June 1986).

12 Chris Harte, *Two tours and Pollock: the Australian cricketers in South Africa 1985-87* (Adelaide, 1988).

13 R. Cashman and A. Weaver, *Wicket women: cricket and women in Australia* (Kensington, 1991).

14 Mulvaney and Harcourt.

15 Genevieve Clare Blades, 'Australian Aborigines, cricket and pedestrianism: culture and conflict, 1880-1910', Bachelor of Human Movement Studies, Hons thesis, University of Queensland (1985), p. 4.

16 Blades, 'Australian Aborigines', p. 144.

17 King played in the 1969-70 season and Mainhardt played from 1980-82.

18 *Referee*, 9 June 1916.

19 Blades, 'Australian Aborigines', pp. 73-4.

20 Brian Stoddart, *Saturday afternoon fever: sport in the Australian culture* (Sydney, 1986), p. 166.

21 Blades, 'Australian Aborigines', pp. 72-5.

22 Chris Harte, *SACA: the history of the South Australian Cricket Association* (Adelaide, 1990), pp. 191-92, pp. 262-63.

23 Harte, *SACA*.

24 Philip Derriman, *True to the blue* (Sydney, 1985).

25 David Montefiore, 'Cricket in the doldrums'.

26 Bill O'Reilly, *'Tiger': sixty years of cricket* (Sydney, 1985), pp. 157-60.

27 Braham Dabscheck, 'Professional Cricketers Association of Australia', *Sporting Traditions*, 8.1 (1991), p. 2-27.

28 Keith A. P. Sandiford, 'English cricket crowds during the Victorian age', *Journal of Sports History*, 9.3 (Winter, 1982), p. 12.

29 Clive Forster, 'Sport, society and space: the changing geography of country cricket in South Australia 1836-1914', *Sporting Traditions*, 2.2 (1986), p. 28.

30 Greg McKie, 'A history of Australian schoolboys' cricket and how educational changes within Victoria have influenced it', MA thesis, La Trobe University (Melbourne, 1993).

Chapter 5: Golf

1 *Sports directory 1993* (Canberra, 1993); National Golf Foundation, *Golf participation in the United States* (Florida, 1991); (One late 1990 survey report put the Australian figure at 26 per cent, or 4.4 million people, but that seems far too high.) Brian Sweeney and Associates, *Australians in sport* (Sydney, 1990).

2 *Australian golf directory — 1993* (Sydney, 1992) is an excellent guide to the full range of activities.

3 *See* Jack Pollard, *Australian golf: the game and the players* (Sydney, 1990), a great source for factual information generally.

4 Gordon Inglis, in his *Sport and pastime in Australia* (London, 1912), p. 220 described golf as 'the most thriving game in the Commonwealth'.

5 *See* David J. Innes, *The story of golf in New South Wales, 1851-1987* (Sydney, 1988), chapters 1-3. For the British story, *see* John Lowerson, 'Golf' in Tony Mason, *Sport in Britain* (Cambridge, 1989), pp. 187-214.

6 Colin Tatz and Brian Stoddart, *The Royal Sydney Golf Club: the first hundred years* (Sydney, 1993), especially chapters 2, 3.

7 Joseph Johnson, *The Royal Melbourne Golf Club: a centenary history* (Melbourne, 1991), especially chapter 3. For Queensland, Murray Phillips, 'Golf and Victorian sporting values', *Sporting Traditions*, 6.2 (May 1990).

8 On course architecture, Geoffrey S. Cornish and Ronald Whitten, *The golf course* (New York, 1981). For Australian representations, Marlene Roeder, *Courses without par in Australia* (Sydney, 1992).

9 Michael White, *Lake Karrinyup Country Club, 1928-1988* (Sydney, 1988), chapter 2.

10 White, chapter 2.

11 Hugh Barry, *Elanora* (Sydney, 1977).

12 Advertising brochure, *Belvedere* (1920).

13 *Golf in Australia*, 16 October 1924.

14 *Golf in Australia*, 5 February 1925.

15 Johnson, p. 88; *Golf in Australia*, 18 September 1924.

16 Johnson, pp. 85-8.

17 *Golf*, 9.2 (February 1928), p. 68; *Golf*, 9.3 (March 1928), p. 37.

18 *Golf*, 7.6 (June 1926), p. 259.

19 *Golf*, 3.9 (September 1924), p. 5.

20 Tatz and Stoddart, pp. 216-21; also Colin de Groot (with Jim Webster), *Pro golf: out of the rough — illustrated history of professional golf in Australia* (Sydney, 1991), pp. 23-5.

21 de Groot, pp. 27-8, p. 44, p. 51. Also, J. Victor East, *Better golf in five minutes* (London, 1958) and Joe Kirkwood, *Links of life* (New York, 1973).

22 G.H. Newman, *The history of the Cottesloe Golf Club (Inc), 1905-1983* (Perth, 1984), p. 32.

23 Tatz and Stoddart, pp. 90-3.

24 Interview material with Royal Canberra personnel. However, compare with *Royal Canberra Golf Club jubilee history, 1926-1976* (Canberra, 1977), p. 60.

25 *See* Marion K. Stell, *Half the race* (Sydney, 1991).

26 Interview with Dale Wharton.

27 Pollard, pp. 257-58.

28 Interview with Robyn Gibson-Quick.

29 For example, *see* Tatz and Stoddart, pp. 45-6.
30 For example, *see* Norman von Nida, *Golf is my business* (London, 1956).
31 *New Zealand Golfing World*, April/May 1993.
32 Pollard, pp. 30-1.
33 de Groot, chapter 2.
34 For example, *see* John Kissling, *Seventy years: the story of the Metropolitan Golf Club* (Melbourne, 1973) for details of that club's relocations.
35 'Special report examines golf and the environment', *Golf Market Today*, 32.6 (November-December 1992)
36 Interview with Australian Broadcasting Corporation golf production personnel.

Chapter 6: Horse Racing and Trotting

1 *Argus*, 1 November 1867.
2 Maurice Cavanough and Meurig Davies, *Cup day. The story of the Melbourne Cup 1861-1960*, (Melbourne, 1960), p. 19.
3 *Argus*, 1 and 4 November 1867.
4 *Argus*, 1 and 4 November 1867.
5 *Argus*, 1 and 4 November 1867.
6 Jack Pollard, *The pictorial history of Australian horse racing* (Sydney, 1971), pp. 75-6; Cavanough and Davies, pp. 17-18.
7 Cavanough and Davies, pp. 19-22, p. 326.
8 *Argus*, 4 November 1867.
9 The population of Grafton and district was below five thousand.
10 *Clarence and Richmond Examiner*, 23 July 1867.
11 O'Hara, *A mug's game: a history of gaming and betting in Australia* (Sydney, 1988), pp. 13-17. Painter and Waterhouse, *The principal club. A history of the Australian Jockey Club* (Sydney, 1992), pp. 4-5. pp. 13-16, p. 32; H. Freedman and A. Lemon *The history of Australian thoroughbred racing* (Melbourne, vol 1, 1987; vol 2, 1990). The first race at this meeting was won by Captain Ritchie's Chase over two two-mile heats.
12 Pollard, p. 11.
13 Pollard, p. 11; Max Agnew, *Australia's trotting heritage* (Mitcham, 1977), p. 21.
14 Agnew, p. 21.
15 *Sydney Gazette*, 5 May 1810. The galloping event was won by the appropriately named Parramatta and the trotting match went to Captain Piper's mare Miss Kitty.
16 *Sydney Gazette*, 29 September, 6 October 1810.
17 Agnew, p. 21.
18 A ban on horse-racing in the northern American states in the early nineteenth century led to a closure of race tracks. This resulted in the roads becoming the testing ground for racing and

the trotter was more suited to the hard roads than was the more fragile thoroughbred. Agnew, pp. 13, 21.

19 Painter and Waterhouse, pp. 9-17; O'Hara, pp. 33-5; N. Penton, *A racing heart. The story of the Australian turf* (Sydney, 1987), p. 17.

20 O'Hara, pp. 11, pp. 35-7; Painter and Waterhouse, pp. 6-12.

21 Douglas M. Barrie, *Turf calvacade, a review of 150 years of horse racing in Australia and of the Australian Jockey Club's hundred years at Randwick* (Sydney, 1960); Penton, pp. 21-3.

22 Painter and Waterhouse, p. 17.

23 Painter and Waterhouse, p. 19.

24 Painter and Waterhouse, p. 40.

25 Freedman and Lemon, pp. 293-95.

26 Freedman and Lemon pp. 280-82; Painter and Waterhouse, p. 15, p. 19.

27 Gate money became an additional revenue source in the 1870s when the main racecourses in each colony were enclosed by perimeter fencing, allowing the clubs to increase prize money further.

28 Penton, p. 36.

29 Cavanough and Davies, pp. 324-25.

30 Freedman and Lemon, pp. 275-76.

31 Freedman and Lemon, p. 349.

32 Freedman and Lemon, pp. 315-32.

33 Freedman and Lemon, pp. 333-42.

34 Freedman and Lemon, p. 363.

35 Painter and Waterhouse, pp. 112-13.

36 Freedman and Lemon, pp. 277-80.

37 O'Hara, p. 103, p. 126; Painter and Waterhouse, pp. 32-40.

38 O'Hara, p. 103.

39 O'Hara, p. 104; Agnew, pp. 22-7, p. 38.

40 Agnew, pp. 42-4.

41 O'Hara, pp. 103-5.

42 Greg Brown, *One hundred years of trotting, 1877-1977* (Sydney, 1981), pp. 61, pp. 69-74; Agnew, p. 67.

43 Brown, pp. 65-71; O'Hara, pp. 155-56.

44 O'Hara, pp. 176-84.

45 Brown, p. 176; Agnew, pp. 105-8, pp. 128-30.

46 Agnew, pp. 169-73.

47 O'Hara, pp. 186-87.

48 Agnew, p. 178.

49 The exception is Tasmania where night trotting has still not been introduced successfully. In that state the two forms of horse-racing alternate each week between Hobart and Launceston, on Saturday afternoons.

50 Brown, p. 138.

51 Although the system used has differed from state to state the

formulas are based on betting turnover, which ensures that the galloping clubs receive more money with which to promote their sport, again ensuring a higher betting turnover. Brown, pp. 259-61.

52 Since the introduction of the TAB, race crowds have decreased by up to 60 per cent. *Sun-Herald*, 28 July 1991.

Notes to Chapter 7: Lawn Bowls

1 *Sydney Morning Herald*, 28 April 1900

2 It is often claimed that this disjuncture between the two games found in England resulted from legislation which stipulated that only land holders whose land was valued at more than one hundred pounds per year could legally build a bowling green. The less well-to-do were then forced to frequent illegal 'alleys' to gamble and drink. For example, see A. T. Holroyd, *Bowls and bowling with the laws and rules of the game* (Sydney 1874), pp. 4-6

3 For example, see E. T. Ayers, *Bowls, bowling greens and bowls players* (London, 1896), p. 36, p. 65. A. H. Haynes, *The story of bowls* (London, 1972), p. 93 refers to the alleys as 'the resort of idle and dissolute persons'.

4 It is interesting to note that the English adopted the more formal Scottish play only after an Australian deputation to encourage the formation of an 'Imperial' Bowling Association in 1899.

5 *Sydney Morning Herald*, 27 May 1935, for example, reported the gift to the New South Wales Bowls Association by Miss Fairfax of hundred-year-old bowls which had been used by the Hon. John Fairfax on his private green 'long before a public green was in existence'.

6 H. E. Quigley, *Bowls in Parramatta 1868-1951* (Parramatta, 1951), p. 20, quoting *Bell's Life* remarked upon the launch of a green at the Boundary Stone Inn, Surry Hills (New South Wales), which linked its opening with the birthday of the Prince of Wales.

7 J. P. Monro, *Handbook of the sixth Australian bowling carnival* (1927) p. 13, citing the *Hobart Town Courier and Van Diemen's Land Gazette*, 4 January 1845 on the opening of Mr Lipscombe's green.

8 Quigley, p. 18. Following the green's opening a club of sorts was initiated where, for an annual sum, the green was reserved for paying players on certain days and times.

9 Monro, p. 17. This 'club' too charged an annual sum of one pound for membership. Monro, p. 13.

10 *Australian Bowling Carnival Sydney 1926*, p. 21; J. Henshaw, O. Glenn, *The first one hundred years of the Royal Victorian Bowls*

Association 1880-1980 (Melbourne, 1979), p. 108, p. 121.

11 L. McCarthy, 'Young, Sir John', in Wray Vamplew, Katharine Moore, John O'Hara, Richard Cashman and Ian F. Jobling (eds), *The Oxford companion to Australian sport* (Melbourne, 1992), p. 387.

12 Others were the Woolpack Inn, Parramatta (est. 1870); Cambridge College Club, Sherwood Scrubs, Parramatta (est. 1872); the King's School (est. 1874), and the Sydney Club (est. 1876); see C. K. Guiney, *Centenary. The history of the Royal New South Wales Bowls Association* (Sydney 1980), pp. 4-5.

13 J. Bower, 'The history of bowls in South Australia', unpublished manuscript, (n.d.) p. 1.

14 W. L. Johnston, *Fifty years of history: Waverley Bowling and Recreation Club* (Sydney, 1944), p. 12.

15 The Sydney Club built by the Governor of New South Wales on the Domain was closed in 1878 when the land was resumed for the Exhibition Building, although members moved to another green (formed at the Police Barracks) which finally closed in 1880. *First annual report of the Sydney Bowling Club 1878* (Sydney 1978), pp. 16-17.

16 For example, see *Rules of the Redfern Club* (Sydney, 1890).

17 R. Healey, *The history, objects, activities and achievements of the City Bowling Club* (supplement to the *Helm*) (Sydney, 1967), p. 41.

18 'Old minute book', pp. 11-12, 13. The clubhouse was designed by Varney Parkes who was given life membership in recognition, p. 15, p. 18.

19 *Souvenir programme of the third Australian bowling carnival* (Adelaide, 1921), pp. 35-9.

20 *Sydney Morning Herald*, 29 January 1892.

21 *Sydney Morning Herald*, 29 January 1892.

22 P. Ashton, *Centennial Park. A history* (Sydney, 1988), p. 111.

23 J. Young, 'Public parks and bowling clubs' in *New South Wales bowlers annual* (Sydney, 1906), p. 23; A. Roberts, 'An ancient game in a new land: bowling and society in New South Wales to 1912', *Journal of the Royal Australian Historical Society*, 65.2 (September 1979), p. 117.

24 Ashton, p. 111.

25 Johnston, p. 12.

26 Even though the moves to introduce a residential qualification in bowls-club membership were consistently defeated, nonetheless the majority of players tended to join clubs within reach of their homes. Indeed, J. Young commented that a number of the clubs established towards the end of the nineteenth century were founded by ex-Annandale men who started up clubs closer to home. J. Young 'History of bowls in New South Wales' in *New South Wales bowlers annual* (1906), p. 18.

27 J. A. Manson, *The complete bowler. Being the history and practice of the ancient and royal game of bowls* (London, 1912), p. 72.

28 Monro, p. 23.

29 *Rules of the Redfern Bowling Club* (1890), p. 8.

30 New South Wales women followed in 1929; South Australia, Queensland and New Zealand in 1930; England in 1931; Wales in 1932; Scotland in 1934; Western Australia and Ireland in 1935; the Tasmanian Bowls Council in 1905; Northern Territory in 1983; Australian Capital Territory in 1993 and the Australian Women's Bowls Council in 1947.

31 The first record of unambiguous female club membership was the Stawell Club, Victoria in 1895; the Perth Club (male) opened in 1894 (the green however in 1895); the Fremantle Club in 1896; the Swan in 1897; the Adelaide Club in 1898 and the Adelaide Oval in 1900. Although another early club, Brighton Beach, began as an exclusively women's club in 1905, following a meeting held in 1906 the club rewrote its rules to allow male 'associate' membership. Henshaw and Glenn, p. 93.

32 *Sydney Morning Herald*, 28 April 1900.

33 Up to 1949 in Queensland all women's clubs were affiliates of men's; of the 162 male clubs, 123 had women's facilities. The first all-woman club was established in Queensland following a vote by one male club not to allow women to join. Lettie Morelle, *The first fifty years: a brief history of the growth and development of the Queensland Ladies Bowling Association* (Brisbane, 1980) chapter 7 (n.p.).

34 G. Sargeant, *Bowls* (1959), p. 112.

35 L. McCarthy, 'Training the body or the mind? Debates about the higher education of women in nineteenth-century New South Wales', unpublished. MA thesis, University of New South Wales (1991).

36 Johnston, p. 19.

37 Young provided tables about the cost of the green's upkeep and the amount realised through paying customers to show that these greens were also profitable in an immediate sense too. Young, 'Public parks', p. 25.

38 *Memento of the first Commonwealth bowling carnival Adelaide, Christmas 1910* (Adelaide, 1910), p. 82.

39 W. D. and H. O. Wills established the Raleigh Park greens in the 1930s, Nestlés, Lysaghts, Federal Match Co., Broken Hill Proprietary, Davis Gelatine, and other companies soon followed. For example, *see* J. Brown, *Principles and practice of Australian bowls* (Melbourne, 1949).

40 The various men's associations were formed in the following years: New South Wales and Victoria, 1880; Western Australia, 1898; Tasmania, 1902; Queensland, 1903; South Australia, 1910; Northern Territory, 1982; Australian Capital Territory, 1983.

41 Monro, p. 63.

42 S. Aylwin, *The gentle art of bowling* (London, 1904), n.p. The prices ranged from fourteen shillings and sixpence to twenty-one shillings in Britain and, although 'wood turners' existed in Australia, many bowls were still imported. The wood needed for the manufacturing of bowls was also imported.

43 The composite bowl's place in the history of Australian bowls is described in J. P. Monro, *The romance of bowls manufacture*, 13th ed. (Melbourne, n.d.).

44 *Sydney Morning Herald*, 18 January 1928.

45 *Sydney Morning Herald*, 8 April 1930.

46 *Sydney Morning Herald*, 4 April 1928. The first Australian Bowls Council ruling on this matter was brought down in February 1926, *see* Guiney, p. 36. In 1931 the Council did adopt the New South Wales standard, which made the Victorians unhappy, *Sydney Morning Herald*, 7 March 1931.

47 *Sydney Morning Herald*, 1 December 1928; *Sydney Morning Herald*, 8 January 1929.

48 *Sydney Morning Herald*, 26 July 1928.

49 Johnston, p. 34.

50 For example, *see Sydney Morning Herald*, 1 February 1928.

51 The Australian Bowls Council legislated to disqualify inappropriately dressed carnival competitors in March 1931 and for pennant matches in July 1931.

52 The Critic, 'Are they bowlers or fishermen? Weird attire on the green', *Bowls in New South Wales*, 1.2 (October 1936), p. 2.

53 *Sydney Morning Herald*, 18 January 1933.

54 *Australian bowling carnival* (Sydney, 1926), p. 72. Commensurate expense is needed in the 1990s; one author estimates that to equip oneself in the regulation clothes would cost $350 on average.

55 Perrin, 'Championships on week-days', *Bowls in New South Wales*, 1.6 (February 1937), p. 20.

56 Monro, p. 41.

57 *Sydney Morning Herald*, 15 November 1933; *see also* A. Dawe, *The Australian bowling team in England . . . 1922*, p. 61 for professionalism versus comradeship; *Australian bowling carnival 1926*, p. 11 for only those 'who have won distinction in professions or business should travel'; *Sydney Morning Herald*, 17 June 1930 for the '£40 000 tour' and arguments for the value of these self-paid tours; *Sydney Morning Herald*, 12 September 1931 for debates concerning New South Wales Bowls Association meeting where the motion to introduce expenses was lost; *Sydney Morning Herald*, 12 September 1928 concerning reimbursement 'disrupt[ing the] traditional order of things. . . [where the] consequences would be disastrous'.

58 R. T. Harrison, 'Should bowlers be paid?', *Bowls in New South*

Wales, 1.6 (February 1937), p. 14; *Sydney Morning Herald*, 15 November 1933; *Sydney Morning Herald*, 29 April 1930.

59 *Australian bowling carnival Sydney 1926*, p. 10: 'Devotion to bowls enrols a man at once in a freemasonry that has no parallel in other sports. . . the majority of players are men who have reached a stage of life to enjoy the companionship of men with whom they find themselves in mental and moral accord.'

60 Dawe, p. 61.

61 Jack High, 'Should players be paid?', *Bowls in New South Wales*, 1.3 (November 1936), p. 5.

62 Dawe, p. 60.

63 Dawe, p. 44, p. 52; and p. 58 for reciprocal tendency to use these occasions to encourage trading links. *See also Sydney Morning Herald*, 27 October 1928 where the next tour was entertained at Windsor Castle. An interesting corollary of this British influence is provided by the White Australia policy's effects on a bowling team's tour:

    Mr J. A. Carruthers, MLA, referred to the effect that federal legislation had upon the game of bowls in New South Wales and other states of the Commonwealth. It was reported, Mr Carruthers said, that whilst on a visit to Japan Mr John Young . . . proposed to bring out a team of bowlers from Japan to Sydney, but that owing to recent legislation by the Federal Parliament regarding aliens the venture had to be dropped. At the same time, remarked the opposition leader, we had in our midst a Japanese [naval] commander with his squadron, and throughout all the States visited by the squadron it was agreed that the Japanese were an important and worthy ally of the British nation.' *Sydney Morning Herald*, 21 September 1903.

64 *Eighth bowling carnival Brisbane 1931* (Brisbane, 1931), p. 23.

65 LSPJ, 'Should players be paid?' *Bowls in New South Wales*, 1.3 (November 1936), p. 5.

66 Johnston, p. 12.

67 Johnston, pp. 16-17.

68 G. T. Caldwell, 'From pub to club: the history of drinking in New South Wales and the growth of registered clubs, 1900-1945', *Australian National University Historical Journal*, 9 (1972), p. 26.

69 G. Sargeant, 'The magical lure of bowls', in J. Pollard (ed.), *Lawn bowls — the Australian way* (Melbourne, 1962), p. 9.

70 H. W. Hawker, 'Country week: The bowlers' Mecca', *Bowls in New South Wales*, 2.1 (March 1937), p. 3. This was true particularly in New South Wales: Victoria had quite a slowing of bowling greens during the same period. The call to have these work-creation schemes build public greens in parks where the unemployed could actually play on them, was not welcomed quite so heartily (*See Sydney Morning Herald* 23 November 1938). Only one such green was ever opened in Sydney by

Sydney City Council in June 1937. *Bowls in New South Wales*, 1.11 (July 1937), p. 19.

71 Bowls in New South Wales, 1.2 (October 1936), p. 3. As much of the 'leased land' was leased from councils it might be safe to argue that over fifty per cent of the New South Wales clubs at least, were on public land.

72 Hawker, *Bowls in New South Wales*, 2.1 (September 1937), p. 2.

73 Phil Irvine, *The first fifty years: Ardlethan Bowling Club 1940-1990* (1990), p. 5.

74 Morelle, chapter 7 (n.p.).

75 Morelle, chapter 7 (n.p.).

76 'A dry game of bowls; Sunday bowls', *Bowls in New South Wales*, 1.5 (January 1937), p. 7.

77 Guiney, p. 55

78 Guiney, p. 56, p. 67, p. 68.

79 Sargeant, in Pollard, p. 9.

80 R. Cashman, 'Parrella, Rob' in Vamplew et al., *The Oxford Companion to Australian Sport*, p. 271.

81 *Sydney Morning Herald*, 28 April 1900.

82 Sargeant, *Bowls* (1959), p. 114.

83 Figures courtesy of Mrs M. Frost, Hon. Secretary Australian Women's Bowls Council, 18 January 1993.

84 'The changing face of women's bowls', *Leisure Life* (Jan/Feb 1982).

85 'Bowling with equal opportunity', *South Australian Bowler* 21.3 (November 1986), p. 16. Furthermore, the difficulties do not end with the successful creation of the club. Many women find it impossible to sustain a gender specific club once it is in operation: there are only ten such in New South Wales and only five out of 229 in South Australia.

86 Johnston, p. 41.

87 Council meeting, *Bowls in New South Wales*, 1.6 (September 1936), pp. 17–18.

88 When the women's world champion, Merle Richardson, was matched with her male counterpart, New Zealander Peter Belliss, in 1986, skill and judgement triumphed where physical strength might have been expected to take the honours.

89 P. N. Sutcliffe, 'It's a woman's game too' in Pollard, p. 51.

90 Sargeant, *Bowls*, p. 51.

91 *Sydney Morning Herald*, 22 April 1985.

92 'Hats off to our women', *Australian Lawn Bowls World*, 1.3 (1991), p. 17.

93 'Statistics show fall in number of bowlers', *Australian Lawn Bowls World*, 1.3 (1991), p. 17.

94 'Hats off', p. 27.

95 Figures provided by Mrs M. Frost, Hon Secretary Australian Women's Bowls Council and the information officer for the Australian Bowls Council, 18 January 1993.

Chapter 8: Lawn Tennis

1 An early English booklet on lawn tennis, one of a series on sports, details the contents of such a tennis kit, suggesting that the necessary implements should cost from one pound five shillings to six guineas, and that the whole should be fitted into a strong box. The booklet, *Lawn tennis (croquet, racquets etc.) illustrated*, acknowledges no author, is undated and published by Ward, Lock and Co. of Salisbury Square, but is clearly written soon after the codification of the rules of tennis by the Marylebone Cricket Club in 1875. Its author still allows the possibility of an hour-glass court shape, while thinking 'the parallel one the better'. The contents of a tennis kit similar to that of Major Wingfield is on display in the sports museum at the Melbourne Cricket Ground.

2 In describing the play in the Geelong Easter tournament of 1894, the correspondent of the *Geelong Times* wrote: 'The position of tennis amongst the popular outdoor pastimes of Australia was much discussed by the onlookers, and a very large majority were convinced the game has receded considerably in public favour during the last few years, this circumstance being, in the opinion of authorities on tennis, almost solely attributable to the absurd introduction of the covered ball onto Australian courts.'

3 Douglas Sladen, *My long life* (London, 1939), p. 57.

4 An insight into these early inter-colonial and interstate matches is gained from the lists of match results and team members in the book by 'Austral' (of the *Referee*) entitled *Lawn tennis in Australasia* (Sydney, 1912).

5 The story of this tournament and of the Geelong Lawn Tennis Club is told in Graeme Kinross-Smith's *The sweet spot: one hundred years of life and tennis in Geelong* (Melbourne, 1982).

6 Handicapping took two main forms. In the first, allocated points known as 'bisques' could be taken by the inferior player at times in the match when these 'free' points were of most use in winning a game. This practice may have stemmed from royal tennis, but its origins are uncertain. In the second form of handicapping the more skilful players were deemed to 'owe' points to their opponents sometimes in each game, sometimes in specified games. Thus, in early male tournament events the 'owe-thirty men' had to win two points (to reach 'owe-fifteen' and then 'love') before they could start to score in a game. In a refinement of this, skilled players might be handicapped '30 2/ 6', for instance, indicating that they had to gain two points before scoring on each second and sixth game.

7 A Melbourne *Argus* report, syndicated in the *Geelong Advertiser* of 26 January 1883.

8 Gordon Inglis, in his *Sport and pastime in Australia* (London,

1912), pp. 158-59, concurs with several other commentators in stressing the importance of the Melbourne 1908 Davis Cup contest in registering tennis for the first time in the general and public mind as well as in the minds of those who were already devotees and practitioners of the sport:

It was really the first success of the two Australasian players, Norman Brookes and Anthony F. Wilding, and the subsequent contests with America, which caused lawn tennis to rank as a serious game in Australasia...We always had plenty of genuine enthusiasts, but public recognition of the game's merits came as a result of the [Davis] Cup. When Brookes and Wilding were fighting so pluckily at Wimbledon the popular sympathy was first enlisted. At previous tournaments I suppose that eight out of every ten people present were directly interested in a game they themselves followed.

But it was the introduction of an international element that drew the outsider. Previously lawn tennis had been hopelessly misunderstood. The scoffer always associated it with afternoon tea; he jibed at its scoring terms and was pleased to burlesque fifteen-love as a term of endearment when recorded in mixed doubles. The ignorant labelled it a 'ladies game' and beneath their notice. When they saw a quartet like Wright, Alexander, Brookes and Wilding fighting out five-sets matches for two hours under a blazing sun, it was made apparent that not only science but also physique, was essential in the making of a champion. The Davis Cup of 1908 removed all misconceptions.

9   Richard Yallop, *Royal South Yarra Lawn Tennis Club: 100 years in Australian tennis* (Melbourne, 1984), p. 39.

10   I am indebted to several sources for the information that goes to make up the picture of Australian and particularly Melbourne tennis painted in the preceding several paragraphs: to Richard Yallop's account of the Royal South Yarra Tennis Club; to wider social accounts such as Dame Mabel Brookes' *Crowded galleries*; and particularly to my several interviews with J. B. (Jack) Hawkes in 1981, and with Mrs 'Muffy' Stogdale of South Yarra concerning her father Gerald Patterson, his life story and his acquaintances.

11   Austral, *Lawn Tennis in Australasia*.

12   Virginia O'Farrell posits such a set of social, economic and religious characteristics as being typical of the membership of Australian tennis clubs in their early days in her essay, 'The unasked questions in Australian tennis' in *Sporting Traditions*, 1.2 (May 1984), p. 74. Her conclusion seems well supported by recourse to the details of pre-war membership of such clubs as the Melbourne Cricket Club, the Royal South Yarra, the Grace Park and the Geelong Lawn Tennis clubs in Victoria, while the pattern in the wider range of Victorian clubs and in Sydney's earlier tennis clubs may be harder to substantiate.

13 The story of the debt of Australian (and particularly New South Wales) tennis to the country nurturing of accomplished players is told in Ron McLean's *Country cracks: the story of New South Wales country tennis* (Gunnedah, 1983).

14 Victor Kalms, son of Fred Kalms, in an interview with the author in November 1987 has recalled his father's verbal accounts of his sense of isolation while on the 1924 Davis Cup tour in America, although Fred Kalms to his knowledge had never committed such detail to paper.

15 Robert Gordon Menzies, 'The great game of tennis', in Allison Danzig and Peter Schwed (eds), *The fireside book of tennis* (New York, 1972), p. 3.

16 *See* Bruce Matthews, *Game, set and glory: a history of the Australian tennis championships* (Melbourne, 1985), p. 11.

17 Matthews, p. 43, and *see* Sir Norman Brookes' assessment of Wynne (Bolton) in R. S. Whitington, *An illustrated history of Australian tennis* (South Melbourne, 1975), p. 40.

18 Matthews, pp. 50-1, p. 62. I am also indebted to Judy Dalton for her information about these events.

19 Yallop, p. 93.

20 A boycott by women players at the Australian Championships — also over the issue of the imbalance between men's and women's prize money — was narrowly averted in the same year.

21 *See* the account of these events in Richard Schickel, *The world of tennis* (New York, 1975), pp. 200-01.

22 Kinross-Smith, p. 99 and in the author's interview with Jack Hawkes, February 1982.

23 Rosemary Alexander, 'Where have all the aces gone?', *Weekend Australian*, 14/15 December 1991.

Chapter 9: Netball

1 'Women's basket ball' in Australia officially became 'netball' in 1970, the word 'women's' deleted, and the name changed to the All Australia Netball Association (AANA). Throughout this chapter the term 'netball' refers to the sport which was called variously women's basket ball or basketball, outdoor basketball or seven-a-side basketball, unless the context of the discussion requires other terminologies.

   The author acknowledges the contribution of Pamela Barham who was co-author of *Netball Australia: a socio-historical analysis*, a report to the Australian Sports Commission and the All Australia Netball Association (AANA), November 1988. This report was undertaken with the support of the AANA through the provision of a grant under the National Sports Research Programme of the Australian Sports Commission.

2 Much of the historical information about the early years of netball in Great Britain has been gleaned from an unpublished

manuscript provided to the author by Christine Maylor, an international player for the All England Netball Association.

3 B. H. Grieve, *The game of netball and how to play it*, third edition, (London, 1916).

4 P. D. Hyland (ed.), *AANA golden jubilee booklet* (Sydney, 1977).

5 Jean Cowan, unpublished manuscript (1977).

6 Jean Cowan, unpublished manuscript (1977).

7 Jean Dolding, correspondence to the author, 21 April 1986.

8 Dorothy Christensen, correspondence to the author, 24 April 1986.

9 Hyland.

10 Activities included a welcome social at the YWCA, a visit to the Bryant and May matches factory in Richmond, a theatre party to the Capitol cinema in Melbourne, an all-day picnic at Belgrave near Melbourne and a visit to the Semco factory at Black Rock.

11 Report of the All Australia Women's Basket Ball Association (AAWBBA), 1929, p. 28.

12 Minutes of the AAWBBA fourth annual general meeting, Sydney, 27 August 1931, p. 45.

13 Beetec, 'Women out of doors', unknown Adelaide newspaper, 1933.

14 Programme of events, information supplied by Jean Dolding, Brisbane.

15 Material supplied to the author by Maisie Mudie, Brisbane. Mudie was a member of the New South Wales team which participated in the first All Australia Basketball Carnival in Melbourne.

16 Material by Mudie.

17 Minutes of the annual general meeting of AAWBBA, 15 August 1938, p. 145.

18 Hyland.

19 Hyland, p. 5.

20 Honorary secretary's report to the AAWBBA, 1937.

21 Report of the AAWBBA, 1937.

22 Edith Hull, 'Report on visit to the New Zealand Basketball Tournament, September 1937', p. 1.

23 Hull pp. 1-2.

24 Hull, p. 2.

25 Hull.

26 Annual report of the AAWBBA, 1938.

27 Hull, p. 1.

28 'Basketball carnival concludes', press clipping, undated, in Jean Cowan scrapbook.

29 'Basketball carnival concludes', in Jean Cowan scrapbook.

30 Minutes of the AAWBBA annual general meeting, 19 August 1938, p. 2.

31 Minutes of adjourned conference between the AAWBBA and the New Zealand Women's Basket Ball Association, NZWB-BA, p. 1.

32 Minutes of AAWBBA annual general meeting, 1938, p. 3.

33 *Annual report of the AAWBBA, 1938*, p. 1.

34 Meeting of the AAWBBA, 29 August 1939.

35 Meeting of the AAWBBA, 15 August 1938. However, it agreed that the AAWBBA would cover 75 per cent of the manageress' and umpire's expenses.

36 Circular to players selected for 1940 New Zealand tour.

37 *Mitiamo Football Club Centenary, 1889-1989 (incorporating Mitiamo Netball Club, 1932-1989)* (Mitiamo, Centenary Committee, 1989), p. 4.

38 Walters, p. 5.

39 Hyland.

40 Walters, p. 9

41 Beverley Harper, *Against the wind: a history of football, hockey and netball in Boort* (Boort, Centenary Committee, 1989), pp. 159–60.

42 Walters, p. 143; All Australia Netball Association, *Annual report 1992*, p. 2.

43 Preliminary meeting of AAWBBA Council, 27 August 1947.

44 Minutes of AAWBBA council meetings, 21 August 1947, 23 August 1947 and addendum to the minutes of AAWBBA council, 23 August 1947. The street uniform was even more elaborate and expensive for the players as they had to pay for the material for a grey skirt and were responsible for either making it, or having it made, according to the Army Women's Service pattern. This uniform also comprised a white blouse made from a light woollen material, long and short-sleeved green pullovers, a grey felt sports hat, a pair of black walking shoes, a green tie and accessories of black gloves and wallet.

45 Hyland.

46 Addendum to minutes of the AAWBBA council, 23 August 1947.

47 Addendum to minutes, 23 August 1947.

48 'Australian team opens NZ tour in Timaru', undated newspaper clipping, Jean Cowan scrapbook.

49 These impressions are taken from reports in various newspaper clippings, Jean Cowan scrapbook.

50 *Annual report of the AAWBBA, 1949*.

51 *Annual report of the AAWBBA, 1953; Annual report of the AAWBBA, 1954*.

52 *Annual report of the AAWBBA, 1955*.

53 Minutes of AAWBBA council, 24 August 1954.

54 Minutes of annual conference, 20 August 1955.

55 *Annual report of the AAWBBA, 1955*.

56 Letter from the AAWBBA to the AENA, 3 August 1955.

A sports mistress at Ascham School had trained two teams in the English game and they had given a demonstration at the 1955 AWBBA interstate carnival.

57 *Manchester Guardian*, 11 April 1956.
58 'Touring team to England, 1956', statement by the AAWBBA.
59 'Bill McGowran's sports diary', *Evening News*, 24 February 1956.
60 *Evening Star*, 7 March 1956.
61 Harper, p. 159.
62 Following sections from Walters, *passim*.
63 *Sunderland Echo*, 14 April 1956.
64 *Annual report of the AAWBBA, 1960*.
65 J. McKay, *No pain, no gain? Sport in Australian culture* (Sydney, 1991).
66 Grieve.

Chapter 10: Rowing and Sculling

1 S. Bennett, 'Professional sculling in New South Wales', *Journal of the Royal Australian Historical Society*, 71.2 (October 1985), p. 127. K. Webb, cited in H. Cleaver, *A history of rowing* (London, 1957), p. 184. There were similar scenes in early colonial South Australia, with the Port River a venue for challenges 'between longboats and lifeboats of immigrant sailing ships' in 1839. R. W. Richardson, *Adelaide Rowing Club. The first hundred seasons. A narrative history 1882-1982* (Adelaide, 1982), p. 5.

2 In one instance in 1827, Captain John Piper's crew lost its backer the large sum of 200 guineas when it was defeated by the men from HMS *Rainbow*. J. Blanch (ed.), *Ampol's sporting records*, rev. fifth edition (Crows Nest NSW, 1978), p. 311.

3 Blanch, p. 311. S. Bennett 'Rowing and sculling', in Wray Vamplew, Katharine Moore, John O'Hara, Richard Cashman and Ian F. Jobling (eds), *The Oxford companion to Australian sport* (Melbourne, 1992), p. 292. R. Ward, *The Australian legend*, second edition (Melbourne, 1966), p. 67. Conducted for the first time in 1837, the Anniversary Regatta recognised the founding of white settlement in New South Wales on 26 January 1788. Similarly, the Royal Hobart Regatta, first held in 1838, commemorated Tasman's naming of Van Diemen's Land on 25 November 1642. G. Inglis, *Sport and pastime in Australia* (London, 1912), pp. 215-16. Webb, cited in Cleaver, p. 184.

4 *Bell's Life in Victoria*, 24 August 1867. In South Australia, a regatta was held on 24 May 1837 at Kingscote Harbour, Kangaroo Island, to celebrate Queen Victoria's birthday. Richardson, p. 5. During the 1857 Newcastle Regatta the town was decorated with flags as 'signs of loyalty' to the monarch. *Bell's Life in Sydney*, 30 May 1857.

5 An early regatta victor was Mr J. Oliver who won the amateur

single sculls on the waters of Port Jackson, and a prize of twenty pounds. Webb, cited in Cleaver, p. 184.

6 Such as Thomas Jordan and Robert Prest, of Sandringham, who agreed to scull the Melbourne regatta course for the prize of a trophy worth ten pounds. *Bell's Life in Victoria*, 1 June 1867.

7 Typical of these was an amateur handicap scullers' match held in Sydney 'for ten pounds and a pair of sculls'. *Bell's Life in Victoria*, 1 June 1867.

8 Bennett, 'Professional sculling', p. 127. Scullers often advertised in the press for opponents, as did the brothers Hickey who, under the heading 'challenge', declared they would 'row any two men in the world, either with oars, double-sculls, or single-handed, for any sum, from £100 to £1000'. *Sydney Morning Herald*, 17 March 1869.

9 A. Brown, 'Edward Hanlan, the world sculling champion visits Australia', *Canadian Journal of History of Sport*, 9.2 (December 1980), p. 1.

10 These were often men with commercial interests, who used champion scullers to advertise their businesses. In New South Wales Bill Beach was sponsored by the publican J. Deeble, and Henry Searle was financed by the pharmacists John and Thomas Spencer. Bennett, 'Professional Sculling', p. 129.

11 C. Dodd, 'Rowing', in T. Mason (ed.), *Sport in Britain. A social history* (Cambridge, 1989), p. 280. Inglis, pp. 227-28. Richard Green, the first Australian to challenge for the world title, was defeated. Subsequently, *Bell's Life in Sydney* suggested that Green had been drugged by his opponents, a charge which could not be substantiated. R. Fotheringham, 'Early sporting diplomacy : the case of R.A.W. Green', *Sporting Traditions*, 5.2 (May 1989), pp. 173-86.

12 As examples, the 1884 Beach versus Hanlan contest attracted an estimated crowd of 100 000 spectators to the banks of the Parramatta River, and the 1904 Tressider versus Towns race drew around 90 000 people to the same championship course. D. Adair, ' "Two dots in the distance": professional sculling as a mass spectacle in New South Wales, 1876-1907', *Sporting Traditions*, 9.1 (Nov. 1992), p. 60, p. 72.

13 As Bennett puts it, 'winning the purses was usually a secondary consideration to a big win in side bets'. S. Bennett, *The Clarence Comet. The career of Henry Searle 1866-89* (Sydney, 1973), p. 11. For example, 'when Searle defeated O'Connor of Canada in 1889, the contest was for £500 a-side, but it was said that the Australians won £30 000 in wagers — and that the Canadians had stood to win much more'. Bennett, 'Professional Sculling', p. 129.

14 Adair, 'Two dots in the distance', pp. 68-73. On promenading as a social ritual, see D. Scobey, 'Anatomy of the promenade:

the politics of bourgeois sociability in nineteenth century New York', *Social History*, 17.2 (May 1992), pp. 203-27.

15 *Sydney Morning Herald*, 10 November 1876.

16 K. Dunstan, *Sports* (Melbourne, 1973), p. 169.

17 For further descriptions, see S. Bennett, *The Clarence Comet*, pp. 83-7; E. H. McSwan, *Champions in sport, Henry Searle and Chimpy Busch* (Maclean, New South Wales, 1973), n.p.; Dunstan, pp. 171-74; Adair, 'Two dots in the distance', pp. 65-7. Despite these demonstrations of public sympathy, a movement to create a monument to commemorate Searle was described as 'a partial failure', for 'not one-half of the subscription lists have been returned'. Letter to the editor by W. A. Blackstone, *Referee*, 10 December 1890. Finally, however, a monument was erected on the Gladesville bank of the Parramatta near Henley Point. McSwan, n.p. The funeral processions of the explorers Burke and Wills (21 January 1863), and the civic leader W. C. Wentworth (6 May 1873), indicate that there were precedents for this type of mass public mourning. T. Bonyhady, *Burke and Wills. From Melbourne to myth* (Balmain, NSW, 1991), pp. 240-46. K. S. Inglis, *The Australian colonists. An exploration of social history 1788-1870* (Melbourne, 1974), pp. 246-56. But Searle may have been the first recipient of sporting martyrdom on such a scale.

18 As an example, Bill Beach, one of the most successful scullers, claimed winnings of £3334 in 1886 alone. And Henry Searle took home £1000 in prize money as well as the world championship title in 1889. N. Wigglesworth, *A social history of English rowing* (London, 1992), p. 79.

19 Brown, 'Edward Hanlan', p. 9, p. 12, pp. 17-18. Hanlan was open to row any man for £1000 a-side. *Bulletin*, 5 January 1884.

20 Although 90 000 people viewed the Towns versus Tressider championship race on the Parramatta in 1904, it was the first world title race in Australia for twelve years. *Sydney Morning Herald*, 25 July 1904. Inglis, *Sport and Pastime*, p. 277.

21 *Referee*, 14 May 1890, 17 December 1890.

22 For fuller explanations, see Adair, 'Two dots in the distance', pp. 68-78; and Brown, 'Edward Hanlan', pp. 13-15, pp. 21-2, pp. 29-30.

23 Bennett, 'Professional Sculling', p. 136.

24 Even the famous Henry Searle was found guilty of shady practices. For details, *see* Bennett, *Clarence Comet*, pp. 40-7; Adair, 'Two dots in the distance', pp. 62-7.

25 Adair, 'Two dots in the distance', pp. 77-8.

26 It is not enough, however, to ascribe signs of sculling's decline in the 1890s to 'personality' factors. Shepherd, for example, argues that Searle's death coincided with sculling's demise. Similarly, Bennett claims that although there were Australian

world champions after Trickett, Beach and Searle, they were not held in as high regard. This could help explain a decline in the sport's public appeal. J. Shepherd (ed.), *Encyclopedia of Australian sport* (Adelaide, 1980), p. 371. Bennett, 'Professional Sculling', p. 137. But *see* Adair, 'Two dots in the distance', pp. 74-8.

27 Bennett, 'Professional Sculling', pp. 139-40.

28 For example, at Brisbane's first regatta day on 10 December 1860, Governor Bowen acted as a race official, as did members of parliament, and they adjudicated in rowing and sailing contests. H. Wetherell, *A short historical sketch of the Commercial Rowing Club* (Brisbane, 1945), p. 8.

29 R. R. Aitken, *Mercantile. A century of rowing* (Melbourne, 1980), p. 3, p. 13. For English precedents, *see* Wigglesworth, pp. 14-31.

30 The 1877 Goolwa Regatta included a 'Duck Hunt', with a prize of one pound ten shillings. The duck had five minutes head start, and was pursued by four-oared boats until it was caught. *Advertiser*, 10 August 1877. The 1860 Brisbane regatta scheduled 'a race for Aborigines in six-oared gigs, the prizes being, 1st. 100 lb of flour and 2 lb of tobacco; 2nd, a bag of sugar; and 3rd, 6 lb of tobacco'. Wetherell, p. 8. Similarly, the rural Victorian Corowa Rowing Club's 1862 New Year's Day Regatta offered a variety of novelty events, including 'a race for Aborigines in bark canoes, with the oarsmen being cheered on by the lubras on the banks'. F. G. Rickards, *Rowing in Victoria : the first hundred years of the Victorian Rowing Association, 1876-1976* (Kew, Vic., 1976), p. 97.

31 The 1859 Port Adelaide Regatta offered amusements for the crowd reminiscent of fair days. People were invited to participate in sack races, jumping with hands tied behind the back and other novelties. M. Stephen, 'The Port Adelaide Regatta, 1838-1914', *The Flinders Journal of History and Politics*, 12 (1987), pp. 9-19.

32 Aitken, pp. 15-16.

33 Rickards, pp. 67-71, pp. 78-88, pp. 102-3.

34 Each committee member was given a black ball, and a padded box was passed around as a nominee's name was announced. If at least two black balls were found in the box afterwards, the nomination was not accepted. Richardson, pp. 5-17.

35 M. Kavanagh, *On these bright waters. A centennial history of Leichhardt Rowing Club 1886-1986* (Leichhardt NSW, 1986), p. 1.

36 Kavanagh, pp. 1-6.

37 A. L. May, *Sydney rows : a centennial history of the Sydney Rowing Club* (Sydney, 1970), p. 12.

38 May, p. 2, pp. 13-14.

39 Arthur Fitzhardinge, cited in May, pp. 13-14.

40 May, p. 15.
41 R. Poke, 'The New South Wales Rowing Association', *Australian Rowing*, 1.2 (October 1978), p. 15.
42 D. G. Lane and I. F. Jobling, 'For honour and trophies: amateur rowing in Australia, 1888-1912', *Sporting Traditions*, 4.1 (November 1987), p. 5, p. 10.
43 See J. A. Mangan, 'Oars and the man : pleasure and purpose in Victorian and Edwardian Cambridge', *The British Journal of Sports History*, 1.3 (December 1984), pp. 245-71; and R. A. Smith, 'The historic amateur-professional dilemma in American college sport', *The British Journal of Sports History*, 2.3 (December 1985), pp. 221-31.
44 Amateur sportsmen who were found to accept cash prizes or wager on a contest were doubly penalised. They were not only barred from amateur competition in their own sport, but in other amateur sports as well. For a case study, see K. Moore and M. Phillips, 'The sporting career of Harold Hardwicke: one example of the irony of the amateur-professional Dichotomy', *Sporting Traditions*, 7.1 (November 1990), pp. 61-76.
45 Disqualification of competitors from amateur competition on occupational grounds was not uncommon. One of the best known was the 'Jack affair' in 1908. E. Jack won the interstate single-sculls championship, but was eventually disqualified because he had been employed in building boats with his father. D. Lane, 'Jack affair', in Vamplew et al., *The Oxford companion to Australian sport*, p. 193.
46 May, p. 67.
47 For example, in 1936 an Australian entry in the Grand Challenge Cup at Henley was refused 'on the grounds that they were policemen and therefore ineligible'. E. Halladay, *Rowing in England: a social history. The amateur debate* (Manchester, 1990), pp. 170-1.
48 Dunstan, pp. 174-75. L. Schlink, 'Bobby the coolest champion', [Adelaide] *Advertiser*, 26 June 1992.
49 For a full discussion, *see* Halladay, pp. 172-93.
50 May, pp. 116-17.
51 Richardson, pp. 54-6, pp. 128-9. Aitken, p. 22, pp. 42-3.
52 *Referee*, 24 February 1887. The Victorian Rowing Association was pragmatic about raising revenue. When Edward Hanlan, the Canadian professional sculler, gave an exhibition at Albert Park Lake, the VRA agreed that one-third of the moneys raised would go to Hanlan, a further third to the VRA and the final third to a 'lake improvement fund'. Brown, 'Edward Hanlan', p. 18.
53 *Referee*, 29 November 1890, p. 19.
54 D. Lane, 'Rowing: intercolonial regattas', in Vamplew et al., *The Oxford companion to Australian sport*, p. 293. The cover of a

programme of the 1905 championships depicts crews rowing before crowded steamers, with elegantly attired ladies waving handkerchiefs from the banks of the river. 'Interstate eight oar sculling championships of Australia', 13 May 1905.

55 S. Bennett, 'King's Cup', in Vamplew et al., *The Oxford companion to Australian sport*, p. 198. Eventually, other prestigious events on the rowing calendar, such as the President's Cup (amateur sculling championship of Australia), and the Head of the River for public schools, supplemented the King's Cup programme. *See*, as examples : *Souvenir programme. The King's Cup, Hamilton Reach, Brisbane River, 6 May 1933* and *Programme, Australian amateur rowing and sculling championships, 18 April 1953*.

56 G. Sherington, R. C. Peterson, and I. Brice, *Learning to lead. A history of girls' and boys' corporate secondary schools in Australia* (Sydney, 1987), pp. 50-1. A. Leicester, *A history of rowing in the Athletic Association of the Greater Public Schools of New South Wales* (Sydney, 1978) pp. 2, 10.

57 *Referee*, 26 August 1896.

58 S. Bennett, 'GPS Head of the River', in Vamplew et al., *The Oxford companion to Australian sport*, p. 162. *See*, as examples, the Greater Public Schools reports in *Australian Rowing*, 3.2 (September 1980), pp. 13-15; *Australian Rowing*, 4.2 (June 1981), pp. 17-19; and *Australian Rowing*, 9.2 (June 1986), pp. 31-2; and F. J. Gorman, *Rowing at Riverview. The first hundred years 1882-1982* (Lane Cove NSW, 1983), pp. 76-7, p. 105.

59 C. Jones, 'Henley on Yarra. The lost festival', *This Australia*, 2.4 (Spring 1983), pp. 7-8.

60 The South Australian Rowing Association organised a Henley-on-Torrens in 1910, but it was held sporadically from then on. The Henley-on-Maribyrnong, rowed on Melbourne's other prominent river, has been more successful since its inception in 1913. Jones, 'Henley on Yarra', pp. 10-11.

61 Jones, 'Henley on Yarra', pp. 10-11.

62 M. K. Stell, *Half the race. A history of Australian women in sport* (Sydney, 1991), p. 8.

63 An early exponent was Eadith Walker of Yaralla, who organised a women's rowing regatta on the Parramatta River in 1886. May, p. 24.

64 Rickards, p. 115.

65 Rickards, p. 115. Blanch, p. 317.

66 May, pp. 66, 81.

67 One of the earliest of these was the Ladies' Boat Club on the Torrens Lake in Adelaide in 1895. J. A. Daly, *Elysian fields: sport, class and community in colonial South Australia* (Adelaide, 1982), p. 183, p. 185. The most famous of the early clubs was Albert Park Lake Ladies' Club in Victoria, formed in 1907 by the ubiquitous

Cassie McRitchie (née Woolley). By 1910, the members 'had constructed their own boat house ... along the lake shore'. The club continued to 1963, when financial problems caused its closure. Rickards, pp. 115-16. Blanch, pp. 317-18.

68 These were the Pioneers Ladies' Professional Sculling Club (1913) and the Double Bay Ladies' Rowing Club (1915). Together with male professionals, the ladies were members of the New South Wales Rowing and Sculling League, although this body declined after 1923. May, p. 81, p. 100.

69 Kavanagh, p. 28.

70 Rickards, pp. 115-16. Blanch, pp. 317-18.

71 Rickards, pp. 115-16.

72 Sherington et al., pp. 52-3, pp. 151-52.

73 Rickards, pp. 115-16.

74 Stell, pp. 58-9.

75 But during the 1930s rowing clubs responded to such fears by insisting that 'women be medically examined as well as being able to swim'. Stell, p. 57, p. 173.

76 Stell, p. 57.

77 Stell, p. 57.

78 Stell, p. 74.

79 May, pp. 133-34, p. 159. Kavanagh, p. 28. Rickards, pp. 117-18.

80 R. Wilson, 'Personality profile — Kath Bennett', *Australian Rowing*, 6.4 (December 1983), p. 30.

81 May, p. 190.

82 Wilson, 'Kath Bennett', p. 30.

83 Wilson, 'Kath Bennett', pp. 30-1. At Leichhardt (New South Wales), for instance, women could become members from 1976, with full voting rights for those over eighteen years of age. Kavanagh, p. 28. Horsham Rowing Club in Victoria accepted women members in 1972, and Anne Mitchell was elected a member of the club committee. When Horsham held its first official regatta in November of 1972, a women's four provided the club with its first win. Rickards stresses that '[t]he enthusiasm of the women rowers was one of the factors which helped the club to survive in later years'. Rickards, p. 100.

84 In Victoria, for example, the Victorian Ladies' Rowing Association was 'staging eight or nine full-scale regattas each year' during the 1970s, and could boast a total of twenty new clubs by the end of 1976. Rickards, pp. 117-19.

85 Women's rowing first appeared at the 1976 Olympics. But no women were sent from Australia, a decision which created controversy in rowing circles. This was a forerunner to subsequent disputes about the non-selection of several women rowers for international meets, which was seen in some quarters as deriving from 'the prejudices of the male-dominated Australian Rowing Council'. Stell, p. 135, p. 267.

86 Among these were a bronze medal to the coxed four (1984 Olympics); a victory to Adair Ferguson in the lightweight sculls (1985 world championships); a gold medal to the women's eight, silver to the coxed four and lightweight four, and gold to Adair Ferguson in the lightweight sculls (1986 Commonwealth Games). The women's junior fours have also tasted success (1989 world championships). Stell, p. 135, p. 267.

87 Problems remain, however. In 1987 a committee of principals overturned the inclusion of a girls' event in the South Australian Head of the River. One of the principals argued that the committee had received 'medical advice that under-fourteen girls should not be racing'. This view was disputed by Dr Barnes of the South Australian Sports Medicine Clinic, and Dr Bill Webb, the Australian national rowing team's medical adviser. Also, the girls had competed in other regattas during the season, and had been in training for six months without showing signs of debilitation. But the committee also argued that they required a year's notice for the girls' event to be rowed. This was despite the fact that in the previous year's programme new boys' events had been brought forward without such notice. With the intervention of Josephine Tiddy, the Equal Opportunity Commissioner for South Australia, the principals' committee relented and the girls were allowed to compete. *Sunday Mail*, 15 March 1987; [Adelaide] *Advertiser*, 18, 21 March 1987. In addition, there has been at least one complaint of problems of access to rowing equipment at mixed clubs, where men have been provided with shells and the women offered restricted use of junior men's shells. Australian Sports Commission, *Women, sport, and sex discrimination* (Sydney, 1992), p. 16. I thank Leonie Randall for this information.

88 S. Mott, 'Adair Ferguson : the making of superwoman', *Weekend Australian*, 15-16 March 1986. W. Oakley, 'Our new golden girl', *Your Sport*, 1.7, (December 1985 — January 1986), pp. 62-4.

89 There were various requirements to be classified veteran. For example, a rower needed to be at least thirty years of age, and have retired from 'active rowing' for at least a year. For a summary of early veteran rowing in Victoria, *see* Rickards, pp. 128-32.

90 D. Todd, 'More veteran gold', *Australian Rowing*, 3.3 (December 1980), pp. 29-31. A. Armstrong, 'Rowing, the growing sport, takes to the masters games', *Australian Rowing*, 8.1 (March 1985), p. 9. D. Bagnall, 'Australian veterans' championships, Canberra', *Australian Rowing*, 10.1 (February 1987), p. 13.

91 N. Hunter, ' "Freedom on the river". Rowing for the disabled', *Australian Rowing*, 10.2 (July 1987), pp. 15-16. N.a., 'Disabled rowing first at major regatta', *Australian Rowing*, 11.2 (May 1988), pp. 16-17.

92   Ian Hill, cited in n.a., 'Disabled rowing first', p. 17. For further discussions, see J. Ashmore, 'We can play too', *Australian Disability Review*, 3.1, 1986, pp. 15-18; and J. Boelen, 'Pleading in favour of disabled rowers', *Australian Rowing*, 11.4 (December 1988), p. 36.

93   [Adelaide] *Advertiser*, 16 October 1992. N.a., *Perth International Dragon Boat Club (Inc.), tenth anniversary year* (Perth, 1990).

94   R. Gaskin, 'The Margaret River Regatta', *Australian Rowing*, 4.1 (March 1981), p. 28.

95   L. Clausen, 'The pain of long-distance rowers', [Adelaide] *Advertiser*, 29 June 1992.

96   In 1973 Warrnambool's Val Bertrand sculled for twenty-one hours and three minutes to set a world hundred-mile record. Rickards, pp. 122-25. In 1980 Adelaide's Hugh McLean and Martin Smart rowed 206.8 kilometres in twenty-three hours eleven minutes, beating the previous world record held by South Australians Mark Hebblewhite and Athol McDonald, of 204 kilometres in a twenty-four-hour period. H. McLean, 'An epic row', *Australian Rowing*, 3.3 (December 1980), p. 21.

97   Banjo Paterson, who rowed briefly for Sydney Rowing Club in 1884, recalled that Hanlan 'had toughened himself up by work as a fisherman', McLean was an axeman 'who could fell any tree' and Searle rowed the Clarence River as a boy 'taking orders and delivering meat on account of a local butcher'. A. B. (Banjo) Paterson, 'On the river', c.1884, cited in May, p. 26, p. 34.

98   Dunstan, pp. 166-7.

99   For further discussions, *see* G. Jones, 'Training, the good old days', *Australian Rowing*, 10.4 (December 1987), pp. 11-12. R. Holt, *Sport and the British. A modern history* (Oxford, 1989), pp. 99-100. Halladay, pp. 212-17.

100 Sherington et al., pp. 151-52. Holt, pp. 97-8.

101 For one shilling the rowing enthusiast could purchase *Style of rowing adopted by the New South Wales Rowing Association 1925*. It even boasted a supplement by former Australian Prime Minister Stanley Bruce entitled, *How to row: how to coach*. Bruce had been a highly successful coach at Cambridge.

102 May, pp. 13-14.

103 In the 1898 Victorian Rowing Association regatta he won three one-mile races on the same day's programme — senior sculls, senior fours and senior eights. Rickards, p. 134.

104 Sherington et al., pp. 50-4, pp. 150-52. D. W. Brown, 'Criticisms against the value-claim for sport and the physical ideal in late nineteenth century Australia', *Sporting Traditions*, 4.2 (May 1988), pp. 153-6.

105 [Sydney] *Daily Telegraph*, 27 February 1882, cited in Brown, 'Value-claim for sport', p. 150.

106 D. Buchanan, *Donkey worship v. hero worship; or, cricket and boat-pulling amongst Australians* (Sydney, 1882), p. 4.

107 [Melbourne] *Age*, n.d., cited in Bennett, *Clarence Comet*, p. 89.

108 While the design was hardy, the clinker shape with overlapping planks created turbulence which reduced boat speed. The idea of using outriggers was 'to extend the fulcrum of the oar outwards and increase the blade poundage'. The sliding seat allowed the rower to move forward with the seat, and back at the completion of the stroke, and this 'effectively lengthened the stroke in the water'. Wigglesworth, pp. 83-6.

109 For example, Michael Rush was no match for Ned Trickett in their race for the world professional sculling championship in 1877. Trickett used the sliding seat, while Rush, who defeated Trickett four years earlier, chose to persist with the fixed seat. The form reversal astonished Rush. Dunstan, pp. 163-64. The sliding seat was also accepted into crew rowing during the 1870s. Wetherell, p. 6.

110 Coaches' Sub-Committee Report to New South Wales Rowing Association, cited in *Style of Rowing*, p. 1. This was sound advice for, increasingly, fixed-pin crews were being soundly defeated by competitors using swivels in international competition. P. Haig-Thomas and M. A. Nicholson, *The English style of rowing. New light on an old method* (London, 1958), p. 46.

111 May, p. 25.

112 Dodd, 'Rowing', pp. 293-94. For fuller explanations, *see* C. Dodd, *Henley Royal Regatta* (London, 1981), pp. 132-8; A. N. Jacobsen, *Australia in world rowing* (Melbourne, 1984), pp. 17-23; and Haig-Thomas and Nicholson, pp. 54-62.

113 May, p. 116. *See also*, Kavanagh, pp. 29-30. For criticisms of the 'Fairbairn' style, *see* Haig-Thomas and Nicholson, p. 64.

114 *Australian Rowing*, 4.4 (December 1981), p. 11. R. Malogier, 'Omega photofinish and timing system: photo-sprint', *Australian Rowing*, 9.3 (December 1986), pp. 18-19.

115 These were first introduced during the 1950s, and they have allowed coaches to monitor athletic performance off-water, and to measure improvements. Kavanagh, pp. 29-30. For recent applications of the ergometer, *see* D. Stuart, 'A comparison of test scores for élite rowers using a Repco and Gjessing rowing ergometer', *Australian Rowing*, 7.3 (September 1984), pp. 25-8. D. C. McKenzie, and E. C. Rhodes, 'Cardiorespiratory and metabolic responses to exercise on a rowing ergometer', *Australian Journal of Sports Medicine*, 14.1 (1982), pp. 21-3.

116 *Australian Rowing*, 7.2 (June 1984), p. 20.

117 *Australian Rowing*, 10.1 (February 1987), p. 12.

118 For example, a 1985 conference of the Australian Rowing Council heard papers on subjects such as 'The biomechanics of rowing', 'Psychological aspects of peak performance', and 'Nutrition and rowing'. *Coaching rowing. A scientific approach.* Papers presented at the Olympic Solidarity Seminar (Canberra, 11-13 October, 1985). Similar discussions have appeared in

Australian Rowing, suggesting their dissemination among rowers and their coaches. See B. Porra, 'A guide to gearing', *Australian Rowing*, 3.1 (March 1980), pp. 14-16; R. Marlow, 'A framework for writing a training programme', *Australian Rowing*, 10.4 (December 1987), pp. 13-14; and S. Gilbert, 'Strength training for rowers', *Australian Rowing*, 11.2 (March 1988), pp. 23-4.

119 C. Muirden, 'The Oarsome Foursome. Rowing from glory to glamour', *Australian* 9-10 May 1992.

120 In the first year twenty-four scholarships, three coaching positions, and $90 000 towards capital equipment were offered by the Commonwealth Government. *Australian Rowing*, 8.3 (September 1985), p. 4. For further details, see N. and S. Whitehouse, 'Rowing at the AIS', *Australian Rowing*, 9.1 (March 1986), pp. 9-10.

121 I. Clubb, 'An Australian boat builder takes up the challenge', *Australian Rowing*, 1.2 (October 1978), pp. 23-4. A. Phillips, 'The all new plastic boat', *Australian Rowing*, 2.1 (April 1979), p. 17.

122 N. Lawrence, 'The winged keel of rowing', *Australian Rowing*, 7.4 (December 1984), pp. 15-16.

123 [Adelaide] *Advertiser*, 24 July 1992.

124 *Australian Rowing*, 11.3 (September 1988), p. 19. For other innovations subsequently banned, see Dodd, 'Rowing', pp. 290-1.

125 *Australian Rowing*, 11.3 (September 1988), p. 19.

126 For an example of this, *see* K. Matts, 'Rower banned', *Australian Rowing*, 11.3 (September 1988), p. 22.

127 An 'Old Member', 'Some rowing club reminiscences. The Leichhardts long ago' *Sportsman*, 25 February 1908, cited in Kavanagh, p. 37.

Chapter 11: Rugby

1 Trevor Arnold, 'Sport in colonial Australia', PhD Thesis, University of Queensland (1979), pp. 33-9.

2 Tom Hickie, 'Rugby union' in Wray Vamplew, Katharine Moore, John O'Hara, Richard Cashman and Ian F. Jobling (eds), *The Oxford companion to Australian sport* (Melbourne, 1992), p. 303.

3 Eric Dunning and Kenneth Sheard, *Barbarians, gentlemen and players: a sociological study of the development of rugby football* (Oxford, 1979), pp. 79-99.

4 Hickie, 'Rugby Union', in Vamplew et al., p. 304.

5 Peter A. Horton, 'Rugby union football and its role in the socio-cultural development of Queensland 1882-91', *International Journal of the History of Sport*, 9.1 (1992), p. 122.

6 Jim Shepherd (ed.), *Rothmans Australian rugby yearbook 1981* (Sydney, 1981), p. 12.

7 Dunning and Sheard, pp. 33-4.

8 Shepherd, p. 10.

9 Shepherd, p. 11.

10 Tom Hickie, *The game for the game itself! The development of sub-district rugby in Sydney: in remembrance of every person who has administered, played for or supported a sub-district rugby club* (Sydney, 1983), p. 14.

11 Shepherd, p. 17.

12 Peter A. Horton, 'A history of rugby union football in Queensland 1882-1891', PhD thesis, University of Queensland (1989), pp. 586-90.

13 Peter A. Horton, 'Rugby union football and its role', p. 124.

14 Jack Pollard, *Australian rugby union: the game and the players* (Sydney, 1984), p. 834, p. 912.

15 Shepherd, pp. 16-17.

16 Hickie, *The game for the game itself*, p. 48.

17 Richard Cashman, *'Ave a go, yer mug!' Australian cricket crowds from larrikin to Ocker* (Sydney, 1984), p. 6.6

18 Horton, 'Rugby union football and its role', p. 125; Hickie, *The game for the game itself*, p. 56.

19 Andrew Moore, 'The curse of the Kalahari: the North Sydney Bears and the ghosts of 1921-1922', *Sporting Traditions*, 5.2 (1989), pp. 148-72.

20 Chris Cunneen, 'The rugby war: the early history of rugby league in New South Wales, 1907-15' in Richard Cashman and Michael McKernan (eds.), *Sport in history: the making of modern history* (Brisbane, 1979), p. 295; Horton, 'Rugby union football and its role', p. 125.

21 Max Howell and Reet Howell, *The greatest game under the sun: the story of rugby league in Queensland* (Brisbane, 1989) p. 4.

22 Max Solling, 'Football in Sydney 1870-1920', *Leichhardt Historical Journal*, 8 (1979), pp. 25-30.

23 'Rugby league', MAN, 2.3 (1937), pp. 72-3.

24 Cunneen, 'The Rugby War', in Cashman and McKernan, pp. 295-6.

25 Gary Lester, *The story of Australian rugby league* (Sydney, 1988), p. 17.

26 Dally Messenger, *The master: the story of H. H. 'Dally' Messenger and the beginning of Australian rugby league* (Sydney), pp. 23-6.

27 Lester, pp. 17, pp. 23-9.

28 Howell and Howell, p. 9.

29 Lester, pp. 30-6.

30 Ian Heads, *The story of the Kangaroos* (Sydney), pp. 9-24.

31 Lester, pp. 56-7.

32 Lester, pp. 58-9.

33 Howell and Howell, p. 49.

34 Chris Cunneen 'J.J. Smith' in Geoffrey Serle et al. (eds.), *Australian dictionary of biography, Volume 11, 1891-1939* (Melbourne, 1988), pp. 650-51.

35 Lester, pp. 60-3, p. 66.
36 Lester, pp. 66-74.
37 Howell and Howell, p. 25.
38 Cunneen, 'The rugby war', in Cashman and McKernan, p. 301.
39 Lester, pp. 75-88.
40 Howell and Howell, p. 34.
41 Cunneen, 'The rugby war', in Cashman and McKennan, p. 295.
42 Ross Mackay, 'Hard times, high stakes: the political culture of South Sydney Rugby League, 1928-1935', unpublished research paper (1982), p. 3.
43 Bret Harris, *Winfield State of Origin 1980-1991* (Sydney, 1992).
44 Cunneen, 'The rugby war', in Cashman and McKernan, p. 298.
45 Moore, 'The curse of the Kalahari', pp. 148-72.
46 *Referee*, 17 June 1908.
47 Murray G. Phillips, 'Australian sport and World War One', PhD thesis, University of Queensland (1991), pp. 23-53.
48 Hickie, *The game for the game itself*, pp. 80-1.
49 W. Bickley, *Maroon: highlights of one hundred years of rugby in Queensland, 1882-1982* (Brisbane, 1982), p. 59.
50 Lester, pp. 100-35.
51 Philip A. Mosely, 'A social history of soccer in New South Wales, 1880-1956', PhD thesis, University of Sydney (1987), p. 159. My thanks are extended to Philip Mosely for the availability of this thesis and other relevant sources.
52 Mackay, p. 4.
53 Marion Stell, *Half the race: a record of women in Australian sport* (Sydney, 1991), pp. 56-7.
54 Manning Clark, *A short history of Australia* (Ringwood, 1992), p. 198.
55 Pollard, pp. 46, 753-57.
56 Mackay, p. 11.
57 Philip A. Mosely, 'The Depression and football patronage: a regional study, Newcastle district 1929-1939', unpublished research paper, (1992), p. 12.
58 Pollard, p. 46.
59 Howell and Howell, pp. 133-42.
60 W.T. Field, 'Sport, war and society: a study of St George District Rugby League Football Club 1939-45', BA (Hons), University of New South Wales (1981).
61 Malcolm Andrews, *ABC of rugby league* (Sydney, 1992), p. 231.
62 Pollard, pp. 47-52.
63 Lester, p. 190.
64 Pollard, pp. 798-801, pp. 780-83, pp. 609-10.
65 Brian Stoddart, *Saturday afternoon fever: sport in the Australian culture* (Sydney, 1986), pp. 178-79.
66 Colin Tatz, *Aborigines in sport* (Adelaide, 1987), pp. 80-4.
67 C. J. Hallinan, 'Aborigines and positional segregation in Aus-

tralian rugby league', *International Review for the Sociology of Sport*, 26.2 (1991), pp. 69-79.

68 Kris Corcoran, 'Between bifurcation and big business: rugby league in Sydney: 1914 to 1952', unpublished research paper (1984), appendix 2.

69 Pollard, pp. 493-94.

70 Bickley, pp. 104-5.

71 Bruce Kidd, 'The campaign against sport in South Africa', *International Journal*, 43.4 (1988), pp. 643-44.

72 Robert Archer and Antoine Bouillon, *The South African game: sport and racism* (London, 1982), p. 62; Keith Quinn, *The encyclopedia of world rugby* (Crows Nest, New South Wales, 1991), p. 267.

73 Stewart Harris, *Political football: the Springbok tour of Australia, 1971* (Melbourne, 1971).

74 Lester, pp. 245-9.

75 Adam Young et al., 'The re-marketing of rugby league', unpublished research paper, (1983), p. 4.

76 Pollard, p. 51.

77 Correspondence, Michael Blucher, Public Promotions Officer, Queensland Rugby Union (August 1992).

78 Lester, pp. 259-68.

79 [Sydney] *Sun-Herald*, 9 June 1991.

80 *Business Review Weekly*, 13 October 1989.

81 Lester, pp. 259-68.

82 *Sydney Morning Herald*, 23 September 1989.

83 Greg Campbell, 'Rugby: the game they play in heaven', *Sport Report*, 12.2 (1992), pp. 8-9.

84 *Australian*, 24 March 1993.

85 Bruce Wilson, 'Pumping up the footy: the commercial expansion of professional football in Australia' in David Rowe and Geoff Lawrence (eds.), *Sport and leisure: trends in Australian popular culture* (Sydney, 1990), pp. 31-2.

86 *Business Review Weekly*, 13 October 1989.

87 *Weekend Australian*, 19-20 September 1992.

88 Interview with Greg Campbell, Australian Rugby Union, 6 April 1993.

89 Interview with Pam Parker, Australian Rugby League, 6 April 1993.

90 Bob Dwyer, *The winning way* (Auckland, 1992), pp. 181-85.

Chapter 12: Soccer

1 *Sydney Monitor*, 25 July 1829.

2 Various forms of football were played in Sydney and Melbourne between 1829 and 1858. *Sydney Morning Herald*, 27 May 1840, p. 2; Leonie Sandercock and Ian Turner, *Up where Cazaly? The*

great Australian game (London, 1981), chapter 2.

3 Philip Mosely, 'A social history of soccer in New South Wales 1880-1957', PhD thesis, University of Sydney, (1987), chapter 1.

4 Mosely, 'A social history of soccer', chapter 1.

5 Mosely, 'A social history of soccer', chapter 1; *Australasian Association Football Conference, held at Sydney, New South Wales 15-16, 21 December 1911*, minutes of proceedings (Mitchell Library, E. S. Marks Sporting Collection Q51 Box 7).

6 The district system also led to a split in Adelaide 1927-28. *South Australian soccer year book* (Adelaide, 1965), pp. 31-2.

7 *Referee*, 14 July 1938; Queensland raised £2286 19s 6d, Victoria £844 13s 3d, Western Australia £246 15s 10d, South Australia £108 12s 7d.

8 Mosely, 'A social history of soccer', pp. 252-53.

9 Mosely, 'A social history of soccer', pp. 81-91; Michael Cigler, *The Czechs in Australia* (Melbourne, 1983), pp. 25-7.

10 Scores, crowds and gate receipts for England's tour of 1951 are provided in J. Houston, *Association football in New Zealand* (Wellington, 1952), p. 119.

11 Mosely, 'A social history of soccer', pp. 114-16.

12 Rory Crowe, *100 years of Queensland soccer* (Brisbane, 1984), p. 3.

13 Commonwealth Department of Immigration, *Consolidated Statistics*, 16 (1990), pp. 12-13.

14 Adelaide City's early soccer history is detailed in *South Australian soccer year book* (Adelaide, 1964), pp. 45-9.

15 Mosely, 'A social history of soccer', p. 297; *Soccer world annual 1966*, p. 27.

16 Blackpool did not play Brisbane. New South Wales Federation of Soccer Clubs, *Official year book* (1959), p. 31; *Soccer World*, 1 July 1960, 30 April 1965.

17 [Hobart] *Mercury*, 18 June 1951, p. 20; *W. A. Soccer Mail*, 9 August 1952, p. 23; *Soccer World*, 27 September 1963, p. 5, 1 November 1963, p. 1, 1 February 1963, p. 2.

18 Geoff Allen, 'They're throttling our sport', *People*, 16 April 1958.

19 *Soccer World*, 28 May 1965; [Melbourne] *Soccer News*, 11 June 1960.

20 Philip Mosely, 'European immigrants and soccer violence in New South Wales 1949-59', *Journal of Australian Studies*, 40 (forthcoming).

21 Mosely, 'European immigrants'.

22 Mosely, 'A social history of soccer', pp. 330-37.

23 'Last ten minutes of Syd Storey', (no author), *Nation*, 6 December 1962.

24 'Last ten minutes', pp. 13-14; Laurie Schwab, *The Socceroos and their opponents* (Melbourne, 1979), p. 30; Philip Mosely 'FIFA

ban on Australian soccer', in Wray Vamplew, Katharine Moore, John O'Hara, Richard Cashman and Ian F. Jobling (eds), *The Oxford companion to Australian sport* (Melbourne, 1992), p. 137.

25 Match descriptions and records are available in Schwab, Robert Lusetich, *Frank Arok: my beloved Socceroos* (Sydney, 1992); G.E. Olivier-Scerri, *Encyclopaedia of Australian soccer 1922-88* (St Leonards, 1988).

26 Noble attempts to qualify were made under coach Frank Arok, especially against Scotland for the 1986 World Cup in Mexico. Lusetich.

Chapter 13: Swimming, Surfing and Surf Lifesaving

1 *Sydney Sportsman*, 9 April 1902.

2 'A fuming McDonald is not "in the swim" ', *Sydney Morning Herald*, 24 January 1990.

3 George Ryley Scott, *The story of baths and bathing* (London, 1939); John Hargreaves, *Sport, power and culture* (Cambridge, 1986), p. 21.

4 Bryan Turner, *The body and society* (Oxford, 1984), p. 157.

5 Michael Foucault, *Discipline and punish* (Harmondsworth, 1979).

6 *Sydney Gazette*, 18 February 1834.

7 Veronica Wood, 'A decent and proper exertion: the rise of women's competitive swimming in Sydney to 1912', unpublished BA Hons thesis, University of New South Wales, (1990), p. 36, p. 37, p. 42.

8 *Sydney Gazette*, 6 October 1810.

9 In 1833 the New South Wales government passed an act (4 William IV, No. 7) prohibiting bathing in Sydney Cove and Darling Harbour between six am and eight pm. [para. 21] In 1838, 2 Victoria II, no. 2 extended the ban on bathing 'near to or within view of any public wharf, quay, bridge, street, road or other place of public resort within the limits of any towns ... between the hours of six o'clock in the morning and eight in the evening'. [para. 21].

10 Richard Holt, *Sport and the British: a modern history* (Oxford, 1989), pp. 89-92.

11 Kathleen McCrone, 'Play up! Play Up! And play the game! Sport and the late Victorian girls' public schools' in, J. A. Mangan and Roberta Park (eds), *From 'fair sex' to feminism: sport and the socialisation of women in the industrial and post industrial eras* (London, 1987), pp. 97-106; Patricia Vertinsky, 'Body shapes: the role of the medical establishment in informing female exercise and physical education in nineteenth century North America', in Mangan and Park, pp. 256-81.

12 Peter Bailey, *Leisure and class in Victorian England: rational recreation and the contest for control* (London, 1978).

13 Wood, p. 49; John Daly, *Elysian fields; sport, class and community in colonial South Australia 1836-1890* (Adelaide, 1982), p. 69.

14 Holt, p. 87.

15 Alan Clarkson, *Lanes of gold: 100 years of the New South Wales Amateur Swimming Association* (Sydney, 1990), p. 11.

16 Wood, p. 43.

17 Wood, pp. 53-7.

18 Ben Finney, 'Surfing in ancient Hawaii', *The Journal of the Polynesian Society*, 68.5 (1959), p. 328.

19 Harold Bradley, *The American frontier in Hawaii: the pioneers 1789-1843* (Gloucester, Mass., 1941), p. 168.

20 Sheldon Dibble cited in Ben Finney and James Houston, *Surfing: the sport of Hawaiian kings* (Johannesburg, 1966), p. 61.

21 Christopher Lasch, *The culture of narcissism* (New York, 1978), p. 49.

22 Mike Featherstone, 'Leisure, symbolic power and the life course' in John Horne, David Jary and Alan Tomlinson (eds), *Sport, leisure and social relations* (London, 1987), pp. 130-31.

23 Peter Stallybrass and Allon White, *The politics and poetics of transgression* (London, 1986), p. 188.

24 'Bathing at Little Coogee', *Sydney Morning Herald*, 9 June 1902.

25 'Commotion at Little Coogee', *Sydney Morning Herald*, 2 June 1902. At Federation in 1901 all existing bans on bathing in New South Wales were inscribed in Section 77 of the Police Offences Act No.5.

26 Letter, Borough of Waverley to the Inspector General of Police, 12 November 1902. Legislative Assembly, Tabled Paper 1902/884, New South Wales Parliamentary Archives.

27 Sub-Inspector J. McDonald to Superintendent N. Larkins, 13 November 1902. Tabled Paper 1902/884.

28 Inspector-General Fosbery to the Chief Secretary, 14 November 1902. Tabled Paper 1902/884.

29 'The sun bath', *Australian Star*, 14 October 1907.

30 'The value of sunshine', *Evening News*, 12 October 1907.

31 Letter, 'A mere man', *Sydney Morning Herald*, 7 February 1907.

32 Letter, 'A mother of girls', *Sydney Morning Herald*, 12 February 1907.

33 Letter, 'Daily dipper', *Sydney Morning Herald*, 1 February 1907.

34 'The new bathing regulations. More opinions', *Evening News*, 14 October 1907.

35 Wood, p. 18.

36 'Surf bathing and swimming-baths. The proposed new regulations', *Evening News*, 14 October 1907.

37 'Surf bathers' revolt. A demonstration at Bondi', *Evening News*, 21 October 1907; Douglas Booth, 'War off water: the Australian

Surf Life Saving Association and the beach', *Sporting Traditions*, 7.2 (1991), 140-42.

38 Local Government Act 1906, Ordinance No. 52, Public Baths and Bathing (New South Wales Government Gazette, 14 May 1908) para. 3.

39 Letter, 'Merman', *Sydney Morning Herald*, 24 January 1907.

40 'Revolt of the surfers against municipal laws', *Daily Telegraph*, 19 October 1907; 'Manly Council and surf bathing', *Manly and North Sydney Daily*, 24 October 1907.

41 Edward Reeve, 'The SLSA [Surf Life Saving Association] rules', *Surf in Australia*, 1 March 1937.

42 Surf Bathing Committee, *Report of the Surf Bathing Committee* (New South Wales Legislative Assembly, 14 February 1912), para. 22.

43 'Surf bathing at Manly — a club formed', *Manly and North Sydney Daily*, 20 July 1907.

44 Barry Galton, *Gladiators of the surf* (Sydney, 1984), pp. 21-2; Mark Doepal, 'The emergence of surf bathing and surf life saving at the holiday resort of Manly, 1850-1920', unpublished BA (Hons) thesis, University of New South Wales, (1985), p. 46.

45 'The surf club', *Manly and North Sydney Daily*, 6 August 1907.

46 Surf Bathing Committee, paras. 148-49, 152, 154-55.

47 Surf Bathing Association of New South Wales, *Fourth Annual Report*, 1912.

48 Wood, pp. 62-7. The historical content of this section draws principally on Wood's study. Her permission for access to the thesis is gratefully acknowledged.

49 'Swimming', *Sydney Sportsman*, 2 April 1902.

50 Wood, pp. 68-70.

51 Wood, pp. 77-82.

52 Wood, pp. 83-4.

53 Wood, pp. 87-9.

54 'Natator', 'Swimming', *Referee*, 13 March 1912.

55 Undated, cited in Wood, p. 94.

56 'Natator', 'Swimming', *Referee*, 13 March 1912.

57 Turner, pp. 101-2.

58 John Rickard, 'For God's sake keep us entertained' in Bill Gammage and Peter Spearritt (eds), *Australians 1938* (Sydney, 1987), p. 348.

59 Muscular torso and limbs, small waist and broad shoulders for males and less pronounced musculature but well-built and well-proportioned frame, with a more rounded contoured shape, for females.

60 John Hargreaves, 'The body, sport and power relations' in Horne et al., pp. 151-52; Hargreaves, pp. 170-71.

61 In Leonie Sandercock, 'Sport' in Gammage and Spearritt, p. 377.

62 Surf Bathing Committee, para. 54.

63 John Rickard, *Australia: a cultural history* (London, 1988), pp. 194-95.

64 'Trunks for men. Recommended by overwhelming majority', *Surf in Australia*, 1 December 1936; 'The burning question — trunks', *Surf in Australia*, 1 January 1937.

65 George Philip, *Sixty years recollections of swimming and surfing in the Eastern suburbs* (Sydney, 1940), p. 44.

66 Surf Life Saving Association of Australia, *Twenty Eighth Annual Report, 1934-35*, (1935).

67 Editorial, 'Trunks and shorts. Youth versus age', *Surf in Australia*, 1 January 1937.

68 [Adelaide] *Advertiser*, 24 January 1938, cited in Gammage and Spearritt, p. 314.

69 Rickard, p. 195.

70 'Who is Sydney's most beautiful surf girl?', *Sydney Times*, 22 February 1920.

71 Marion Stell, *Half the race: a history of Australian women in sport* (Sydney, 1991), p. 165, pp. 188-91.

72 Surf Life Saving Association of Australia, *Nineteenth Annual Report, 1926-27* (1927).

73 'Believes women "too weak" for surf events', *Sydney Morning Herald*, 11 March 1953. The ban on women lifesavers was temporarily lifted during the Second World War.

74 Reg Harris, *Heroes of the surf: fifty years' history of Manly Life Saving Club* (Sydney, 1961), pp. 53-4; Jack Finlay, 'A blast from the past', *Tracks*, November 1980.

75 Surf Life Saving Association of Australia, *Twentieth Annual Report, 1927-28*, (1928).

76 C. Justin 'Snow' McAlister in Galton, p. 26.

77 'Surf board club likely at Bondi', *Surf in Australia*, 8 December 1941.

78 Trudge, 'Swimming', *Sydney Sportsman*, 16 April 1902.

79 Personal interview, Syd Grange (former member of Maroubra Surf Life Saving Club, secretary of the New South Wales Amateur Swimming Association, Manager of the Australian Swimming Team and chairman of the Australian Olympic Federation), 19 August 1992; quotes from, Clarkson, pp. 57-8.

80 Clarkson, p. 60.

81 Dennis Phillips, *Australian women at the Olympic Games* (Sydney, 1992), p. 98. *See also* Clarkson, chapter 7.

82 A balsa-wood fibreglass-covered board weighing about twenty-five pounds (11.34 kilograms). The name derived from the Californian beach where it first became popular.

83 Leonard Lueras, *Surfing: the ultimate pleasure* (New York, 1984), p. 119.

84 Kent Pearson, *Surfing sub-cultures of Australia and New Zealand*

(St Lucia, 1979), p. 59; Galton, p. 35; Craig McGregor, *Profile of Australia* (Chicago, 1968), pp. 285-88.

85 Personal interview, Dennis Heussner (Surf Life Saving Association of Australia director), 26 August 1992; Barry Bennett, foam-blank manufacturer, 12 September 1992.

86 The Surf Life Saving Association of Australia's active membership increased by 18.97 per cent between 1953 (8267) and 1958 (10 203) and by 19.87 per cent between 1958 (10 203) and 1963 (12 734). Annual reports.

87 John Clarke, Stuart Hall, Tony Jefferson and Brian Roberts, 'Sub-cultures, cultures and class' in Hall and Jefferson (eds), *Resistance through rituals* (London, 1976), p. 67.

88 Hall and Jefferson, p. 62.

89 Hall and Jefferson, p. 70.

90 Nat Young, *The history of surfing* (Sydney, 1983), p. 117.

91 Letter, *Tracks*, October 1970.

92 Quoted in Irwin Silber, *The cultural revolution: a Marxist analysis* (New York, 1970), p. 58.

93 Robert Conneeley interview, *Tracks*, April 1978; Ted Spencer interview, *Tracks*, August 1974.

94 Ted Spencer interview, *Tracks*, August 1974; David Caute, *Sixty-eight: the year of barricades* (London, 1988), p. 40.

95 Clarke et al, p. 67.

96 Turner, pp. 111-12.

97 For example, see Vyv Simpson and Andrew Jennings, *The lords of the rings* (London, 1992).

98 Booth, pp. 151-55.

99 Personal interview, Midget Farrelly, 21 October 1992.

100 'Doyle does it at the Duke', *Surfer Magazine*, 10.1, 1969, p. 78. The Duke followed the Durban (later Gunston) 500, which is regarded as the first professional contest.

101 Personal interview, Terry Fitzgerald, 29 September 1992.

102 Peter Townend, 'ASP world tour, take one' in Association of Surfing Professionals, *Media guide and year book* (1992), pp. 54-5.

103 Fred Hemmings, 'Professionalism is white', *Surfer Magazine*, 10.5 (1969), pp. 64-5.

104 Interview, *Tracks*, April 1977.

105 'A profile of Graham Cassidy', *Tracks*, December 1977.

106 'The Australian Professional Surfers Association', *Tracks*, May 1975.

107 Interview, *The Surfers Journal*, 1.2 (1992), p. 90.

108 Jame Brisick quoted in, 'Surfers on why they surf', *Tracks*, October 1991.

109 Mike Featherstone, 'The body in consumer culture' in Mike Featherstone, Mike Hepworth and Bryan Turner (eds), *The body* (London, 1991), pp. 170-96.

110 In Stallybrass and White, p. 189.

111 Dawn Fraser and Harry Gordon, *Gold medal girl: the confessions of an Olympic champion* (Melbourne, 1965), p. 117.
112 Featherstone, *The body*, pp. 170-96.
113 'The apple and pear generation', *Bulletin*, 15 January 1991.

Chapter 14: Track and Field

1 John A. Daly, 'Athletics' in Wray Vamplew, Katharine Moore, John O'Hara, Richard Cashman and Ian F. Jobling (eds), *The Oxford companion to Australian sport* (Melbourne, 1992), p. 20.
2 [Adelaide] *Register*, 12 November 1845.
3 R. White and M. Harrison, *A hundred years of the NSWAAA [New South Wales Amateur Athletics Association]: 1887-1987* (Sydney, 1987), p. 15.
4 Keith Dunstan, *Sports* (Melbourne, 1973), p. 280. *See also* Percy Mason, *Professional Running in Australia* (Adelaide, 1985), p. 12.
5 White and Harrison, p. 16.
6 John A. Daly, *Elysian fields: sport, class and community in colonial South Australia 1856-1890* (Adelaide, 1982), pp. 86-8.
7 A. Mancini and G. M. Hibbins, *Running with the ball* (Melbourne, 1987), p. 117.
8 White and Harrison, p. 16.
9 [Adelaide] *Register*, 7 June 1870.
10 Daly, *Elysian fields*, p. 88.
11 White and Harrison, p. 9.
12 G. Henniker and I. Jobling, 'Richard Coombes and the Olympic Movement in Australia', *Sporting Traditions*, 6.1 (1989).
13 W. F. Mandle, 'Richard Coombes' in *Australian dictionary of biography* (Canberra, 1981), pp. 104-5.
14 *See* Pierre de Coubertin, *The Olympic idea: discourses and essays* (Stuttgart, 1967), p. 133.
15 Daly in Vamplew et al., *The Oxford companion to Australian sport*, p. 21.
16 Doris Magee, cited in Dennis Phillips, *Australian women at the Olympic Games* (Sydney, 1992), p. 41.
17 Magee in Phillips, p. 41.
18 Phillips, p. 7.
19 *See* P. Mason, *Professional athletics in Australia* (Adelaide, 1985), pp. 42-54.
20 Colin Tatz, 'Aborigines in sport' in Vamplew et al., p. 3.
21 Daly in Vamplew et al., *The Oxford companion to Australian sport*, p. 140.
22 Cited in Reet Howell and Max Howell, *Aussie gold: the story of Australia at the Olympics* (Brisbane, 1988), p. 11.
23 *See* John A. Daly, 'Australia's national sport — winning!', *Australian Journal of Physical Education* (September, 1972).

Chapter 15: Reflections Past and Present

1 For some comparisons here *see* Melvin J. Adelman, *A sporting time: New York City and the rise of modern athletics* (Champaign-Urbana, 1986); Allen Guttmann, *From ritual to records: the nature of modern sports* (New York, 1978) and John Hargreaves, *Sport, power and culture* (London, 1986).

2 This was written in the midst of Australia's very public 1993 republican debate.

3 *See* Richard Cashman, 'The making of Australian sporting traditions, 1977-87', *International Journal of the History of Sport*, 4.1 (May, 1987).

4 Shayne P. Quick, 'What a catch! Cricket's establishment on Australian commercial television', *Media Information Australia* (August, 1991) makes some interesting points.

5 This is seen repeatedly in reviews and in journalistic comment.

6 For some aspects of this general debate *see* Tony Mason, *Association football and English society, 1863-1915* (London, 1980) which should be compared with Alan Tomlinson and Garry Whannel (eds), *Off the ball* (London, 1986). For another fascinating insight *see* Nick Hornby, *Fever pitch: a fan's life* (London, 1992).

7 During 1993 the Australian Sports Commission funded two public seminars involving prominent athletes to emphasise and foster such perceived similarities between sport and business.

8 The volunteers' programme was a 1993 initiative launched by the Australian Sports Commission.

9 In the Australian context, see: Helen King, 'The sexual politics of sport: an Australian perspective' in Richard Cashman and Michael McKernan (eds.), *Sport in history* (Sydney, 1979); Marion K. Stell, *Half the race: a history of women in Australian sport* (Sydney, 1991).

10 *See* Brian Stoddart, *Women, sport and the media: 1992* (report to Standing Committee of Ministers of Recreation and Sport, 1993).

11 Bret Harris, *The proud champions: Australia's Aboriginal sporting heroes* (Sydney, 1989); Colin Tatz, *Aborigines in sport* (Adelaide, 1987).

12 Brian Stoddart, 'Ethnic influences' in Wray Vamplew, Katharine Moore, John O'Hara, Richard Cashman and Ian F. Jobling (eds), *The Oxford companion to Australian sport* (Melbourne, 1992).

13 For comparisons, *see* the vast literature on the role and place of African-Americans in American (especially professional and college) sports.

14 Brian Stoddart, *Saturday afternoon fever: sport in the Australian culture* (Sydney, 1986). For commentary and alternative views,

see: 'A debate in sports history: three views on Saturday after-noon fever' in *Sporting Traditions*, 4.1 (November, 1987), essays by Richard Cashman, David Rowe and Robert J. Paddick; Bob Stewart, 'Stoddart on sport', *Sporting Traditions*, 3.1 (November, 1986).

15 *See*, for comparative example, James Bradley, 'The MCC [Marylebone Cricket Club], Society and Empire: a portrait of cricket's ruling body, 1860-1914', *International Journal of the History of Sport*, 7.1 (May, 1990).

16 For example, the Women In Sport Unit, Australian Sports Commission.

17 As applied to sport, Norbert Elias and Eric Dunning, *Quest for excitement: sport and leisure in the civilizing process* (Oxford, 1986).

18 Jim McKay, *No pain, no gain? Sport and Australian culture* (Sydney, 1991). *See also* Geoff Lawrence and David Rowe (eds), *Power play: essays in the sociology of Australian sport* (Sydney, 1986) and David Rowe and Geoff Lawrence (eds), *Sport and leisure: trends in Australian popular culture* (Sydney, 1990).

19 For some interesting views *see* Alan Metcalfe, 'Power: a case study of the Ontario Hockey Association, 1890-1936', *Journal of Sport History*, 19.1 (Spring, 1992).

20 Wray Vamplew, *Pay up and play the game: professional sport in Britain, 1875-1914* (Cambridge, 1988).

21 For the British case *see* Tony Mason (ed.), *Sport in Britain: a social history* (Cambridge, 1989), and Richard Holt, *Sport and the British: a modern history* (Oxford, 1989). For comparative views on one set of sports professionals: Lauren St John, *Shooting at clouds: inside the PGA European tour* (Edinburgh, 1991) and William Wartman, *Playing through: behind the scenes on the American PGA tour* (New York, 1990).

22 This is best demonstrated by the case of Adelaide's vigorous but unsuccessful bid to stage the 1998 Commonwealth Games at a time when South Australia was heading towards deep financial crisis.

23 As an example, *see* John Nauright, 'Sport, manhood and Empire: British responses to the New Zealand rugby tour of 1905', *International Journal of the History of Sport*, 8.2 (September, 1991).

24 From the expanding literature *see*: Garry Whannel, *Fields in vision: television sport and cultural transformation* (London, 1992); Steven Barnett, *Games and sets: the changing face of sport on television* (London, 1990); Lawrence Wenner (ed.), *Media, sports and society* (San Francisco, 1989); Joan M. Chandler, *Television and national sport: the US and Britain* (Champaign-Urbana, 1988); John Goldlust, *Playing for keeps: sport, the media and society* (Melbourne, 1987); Benjamin J. Rader, *In its own*

image: how television has transformed sport (New York, 1984);
Leonard W. Koppett, *Sports illusion, sports reality: a reporter's view of sports, journalism and society* (Boston, 1981).

25 For an example, David Rowe, 'How TV turned sportsmen into media playthings', *Australian*, 19 May 1993.

26 The task might be as big, if possibly not so important, as that outlined in the famous manifesto!

27 The model is J. A. Mangan, *Athleticism in the Victorian and Edwardian public school: the emergence and consolidation of an educational ideology* (Cambridge, 1981).

28 Australian beginnings may be seen in Bob Stewart, 'Athleticism revisited: sport, character building and Protestant school education in nineteenth century Melbourne', *Sporting Traditions*, 9.1 (November 1992) and Ray Crawford, 'Athleticism, gentlemen and Empire in Australian public schools: L. A. Adamson and Wesley College' (unpublished paper).

29 Adrian McGregor's books on Wally Lewis at least attempt to set a cultural context.

30 Compare with Francis Fukuyama, *The end of history and the last man* (London, 1992). Perhaps predictably, sport does not appear in the index of Paul Kennedy, *Preparing for the twenty-first century* (London, 1993).

31 On literature, Barry Andrews: 'The willow tree and the laurel: Australian sport and Australian literature' in Cashman and McKernan, and Brian Stoddart, 'Cricket, literature and culture: windows on the world', *Notes and Furphies*, 30 (April 1993).

Index

Note that all organisations are referred to by their full name rather than by their initials, for example, Australian Soccer Federation *not* ASF.